The Works

of

THOMAS CAMPION

WALTER R. DAVIS received his Ph.D. from Yale University and has taught at the University of Rochester, Dickenson College, Williams College, and M.I.T. He is now professor of English at the University of Notre Dame. His books include *A Map of Arcadia: Sidney's Romance in its Tradition* (1965) and *Idea and Act in Elizabethan Fiction* (1969).

THE NORTON LIBRARY

SEVENTEENTH-CENTURY SERIES

J. MAX PATRICK, *General Editor*

The Works
of
THOMAS CAMPION

*Complete Songs, Masques, and Treatises
with a Selection of the Latin Verse*

EDITED WITH AN INTRODUCTION
AND NOTES BY
WALTER R. DAVIS

GENERAL EDITOR: J. MAX PATRICK

The Norton Library
W · W · NORTON & COMPANY · INC ·
NEW YORK

W. W. Norton & Company, Inc. also publishes *The Norton Anthology of English Literature,* edited by M. H. Abrams et al; *World Masterpieces,* edited by Maynard Mack et al; *The Norton Reader,* edited by Arthur M. Eastman et al; *The Norton Facsimile of the First Folio of Shakespeare,* prepared by Charlton Hinman; and the Norton Critical Editions.

SBN 393 00439 2

PRINTED IN THE UNITED STATES OF AMERICA

1 2 3 4 5 6 7 8 9 0

To the Memory
of
Noah Greenberg

Foreword to the Norton Library Edition

To this reprint of the original edition I have added one doubtful poem, "Tarry sweet love," and have made some corrections, mostly in the music; I wish to thank David Greer, Edward Doughtie, and Seymour L. Gross for calling my attention to my errors.

Since this edition was first published, three items of particular importance to Campion studies have appeared: an edition of *The Lords' Masque,* modernized and with detailed and valuable commentary, by I. A. Shapiro in *A Book of Masques in Honour of Allardyce Nicoll* (Cambridge, 1967) ; an interesting attempt to reconstruct the entertainment at Brougham Castle, "Campion's Entertainment at Brougham Castle, 1617," by Ian Spink, in *Music in Renaissance Drama,* edited by John H. Long (Lexington, Kentucky, 1968) ; and a physician's view of Campion, "Thomas Campion: Lyrick-Doctor in Physicke," by Paul J. Davis, M.D. (no relation) in *The Journal of the American Medical Association,* CCVIII (April, 1969), 115-19.

WALTER R. DAVIS

Notre Dame, Indiana
January, 1970

Preface

This edition would have been impossible without the aid of two people: my wife, Yolanda Leiss Davis, who undertook the work of transcribing the music and gave me advice on musical matters; and John P. Cutts, who lent me generous portions of his library of microfilmed songbooks and took the time to check several items for me. My thanks are also due to John P. Turley, Francis Lazenby, and Phyllis S. Smith for their advice on Campion's Latin; and to J. Max Patrick, the late Noah Greenberg, Rev. C. A. Soleta, C.S.C., Leni Coral, Gregory Theissen, and H. B. Martin for invaluable aid of various sorts. I wish to thank the Trustees of the British Museum, the Governing Body of Christ Church, Oxford, the Trustees of the National Library of Scotland, and the New York Public Library for permission to transcribe various materials; and the Folger Shakespeare Library, the Huntington Library, and the Trustees of the Chatsworth Settlement for permission to reproduce materials in the plates. Finally, I wish to thank the editors of *Modern Language Quarterly* and *Criticism* for permission to include material that originally appeared in their journals in my Introduction and Notes.

W.R.D.

The University of Notre Dame

Contents

Songs Reproduced with Music

Introduction

That no edition of Thomas Campion has appeared in the nearly sixty years since Percival Vivian's indicates the necessity for the re-examination to which the present edition is dedicated. Campion's reputation has fluctuated widely: a controversial figure to his contemporaries,[1] he was virtually forgotten from the middle of the seventeenth century until his rediscovery in 1887 by A. H. Bullen, who issued the very first collected edition of his works two years later. So enthusiastically was his reappearance on the scene greeted by critics that by 1903 his original discoverer expressed fear lest he become "the object of uncritical adulation."[2] Bullen's fear—for better or worse—was not warranted; for, while a handful of Campion's lyrics have endured as standard anthology pieces, he seems to have settled rather firmly into the ranks of the minor poets.

A major cause for the decline of Campion's reputation over these sixty years was T. S. Eliot's domination of the literary scene in the 1920s and after, with the resultant elevation of John Donne and the "metaphysical" poets to major status as the really important poets of the English Renaissance, and of metaphysical wit and the complex image as the major evidences of literary worth. Eliot's revaluations soon hardened into dogma: under the shadow of Donne, even Milton's reputation paled, and lesser poets such as

[1] For the attacks on Campion by Samuel Daniel and Ben Jonson, see headnotes to *Observations in the Art of English Poesie* and *The Somerset Masque*, respectively.

[2] A. H. Bullen, ed., *Thomas Campion, Songs and Masques, with Observations in the Art of English Poesy* (London and New York, 1903), p. viii.

Jonson, Campion, and Herrick, who, like Milton, subordinated image to argument, found little or no room in the literary establishment at all.

But there has been a turn in taste away from the Eliot canon in the past decade. Frank Kermode's *Romantic Image* was the first important public assertion that an image-centered poetic was not an esthetic absolute but a product of Romantic and Symbolist polemics; new British poets such as Donald Davie and Philip Larkin have been more interested in "purity of diction" and energetic syntax than in image; and we have seen an important American poet like Robert Lowell move from a packed imagistic poetry to a relaxed and plainer epistolary style. Within this new creative context, we have witnessed a decline in Donne's reputation and the ascendance in his place of Sidney, Spenser, and Milton; and recent important studies have brought the taut lyric definitions of Ben Jonson and the ceremonious retreats of Robert Herrick once more into poetic currency.

Campion is a poet—perhaps *the* poet—of the auditory rather than the visual imagination; more fully than any other song writer of his age, he offers us experiences that strike the ear: structures of sound, the implications of words, tones of voice. So little concerned is he with specificity of image, color, or shape that when we encounter an occasional "yellow Frog" or "Gray Snakes" we react with surprise—until we realize that the primary effect of such images is to subtly overplay a fearful state of mind ("So quicke, so hot"); it is far more typical of him to reach out and convert visual experience into auditory terms, as when he calls Lawra's face "thy beawties / Silent musick" ("Rose-cheekt *Lawra*"). As Catherine Ing says, "His Corinnas and Lesbias and Bessies may be related to the Delias and Chloes and sweet Kates, but they have their individuality, and it arises partly from the fact that Campion draws attention to qualities in them hardly noticed by other poets. They may have golden wires for hair and pearls for teeth, but he is not particularly interested if they have. Yet if they move or speak or sing, his awareness quickens at once."[3]

Campion's pursuit of the movements of sound is recorded in that strange but subtle treatise, *Observations in the Art of English Poesie*, and its fruits are preserved in his songbooks. His theoretical speculations on the emotional effect of a final unaccented syllable,

[3] Catherine M. Ing, *Elizabethan Lyrics: A Study in the Development of English Metres and Their Relation to Poetic Effect* (London, 1951), p. 173.

the march-like effect of iambs in short lines, or the quickening of the pulse by a trochee gave rise to his mastery of metrical effect in the songs; witness, for example, the totally different metrical shapes given to the following pentameter lines by variations in stress and pause: "My sweetest Lesbia, let us live and love," "Follow thy faire sunne, unhappy shaddowe," "Follow your Saint, follow with accents sweet." His efforts to contain movement in "stands" produced in his songs a variety of interesting stanzaic forms, some of them giving an effect of articulation without stoppage, others using rime (which he had denied himself in the *Observations*) to dilate movement before contracting it into a couplet, or to balance contrasting movements, or even to quiet action by following accentual lines by quantitative ones.

His theoretical care to measure the exact length of vowel sounds and ensure their independence by regularly intervening consonants, as well as his use of echo-effects to fix metrical equivalences, led him in his songs to use sound as a means of organization. Sometimes he centered individual lines on variations of one vowel sound, as in "O then I'le shine forth as an Angell of light," "Though you are yoong and I am olde," "There is ever one fresh spring abiding," or "Follow her whose light thy light depriveth." And often he conceived of an entire strophe as a unit of massed sounds, as in the first strophe of "Shall I come, sweet Love" where the *l*-sounds beginning every line but one frame a movement from the first four lines, dominated by "sweet," "thee," "beames," "be" and related sounds, to the last two dominated by the *o*-sounds of "for," "more," "your dore," and other words, the movement of sounds delineating a change in tone.

Campion was concerned in these technical matters with the effects of meter and massed sounds on tone; they represent therefore only the bare means by which the accents of a voice full of meaning fall upon the ear.

Campion's management of diction is both precise and significant. Sometimes he will juxtapose two nearly cognate words for an effect of precise definition gained with ease, as in "All their pleasure is content" (*"Jacke* and *Jone"*). At other times he uses diction to suggest imagery briefly by action, as when he applies "dive" to suns and "set" to lovers, thus by two verbs uniting opposed terms ("My sweetest Lesbia"). In this respect, it will be instructive to read "Now winter nights" with the following comment by Yvor Winters in mind, for most of the imagistic effects Winters notes are created by well-chosen single words, usually verbs: "one should note the vastness of night suggested in the first four lines, the fusion in images of light of the fire, wine, and wax, the continuation of this suggestion in the word 'honey' used, however, metaphorically, and the way the spirits of the convivialists leap in the line subsequent to that in which the cups overflow."[4]

Most frequently, Campion will place the telling word where it will reverse the tone and show movement of mind, as does that "Comfit-makers" oath (as Hotspur calls it in *Henry IV*, Part I) "forsooth" in "I care not for these Ladies." Similarly, "Blame not my cheeks" takes us to a new tone at the end by a switch in levels of diction: the lover's involved physiological argument linking pale cheeks to flaming heart leads in the second strophe to satire of other lovers whose "fat love lyes in their outward parts," and ends with plain low diction and the comic spatial image of Cupid as a cold little boy:

> But in their brests, where love his court should hold,
> Poore Cupid sits and blowes his nailes for cold.

Tonal complexity—whether produced by diction or by other means—is one of Campion's most pervasive qualities. "When thou must home," for example, suspends the mistress in a romantic classical Hades with the shades of "White Iope, blith Hellen, and the rest" until the last line, which suddenly cuts beneath the romance to assimilate Hades to the Christian Hell reserved for sinners, and to show the real brutality of the celebrated mistress, all by means of the final verb: "Then tell, O tell, how thou didst murther me." On the other hand, "Thou art not faire" turns at the end by a witty epigrammatic twist to make the lover's condemnation of his mistress the very reason for her granting his desires. In "Though your strangenesse frets my hart" complexity is achieved by the devastating juxtaposition of the lady's excuses (which, couched in easy sentimental clichés, illustrate her brutal indifference) to the lover's plain hard comments; he resolves his attitudes of complaint and sarcasm by careless irony at the end:

> Would my Rival then I were,
> Some els your secret friend:
> So much lesser should I feare,
> And not so much attend.

Tonal complexity sometimes reveals a rather dark side of Campion, as in "the humanity and wise disillusionment" Winters finds in

[4] Yvor Winters, "The 16th Century Lyric in England: Part III," *Poetry: A Magazine of Verse*, LIV (1939), 37.

"Now winter nights," or in the gradual revelation in "I must complain" that the lover who scores the deceit of a fair woman is himself tired and cynical.

Perhaps the most apparent evidence of the fiber beneath the grace and polish of Campion's verse is his command of structure, for it is no exaggeration to say that Campion took the loose and repetitive lyric form of his time and disciplined it by argumentative and even logical means. Ralph W. Berringer writes, "In his favorite two-stanza form, the second stanza answers the first by application or conclusion, the whole giving much the same effect as a well-constructed sonnet. The point is frequently driven home by an epigrammatic turn, sometimes lightly accenting each stanza, more often clinching the whole with an unexpected ending."[5] The logicality of such structure is frequently indicated by the syntax, as in "When to her lute" (which we shall examine in more detail, with its music, below), "Thou art not faire," or "Breake now my heart." "Thus I resolve" proceeds from the condition the lover finds himself in (lines 1–3), to the resolve based on it (line 4), to an emotional stasis arising from the resolve (lines 5–6) in the first strophe; the second strophe proceeds to explain the necessity of such a resolve by reference to the full context of man's life in Nature.

The combination of grace and strength pervades all of Campion's verse but does not define the limits of his accomplishment. He has, in fact, two manners, the "light" and the "solid." Most of the lyrics we have examined so far are examples of the former style; "Though your strangenesse" and "I must complain" are examples of the latter, as is "Where are all thy beauties now," which deserves some quotation. The harsh condemnation of the subject's vanity is continued from the first into the second strophe:

> Thy rich state of twisted gold to Bayes is turned;
> Cold as thou art, are thy loves that so much burned:
> Who dye in flatt'rers armes are seldome mourned.

But the song is not content with simplistic pious rebuke; the fineness of tone with which it is conceived dictates that it end with full justice, with honest respect for the subject in spite of scorn:

> When thy story, long time hence, shall be perused,
> Let the blemish of thy rule be thus excused:
> None ever liv'd more just, none more abused.

[5] Ralph W. Berringer, "Thomas Campion's Share in *A Booke of Ayres*," *PMLA*, LVIII (1943), 942.

The songs of this manner are not always love songs; when they are, they usually relate love to a context larger than the romantic, such as society, Nature, or even theology (as in the continual play on faith, hope, and love in "Shall I then hope when faith is fled"). They eschew romance for naturalism and even the doggedly empirical (as in "Vaine men, whose follies"). They are couched in a plain literal style that limits imagery to illustration of a stated point and almost completely exorcises metaphorical diction. They are not conceived as dramatic moments in the love game when the lover tries to persuade his mistress to grant his desires, but rather as attempts at *definition* of a given concept or stance clearly and in all its specificity. As such, they allow the tonal complexity we saw in the "light" songs to take the center of the stage, and the result is that such complexity is both deepened and broadened by wide reference.

One of the finest examples of the complex and responsible attitude achieved in these songs is "Were my hart as some mens are." In the first strophe the lover establishes himself as an honest man both by his conversational style and by his balanced view of himself: he is less patient than some lovers but his very impatience is a token of his concern for the beloved. Her faults, moreover, are forgiven but not at all mitigated by his confession of his own faults:

Were my hart as some mens are, thy errours would not move me:
But thy faults I curious finde, and speake because I love thee;
Patience is a thing divine and farre, I grant, above mee.

This man explains his stance in the second strophe by reference to friendship's duty to reveal faults to the friend, and gives his explanation substance by opposing "th' obsequious bosome guest" who flatters to destroy. Finally, by a sentence that starts as an oath of allegiance but turns to a hard-headed promise (thus utilizing syntax for tone), he reaches a final balance of critic, servant ("observer"), and detached though tender well-wisher:

While I use of eyes enjoy, and inward light of reason,
Thy observer will I be, and censor, but in season:
Hidden mischiefe to conceale in State and Love is treason.

By relating his finely balanced attitude to those proper to serious affairs in life such as State and Friendship, the lover impresses on the reader the fact that his kind of love is just such a serious affair, and demands fully as much care.

Campion's "light" manner dominates his early productions, his "solid" manner the later ones. A brief sketch of his literary career will reveal some of the motives and means that brought his manner from the one to the other.

II

Campion began his literary career as a disciple of Sir Philip Sidney. In his first published verse, the set of five songs gathered together with work by Daniel and Greville and included in *Poems and Sonets of Sundrie Other Noblemen and Gentlemen* appended to Thomas Newman's surreptitious quarto of *Astrophel and Stella* in 1591, he exhibits the typically Sidneian traits of tonal flexibility, ease of articulation, and complex stanzaic pattern. These songs show traces of two entirely unrelated forms of Elizabethan "classicism." The first is indicated by the fact that one of the songs is an experiment in the classical Asclepiadic meter after "O sweet woods" in Sidney's *Arcadia;* for Campion was to become the last champion of that Quixotic attempt Sidney had inaugurated in the 1570s to adapt the accentual English language to the quantitative scansion and verse forms of Latin poetry. Unfortunately, by the time Campion's *Observations in the Art of English Poesie* was published (eleven years later, in 1602), the issue had been dead for a decade; he failed to resuscitate it and soon abandoned the attempt. The second form of classicism, exhibited most fully in the first of the five songs, is a tendency to see life in a heady atmosphere of classical myth, a tendency whose roots lie in the work of Spenser, Tasso, and, ultimately, Ovid. This trait permeates Campion's work much more fully than the first; it reappears in his second publication, the Latin *Poemata* of 1595; here there are many Latin echoes of Spenser and a style, with its sound effects, turns on words, and static psychological analyses by dichotomy, that is especially Ovidian. Especially Ovidian too is Campion's attempt to explore human archetypes by means of myths of origin; in *Umbra,* for example, he seeks to explain the paradoxes of love by reference to a great transformation myth involving the recurrent painful juncture of the inseminating male principle (hot, dry, and light) to its opposite, the cold, wet, dark female potentiality in nature.

In the masques Campion wrote for the Court of James I between 1607 and 1613, myth became symbolic. The masque form (which Campion helped to solidify)[6] by nature encouraged symbolism, for it attempted at one and the same time to both celebrate a specific court event and develop its broadest applications; and Campion made full use of all the symbolic media the form offered: traditional iconography, number symbolism, the use of music to transform emotions, and dance as an emblem of order. By means such as these, the graceful myth invented for the wedding of the Lord Hay in 1607 proliferates meanings in the political, psychological, and cosmic dimensions.

Throughout his career as a masque composer, Campion conceived of the movement of the entertainment—and of the marriage or political occasion it celebrated—as an exchange of chaos for order. But while his theme remained fixed, the means he chose to embody it changed. His means became progressively more spare: in the entertainments composed after *The Lord Hay's Masque,* he de-emphasized myth in order to present nakedly the civilizing power of language; and by the time of his last masque for the Earl of Somerset he had stripped the form down to a spare diagram consisting of little more than an antimasque in pantomime followed by a spectacular transformation scene. It was also in this masque that he demythologized the form. "In our dayes," he wrote in a prefatory section, the great myths, "although they have not utterly lost their use, yet finde they . . . litle credit." By grounding his device in an enchantment instead of a myth, he shifted his emphasis from the symbolic ramifications of life to the confusion of appearance and reality that so plagues human experience. And his audience thereby experienced a clarification of what in fact their quotidian life was like, instead of an ennoblement of it. What they saw at the beginning of the masque was a tumult of elements, continents, and other personifications (an illusion); what they saw at its end was a crew of sailors coming up the Thames, disembarking, and dancing a hornpipe.

The five books of songs Campion produced between 1601 and 1617 show a similar progress from a relatively luxuriant mode of poetry to a spare and naturalistic mode. The keynote of his first volume, *A Booke of Ayres* (1601), is variety, proceeding from a sense of the copiousness of experience. There are divine and moral songs here (one of them in classical meters), songs which envelop

[6] See Enid Welsford's remarks on *Gesta Grayorum,* in which Campion participated: *The Court Masque* (Cambridge, 1927), pp. 163–66; also Stephen Orgel, *The Jonsonian Masque* (Cambridge, Massachusetts, 1965), pp. 8–18.

experience in a heady aura of myth (Nos. i, xx, and xix—the last reprinted from the *Astrophel and Stella* appendix), songs cultivating a refined courtly sentiment whose roots lie in Petrarch (Nos. iv, x, and xiii), and, in contrast, sensuous and humorous country ballads (Nos. iii, v, and viii), with their "anti-Petrarchan naturalism."[7] Whatever their differences in subject matter and treatment, all the songs exhibit Campion's characteristic traits: the suavity of his sounds, his use of various levels of diction to effect tonal changes, and tight structure. Poetic structure in this book is basically of two kinds. There is the Sidneian kind of song, copious and leisurely in development but made coherent by patterns of complex rime, refrain, or rhetorical parallelism. And there is the song of two strophes that proceeds by the quasi-logical method of laying down terms and then collecting them, and ends with a surprising turn of thought. This latter type conforms to Campion's characterization of the solo song in his preface, where he wrote, "What Epigrams are in Poetrie, the same are Ayres in musicke, then in their chiefe perfection when they are short and well seasoned."

The radical concept of the lyric as epigram, announced but not totally fulfilled in *A Booke of Ayres,* was to govern Campion's later development as a lyric poet. He reiterated this concept in the preface to *Two Bookes of Ayres, The First Contayning Divine and Morall Songs: The Second, Light Conceits of Lovers* (ca. 1613), and, in its body of verse, developed it in two separate directions. In the divine and moral songs (which constitute his least distinguished production), he cultivated a plain style of literal statement that eschews metaphor, incorporates a non-sensuous diction consisting for the most part of abstract but specific nouns (whether the standard terms of religious discourse such as "grace" or "Patience" or not, as in "Making trouble their content"), and concentrates on rhetorical devices for relating precise terms concisely, as in lines like these:

> The Lord exceeds in mercy as in might;
> His ruth is greater, though thy crimes be great.

In the love songs, he achieved a new contemporaneity and realism by showing love and its problems of courtship, marriage, and adultery in a social context rather than abstractly, and by intensifying his psychological focus; the pleading lover in these songs, for instance, is not the abject sufferer of "Follow your Saint," but the cynic or the disabused or the man of wit offering argument.

[7] Berringer, p. 941, n. 9.

The dual development in these two books constitutes a further realization of the power of the epigrammatic mode in lyric; for, as Martial had been the first to show,[8] the epigram's immediacy of effect was due not only to its brevity but also to its direct confrontation of the reader as an epistle in plain style concerning his own quotidian life instead of remote romantic myth.

It is in *The Third Booke of Ayres* (not in *The Fourth Booke,* a retrospective volume published along with it ca. 1617) that these separate strands come together. The songs of Campion's late manner are, first of all, terse: that is, they are not only briefer than the previous songs, but they are compressed. The devices of compression are largely those stressing the relationships of individual words developed in the plain style of *The First Booke,* but the lines often are drawn so tightly as to achieve an Augustan couplet-rhetoric of turn, balance, and antitheses (as in "O griefe, O spight"); beyond these, there is the new device of the aphorism, whereby distillations of general experience in diverse aspects of life are let into a song. These mature songs are plain in style, approaching their subjects directly and literally; in the few cases where they are not, they treat metaphor wittily as the tinsel any experienced lover can manipulate with ease (as in "Be thou then my beauty named"). They are realistic, not only in their use of naturalistic and societal details, but in the many allusions to specific situations and persons which their frequently occasional nature (as established in the verse epistle to Monson) demands.

But the most distinctive trait of *The Third Booke* is its concern with tone and tonal modulation—with the civilized art of taking a wide range of possible attitudes toward a situation and creating some adjustment among them rather than excluding some and cultivating others. This concern appears first in the way emotions are compared and modified in the epistle to Monson; then in the complex voices of "Breake now my heart and dye"; or in the adjustment of lightly cynical, heavily sarcastic, and finally sincerely laudatory attitudes in "Silly boy." Songs like "Thus I resolve" and, especially, "Were my hart as some mens are" are explicitly concerned with establishing and exploring viable attitudes, usually by indicating a delicate combination of diverse responses, and "Shall I then hope when faith is fled" develops an especially complex tone by presenting a series of ethical and psychological paradoxes.

The spare plain style arises out of a heightened sense of the real and the necessity of confronting it directly; and this impulse in-

---

[8] See, e.g., *Epigrams* IV. xlix, X. iv, and the prefatory letter to Book II.

volves both an attempt to define the real and an assumption of complex attitudes toward it, in the belief that only thus can human truth (instead of some standard oversimplification) be reached. This was the task Campion set for his songs at the end of his career. Whereas in the masques he had proceeded rather simply from decorative myth toward terse realism, his progress in the songs was toward a deepening complexity within that realistic vision; within the mode of the epigrammatic, he worked to make the neat and graceful ayre, rich yet spare in its means, into the vehicle for a full and sententious exploration of reality. His final achievement has the true ring of the classical tone he had sought in vain during his early classicist imitations.

III

That Campion is the primary poet of the auditory imagination is due to his combining the roles of poet and composer in a manner unique in the history of English literature. The concept of the lyric as epigram we explored above was not merely a poetic concept but a radically new theory involving music and poetry as an undifferentiated unit of sound, a theory of the short, simple, un-repetitive ayre (music) as terse and pointed epigram (poetry). Part of the epigrammatic effect of "When to her lute," for ex-ample, depends on its music: the suspense proper to the logical condition set up in the first four lines of each strophe is intensified in the melody by phrases ending in the dominant d, but constantly frustrated in their movement toward closure and rest in the tonic g. The new condition arising in the fifth line ("But when she doth of mourning speake") supersedes the first condition and therefore is represented by repeating the melodic pattern of the first line and then reversing direction; from this point, the music leads us toward the climax by building suspense in a sequence on "her sighes" (and "my hart"), then displacing the rhythm and subsiding to the tonic on the nodal phrase "the strings doe breake" (which is punctuated by a dissonant chord in the lute part). The rich effect of a song like this one comes neither from strikingly complex music nor from conceited or strong-lined texts, but rather from the meaningful sounds of words inextricable from notes.

Therefore it is to Campion especially among the lutenist song writers that one looks for sophisticated examples of the ways in which music and poetry can so combine as to extend or give depth to the implications of words. The ways are many.

Perhaps the most obvious way is by allusion, where the music recalls relevant associations left unstated in the text. For example, when the music of "The peacefull westerne winde" incorporates the well-known traditional melody "Westron Wynde," the listener hears along with Campion's song the mordant old words which give a new dimension to the text:

> Westron wynde when wyll thow blow
> the small rayne down can rayne
> Cryst yf my love wer in my armys
> And I yn my bed agayne.

Similarly, when the London street seller's cry "Cherry ripe, cherry ripe" bursts into the musical refrain of "There is a Garden in her face," it breaks the tone and totally revalues the previous part of the song.

The madrigalists had contrived many other ways (few of them very subtle) for music to underline the meaning of words. In this representative passage, Thomas Morley gave a few basic prescriptions to musicians:

Moreover you must have a care that when your matter signifieth 'ascending,' 'high,' 'heaven,' and such like you must make your music ascend; and by the contrary where your ditty speaketh of 'descending,' 'lowness,' 'depth,' 'hell,' and others such you must make your music descend; for as it will be thought a great absurdity to talk of heaven and point downwards to the earth, so will it be counted great incongruity if a musician upon the words 'he ascended into heaven' should cause his music descend, or by the contrary upon the descension should cause his music to ascend.[9]

Campion used such devices of "word-painting" frequently—for example, in repeating "but a little higher" each time a note above the preceding musical phrase ("Beauty, since you so much desire"); or in stressing the weariness of "long houres" by a repeated long descending phrase ("Shall I come, sweet Love, to thee"); or in expressing "my dying spright" by a falling phrase, "wander as a stray" by an uncertain cross rhythm, and "mists and darkness" by a tonally unstable chromatic phrase ("Author of light").[10] In Campion's hands such effects often took on fuller meaning than

[9] *A Plaine and Easie Introduction to Practicall Musicke* (1597), ed. R. Alec Harman (New York, 1952), p. 291.

[10] See Miles M. Kastendieck, *England's Musical Poet, Thomas Campion* (New York, 1938), pp. 113–14 and 157–58.

those implied in Morley's limited rules. In "Followe thy faire sunne," for instance, the up-down movement of the first line obviously repeats the idea of relentless walking; but when the music first falls and then rises on "blacke as night, / And she made all of light," not only is the movement broken momentarily, but Campion's favorite light-dark imagery receives a new, a spatial, dimension: light is high, dark is low, and she becomes even more firmly established with the sun in its element of air while he, her shadow, is bound to the dark and heavy element of earth he falls upon.

But Campion mocked Morley's techniques in the preface to *A Booke of Ayres,* and asserted that music ought chiefly to give stress to necessary portions of the text. In practice, this precept frequently amounted to indicating the structure of a text by melody. In "My sweetest Lesbia" this is done by setting to an identical descending phrase (which is, by the way, the only repeated phrase in the entire song) the words "live and love" and "ever-during night"—the terms standing for the concepts of love and the hostile universe whose conflict, strophe by strophe, determines the development of the whole lyric. "Though you are yoong" intensifies the conflict of youth and age in each half line by· using a different rhythmical motif for each, and emphasizes age's reversal over youth at the end by setting age to the motif hitherto associated with youth. Here, the music does not merely point up the basic terms of the song; it is making a pervasive structural statement.

Two other songs suggest further possibilities. In "Come, chearfull day," each strophe contains a little *peripeteia* in which the couplet totally revalues the opening statement. The music emphasizes the nature of the reversal in the last line by symmetry, since "we live we live" is set to the music of "So ev'ry day," itself the near retrograde of the first phrase of the song. Here the music shows not only the structure of the text but the same kind of structure in itself, separately. "Tune thy Musicke to thy hart" presents a more complex case of such "mirroring" of the text in the music. The lyric's construction is quite simple: in each strophe two stylistic directions are usually followed by a longer affirmation which gives substance to the imperatives; as the lyric attempts to unite religion and art, so a religious statement justifies the directions for style. The music expresses perfectly the relation of the second half of the strophe to the first, both transcending it and explaining it. The basic musical idea of the song is a tetrachord from c to g with each of the notes repeated, as established in the descending motion of the first line. The second line works this in retrograde in an obvious movement toward symmetry, but the symmetry is broken

after the *b*-flat and never reaches the necessary repeated *c*. The
second half of the strophe reworks the second line, starting again
on the repeated *g;* but it augments the motif by repetitions, by
adding half steps (thus giving a plaintive chromatic tone to the
upward movement), and by rising above the tetrachord once
only, on "the rich." It also pushes the song finally to the symmetry
it had been seeking and makes it end where it began. In this song
Campion created a musical form, independent of the verbal
structure but inspired by it, which perfects the lyrical statement.
By forcing on the listener a desire for completion of a pattern
which cannot be satisfied until he reaches the religious level of
thought at the end, it implies that devotion is necessary to art not
only for its inspiration but for fulfillment of its being, its form as
well.

IV

The present edition is designed both to bring Campion to light
as a poet once more and to present the reader with a more
accurate text of his work than has been hitherto available. To the
latter end, considerable new manuscript material and scholarship
on the Campion canon that have appeared since Vivian's edition
of 1909 have been incorporated, and an attempt has been made
to correct Vivian's errors of transcription. In this edition the
reader will find the complete English works of Thomas Campion:
the songs, the masques, and the two treatises on metrics and
music, as well as his occasional verse. In addition, a reasonably
cautious collection of the verse whose attribution to Campion is
doubtful has been included at the end of the volume. Original
spellings have been retained, save for a few expansions of abbre-
viations and the regularization of *u* and *v, i* and *j;* punctuation
has been modernized wherever necessary for clarity. The original
typography of the masques has been regularized slightly by
reserving speeches and songs for roman type and printing all
other material in italics. Because Campion's Latin verse is of
considerable importance, it was found feasible to include a
selection of it, with translations especially prepared for this
edition by Phyllis S. Smith.

Finally, so that the reader may have some sense of the songs as
songs, I have included a sampling of twenty-six of them with
Campion's original music, as well as the music printed with
The Somerset Masque. Because the transcriptions of the music are

intended primarily for study, they have been made as close to literal facsimiles as possible. A few obvious errors in the original editions have been corrected, as noted in the Textual Notes, and some bracketed editorial accidentals in the voice-parts have been added for clarity. The original note-values (which should usually be halved in performance) have been retained, with the exception of "I care not for these Ladies." The frequently inconsistent barring of the original (which usually indicates phrasing rather than meter) has been retained, but the equally inconsistent placing of repeat-dots has been rectified wherever it might lead to confusion (on pages 49, 67, 71, 78 and 281 of this edition). The tablature for the lute accompaniment has been realized for modern keyboard performance. The musician desiring a complete practical edition of the songs is referred to that of Edmund H. Fellowes in "The English School of Lutenist Song Writers" series.

Biographical Outline

1567 (February 12): Thomas Campion born to John and Lucy Campion in London; christened at St. Andrewes Church, Holborne.

1576 (October): John Campion died; Lucy Campion remarried, to Augustine Steward, August 21, 1577.

1580 (March): Thomas Campion left an orphan by his mother's death; Steward undertook sole guardianship of him and his sister Rose.

1581: Thomas Campion entered Peterhouse, Cambridge.

1584: Campion left Cambridge, apparently without a degree.

1586 (April 27): Campion admitted to Gray's Inn to study law.

1588 (January 17): Campion played the parts of "Hidaspes" and "Melancholy" in revels presented by Gray's Inn at Court.

1591: Five songs by Campion (under the pseudonym "Content") appeared appended to Newman's surreptitious quarto of Sidney's *Astrophel and Stella*.

1591–1592: Campion probably served under Sir Robert Carey in Essex's Norman expedition sent to aid Henri IV against the Catholic League.

1594 (Shrovetide): Campion composed one or more songs for *Gesta Grayorum*, a revels presented at Court.

1595: *Thomae Campiani Poemata* published (entered December 2, 1594).

1601: *A Booke of Ayres* published in collaboration with Philip Rosseter, lutenist.

1602: *Observations in the Art of English Poesie* published.

1603: Samuel Daniel's *A Defence of Ryme* published in answer to the *Observations*.

1605 (February 10): Campion received the degree of M.D. from the University of Caen in France, and probably returned to London to practice medicine shortly thereafter. He had presumably been away on the Continent since 1602; it has not been definitely established whether he became a convert to Roman Catholicism at this or any other time.

1607 (January 6): *The Lord Hay's Masque* performed at Court.

1613 (?): *Two Bookes of Ayres* published.

1613: *Songs of Mourning* on the death of Prince Henry (died November 6, 1612) published, "worded" by Campion, the music by Giovanni Coperario.

—— (February 14): *The Lords' Masque* for the wedding of the Princess Elizabeth performed.

—— (April 27–28): *The Caversham Entertainment* for Queen Anne performed.

—— (December 26): *The Somerset Masque* performed at Court.

1613–1614 (?): *A New Way of Making Fowre Parts in Counter-point* published.

1615 (October 26): Campion examined and cleared of complicity in the murder of Sir Thomas Overbury.

1616 (January 14): Campion allowed to administer physic to his friend Sir Thomas Monson, who was imprisoned in the Tower for the murder of Overbury.

1617 (?): *The Third and Fourth Booke of Ayres* published.

1617 (August): *The Ayres That Were Sung and Played at Brougham Castle* by George Mason and John Earsden, perhaps with words by Campion, performed for James I's return from Scotland; published in 1618.

1619: *Tho. Campiani Epigrammatum Libri II* published (entered August 21).

1620 (March 1): Campion died and was buried at St. Dunstan's in the West, Fleet Street.

SONGS AND POEMS

SONGS APPENDED TO
SIDNEY'S *ASTROPHEL AND STELLA*

This set of five songs signed "Content," which appeared in the *Poems and Sonets of Sundrie Other Noblemen and Gentlemen* appended to Thomas Newman's surreptitious edition of Sidney's *Astrophel and Stella* (1591) along with poems by Daniel and Greville, constitutes Campion's first publication. The identification of Campion as "Content" is ensured beyond reasonable doubt by his inclusion of *Canto Primo* as song xix in *A Booke of Ayres* in 1601 and his very close translations of *Canto tertio* and *Canto quarto* into Latin epigrams in the *Poemata* of 1595. The imprint of Sidney on these early pieces is unmistakable: in the romantic cast of the first two songs, in the quantitative experiment in Asclepiadics after Sidney's example, and in the spirit of formal experimentation in which they are all written.

It is quite likely that these songs were originally written for a lost masque. The designation of "Canto primo," etc., was usual in labeling music appended to a masque (for instance, in Campion's own *Somerset Masque*). There seems to be narrative continuity between the awakening of ladies to love in the first song and their appearance to the forsaken knights in the second (which itself reads like a presenter's speech); the two, moreover, outline a usual masque situation where ladies free enchanted knights by their love (as, for example, in the speeches at Quarrendon of August 1592, attributed to John Lyly). Likewise, the last song celebrating the brilliance of a moment is peculiarly appropriate to the ending of a masque, and reflects Campion's sentiments in both the last song appended to *The Lord Hay's Masque* and the prefatory poem to Lord and Lady Hay. Finally, the two songs of a single strophe each may have been written to dances in a masque, as the last three songs appended to *The Lord Hay's Masque* were. Unfortunately, the absence of Revels Office accounts after 1587 makes identification of a masque to which these songs may belong impossible.

CANTO PRIMO.[1]

Harke, all you Ladies that doo sleepe:
The Fairie Queene *Proserpina*
Bids you awake, and pitie them that weepe:
  You may doo in the darke
  What the day doth forbid: 5
  Feare not the doggs that barke,
  Night will have all hid.

But if you let your Lovers mone,
The Fairie Queene *Proserpina*
Will send abroad hir Fairies everie one, 10
  That shall pinch blacke and blew
  Your white hands and faire armes,
  That did not kindly rewe[2]
  Your Paramours harmes.

In myrtle arbours on the downes, 15
The Fairie Queene *Proserpina,*
This night by Moone shine leading merrie rounds,
  Holds a watch with sweete Love;
  Downe the dale, up the hill,
  No plaints nor grieves may move 20
  Their holy vigill.

All you that will hold watch with Love,
The Fairie Queene *Proserpina*
Will make you fairer than *Dianas* Dove;

[1] This song is based on the late Latin poem *Pervigilium Veneris,* "The Vigil of Venus." The third strophe outlines the situation of the whole *Pervigilium;* ll. 15–16 are derived from ll. 4–5 of the Latin:

> *cras amorum copulatrix inter umbras arborum*
> *inplicat casas virentes de flagello myrteo*

[tomorrow the joiner of loves will weave green bowers out of myrtle branches amid the shadows of trees];
and the whole fifth strophe expands the Latin refrain, *cras amet qui numquam amavit, quique amavit cras amet* [tomorrow he will love who never before has loved, and he who has loved will love tomorrow]. The music to this song (see *A Booke of Ayres,* Part I, xix, below) reveals that the last three lines of each strophe are quantitative, and approach a kind of Sapphic strophe. Ode 14 of Barnabe Barnes's *Parthenophil and Parthenope* appears to be an answer to this song.

[2] pity out of love.

Roses red, Lillies white,   25
And the cleere damaske hue,[3]
Shall on your cheekes alight:
Love will adorne you.

All you that love, or lov'd before,
The Fairie Queene *Proserpina*   30
Bids you increase that loving humour more:
They that have not yet fed
On delight amorous,
She vowes that they shall lead
Apes in *Avernus*.[4]   35

[3] pink, the color of a damask rose.

[4] Leading apes in hell was a proverbial punishment for old maids, perhaps in revenge for their unwillingness to choose a mate in life. See Samuel Rowlands, *'Tis Merry When Gossips Meete,* 1602 (in the Hunterian Club reprint, Glasgow, 1880), p. 23:

There's an old grave Proverbe tell's us that
Such as die *Maydes* doe all lead Apes in hell.

CANTO SECUNDO.[5]

What faire pompe have I spide of glittering Ladies;
With locks sparckled abroad, and rosie Coronet
On their yvorie browes, trackt to the daintie thies
With roabs[6] like *Amazons*, blew as Violet,
With gold Aglets[7] adornd, some in a changeable   5
Pale,[8] with spangs[9] wavering, taught to be moveable.

Then those Knights that a farre off with dolorous viewing
Cast their eyes hetherward: loe, in an agonie,
All unbrac'd, crie aloud, their heavie state ruing:
Moyst cheekes with blubbering, painted as *Ebonie*   10
Blacke; their feltred[10] haire torne with wrathfull hand:
And whiles astonied, starke in a maze they stand.

But hearke, what merry sound! what sodaine harmonie!
Looke, looke neere the grove where the Ladies doe tread
With their knights the measures waide[11] by the melodie!   15
Wantons, whose travesing[12] make men enamoured!
Now they faine an honor,[13] now by the slender wast
He must lift hir aloft,[14] and seale a kisse in hast.

Streight downe under a shadow for wearines they lie
With pleasant daliance, hand knit with arme in arme;   20
Now close, now set aloof, they gaze with an equall eie,[15]
Changing kisses alike; streight with a false alarme,
Mocking kisses alike, powt with a lovely lip.
Thus drownd with jollities, their merry daies doe slip.

[5] The meter is rimed Asclepiadic, after Sidney's "O sweet woods the delight of solitarines" in *Arcadia;* the quantitative scansion is: − − − ⌣ ⌣ − − ⌣ ⌣ − ⌣ ⌣.
[6] with their tunics pulled up to their thighs.
[7] metal ends of laces.   [8] pall, cloak.   [9] spangles.   [10] matted.
[11] weighed, marked off.   [12] traversing, movement.   [13] bow.
[14] The dance is a Volta, where each measure ends with the man assisting the lady in a "leap" into the air.
[15] with the same intense gaze.

But stay! now I discerne they goe on a Pilgrimage   25
Toward Loves holy land, faire *Paphos* or *Cyprus*.[16]
Such devotion is meete for a blithesome age;
With sweet youth it agrees well to be amorous.
Let olde angrie fathers lurke in an Hermitage:
Come, weele associate[17] this jollie Pilgrimage!   30

[16] legendary dwellings of Venus; the pilgrimage thither is a mediaeval tradition best embodied in the famous *Hypnerotomachia Poliphili* (Venice, 1499).

[17] join.

CANTO TERTIO.[18]

My Love bound me[19] with a kisse
That I should no longer staie;
When I felt so sweete a blisse,
I had lesse power to passe away:
Alas, that women do not knowe,
Kisses make men loath to goe.

CANTO QUARTO.[20]

Love whets the dullest wittes,[21] his plagues be such;
But makes the wise, by pleasing, doat as much.
So wit[22] is purchast by this dire disease:
Oh let me doat, so Love be bent to please.

[18] Compare Campion's Latin version, *"In Melleam"* in *Epigrammatum Liber* II, 12, below; this epigram was included in both the 1595 and 1619 collections. For additional stanzas to this song by Campion or someone else, see textual notes.

[19] made me promise.

[20] Compare Campion's very close Latin version, *"Ad Amorem"* in *Epigrammatum Liber* II, 54, below; this epigram was included in both the 1595 and 1619 collections.

[21] brains.   [22] intelligence.

CANTO QUINTO.[23]

A daie, a night, an houre of sweete content
Is worth a world consum'd in fretfull care.
Unequall[24] Gods, in your Arbitrement
To sort[25] us daies whose sorrowes endles are!
   And yet what were it? as a fading flower: 5
   To swim in blisse a daie, a night, an hower.[26]

What plague is greater than the griefe of minde?
The griefe of minde that eates in everie vaine,
In everie vaine that leaves such clods[27] behind,
Such clods behind as breed such bitter paine,   10
   So bitter paine that none shall ever finde
   What plague is greater than the griefe of minde.

Doth sorrowe fret thy soule? o direfull spirit!
Doth pleasure feede thy heart? o blessed man!
Hast thou bin happie once? o heavie plight!   15
Are thy mishaps forepast? o happie than![28]
   Or hast thou blisse in eld?[29] o blisse too late!
   But hast thou blisse in youth? o sweete estate!

Finis. CONTENT.

[23] The second strophe, as Vivian observes in his edition of Campion, is Puttenham's "heel treading kind of verse" where the first words of each line repeat the last words of the preceding line; for other examples, see Sidney's "Beautie hath force to catch the humane sight" (*Arcadia,* Book III) and "Since wayling is the bud of causefull sorowe" (*Arcadia,* Fourth Eclogues).

[24] unjust.   [25] to allot by fate.

[26] And yet to swim in bliss for a day or a night or an hour is only to be like a fading flower.

[27] blood clots in the veins.   [28] then.   [29] old age.

A
BOOKE OF
AYRES,

Set foorth to be song
to the Lute, Orpherian, and
Base Violl, by *Philip Rosseter*
Lutenist: And are to be solde
at his house in Fleetstreete
neere to the Gray-
hound.

1601

A Booke of Ayres appeared in 1601 as a manifesto of the new ayre or solo song's ascendancy over the older polyphonic madrigal, whose pinnacle had been reached the same year with Thomas Morley's *The Triumphs of Oriana* (see Kastendieck, *England's Musical Poet,* chapter IV). Earlier books of ayres—John Dowland's of 1597 and 1600, Michael Cavendish's of 1598, and Robert Jones's of 1600—had allowed for alternative performances of their songs as solos or as part songs, like madrigals, of two, four, or even five voices; but Campion and Rosseter insisted on performance by a single voice accompanied by a single instrument, the lute (whose Bass line might be doubled by a viola da gamba). The insistence on a single voice threw new emphasis on the significance and clarity of the words, and this new emphasis demanded in turn a new esthetic that rejected the characteristic devices by which the madrigal managed to bury the words in polyphonic texture, and indicated new ways for music to serve poetry, often by insisting on music's analogy to poetry. Sketched out in the preface "To the Reader," the esthetic is really a musico-poetic manifesto. By finding the analogue to the ayre in the epigram, it carries the literary cult of brevity, started in the late 1590s, into the realm of music.

As originally published, the songs appeared with a vocal line, a lute part in tablature below it, and a Bass line for viola da gamba above it and upside-down (for reading across a table). As the title page indicates, the lute part could also be played on the orpheoreon or orpharean, a large member of the cittern family (flat-backed instead of rounded, as the lute was, and strung with wire instead of gut) popular in the first decade of the seventeenth century. While in most of the songs the Bass line for viola da gamba merely doubles the bottom line of the lute, in some it nearly becomes a separate part; in the transcription of "Though you are yoong" (ii) prepared for this edition, such a part has been printed beneath the realization of the lute part.

Campion's collaborator in this volume, Philip Rosseter (ca. 1575–1623), was, like John Dowland, one of the new school of professional lutenists whose rise to prominence paralleled that of the solo song. On November 8, 1604, he was created King's lutenist at a total stipend of £36/2/6 per annum; his later activities include compilation of *Lessons for Consort* (1607) and management of the Court Revels (on January 4, 1610, he, along with Philip Kingman, Robert Jones, and Ralph Reeve, was granted a patent to keep the Children of the Revels to the Queen in Whitefriars). Rosseter remained a close friend of Campion's until the poet's death, being named sole legatee in his will. Rosseter was certainly the sole composer of both the words and music of Part II of *A Booke of Ayres;* but, since previous editors have attributed Part II to Campion, it is printed in the present edition among Doubtful Poems.

Sir Thomas Monson (1564–1641), whose coat of arms appears on the reverse of the title page facing the dedication in the original edition, was a prominent Roman Catholic, a dependent of the powerful Howards and a favorite with King James, who made him first his Master Falconer and later (in 1611) Master of the Armoury at the Tower. This latter position involved him in the Overbury murder case (see headnote to *The Somerset Masque*); when he finally emerged from prison with a pardon in 1617, he was financially and politically ruined. In his heyday, Monson was well known for his musical entertainments and his patronage of young singers (including John Dowland's son Robert), some of whom he had educated in Italy; it is possible that Monson's familiarity with contemporary developments in Italian music made some imprint on the monodic art of *A Booke of Ayres,* as well as on Campion's harmonic knowledge in the later (ca. 1613, 1614) treatise on counterpoint.

TO THE RIGHT VERTUOUS
AND WORTHY KNIGHT, SIR
THOMAS MOUNSON.

SIR, the generall voice of your worthines, and the manie particular favours which I have heard Master *Campion*, with dutifull respect, often acknowledge himselfe to have received from you, have emboldned mee to present this Booke of Ayres to your favourable judgement and gracious protection; especially because the first ranke of songs are of his owne composition, made at his vacant houres, and privately emparted to his friends, whereby they grew both publicke, and (as coine crackt in exchange) corrupted: some of them, both words and notes unrespectively, challenged by others. In regard of which wronges, though his selfe neglects these light fruits as superfluous blossomes of his deeper Studies, yet hath it pleased him, upon my entreaty, to grant me the impression of part of them, to which I have added an equall number of mine owne. And this two-faced *Janus,* thus in one bodie united, I humbly entreate you to entertaine and defend, chiefely in respect of the affection which I suppose you beare him, who, I am assured, doth above all others love and honour you. And for my part, I shall thinke my selfe happie if in anie service I may deserve this favour.

Your Worships humbly devoted,

PHILIP ROSSETER.

TO THE READER.

WHAT Epigrams are in Poetrie, the same are Ayres in musicke, then in their chiefe perfection when they are short and well seasoned. But to clogg a light song with a long Praeludium,[1] is to corrupt the nature of it. Manie rests in Musicke were invented either for necessitie of the fuge,[2] or granted as a harmonicall licence in songs of many parts: but in Ayres I find no use they have, unlesse it be to make a vulgar and triviall modulation seeme to the ignorant strange, and to the judiciall tedious. A naked Ayre without guide, or prop, or colour but his owne, is easily censured of everie eare, and requires so much the more invention to make it please. And as *Martiall* speakes in defence of his short Epigrams, so may I say in th' apologie of Ayres, that where there is a full volume, there can be no imputation of shortnes.[3] The Lyricke Poets among the Greekes and Latines were first inventers of Ayres, tying themselves strictly to the number and value of their sillables, of which sort, you shall find here onely one song in Saphicke verse; the rest are after the fascion of the time, eare-pleasing rimes without Arte. The subject of them is for the most part amorous, and why not amorous songs, as well as amorous attires? Or why not new Ayres, as well as new fascions? For the Note and Tableture, if they satisfie the most, we have our desire; let expert masters please themselves with better. And if anie light error hath escaped us, the skilfull may easily correct it, the unskilfull will hardly perceive it. But there are some, who to appeare the more deepe and singular in their judgement, will admit no Musicke but that which is long, intricate, bated with fuge, chaind with sincopation, and where the nature of everie word is precisely exprest in the Note, like the old exploided action in Comedies, when if they did pronounce *Memini*,[4] they would point to the hinder part of their heads, if *Video*,[5] put their finger in their eye. But such childish observing of words is altogether ridiculous, and we ought to maintaine as well in Notes, as in action, a manly cariage, gracing no word, but that which is eminent, and emphaticall. Neverthelesse, as in Poesie we give the preheminence to the Heroicall Poeme, so in Musicke we yeeld the chiefe place to the grave

---

[1] prelude.

[2] Frequent rests in the various voices of a polyphonic piece allow the imitative or fugal structure to be heard.

[3] Martial makes remarks of this general tenor several times: see, e.g., *Epigrams* I. xlv; VII. lxxxv; VIII. xxix; and IX. l.

[4] "I remember."   [5] "I see."

and well invented Motet, but not to every harsh and dull confused Fantasie, where in multitude of points the Harmonie is quite drowned. Ayres have both their Art and pleasure, and I will conclude of them, as the Poet did in his censure of *Catullus* the Lyricke, and *Vergil* the Heroicke writer:

> *Tantum magna suo debet Verona Catullo:*
> *Quantum parva suo Mantua Vergilio.*[6]

[6] Martial, *Epigrams* XIV. cxcv: "Great Verona owes as much to her Catullus as tiny Mantua owes to her Virgil."

A Table of halfe the Songs contained
in this Booke, by T. C.

I.[7]

My sweetest Lesbia, let us live and love,
And, though the sager sort our deedes reprove,
Let us not way them: heav'ns great lampes doe dive
Into their west, and strait againe revive,
But, soone as once set is our little light,   5
Then must we sleepe one ever-during night.

If all would lead their lives in love like mee,
Then bloudie swords and armour should not be,
No drum nor trumpet peacefull sleepes should move,
Unles alar'me came from the campe of love: 10
But fooles do live, and wast their little light,
And seeke with paine their ever-during night.

When timely death my life and fortune ends,
Let not my hearse be vext with mourning friends,
But let all lovers, rich in triumph, come,   15
And with sweet pastimes grace my happie tombe;
And, Lesbia, close up thou my little light,
And crowne with love my ever-during night.

[7] This song is based on the well-known lines of Catullus V:

> Vivamus, mea Lesbia, atque amemus,
> rumoresque senum severiorum
> omnes unius aestimemus assis.
> soles occidere et redire possunt:
> nobis cum semel occidit brevis lux,
> nox est perpetua una dormienda

[Let us live, my Lesbia, and love, and value at a mere farthing all the talk of severe old men. Suns can set and rise again; but, when once our short light dies out, we must sleep one perpetual night].

The second strophe, as J. V. Cunningham has shown ("Campion and Propertius," *Philological Quarterly*, XXXI [1952], 96), depends heavily on Propertius II. xv, especially ll. 41 and 43:

> qualem si cuncti cuperent decurrere vitam, . . .
> non ferrum crudele neque esset bellica navis

[If only all men would pass their lives thus, . . . there would be no cruel steel nor ships of war].

Translations and imitations of Catullus' poem are frequent in the seventeenth century; they include Jonson's "Come, my Celia" (*The Forest*, V), Crashaw's "Come and let us live, my Deare" (*The Delights of the Muses*), "Come Laura come letts live and love," an anonymous song in MS Don. c. 57 (fos. 50–51), and "My deerest mistresse, let us live and love" in William Corkine's *Second Booke of Ayres*. For this last, see Doubtful Poems, below.

My sweet-est Les - bia, let us live and love, And, though the

sa - ger sort our deedes re - prove, Let us not

way them: heav'ns great lampes doe dive In - to their

west, and strait a - gaine re - vive,

But, soone as once set is our lit - tle light, Then must we

sleepe one e - ver - dur- ing night, e - ver - dur - ing night.

II.

Though you are yoong and I am olde,
Though your vaines hot and my bloud colde,
Though youth is moist and age is drie,
Yet embers live when flames doe die.

The tender graft is easely broke,   5
But who shall shake the sturdie Oke?
You are more fresh and faire then I,
Yet stubs doe live, when flowers doe die.

Thou that thy youth doest vainely boast,
Know buds are soonest nipt with frost;   10
Thinke that thy fortune still doth crie,
Thou foole, tomorrow thou must die.

III.

I care not for these Ladies
That must be woode and praide,
Give me kind Amarillis
The wanton countrey[8] maide;
Nature art disdaineth,   5
Her beautie is her owne;
    Her when we court and kisse,
    She cries, forsooth, let go:
    But when we come where comfort is,
    She never will say no.   10

If I love Amarillis,
She gives me fruit and flowers,
But if we love these Ladies,
We must give golden showers;
Give them gold that sell love,   15
Give me the Nutbrowne lasse,
    Who when we court and kisse,
    She cries, forsooth, let go:
    But when we come where comfort is,
    She never will say no.   20

These Ladies must have pillowes,
And beds by strangers wrought,
Give me a Bower of willowes,
Of mosse and leaves unbought,
And fresh Amarillis,   25
With milke and honie fed,
    Who when we court and kisse,
    She cries, forsooth, let go:
    But when we come where comfort is,
    She never will say no.   30

[8] with the common obscene pun (see *Hamlet*, III, ii, 123), a pun reinforced by the alliteration on *c* and the assonance of words in l. 9. The rustic quality of the song is stressed by the meter (in part, the old-fashioned "poulter's measure" of the 1560s and '70s) and the music, for it is set to a country dance tune, a jig.

I care not for these La - dies That must be woode and praide,
Give me kind A - ma - ril - lis The wan - ton coun - trey maide;

Na - ture art dis - dain - eth, Her beau - tie is her owne;

Her when we __ court and kisse, She cries, for - sooth, let go:

But when we come where com - fort is, she ne - ver __ will say no.

IV.[9]

Followe thy faire sunne, unhappy shaddowe:
Though thou be blacke as night,
And she made all of light,
Yet follow thy faire sunne, unhappie shaddowe.

Follow her whose light thy light depriveth: 5
Though here thou liv'st disgrac't,
And she in heaven is plac't,
Yet follow her whose light the world reviveth.

Follow those pure beames whose beautie burneth,
That so have scorched thee,   10
As thou still blacke must bee,
Til her kind beames thy black to brightnes turneth.

Follow her while yet her glorie shineth:
There comes a luckles night,
That will dim all her light;   15
And this the black unhappie shade devineth.

Follow still since so thy fates ordained:
The Sunne must have his shade,
Till both at once doe fade,
The Sun still prov'd,[10] the shadow still disdained. 20

[9] The setting for this song was also used for "Seeke the Lord, and in his wayes persever," *The First Booke*, xviii.
[10] approved.

Fol - lowe thy   faire   sunne,   un - hap - py   shad - dowe:

Though   thou,   though thou be blacke as   night,   And she made all   of

light,   Yet fol - low   thy faire sunne, un - hap   -   pie   shad   -   dowe.

V.

My love hath vowd hee will forsake mee,
And I am alreadie sped.[11]
Far other promise he did make me
When he had my maidenhead.
If such danger be in playing,   5
And sport must to earnest turne,
I will go no more a-maying.

Had I foreseene what is ensued,
And what now with paine I prove,[12]
Unhappie then I had eschewed   10
This unkind event[13] of love:
Maides foreknow their own undooing,
But feare naught till all is done,
When a man alone is wooing.

Dissembling wretch, to gaine thy pleasure,   15
What didst thou not vow and sweare?
So didst thou rob me of the treasure
Which so long I held so deare;
Now thou prov'st to me a stranger,
Such is the vile guise of men   20
When a woman is in danger.

That hart is neerest to misfortune
That will trust a fained toong;
When flattring men our loves importune,
They entend us deepest wrong;   25
If this shame of loves betraying
But this once I cleanely shun,
I will go no more a-maying.

[11] undone.   [12] experience.   [13] unhappy result.

VI.[14]

When to her lute Corrina sings,
Her voice revives the leaden[15] stringes,
And doth in highest noates appeare
As any challeng'd[16] eccho cleere;
But when she doth of mourning speake,   5
Ev'n with her sighes the strings do breake.

And, as her lute doth live or die,
Led by her passion, so must I:
For when of pleasure she doth sing,
My thoughts enjoy a sodaine spring;   10
But if she doth of sorrow speake,
Ev'n from my hart the strings doe breake.

[14] This song may have been suggested by Propertius II. iii. 19–22, where a woman arousing her lover by her lyre playing is assimilated to the Boeotian poetess Corinna:

> et quantum, Aelio cum temptat carmina plectro,
>   par Aganippeae ludere docta lyrae;
> et sua cum antiquae committit scripta Corinnae,
>   carminaque Erinnes non putat aequa suis

[all the more, when she sings to the Aeolian harp, she equals the lyre of Aganippe in her skill of playing, and with her verse she rivals the writings of ancient Corinna, and does not deem Erinna's songs the equals of her own].

John Hollander notes (*The Untuning of the Sky*, pp. 204–5) that "to her lute" in l. 1 may mean both "accompanied by her lute" and "addressing her lute."

[15] heavy (lute strings were made of gut).   [16] aroused.

When to her lute Cor - ri - na sings, Her voice re - vives ____ the ____ lea - den stringes, And doth in high - est noates ap - peare As a - ny chal - leng'd ec - cho cleere; But when she doth of mourn - ing speake, Ev'n with her sighes, her sighes, her sighes, the strings do breake, the ____ strings do breake.

VII.

Turne backe, you wanton[17] flyer,
And answere my desire
With mutuall greeting;
Yet bende a little neerer,
True beauty stil[18] shines cleerer   5
In closer meeting.
Harts with harts delighted
Should strive to be united,
Either others armes with armes enchayning:
Harts with a thought, rosie lips   10
With a kisse still entertaining.

What harvest halfe so sweete is
As still to reape the kisses
Growne ripe in sowing,[19]
And straight to be receiver   15
Of that which thou art giver,
Rich in bestowing?
There's no strickt observing
Of times, or seasons changing,
There is ever one fresh spring abiding: 20
Then what we sow with our lips
Let us reape, loves gaines deviding.

---

[17] frisky.   [18] always (the usual meaning of "still" in this period).
[19] Compare Catullus XLVIII. 5–6:

> *non si densior aridis aristis*
> *sit nostrae seges osculationis*

[not if the harvest of our kisses were thicker than the ripe ears of grain].

VIII.[20]

It fell on a sommers day,
While sweete Bessie sleeping laie
In her bowre, on her bed,
Light with curtaines shadowed;
Jamy came, shee him spies,   5
Opning halfe her heavie eies.

Jamy stole in through the dore,
She lay slumbring as before;
Softly to her he drew neere,
She heard him, yet would not heare;   10
Bessie vow'd not to speake,
He resolv'd that dumpe[21] to breake.

First a soft kisse he doth take,
She lay still, and would not wake;
Then his hands learn'd to woo,   15
She dreamp't not what he would doo,
But still slept, while he smild
To see love by sleepe beguild.

Jamy then began to play,
Bessie as one buried lay,   20
Gladly still through this sleight
Deceiv'd in her owne deceit;
And, since this traunce[22] begoon,
She sleepes ev'rie afternoone.

[20] See Campion's two Latin versions of this song, *"In Lycium et Clytham," Epigrammatum Liber* II, 60, below, and its early version, *"De Thermanio et Glaia"* (textual notes).
[21] reverie.   [22] dazed state or ecstasy.

IX.

The Sypres[23] curten of the night is spread,
And over all a silent dewe is cast.
The weaker cares by sleepe are conquered;
But I alone, with hidious griefe agast,
In spite of Morpheus charmes a watch doe keepe   5
Over mine eies, to banish carelesse sleepe.

Yet oft my trembling eyes through faintnes close,
And then the Mappe of hell before me stands,
Which Ghosts doe see, and I am one of those
Ordain'd to pine in sorrowes endles bands,   10
Since from my wretched soule all hopes are reft
And now no cause of life to me is left.

Griefe, ceaze[24] my soule, for that will still endure
When my cras'd[25] bodie is consum'd and gone;
Beare it to thy blacke denne, there keepe it sure,   15
Where thou ten thousand soules doest tyre[26] upon:
Yet all doe not affoord such foode to thee
As this poore one, the worser part of mee.

X.[27]

Follow your Saint, follow with accents sweet,
Haste you, sad noates, fall at her flying feete;
There, wrapt in cloud of sorrowe, pitie move,
And tell the ravisher of my soule I perish for her love.
But if she scorns my never-ceasing paine,   5
Then burst with sighing in her sight, and nere returne againe.

All that I soong still to her praise did tend,
Still she was first, still she my songs did end.
Yet she my love and Musicke both doeth flie,
The Musicke that her Eccho is, and beauties simpathie;   10
Then let my Noates pursue her scornefull flight:
It shall suffice that they were breath'd, and dyed, for her delight.

[23] a thin material like crape, usually dyed black and used for mourning.
[24] seize.   [25] crazed, broken-down.
[26] tear with the beak like a falcon, prey upon.
[27] The setting of this song was also employed for "Love me or not," *The Fourth Booke*, x.

XI.

Faire, if you expect admiring,
Sweet, if you provoke desiring,
Grace deere love with kinde requiting.[28]
Fond, but if thy sight be blindnes,
False, if thou affect unkindnes,   5
Flie both love and loves delighting.[29]
Then when hope is lost and love is scorned,
Ile bury my desires, and quench the fires that ever yet in vaine have
        burned.

Fates, if you rule lovers fortune,
Stars, if men your powers importune,   10
Yield reliefe by your relenting.
Time, if sorrow be not endles,
Hope made vaine, and pittie friendles,
Helpe to ease my long lamenting.
But if griefes remaine still unredressed,   15
I'le flie to her againe, and sue for pitie to renue my hopes distressed.

---

[28] i.e., grace love by returning it in kind.
[29] i.e., false if you show your "love" of unkindness by fleeing from love
and delight.

XII.[30]

Thou art not faire, for all thy red and white,
For all those rosie ornaments in thee;
Thou art not sweet, though made of meer delight,
Nor faire nor sweet, unlesse thou pitie mee.
I will not sooth thy fancies: thou shalt prove[31]   5
That beauty is no beautie without love.

Yet love not me, nor seeke thou to allure
My thoughts with beautie, were it more devine;
Thy smiles and kisses I cannot endure,
I'le not be wrapt up in those armes of thine.   10
Now shew it, if thou be a woman right:
Embrace, and kisse, and love me, in despight.

[30] Compare the Latin version of this song, "*Ad Caspiam,*" *Epigrammatum Liber* II, 53, below. The source of this song is probably Propertius' tirade against cosmetics in II. xviii. 25–30:

> *ut natura dedit, sic omnis recta figura est:*
> *turpis Romano Belgicus ore color.*
> *illi sub terris fiant mala multa puellae,*
> *quae mentita suas vertit inepta comas!*
> *deme: mihi certe poteris formosa videri;*
> *mi formosa satis, si modo saepe venis*

[The form is always right as nature made it: Belgian rouge looks dirty on Roman cheeks. May many evils in hell befall that girl who dyes her hair with a lying color foolishly! Away with such things! To me surely you can seem beautiful: to me you will be beautiful enough if only you come to me often].

[31] find.

Thou art not faire, for all thy red and white,
Thou art not sweet, though made of meer de-light,
For all those ro-sie or-na-ments in thee;
Nor faire nor sweet, un-lesse thou pi-tie mee.
I will not sooth thy fan-cies: thou shalt prove
That beau-ty is no beau-tie with-out love.

XIII.

See where she flies enrag'd from me,
View her when she intends despite:
The winde is not more swift then shee,
Her furie mov'd such terror makes
As, to a fearfull guiltie sprite,   5
The voice of heav'ns huge thunder cracks.
But, when her appeased minde yeelds to delight,
All her thoughts are made of joyes,
Millions of delights inventing:
Other pleasures are but toies   10
To her beauties sweete contenting.

My fortune hangs upon her brow,
For, as she smiles or frownes on mee,
So must my blowne[32] affections bow;
And her proude thoughts too well do find   15
With what unequall tyrannie
Her beauties doe command my mind.
Though, when her sad planet raignes, froward she bee,
She alone can pleasure move,
And displeasing sorrow banish: 20
May I but still hold her love,
Let all other comforts vanish.

[32] full-blown like flowers.

XIV.[33]

Blame not my cheeks, though pale with love they be;
The kindly heate unto my heart is flowne,
To cherish it that is dismaid by thee,
Who art so cruell and unsteedfast growne:
For nature, cald for by distressed harts,   5
Neglects and quite forsakes the outward partes.

But they whose cheekes with careles blood are stain'd
Nurse not one sparke of love within their harts,
And, when they woe, they speake with passion fain'd,
For their fat love lyes in their outward parts: 10
But in their brests, where love his court should hold,
Poore Cupid sits and blowes his nailes for cold.

[33] Compare Ovid *Amores* II. xix. 19–26, especially ll. 25–26, which
contain the phrase *pinguis amor* [fat love].

Blame not my cheeks, though pale with love they be;
To cher - ish it that is dis - maid by thee,

The kind - ly heate un - to my heart is flowne,
Who art so cru - ell and un - steed - fast growne:

For na - ture, cald for _ by _ dis - tres - sed harts,

Neg - lects and quite for - sakes the out - ward partes.

XV.

When the God of merrie love
As yet in his cradle lay,
Thus his wither'd nurse did say:
Thou a wanton[34] boy wilt prove
To deceive the powers above;   5
For by thy continuall smiling
I see thy power of beguiling.

Therewith she the babe did kisse,
When a sodaine fire out came
From those burning lips of his,   10
That did her with love enflame;
But none would regard the same,
So that, to her daie of dying,
The old wretch liv'd ever crying.

[34] mischievous.

XVI.[35]

Mistris, since you so much desire
To know the place of Cupids fire,
In your faire shrine that flame doth rest,
Yet never harbourd in your brest;
It bides not in your lips so sweete,   5
Nor where the rose and lillies meete,
But a little higher, but a little higher:
There, there, O there lies Cupids fire.

Even in those starrie pearcing eyes,
There Cupids sacred fire lyes;   10
Those eyes I strive not to enjoy,
For they have power to destroy;
Nor woe I for a smile, or kisse,
So meanely triumph's not my blisse;
But a little higher, but a little higher,   15
I climbe to crowne my chast desire.

[35] Compare "Beauty, since you so much desire," *The Fourth Booke,*
xxii.

XVII.[36]

Your faire lookes enflame my desire:
   Quench it againe with love.
Stay, O strive not still to retire,
   Doe not inhumane prove.
If love may perswade,   5
   Loves pleasures, deere, denie not;
Heere is a silent grovie shade:
   O tarrie then, and flie not.

Have I seaz'd my heavenly delight
   In this unhaunted grove?   10
Time shall now her furie requite
   With the revenge of love.
Then come, sweetest, come,
   My lips with kisses gracing:
Here let us harbour all alone,   15
   Die, die[37] in sweete embracing.

Will you now so timely depart,
   And not returne againe?
Your sight lends such life to my hart
   That to depart is paine.   20
Feare yeelds no delay,
   Securenes helpeth pleasure:
Then, till the time gives safer stay,
   O farewell, my lives treasure!

[36] Compare "Your faire lookes urge my desire," *The Fourth Booke,* xxiii.

[37] the famous Elizabethan die pun: reach consummation.

XVIII.[38]

The man of life upright,
　Whose guiltlesse hart is free
From all dishonest deedes,
　Or thought of vanitie,

The man whose silent dayes   5
　In harmeles joyes are spent,
Whome hopes cannot delude,
　Nor sorrow discontent,

That man needes neither towers
　Nor armour for defence,   10
Nor secret vautes to flie
　From thunders violence.

Hee onely can behold
　With unafrighted eyes
The horrours of the deepe,   15
　And terrours of the Skies.

Thus, scorning all the cares
　That fate, or fortune brings,
He makes the heav'n his booke,
　His wisedome heev'nly things,   20

Good thoughts his onely friendes,
　His wealth a well-spent age,
The earth his sober Inne,
　And quiet Pilgrimage.

[38] This song is attributed to Sir Francis Bacon in several manuscripts.
Lines 1–16 are a free paraphrase of Horace *Odes* I. xxii. 1–8:

> *Integer vitae scelerisque purus*
> *non eget Mauris iaculis neque arcu*
> *nec venenatis gravida sagittis,*
> 　　*Fusce, pharetra,*
> *sive per Syrtes iter aestuosas*
> *sive facturus per inhospitalem*
> *Caucasum vel quae loca fabulosus*
> 　　*lambit Hydaspes*

[He who is upright in his life and free from crime does not need Moorish
darts nor a bow nor a quiver loaded with poisoned arrows, Fuscus, whether
he makes his way through the burning Syrtes or the forbidding Caucasus
or the regions that fabled Hydaspes washes].

Compare also George Herbert's "Constancie."

XIX.[39]

Harke, al you ladies that do sleep:
   the fayry queen Proserpina
Bids you awake and pitie them that weep;
   you may doe in the darke
What the day doth forbid: 5
   feare not the dogs that barke,
        Night will have all hid.

But if you let your lovers mone,
   the Fairie Queene Proserpina
Will send abroad her Fairies ev'rie one,   10
   that shall pinch blacke and blew
Your white hands, and faire armes,
   that did not kindly rue
        Your Paramours harmes.

In Myrtle Arbours on the downes,   15
   the Fairie Queene Proserpina,
This night by moone-shine leading merrie rounds,
   holds a watch with sweet love;
Downe the dale, up the hill,
   no plaints or groanes may move   20
        Their holy vigill.

All you that will hold watch with love,
   the Fairie Queene Proserpina
Will make you fairer then Diones dove;
   Roses red, Lillies white,   25
And the cleare damaske hue,
   shall on your cheekes alight:
        Love will adorne you.

All you that love, or lov'd before,
   the Fairie Queene Proserpina   30
Bids you encrease that loving humour more:
   they that yet have not fed
On delight amorous,
   she vowes that they shall lead
        Apes in Avernus.   35

[39] See footnotes [1-4] to the earlier printing of this song as *"Canto Primo"* in the *Astrophel and Stella* appendix.

Harke, al you lad·ies that do sleep: the fay·ry queen Pro·

ser·pin·a Bids you a·wake and pi·tie them that weep;

you may doe in the darke What the day doth for·bid:

feare not the dogs that barke, Night will have all hid.

XX.[40]

When thou must home to shades of under ground,
And there ariv'd, a newe admired guest,
The beauteous spirits do ingirt thee round,
White Iope, blith Hellen, and the rest,
To heare the stories of thy finisht love,   5
From that smoothe toong whose musicke hell can move:

Then wilt thou speake of banqueting delights,
Of masks and revels[41] which sweete youth did make,
Of Turnies and great challenges of knights,
And all these triumphes for thy beauties sake: 10
When thou hast told these honours done to thee,
Then tell, O tell, how thou didst murther me.

[40] Bullen in his edition of Campion has indicated the source of this song as Propertius II. xxviii. 49–52:

> *sunt apud infernos tot milia formosarum:*
> *pulchra sit in superis, si licet, una locis.*
> *vobiscum est Iope, vobiscum candida Tyro,*
> *vobiscum Europe nec proba Pasiphae*

[There are so many thousands of beauties among the dead: let just one beauty stay above, if it may be. With you is Iope, with you white Tyro, with you is Europa, and impious Pasiphae].

[41] masques and other entertainments.

When thou must home to shades of un - der - ground,
The beau - teous spi - rits do in - girt thee round,

And there a - riv'd, a newe ad - mi - red guest,
White I - o - pe, blith Hel - len, and the rest,

To heare the sto - ries of thy fin - isht love,

From that smoothe toong whose mu - sicke hell can move:

XXI.[42]

Come, let us sound with melody the praises
Of the kings king, th'omnipotent creator,
Author of number, that hath all the world in
        Harmonie framed.

Heav'n is his throne perpetually shining,   5
His devine power and glorie thence he thunders,
One in all, and all still in one abiding,
        Both Father, and Sonne.

O sacred sprite, invisible, eternall,
Ev'ry where, yet unlimited, that all things   10
Canst in one moment penetrate, revive me,
        O holy Spirit.

Rescue, O rescue me from earthly darknes,
Banish hence all these elementall objects,
Guide my soule that thirsts to the lively Fountaine   15
        Of thy devinenes.

Cleanse my soule, O God, thy bespotted Image,
Altered with sinne so that heav'nly purenes
Cannot acknowledge me but in thy mercies,
        O Father of grace.   20

But when once thy beames do remove my darknes,
O then I'le shine forth as an Angell of light,
And record, with more than an earthly voice, thy
        Infinite honours.

FINIS.

[42] a free paraphrase of Psalm 19, *Coeli Enarrant,* in the Sapphic meter;
this is the one song in classical meters Campion mentions in the preface
"To the Reader." Campion here uses the "pure" form of Sapphic which
Sidney established in "If mine eyes can speake" in *Arcadia* rather than
the three free varieties he created for himself in the *Observations.* As
Catherine Ing has observed, the music ensures a correct scansion, the al-
ternating minims and crotchets regulating three lines — ∪ — — — ∪ ∪ — ∪ — —
and a short fourth line — ∪ ∪ — — (*Elizabethan Lyrics,* p. 154; see also pp.
162–63 on its sound effects).

Come, let us sound with melody the prai-
ses Of the kings king, th'om·ni·po-tent crea - tor,
Au-thor of num·ber, that hath all the world in Har·mo·nie fram - ed.

TWO BOOKES
OF
AYRES.

THE FIRST
Contayning Divine and Morall Songs:

THE SECOND,
Light Conceits of Lovers.

To be sung to the *Lute* and *Viols*, in two,
three, and foure Parts: or by one *Voyce*
to an INSTRUMENT.

Composed
By
Thomas Campian.

Two Bookes of Ayres, The First Contayning Divine and Morall Songs: The Second, Light Conceits of Lovers appeared without date. But the reference to the youth of Henry, Lord Clifford (born in 1591) suggests a date somewhat before 1615; and the close relation of one of the songs to *The Lords' Masque* of February 14, 1613, as well as the addition of an elegy on Prince Henry (who died November 6, 1612) to the end of *The First Booke,* suggests a date late in 1612 or early in 1613.

Francis and Henry Clifford, father and son, to whom Campion dedicated his two books, were prominent North Country patrons of music; their household records, which have been summarized by Walter L. Woodfill (*Musicians in English Society from Elizabeth to Charles I,* Princeton Studies in History, 9 [Princeton, 1953], pp. 256–60), show constant expenditures for instruments and performances by local musicians. Giovanni Coperario seems to have worked for them, and George Mason was household musician to Francis, Earl of Cumberland, from at least 1611 to after 1618. It may be that Campion, who seems to have experienced Cumberland's hospitality, also wrote the words to Mason's music for the reception of King James at Brougham Castle in 1617 (see Doubtful Poems).

Campion made it clear that the two books of this publication were organized around a single large contrast of subject matter (sacred and secular), style, and, hence, of appeal (to age and youth). *The First Booke,* which was, incidentally, the first English collection of sacred ayres (though, unfortunately, not a very successful one), has considerable variety, including as it does paraphrases of psalms, moral verse in the Horatian manner, a thanksgiving ode, elegy, allegorical vision, and several pieces in the "witty" tradition of mediaeval Latin hymnody. The love songs of *The Second Booke* form a contrast to the first not only in subject matter but in context, for they are mundane and social instead of idealistic love songs, and both their themes of marriage and adultery (which frequently give a wry twist to moribund courtly love themes) and their personae of cynical or tired lovers contrast strikingly the moods generated by the divine songs.

The style of *The First Booke* is typically that of pithy literal statement (perhaps encouraged by the tradition of paraphrasing psalms), concentrating on clarity of outline and terseness, its main aims precise definition of a situation and wholeness of vision (see iii, "Where are all thy beauties now," for an example of poised judgment); within this mode, Campion sometimes achieves a real intellectual wit (as in the turn the second strophe of xvii takes), as well as an occasional knotty "strong line" (xvi, lines 8–9, for example, or xvii, line 11). On the other hand, the love songs of *The Second Booke* are luxuriant and insistently figured in mode, whether they be allegorical, imagistic, or conceited; sometimes it is an image which serves as the hinge for a reversal in tone (as in the middle strophe of "Vaine men"), and frequently the song concludes with a complex or paradoxical conceit (as vi, viii, and xvii do).

For all the differences between Campion's two books, there is some pressure toward unity in tonal modulations, most notably where the two meet. The first song of *The Second Booke*, "Vaine men, whose follies make a God of Love," is a critique of love carrying some of *The First Booke*'s moral pressure into the second; likewise, in the elegy at the end of *The First Booke*, Prince Henry is treated as a fertility figure rather than as sacred, and the preceding song on Jack and Jone takes a light and sometimes comic view of its homely exemplars of virtue.

In this publication Campion reversed his position in *A Booke of Ayres* by arranging his songs for four, three, or two parts. The printing in parts was surely, as Campion admits, a concession to popular practice in singing; but two additional considerations may be brought forth to account for it. First, his concept of the inner parts as filling in the auditory "space" between Bass line and Cantus shows that he was already thinking in the "vertical" harmonic terms characteristic of baroque music theory, and given full development in his treatise on counterpoint. Second, by setting most of the sacred songs of *The First Booke* to four parts, Campion assimilated his religious ayres to "the grave and well invented Motet," which he had compared earlier to the epic poem in verse. Plate II of the present edition presents one of these four-part settings.

TO THE RIGHT
HONOURABLE, BOTH
in Birth and Vertue, FRANCIS, Earle
of CUMBERLAND.

What Patron could I chuse, great *Lord,* but you?
Grave words your years may challenge as their owne,
   And ev'ry note of Musicke is your due,
Whose House the *Muses* pallace I have knowne.

To love and cherish them, though it descends   5
With many honours more on you, in vaine
   Preceding fame herein with you contends,
Who have both fed the *Muses,* and their trayne.

These Leaves I offer you, Devotion might
Her selfe lay open, reade them, or else heare   10
   How gravely with their tunes they yeeld delight
To any vertuous, and not curious[1] eare.
   Such as they are accept them, Noble *Lord;*
   If better, better could my zeale afford.

Your Honors,

THOMAS CAMPIAN.

[1] prying.

TO THE READER.

OUT of many Songs which, partly at the request of friends, partly for my owne recreation, were by mee long since composed, I have now enfranchised a few, sending them forth divided, according to their different subject, into severall Bookes. The first are grave and pious; the second, amorous and light. For hee that in publishing any worke, hath a desire to content all palates, must cater for them accordingly.

> ———*Non omnibus unum est*
> *Quod placet, hic Spinas colligit, ille Rosas.*[2]

These Ayres were for the most part framed at first for one voyce with the Lute, or Violl, but, upon occasion, they have since beene filled with more parts, which who so please may use, who like not may leave. Yet doe wee daily observe, that when any shall sing a Treble to an Instrument, the standers by will be offring at an inward part out of their owne nature; and, true or false, out it must, though to the perverting of the whole harmonie. Also, if wee consider well, the Treble tunes, which are with us commonly called Ayres, are but Tenors mounted eight Notes higher, and therefore an inward part must needes well become them, such as may take up the whole distance of the *Diapason*,[3] and fill up the gaping betweene the two extreame parts; whereby, though they are not three parts in perfection, yet they yeeld a sweetnesse and content both to the eare and minde, which is the ayme and perfection of Musicke. Short Ayres, if they be skilfully framed, and naturally exprest, are like quicke and good Epigrammes in Poesie, many of them shewing as much artifice, and breeding as great difficultie, as a larger Poeme. *Non omnia possumus omnes,* said the *Romane* Epick Poet.[4] But some there are who admit onely *French* or *Italian* Ayres, as if every Country had not his proper Ayre, which the people thereof naturally usurpe in their Musicke. Others taste nothing that comes forth in Print, as if *Catullus* or *Martials* Epigrammes were the worse for being published. In these *English* Ayres, I have chiefely aymed to couple my Words and Notes lovingly together, which will be much for him to doe that hath not power over both. The light of this will best appeare to him who hath pays'd[5] our Monasylla-

---

[2] "There is not one thing that pleases all: this one picks thorns, that one, roses."

[3] the octave.

[4] Virgil *Eclogue* VIII. 63: "We cannot all do all things."   [5] weighed.

bles and Syllables combined, both which are so loaded with Consonants, as that they will hardly keepe company with swift Notes, or give the Vowell convenient liberty. To conclude: mine owne opinion of these Songs I deliver thus:

> *Omnia nec nostris bona sunt, sed nec mala libris;*
> *Si placet hac cantes, hac quoque lege legas.*[6]

Farewell.

[6] "All the things in our book are not good, but neither are all of them bad; if you please, you may sing them, or, by agreement, read them." The implication seems to be that some of the buyers are good singers (just as some of the songs are good), and some are not; the latter are advised to read the book rather than sing. See Martial I. xvi.

A TABLE OF ALL THE SONGS
contayned in these Bookes.

In the first Booke.

Songs of 4. Parts.

Songs of 3. Parts.

Of 2. Parts.

In the second Booke.

Songs of 3. Parts.

Of 2. Parts.

THE FIRST BOOKE

I.[7]

Author of light, revive my dying spright,
Redeeme it from the snares of all-confounding night.
      Lord, light me to thy blessed way:
For, blinde with worldly vaine desires, I wander as a stray.
      Sunne and Moone, Starres and underlights I see,   5
But all their glorious beames are mists and darknes, being
      compar'd to thee.

Fountaine of health, my soules deepe wounds recure,
Sweet showres of pitty raine, wash my uncleannesse pure.
      One drop of thy desired grace
The faint and fading hart can raise, and in joyes bosome place.[8] 10
      Sinne and Death, Hell and tempting Fiends may rage;
But God his owne will guard, and their sharp paines and
      griefe in time asswage.

[7] See the reproduction of this song as it originally appeared, Plate II. For an incisive analysis, see Wilfrid Mellers, "Words and Music in Elizabethan England," *The Age of Shakespeare,* ed. Boris Ford, 407–8.

[8] place the heart in joy's bosom.

II.[9]

The man of life upright,
  Whose chearfull minde is free
From waight of impious deedes,
  And yoake of vanitee,

The man whose silent dayes   5
  In harmelesse joyes are spent:
Whom hopes cannot delude,
  Nor sorrowes discontent,

That man needes neyther towres,
  Nor armour for defence: 10
Nor vaults his guilt to shrowd
  From thunders violence;

Hee onely can behold
  With unaffrighted eyes
The horrors of the deepe,   15
  And terrors of the Skies.

Thus, scorning all the cares
  That fate or fortune brings,
His Booke the Heav'ns hee makes,
  His wisedome heav'nly things.   20

Good thoughts his surest friends,
  His wealth a well-spent age,
The earth his sober Inne,
  And quiet pilgrimage.

[9] a slight revision of *A Booke of Ayres,* Part I, xviii.

III.

Where are all thy beauties now, all harts enchayning?
Whither are thy flatt'rers gone with all their fayning?
All fled; and thou alone still here remayning.

Thy rich state[10] of twisted gold to Bayes[11] is turned;
Cold as thou art, are thy loves that so much burned: 5
Who dye in flatt'rers armes are seldome mourned.

Yet, in spight of envie, this be still proclaymed,
That none worthyer then thy selfe thy worth hath blamed:
When their poore names are lost, thou shalt live famed.

When thy story, long time hence, shall be perused,   10
Let the blemish of thy rule be thus excused:
None ever liv'd more just, none more abused.

[10] a throne with a canopy.   [11] baize, a coarse woolen cloth.

IV.[12]

Out of my soules deapth to thee my cryes have sounded:
Let thine eares my plaints receive, on just feare grounded.
Lord, should'st thou weigh our faults, who's not confounded?

But with grace thou censur'st thine when they have erred,
Therefore shall thy blessed name be lov'd and feared: 5
Ev'n to thy throne my thoughts and eyes are reared.

Thee alone my hopes attend, on thee relying;
In thy sacred word I'le trust, to thee fast flying,
Long ere the Watch shall breake, the morne descrying.

In the mercies of our God who live secured,   10
May of full redemption rest in him assured;
Their sinne-sicke soules by him shall be recured.

[12] a paraphrase of Psalm 130, *De Profundis.*

V.[13]

View mee, Lord, a worke of thine:
Shall I then lye drown'd in night?
Might thy grace in mee but shine,
I should seeme made all of light.

But my soule still surfets so   5
On the poysoned baytes of sinne,
That I strange and ugly growe,
All is darke and foule within.

Clense mee, Lord, that I may kneele
At thine Altar, pure and white: 10
They that once thy Mercies feele
Gaze no more on earths delight.

Worldly joyes like shadowes fade,
When the heav'nly light appeares;
But the cov'nants thou hast made,   15
Endlesse, know nor dayes, nor yeares.

In thy word, Lord, is my trust,
To thy mercies fast I flye;
Though I am but clay and dust,
Yet thy grace can lift me high.   20

[13] Compare Donne, *Holy Sonnet* I.

VI.[14]

Bravely deckt, come forth, bright day,
Thine houres with Roses strew thy way,
    As they well remember.
Thou receiv'd shalt be with feasts:
Come, chiefest of the *British* ghests,   5
    Thou fift of *November*.
Thou with triumph shalt exceede
    In the strictest ember;[15]
For by thy returne the Lord records his blessed deede.

Britaines, frolicke at your bourd,[16]   10
But first sing praises to the Lord
    In your Congregations.
Hee preserv'd your state alone,
His loving grace hath made you one
    Of his chosen Nations.   15
But this light must hallowed be
    With your best Oblations;
Prayse the Lord, for onely great and mercifull is hee.

Death had enter'd in the gate,
And ruine was crept neare the State;   20
    But heav'n all revealed.
Fi'ry Powder hell did make,
Which, ready long the flame to take,
    Lay in shade concealed.
God us helpt of his free grace,   25
    None to him appealed;
For none was so bad to feare the treason or the place.

God his peacefull Monarch chose,
To him the mist he did disclose,[17]
    To him, and none other;   30
This hee did, O King, for thee,

[14] This ode commemorates the discovery of the Gunpowder Plot to blow up the Houses of Parliament on November 5, 1605; the last three lines also allude to the death of Prince Henry on November 6, 1612. Compare Milton's series of Latin poems on the Plot, as translated in *The Complete English Poems of John Milton,* ed. John T. Shawcross (New York: Doubleday Anchor Books, 1963), pp. 11–19.

[15] period or revolution of time. [16] banquet table. [17] disperse.

That thou thine owne renowne might'st see,
        Which no time can smother.
May blest *Charles* thy comfort be,
        Firmer then his Brother: 35
May his heart the love of peace, and wisedome learne from thee.

VII.

To Musicke bent is my retyred minde,
And faine would I some song of pleasure sing:
But in vaine joyes no comfort now I finde:
From heav'nly thoughts all true delight doth spring.
Thy power, O God, thy mercies to record　　　　5
Will sweeten ev'ry note, and ev'ry word.[18]

All earthly pompe or beauty to expresse,
Is but to carve in snow, on waves to write.
Celestiall things, though men conceive them lesse,
Yet fullest are they in themselves of light:　　　　10
Such beames they yeeld as know no meanes to dye:
Such heate they cast as lifts the Spirit high.

VIII.

Tune thy Musicke to thy hart,
Sing thy joy with thankes, and so thy sorrow:
Though Devotion needes not Art,
Sometime of the poore the rich may borrow.

Strive not yet for curious[19] wayes:　　　　5
Concord pleaseth more, the lesse 'tis strained;
Zeale affects[20] not outward prayse,
Onely strives to shew a love unfained.

Love can wondrous things effect,
Sweetest Sacrifice, all wrath appeasing;　　　　10
Love the highest doth respect,
Love alone to him is ever pleasing.

[18] to record God's power and mercies will sweeten the song.
[19] elaborate.　[20] desires.

Tune thy Mu·sicke to thy hart, Sing thy joy with thankes, and so thy sor·row: Though De·vo·tion needes not Art, Some·time of the poore the rich may bor·row.

IX.

Most sweet and pleasing are thy wayes, O God,
Like Meadowes deckt with Christall streames and flowers:
Thy paths no foote prophane hath ever trod,
Nor hath the proud man rested in thy Bowers.
There lives no Vultur, no devouring Beare,   5
But onely Doves and Lambs are harbor'd there.

The Wolfe his young ones to their prey doth guide;
The Foxe his Cubbs with false deceit endues;
The Lyons Whelpe suckes from his Damme his pride;
In hers the Serpent malice doth infuse: 10
The darksome Desart all such beasts contaynes,
Not one of them in Paradice remaynes.

X.

Wise men patience never want,
Good men pitty cannot hide:
Feeble spirits onely vant[21]
Of revenge, the poorest pride.
Hee alone forgive that can   5
Beares the true soule of a man.

Some there are, debate that seeke,
Making trouble their content,
Happy if they wrong the meeke,
Vexe them that to peace are bent: 10
Such undooe the common tye
Of mankinde, societie.

Kindnesse growne is, lately, colde;
Conscience hath forgot her part;
Blessed times were knowne of old,   15
Long ere Law became an Art:
Shame deterr'd, not Statutes then,
Honest love was law to men.

Deeds from love, and words, that flowe[22]
Foster like kinde *Aprill* showres;   20
In the warme Sunne all things grow,
Wholsome fruits and pleasant flowres;
All so thrives his gentle rayes,
Where on humane love displayes.[23]

[21] vaunt or boast.   [22] deeds and words that flow from love.
[23] His gentle rays make thrive all things over which the water of human love has spread itself.

XI.[24]

Never weather-beaten Saile more willing bent to shore,
Never tyred Pilgrims limbs affected[25] slumber more,
Then my weary spright[26] now longs to flye out of my troubled brest.
    O come quickly, sweetest Lord, and take my soule to rest.

Ever-blooming are the joyes of Heav'ns high paradice,
Cold age deafes not there our eares, nor vapour dims our eyes;
Glory there the Sun outshines, whose beames the blessed onely see:
    O come quickly, glorious Lord, and raise my spright to thee.

[24] Vivian (in his edition of Campion) has shown that this song was
popular as a hymn into the eighteenth century; on its metrical characteris-
tics, see Ing, *Elizabethan Lyrics*, pp. 157–58.

[25] longed for. [26] spirit.

Ne · ver wea · ther · bea · ten Saile more wil · ling bent to shore,
Ne · ver ty · red Pil · grims limbs af · fe · cted slum · ber more,

Then my__ wea · ry__ spright now__ longs to flye__ out__ of my

trou · bled__ brest.   O   come quick · ly,   O   come quick · ly,

O   come quick · ly, sweet · est__ Lord, and__ take__ my__ soule to rest.

XII.

Lift up to heav'n, sad wretch, thy heavy spright,
What though thy sinnes thy due destruction threat?
The Lord exceedes in mercy as in might;
His ruth is greater, though thy crimes be great.
Repentance needes not feare the heav'ns just rod,   5
It stayes ev'n thunder in the hand of God.

With chearefull voyce to him then cry for grace,
Thy Faith, and fainting Hope, with Prayer revive;
Remorce for all that truely mourne hath place;
Not God, but men of him themselves deprive: 10
Strive then, and hee will help; call him, hee'll heare:
The Sonne needes not the Fathers fury feare.

XIII.

Loe, when backe mine eye,
 Pilgrim-like, I cast,
What fearefull wayes I spye,
Which, blinded, I securely past!

But now heav'n hath drawne   5
 From my browes that night;
As when the day doth dawne,
So cleares my long imprison'd sight.

Straight the caves of hell
 Drest with flowres I see,   10
Wherein false pleasures dwell,
That, winning most, most deadly be.

Throngs of masked Feinds,
 Wing'd like Angels, flye,
Ev'n in the gates of Friends;   15
In faire disguise blacke dangers lye.

Straight to Heav'n I rais'd
 My restored sight,
And with loud voyce I prais'd
The Lord of ever-during light.   20

And, since I had stray'd
 From his wayes so wide,
His grace I humbly pray'd
Hence-forth to be my guard and guide.

XIV.[27]

As by the streames of *Babilon,*
Farre from our native soyle we sat,
Sweet *Sion,* thee we thought upon,
And ev'ry thought a teare begat.

Aloft the trees that spring up there   5
Our silent Harps wee pensive hung:
Said they that captiv'd us, Let's heare
Some song which you in *Sion* sung.

Is then the song of our God fit
To be prophan'd in forraine land?   10
O *Salem,* thee when I forget,
Forget his skill may my right hand!

Fast to the roofe cleave may my tongue,
If mindelesse I of thee be found:
Or if, when all my joyes are sung,   15
Jerusalem be not the ground.[28]

Remember, Lord, how *Edoms* race
Cryed in *Jerusalems* sad day,
Hurle downe her wals, her towres deface;
And, stone by stone, all levell lay.   20

Curst *Babels* seede! for *Salems* sake
Just ruine yet for thee remaines!
Blest shall they be, thy babes that take,
And 'gainst the stones dash out their braines!

[27] a paraphrase of Psalm 137, *Super Flumina.*
[28] the basic melody on which variations are built (as well as the place where one stands).

XV.[29]

Sing a song of joy,
    Prayse our God with mirth:
His flocke who can destroy?
Is hee not Lord of heav'n and earth?

Sing wee then secure,   5
    Tuning well our strings:
With voyce, as Eccho pure,
Let us renowne[30] the King of Kings.

First who taught the day
    From the East to rise?   10
Whom doth the Sunne obey
When in the Seas his glory dyes?

Hee the Starres directs
    That in order stand:
Who heav'n and earth protects,   15
But hee that fram'd them with his hand?

Angels round attend,
    Wayting on his will;
Arm'd millions he doth send
To ayde the good or plague the ill.   20

All that dread his Name,
    And his Hests observe,
His arme will shield from shame:
Their steps from truth shall never swerve.

Let us then rejoyce,   25
    Sounding loud his prayse:
So will hee heare our voyce,
And blesse on earth our peacefull dayes.

[29] a very free paraphrase of the first five verses of Psalm 104, *Benedic, Anima Mea.*
[30] celebrate.

XVI.

Awake, awake, thou heavy spright,
That sleep'st the deadly sleepe of sinne;
  Rise now, and walke the wayes of light:
'Tis not too late yet to begin.
    Seeke heav'n earely, seeke it late,   5
    True Faith still[31] findes an open gate.

Get up, get up, thou leaden man:
Thy tracks to endlesse joy or paine
  Yeelds but the modell of a span;[32]
Yet burnes out thy lifes lampe in vaine.   10
    One minute bounds thy bane, or blisse,
    Then watch, and labour while time is.

XVII.

Come, chearfull day, part of my life, to mee:
For, while thou view'st me with thy fading light,
Part of my life doth still depart with thee,
And I still onward haste to my last night.
    Times fatall wings doe ever forward flye,   5
    Soe ev'ry day we live, a day wee dye.

But, O yee nights ordain'd for barren rest,
How are my dayes depriv'd of life in you,
When heavy sleepe my soule hath dispossest,
By fayned death life sweetly to renew!   10
    Part of my life, in that, you life denye:
    So ev'ry day we live, a day wee dye.

[31] always.

[32] a syntactically ambiguous passage: your daily steps are leading you toward eternal reward or punishment, *but* they are minute (a span, the measure of a hand) compared to the extent of time they foreshadow. Compare Psalm 39:5, "Behold, thou hast made my days as an handbreadth," and Sir Thomas Browne, *Urne-Burial*, Chapter V: "our dayes of a span long make not one little finger."

Come, chear-full day, Come, chear-full day, part of my life, to mee: For, while thou view'st me with thy fa - ding light, Part of my life doth still de - part with thee, And I still on - ward haste to my last night. Times fa - tall wings doe e - ver for - ward flye, Soe ev' - ry day,

soe   ev-ry day we live, we   live,   a   day   wee   dye.

XVIII.[33]

Seeke the Lord, and in his wayes persever:
  O faint not, but as Eagles flye,
  For his steepe hill is high;
Then, striving, gaine the top, and triumph ever.

When with glory there thy browes are crowned,   5
  New joyes so shall abound in thee,
  Such sights thy soule shall see,
That wordly thoughts shall by their beames be drowned.

Farewell, World, thou masse of meere confusion,
  False light with many shadowes dimm'd,   10
  Old Witch with new foyles trimm'd,[34]
Thou deadly sleepe of soule, and charm'd illusion.

I the King will seeke of Kings adored,
  Spring of light, tree of grace and blisse,
  Whose fruit so sov'raigne[35] is   15
That all who taste it are from death restored.

[33] This song utilizes the music of "Followe thy faire sunne," *A Booke of Ayres,* Part I, iv, perhaps in sacred parody.
[34] covered with fresh foil, like an old statue renovated.
[35] supreme, and superlative as medicine.

XIX.

Lighten, heavy hart, thy spright,
 The joyes recall that thence are fled;
Yeeld thy brest some living light:
 The man that nothing doth is dead.
Tune thy temper[36] to these sounds,   5
 And quicken so thy joylesse minde;
Sloth the worst and best confounds:
 It is the ruine of mankinde.

From her cave rise all distasts,[37]
 Which unresolv'd Despaire pursues;   10
Whom soone after Violence hasts,
 Her selfe ungratefull to abuse.
Skies are clear'd with stirring windes,
 Th' unmoved water moorish[38] growes;
Ev'ry eye much pleasure findes   15
 To view a streame that brightly flowes.

[36] temperament; the mind is conceived as a musical instrument to be
"tempered" or tuned.
[37] disgusts. [38] sluggish.

XX.

Jacke and *Jone,* they thinke no ill,
But loving live, and merry still;
Doe their weeke dayes worke, and pray
Devotely on the holy day;
Skip and trip it on the greene,   5
And help to chuse the Summer Queene;
Lash out,[39] at a Country Feast,
Their silver penny with the best.

Well can they judge of nappy Ale,[40]
And tell at large a Winter tale;   10
Climbe up to the Apple loft,
And turne the Crabs[41] till they be soft.
Tib is all the fathers joy,
And little *Tom* the mothers boy.
All their pleasure is content;   15
And care, to pay their yearely rent.

Jone can call by name her Cowes,
And decke her windowes with greene boughs;
Shee can wreathes and tuttyes[42] make,
And trimme with plums a Bridall Cake.   20
Jacke knowes what brings gaine or losse,
And his long Flaile can stoutly tosse;
Make the hedge, which others breake,[43]
And ever thinkes what he doth speake.

Now, you Courtly Dames and Knights,   25
That study onely strange delights,
Though you scorne the home-spun gray,
And revell in your rich array;
Though your tongues dissemble deepe,
And can your heads from danger keepe;   30
Yet, for all your pompe and traine,
Securer lives the silly Swaine.

[39] fling out.   [40] heady or strong ale.
[41] crab apples, usually roasted.   [42] nosegays.
[43] a satirical thrust: it is the nobility that breaks the hedges while hunting.

XXI.[44]

All lookes be pale, harts cold as stone.
For *Hally* now is dead, and gone,
     Hally, in whose sight,
      Most sweet sight,
       All the earth late tooke delight.   5
  Ev'ry eye, weepe with mee,
  Joyes drown'd in teares must be.

His Iv'ry skin, his comely hayre,
His Rosie cheekes, so cleare and faire,
     Eyes that once did grace   10
      His bright face,
       Now in him all want their place.
  Eyes and hearts, weepe with mee,
  For who so kinde as hee?

His youth was like an *Aprill* flowre,   15
Adorn'd with beauty, love, and powre;
     Glory strow'd his way,
      Whose wreaths gay
      Now are all turn'd to decay.
  Then againe weepe with mee,   20
  None feele more cause then wee.

No more may his wisht sight returne,
His golden Lampe no more can burne;
     Quencht is all his flame,
      His hop't fame   25
       Now hath left him nought but name.
  For him all weepe with mee,
  Since more him none shall see.

[44] an elegy on Prince Henry, who died in 1612; see headnote to *Songs of Mourning.*

THE
SECOND BOOKE
OF
AYRES.

Containing
Light Conceits of Lovers.

TO THE RIGHT
NOBLE, AND VERTUOUS,
HENRY LORD CLIFFORD, Sonne and Heyre to
the Right Honourable, FRANCIS, Earle of
CUMBERLAND.

Such dayes as weare the badge of holy red
Are for devotion markt, and sage delight;
 The vulgar Low-dayes, undistinguished,
Are left for labour, games, and sportfull sights.

This sev'rall and so diff'ring use of Time   5
Within th' enclosure of one weeke wee finde;
 Which I resemble in my Notes and Rime,
Expressing both in their peculiar kinde.

Pure Hymnes, such as the seaventh day loves, doe leade;
Grave age did justly chalenge those of mee: 10
 These weeke-day workes, in order that succeede,
Your youth best fits, and yours, yong Lord, they be:
  As hee is, who to them their beeing gave;
  If th' one, the other you of force must have.

Your Honors,

THOMAS CAMPIAN.

TO THE READER.

That holy Hymnes with Lovers cares are knit
Both in one Quire[1] here, thou maist think't unfit;
Why do'st not blame the Stationer as well,
Who in the same Shop sets all sorts to sell?
Divine with stiles prophane, grave shelv'd with vaine;
And some matcht worse, yet none of him complaine.

I.[2]

Vaine men, whose follies make a God of Love,
Whose blindnesse beauty doth immortall deeme:
Prayse not what you desire, but what you prove,[3]
Count those things good that are, not those that seeme:
I cannot call her true that's false to me,   5
Nor make of women more then women be.

How faire an entrance breakes the way to love!
How rich of golden hope, and gay delight!
What hart cannot a modest beauty move?
Who, seeing cleare day once, will dreame of night?   10
Shee seem'd a Saint, that brake her faith with mee,
But prov'd a woman, as all other be.

So bitter is their sweet, that true content
Unhappy men in them may never finde;
Ah, but without them, none; both must consent,   15
Else uncouth are the joyes of eyther kinde.
Let us then prayse their good, forget their ill:
Men must be men, and women women still.

[1] a play on "choir" and "quire."   [2] Compare Donne, "Loves Deity."
[3] test for genuine value.

II.

How eas'ly wert thou chained,
Fond hart, by favours fained!
Why liv'd thy hopes in grace,
Straight to dye disdained?
But, since th' art now beguiled   5
By Love that falsely smiled,
In some lesse happy place
Mourne alone exiled.
My love still here increaseth,
And with my love my griefe,   10
While her sweet bounty ceaseth,
That gave my woes reliefe.
Yet 'tis no woman leaves me,
For such may prove unjust:
A Goddesse thus deceives me,   15
Whose faith who could mistrust?

A Goddesse so much graced
That Paradice is placed
In her most heav'nly brest,
Once by love embraced;   20
But love, that so kinde proved,
Is now from her removed,
Nor will he[4] longer rest
Where no faith is loved.
If Powres Celestiall wound us   25
And will not yeeld reliefe,
Woe then must needs confound us,
For none can cure our griefe.
No wonder if I languish
Through burden of my smart;   30
It is no common anguish
From Paradice to part.

[4] the god of Love.

How eas' - ly wert _ thou chai - ned, Fond hart, by fa - vours
But, since th'art now _ be - gui - led By Love that fals - ely

fai - ned! Why liv'd thy hopes in grace, Straight to dye, straight to
smi - led, in some lesse hap - py place Mourne a - lone, mourne a -

dye dis - dai - ned? My love still here in -
lone ex - i - led. Yet 'tis no wo - man

crea - seth, And with my love my griefe, While
leaves me, For such may prove un - just; A

her sweet boun - ty cea - seth, That gave my woes re - liefe.
God - desse thus de - ceives me, Whose faith who could mis - trust?

III.[5]

Harden now thy tyred hart with more then flinty rage;
Ne'er let her false teares henceforth thy constant griefe asswage.
Once true happy dayes thou saw'st, when shee stood firme and kinde,
Both as one then liv'd, and held one eare, one tongue, one minde.
But now those bright houres be fled, and never may returne: 5
What then remaines, but her untruths to mourne?

Silly Tray-tresse,[6] who shall now thy carelesse tresses place?
Who thy pretty talke supply? whose eare thy musicke grace?
Who shall thy bright eyes admire? what lips triumph with thine?
Day by day who'll visit thee and say, th' art onely mine?   10
Such a time there was, God wot, but such shall never be:
Too oft, I feare, thou wilt remember me.

[5] based on Catullus VIII; compare especially ll. 11–18:

> sed obstinata mente perfer, obdura.
> vale, puella. iam Catullus obdurat,
> nec te requiret nec rogabit invitam:
> at tu dolebis, cum rogaberis nulla,
> scelesta, nocte. quae tibi manet vita?
> quis nunc te adibit? cui videberis bella?
> quem nunc amabis? cuius esse diceris?
> quem basiabis? cui labella mordebis?

[but persevere with an unmoved mind, be hard. Farewell, my girl. Now Catullus has hardened; he will not·seek you nor ask for you against your will. But you will be sorry when you are asked by no one at night, poor wretch. What life is left to you? Who will now come to you? to whom will you seem pretty? whom will you love now? whose will you be called? whom will you kiss? whose lips will you bite?].

See John B. Emperor, *The Catullian Influence in English Lyric poetry circa 1600–50,* University of Missouri Studies, III, 3 (Columbia, 1928), p. 25.

[6] Fellowes observes in his edition of Campion that the original spelling here forces wordplay with "tresses."

IV.

O what unhop't for sweet supply!
  O what joyes exceeding!
What an affecting charme feele I,
  From delight proceeding!
That which I long despair'd to be,   5
  To her I am, and shee to mee.

Shee that alone in cloudy griefe
  Long to mee appeared,
Shee now alone with bright reliefe
  All those clouds hath cleared.   10
Both are immortall, and divine,
  Since I am hers, and she is mine.

V.[7]

Where shee her sacred bowre adornes,
    The Rivers clearely flow:
The groves and medowes swell with flowres,
    The windes all gently blow:
Her Sunne-like beauty shines so fayre,   5
    Her Spring can never fade:
Who then can blame the life that strives
    To harbour in her shade?

Her grace I sought, her love I wooed;
    Her love though I obtaine,   10
No time, no toyle, no vow, no faith
    Her wished grace can gaine.[8]
Yet truth can tell my heart is hers,
    And her will I adore:
And from that love when I depart,   15
    Let heav'n view me no more.[9]

Her roses with my prayer shall spring;
    And when her trees I praise,
Their boughs shall blossome, mellow fruit
    Shall straw her pleasant wayes.   20
The words of harty zeale have powre
    High wonders to effect;
O why should then her Princely eare
    My words, or zeale neglect?

If shee my faith misdeemes, or worth,   25
    Woe-worth my haplesse fate:
For, though time can my truth reveale,
    That time will come too late.
And who can glory in the worth
    That cannot yeeld him grace?   30
Content in ev'ry thing is not,
    Nor joy in ev'ry place.

---

[7] The analogy between the anatomy of the mistress and architecture stems from a mediaeval tradition—e.g., *"O comes amoris, dolor"* in the *Carmina Burana* (No. 162) and *Le Roman de la Rose*. Compare also Donne, Elegy XIX, and Carew, "A Rapture."

[8] The technical antithesis here, as elsewhere, is between "love" or affection and "grace" or sexual favors.

[9] This line could mean either let me die, or let me be damned.

> But, from her bowre of Joy since I
>   Must now excluded be,
> And shee will not relieve my cares,   35
>   Which none can helpe but shee:
> My comfort in her love shall dwell,
>   Her love lodge in my brest;
> And though not in her bowre, yet I
>   Shall in her temple rest.   40

VI.

Faine would I my love disclose,
Aske what honour might denye;
But both love and her I lose,
From my motion if shee flye.
Worse then paine is feare to mee: 5
Then hold in fancy, though it burne;
If not happy, safe Ile be,
And to my clostred cares returne.

Yet, o yet, in vaine I strive
To represse my school'd[10] desire;   10
More and more the flames revive,
I consume in mine owne fire.
She would pitty, might shee know
The harmes that I for her endure:
Speake then, and get comfort so: 15
A wound long hid growes past recure.[11]

Wise shee is, and needs must know
All th' attempts that beauty moves:
Fayre she is, and honour'd so
That she, sure, hath tryed some loves.   20
If with love I tempt her then,
'Tis but her due to be desir'd:
What would women thinke of men,
If their deserts were not admir'd?

Women, courted, have the hand   25
To discard what they distaste:[12]
But those Dames whom none demand
Want oft what their wils[13] imbrac't.
Could their firmnesse iron excell,
As they are faire, they should be sought: 30
When true theeves use falsehood well,
As they are wise, they will be caught.[14]

[10] disciplined.   [11] recovery; see textual notes.

[12] dislike; the terms are those of a card game.

[13] desires, often with a sexual implication (see, e.g., Shakespeare, Sonnet 135).

[14] they are deliberately trying to be caught.

VII.

Give beauty all her right,
Shee's not to one forme tyed;
Each shape yeelds faire delight,
Where her perfections bide.
Hellen, I grant, might pleasing be;   5
And *Ros'mond*[15] was as sweet as shee.

Some the quicke eye commends,
Some smelling[16] lips and red;
Pale lookes have many friends,
Through sacred sweetnesse bred.   10
Medowes have flowres that pleasure move,
Though Roses are the flowres of love.[17]

Free beauty is not bound
To one unmoved clime:
She visits ev'ry ground,   15
And favours ev'ry time.
Let the old loves with mine compare,
My sov'raigne is as sweet, and fayre.

[15] Rosamond Clifford, mistress of King Henry II (ruled 1154–1189), a favorite romantic heroine with the Elizabethans; see Daniel's *The Complaynt of Rosamond* (1592). Her mention here forms an obvious compliment to the Clifford family.

[16] sweetly smelling; the unfavorable connotation is modern.

[17] Compare the second strophe of "Now hath *Flora*" in *The Lord Hay's Masque,* p. 215 below.

VIII.

O deare, that I with thee might live,
    From humane trace removed:
Where jealous care might neither grieve,
    Yet each dote on their loved.
While fond feare may colour[18] finde, Love's seldome pleased;   5
But much like a sicke mans rest, it's soone diseased.[19]

Why should our mindes not mingle so,
    When love and faith is plighted,
That eyther might the others know,
    Alike in all delighted?   10
Why should frailtie breed suspect, when hearts are fixed?
Must all humane joyes of force with griefe be mixed?

How oft have wee ev'n smilde in teares,
    Our fond mistrust repenting?
As snow when heav'nly fire appeares,   15
    So melts loves hate relenting.
Vexed kindnesse[20] soone fals off, and soone returneth:
Such a flame the more you quench, the more it burneth.

[18] excuse.   [19] disturbed (as well as tainted).   [20] love.

IX.

Good men, shew, if you can tell,
Where doth humane pittie dwell?
Farre and neere her would I seeke,
So vext with sorrow is my brest.
She (they say) to all is meeke,   5
And onely[21] makes th' unhappie blest.

Oh! if such a Saint there be,
Some hope yet remaines for me:
Prayer or sacrifice may gaine
From her implored grace reliefe,   10
To release mee of my paine,
Or at the least to ease my griefe.

Young am I, and farre from guile;
The more is my woe the while:
Falshood with a smooth disguise   15
My simple meaning hath abus'd,
Casting mists before mine eyes,
By which my senses are confus'd.

Faire he is, who vow'd to me
That he onely mine would be: 20
But, alas, his minde is caught
With ev'ry gaudie bait he sees.
And too late my flame is taught
That too much kindnesse makes men freese.

From me all my friends are gone,   25
While I pine for him alone;
And not one will rue my case,
But rather my distresse deride:
That I thinke there is no place
Where pittie ever yet did bide.   30

[21] especially; the modern meaning, "exclusively," obtains in l. 20 below.

X.[22]

What harvest halfe so sweet is,
As still to reape the kisses
    Growne ripe in sowing?
And straight to be receiver
Of that which thou art giver,   5
    Rich in bestowing?
Kisse then, my harvest Queene,
    Full garners heaping;
Kisses, ripest when th' are greene,
    Want onely reaping.   10

The Dove alone expresses
Her fervencie in kisses,
    Of all most loving:
A creature as offencelesse
As those things that are sencelesse   15
    And void of moving.
Let us so love and kisse,
    Though all envie us:
That which kinde, and harmelesse is,
    None can denie us.   20

[22] The first six lines are repeated from *A Booke of Ayres*, Part I, vii,
ll. 12–17. Compare Catullus XLVIII. ll. 3–6:

> *usque ad milia basiem trecenta,*
> *nec mi umquam videar satur futurus,*
> *non si densior aridis aristis*
> *sit nostrae seges osculationis*

[I would kiss (your eyes) three hundred thousand times, nor would I ever
seem to have enough, not even if our kisses were thicker than the ripe ears
of grain].

What_ har - vest halfe so sweet is, _ As _
And _ straight to be re - cei - ver _ Of _

still to reape the kiss - es Growne ripe in sow - ing?
that which thou art giv - er, Rich in bes - tow - ing?

Kisse _ then, my har - vest _ Queene, Full gar - ners _ heap - ing;

Kiss - es, _ ri - pest _ when th'are greene, Want one - ly reap - ing.

XI.[23]

Sweet, exclude mee not, nor be divided
    From him that ere long must bed thee:
All thy maiden doubts Law hath decided;
    Sure[24] wee are, and I must wed thee.
    Presume then yet a little more: 5
      Here's the way, barre not the dore.

Tenants, to fulfill their Land-lords pleasure,
    Pay their rent before the quarter:[25]
'Tis my case, if you it rightly measure;
    Put mee not then off with laughter.   10
    Consider then a little more:
      Here's the way to all my store.[26]

Why were dores in loves despight devised?
    Are not Lawes enough restrayning?
Women are most apt to be surprised   15
    Sleeping, or sleepe wisely fayning.
    Then grace me yet a little more:
      Here's the way, barre not the dore.

[23] This song was perhaps inspired by Ovid *Amores* I. vi, with its refrain *excute poste seram* [unbar the door]; the complaint of the lover before his mistress' door had the status of a minor genre among the Roman elegiac poets, with examples in Tibullus and Propertius as well as Ovid. Compare also "Hide not, sweetest Love" in Doubtful Poems, below.

[24] betrothed.

[25] the quarter day; rents fell due on March 25, June 24, September 29, and December 25.

[26] goods.

XII.[27]

The peacefull westerne winde
The winter stormes hath tam'd,
And nature in each kinde
The kinde[28] heat hath inflam'd.
The forward buds so sweetly breathe   5
Out of their earthy bowers,
That heav'n, which viewes their pompe beneath,
Would faine be deckt with flowers.

See how the morning smiles
On her bright easterne hill,   10
And with soft steps beguiles
Them that lie slumbring still.
The musicke-loving birds are come
From cliffes and rockes unknowne,
To see the trees and briers blome   15
That late were over-flowne.[29]

What Saturne[30] did destroy,
Loves Queene revives againe;
And now her naked boy[31]
Doth in the fields remaine: 20
Where he such pleasing change doth view
In ev'ry living thing,
As if the world were borne anew
To gratifie the Spring.

If all things life present,   25
Why die my comforts then?
Why suffers my content?
Am I the worst of men?
O beautie, be not thou accus'd
Too justly in this case: 30
Unkindly if true love be us'd,
'Twill yeeld thee little grace.

[27] The theme of the season's rebirth and the lover's deathliness in spring was early transferred from the pastoral elegy to the romantic lyric of Provence and Italy; see especially Petrarch's *Zefiro torna* (Sonnet cccx) with its many imitations (one by Surrey, one set by Monteverdi). Campion's setting forms a musical allusion to the traditional melody "Westron Wynde" (it appears most clearly in the first eight notes of the Cantus part), a very popular tune which had earlier supplied John Taverner (ca. 1495–1545) with the *cantus firmus* of an entire mass. Compare the version of this song in "poulter's measure" in Doubtful Poems, below.   [28] loving.

[29] flooded or drenched (Vivian's note).   [30] the god of winter.   [31] Cupid.

The peace-full wes-terne winde The win-ter stormes hath
And na-ture in each kinde The kinde heat hath in-

tam'd, The for-ward buds so sweet-ly breathe Out
flam'd.

of their ear-thy bowers, That heav'n, which viewes their

pompe be-neath, Would faine be deckt with flowers.

XIII.[32]

There is none, O none but you,
    That from mee estrange your sight,
Whom mine eyes affect to view
    Or chained eares heare with delight.

Other beauties others move,   5
    In you I all graces finde:
Such is the effect of love,
    To make them happy that are kinde.

Women in fraile beauty trust,
    Onely seeme you faire to mee;   10
Yet prove truely kinde and just,
    For that may not dissembled be.

Sweet, afford mee then your sight,
    That, survaying all your lookes,
Endlesse volumes I may write,   15
    And fill the world with envyed bookes:

Which when after ages view,
    All shall wonder, and despaire,
Woman to finde man so true,
    Or man a woman halfe so faire.[33]   20

[32] Compare Sir Robert Ayton's "There is none, noe none but I."
[33] Compare Donne, "The Relique."

XIV.

Pin'd I am, and like to die,
And all for lacke of that which I
    Doe ev'ry day refuse.
If I musing sit, or stand,
Some puts it daily in my hand,   5
    To interrupt my muse.
The same thing I seeke, and flie,
And want that which none would denie.

In my bed, when I should rest,
It breeds such trouble in my brest   10
    That scarce mine eyes will close:
If I sleepe, it seemes to be
Oft playing in the bed with me,
    But, wak't, away it goes.
Tis some spirit, sure, I weene,   15
And yet it may be felt, and seene.

Would I had the heart and wit
To make it stand, and conjure it,[34]
    That haunts me thus with feare.
Doubtlesse tis some harmlesse spright,   20
For it by day, as well as night,
    Is ready to appeare.
Be it friend, or be it foe,
Ere long Ile trie what it will doe.

[34] Perhaps the innuendos are too obvious for annotation; but compare this line with *Romeo and Juliet,* II, i, 23–26:

    This cannot anger him; 'twould anger him
    To raise a spirit in his mistress' circle,
    Of some strange nature, letting it there stand
    Till she had laid it and conjured it down.

XV.

So many loves have I neglected
    Whose good parts might move mee,
That now I live of all rejected,
    There is none will love me.
Why is mayden heate so coy?   5
    It freezeth when it burneth,
Looseth what it might injoy,
    And, having lost it, mourneth.

Should I then wooe, that have been wooed,
    Seeking them that flye mee?   10
When I my faith with teares have vowed,
    And when all denye mee,
Who will pitty my disgrace,
    Which love might have prevented?
There is no submission base   15
    Where error is repented.

O happy men, whose hopes are licenc'd
    To discourse their passion,
While women are confin'd to silence,
    Loosing wisht occasion.   20
Yet our tongues then theirs, men say,
    Are apter to be moving:
Women are more dumbe then they,
    But in their thoughts more roving.

When I compare my former strangenesse   25
    With my present doting,
I pitty men that speake in plainenesse,
    Their true hearts devoting;
While wee with repentance jest
    At their submissive passion: 30
Maydes, I see, are never blest
    That strange[35] be but for fashion.

[35] reserved.

XVI.

Though your strangenesse frets my hart,
Yet may not I complaine:
You perswade me, 'tis but Art,
That secret love must faine.
If another you affect,[36]   5
'Tis but a shew t' avoid suspect.
Is this faire excusing? O no, all is abusing.

Your wisht sight if I desire,
Suspitions you pretend;
Causelesse you your selfe retire,   10
While I in vaine attend.
This a Lover whets, you say,
Still made more eager by delay.
Is this faire excusing? O no, all is abusing.

When another holds your hand,   15
You sweare I hold your hart:
When my Rivals close doe stand
And I sit farre apart,
I am neerer yet then they,
Hid in your bosome, as you say.   20
Is this faire excusing? O no, all is abusing.

Would my Rival then I were,
Some els your secret friend:[37]
So much lesser should I feare,
And not so much attend.   25
They enjoy you, ev'ry one,
Yet I must seeme your friend alone.
Is this faire excusing? O no, all is abusing.

[36] favor. [37] lover.

Though your strange- nesse frets my hart, Yet may not I com - plaine:
You per - swade me, 'tis but Art, That se - cret love must faine.

If a - no - ther you af - fect, 'Tis but a shew t'a - void su - spect. Is

this faire ex - cu - sing? O no, all is a - bus - ing.

XVII.[38]

Come away, arm'd with loves delights,
   Thy sprightfull graces bring with thee:
When loves longing fights,
   They must the sticklers be.[39]
Come quickly, come, the promis'd houre is wel-nye spent,   5
And pleasure, being too much deferr'd, looseth her best content.

Is shee come? O, how neare is shee?
   How farre yet from this friendly place?
How many steps from me?
   When shall I her imbrace?   10
These armes Ile spred, which onely at her sight shall close,
Attending as the starry flowre[40] that the Suns noone-tide knowes.

[38] This song bears a very strong resemblance to the song "Come away" in *The Lords' Masque,* and very likely uses its setting; compare especially ll. 4–6 of each song (p. 252).

[39] "Sticklers" can mean either umpires in a tournament or combatants; though the passage is obscure, the former meaning seems more appropriate here: her graces must umpire the erotic battle between her (armed with love's delights) and him (armed with love's longing).

[40] the heliotrope. Compare Lyly, *Euphues and His England,* ed. M. W. Croll and H. Clemons (London, 1916), p. 395: "A lover is like the herb Heliotropium, which always inclineth to that place where the sun shineth, and being deprived of the sun dieth."

XVIII.[41]

Come, you pretty false-ey'd wanton,
    Leave your crafty smiling:
Thinke you to escape me now
    With slipp'ry words beguiling?
No; you mock't me th' other day,   5
    When you got loose, you fled away;
But, since I have caught you now,
    Ile clip your wings for flying:
Smothring kisses fast Ile heape,
    And keepe you so from crying.   10

Sooner may you count the starres,
    And number hayle downe pouring,
Tell the Osiers[42] of the *Temmes,*
    Or *Goodwins*[43] Sands devouring,[44]
Then the thicke-showr'd kisses here   15
    Which now thy tyred lips must beare.
Such a harvest never was,
    So rich and full of pleasure,
But 'tis spent as soone as reapt,
    So trustlesse[45] is loves treasure.   20

Would it were dumb midnight now,
    When all the world lyes sleeping:
Would this place some Desert were,
    Which no man hath in keeping.

[41] a song in the tradition of the Provençal *pastorella;* the meter—old-fashioned "fourteeners"—underlines its rustic flavor.

[42] willows.

[43] Goodwin Sands, a sand bank ten miles long in the north Dover Strait.

[44] Emperor, p. 25, compares Catullus VII, especially ll. 1–3 and 7–8:

> *Quaeris, quot mihi basiationes*
> *tuae, Lesbia, sint satis superque.*
> *quam magnus numerus Libyssae harenae . . .*
> *aut quam sidera multa, cum tacet nox,*
> *furtivos hominum vident amores*

[You ask how many of your kisses are enough for me and more than enough, Lesbia. As great a number as the grains of Libyan sand . . . or as many as there are stars that see the furtive loves of men when night lies quiet].

Compare Ben Jonson's imitation of these lines in *The Forest,* VI, ll. 13 ff.

[45] undependable or treacherous.

My desires should then be safe,   25
    And when you cry'd then would I laugh;
But if ought might breed offence,
    Love onely should be blamed:
I would live your servant still,
    And you my Saint unnamed.   30

XIX.[46]

A secret love or two, I must confesse,
    I kindly welcome for change in close playing:
Yet my deare husband I love ne'erthelesse,
    His desires, whole or halfe, quickly allaying,
At all times ready to offer redresse.   5
    His owne he never wants, but hath it duely,
    Yet twits me, I keepe not touch[47] with him truly.

The more a spring is drawne, the more it flowes;
    No Lampe lesse light retaines by lighting others:
Is hee a looser his losse that ne're knowes?   10
    Or is he wealthy that wast treasure smothers?
My churle vowes no man shall sent[48] his sweet Rose:
    His owne enough and more I give him duely,
    Yet still he twits mee, I keepe not touch truly.

Wise Archers beare more then one shaft to field,[49]   15
    The Venturer[50] loads not with one ware his shipping:
Should Warriers learne but one weapon to weilde?
    Or thrive faire plants ere the worse for the slipping?
One dish cloyes, many fresh appetite yeeld:
    Mine owne Ile use, and his he shall have duely,   20
    Judge then what debter can keepe touch more truly.

[46] The argument of this song is reminiscent of Chaucer's Wife of Bath, whom Campion mentioned in the first elegy of the 1595 *Poemata;* see below.

[47] To "keep touch" is to live up to one's part in a covenant, but "touch" is also a common euphemism for sexual contact; there is play on these senses of the word throughout the song.

[48] either to smell it or to add his scent to it; the rose is a common sexual image.

[49] Compare Fulke Greville, *Caelica,* XIX, 9: "Good Archers ever have two bowes at least."

[50] a merchant speculating in foreign trade.

XX.

Her rosie cheekes, her ever smiling eyes,
Are Spheares and beds where Love in triumph lies:
Her rubine[51] lips, when they their pearle unlocke,
Make them seeme as they did rise
All out of one smooth Currall[52] Rocke.   5
Oh, that of other Creatures store I knew
More worthy, and more rare:
For these are old, and shee so new,
That her to them none should compare.

Oh, could she love, would shee but heare a friend,   10
Or that shee onely knew what sighs pretend.[53]
Her lookes inflame, yet cold as Ice is shee.
Doe or speake, all's to one end,
For what shee is, that will shee be.[54]
Yet will I never cease her prayse to sing,   15
Though she gives no regard:
For they that grace a worthlesse thing
Are onely greedy of reward.

XXI.

Where shall I refuge seeke, if you refuse mee?
In you my hope, in you my fortune lyes;
In you my life, though you unjust accuse me,
My service scorne, and merit underprise.
    Oh bitter griefe, that exile is become   5
    Reward for faith, and pittie deafe and dumbe.

Why should my firmnesse finde a seate so wav'ring?
My simple vowes, my love you entertain'd,
Without desert the same againe disfav'ring;
Yet I my word and passion hold unstain'd.   10
    Oh wretched me, that my chiefe joy should breede
    My onely griefe, and kindnesse pitty neede.

FINIS.

[51] ruby-colored. [52] coral. [53] claim as reward. [54] i.e., a virgin.

Songs of Mourning:
BEWAILING
the untimely death of
Prince *Henry*.

Worded by THO. CAMPION.

And set forth to bee sung with one voyce
to the Lute, or Violl:

By JOHN COPRARIO.

1613

Henry Frederick, Prince of Wales (1594–1612) held for his time some of the peculiar fascination that Sir Philip Sidney had held for the previous generation—much increased, of course, by the promise of his eventual kingship. A figure of great chivalric appeal, he made his first great public impression in the *Barriers* of 1610 (whose speeches were composed by Jonson); a scholar of some promise, he extended his patronage to many men of letters; he was an earnest student of the arts of war, and took an active interest in the voyages of discovery and colonization. He combined great personal charm with a rather fervent religious nature, leaning toward the kind of strict Protestant position represented by his favorite divine and chaplain Joseph Hall, and taking a far more active interest in the European Protestant cause than his father ever had—an interest that raised great hope in the minds of Protestant intellectuals of the time. For these reasons he viewed coldly prospective French and Spanish marriages for himself and welcomed with joy the match of his sister Elizabeth with Frederic, Count Palatine, with whom he formed a warm friendship in the short space of time between Frederic's arrival in England and his own death. He died on November 6, 1612, of typhoid fever aggravated by overindulgence in exercise.

Prince Henry's popularity and virtues combined with the usual romantic aura about the death of the young to produce a flood of elegies on him by the major and minor poets of the age, including John Donne, Sir Edward Herbert, Cyril Tourneur, Henry King, Sir Henry Goodyere, John Webster, George Chapman, Sir John Davies, William Drummond, Giles Fletcher, and William Browne. Not the least of the elegies was *Songs of Mourning* (1613), "worded" by Thomas Campion and set by the Prince's music tutor Giovanni Coperario. "Giovanni Coperario" (ca. 1575–1626) was born John Cooper; but after an extended visit to Italy in 1604, he Italianized his name and returned to England to bring the art of viola da gamba playing to new heights and to give impetus to the homophonic style of song writing so fully perfected in his pupils William and Henry Lawes. A lutenist, gambist, and composer, he taught all the royal children and was a particular favorite of Charles, upon whose accession he became composer-in-ordinary; among his works are *Funeral Teares* for the Earl of Devonshire (1606), many fine instrumental fantasias, and a treatise, *Rules how to Compose*. Coperario's collaboration with Campion in the year 1613 was quite intense, extending to work on both

The Lords' Masque and *The Somerset Masque* as well as *Songs of Mourning.*

Ruth Wallerstein has established a full context for *Songs of Mourning* in her brilliant study of the elegies on Prince Henry (*The Laureate Hearse: The Funeral Elegy and Seventeenth-Century Aesthetic* in *Studies in Seventeenth-Century Poetic* [Madison, 1950], pp. 59–95). The main stylistic streams she finds are the "drab" or mediaeval survival (in the Scots poets James Maxwell and Sir William Alexander), the Spenserians, usually channeling their laments into the pastoral elegy (Drummond, Fletcher, Browne) and the strong-lined, speculative metaphysicals (Donne and his circle of friends Herbert, King, and Goodyere). Campion's contribution falls into none of these groups; it is unique in at least two respects, in its concrete historical treatment of Prince Henry and in its meditative structure. Both the Spenserians and the metaphysicals attempted to relate this particular event to the most general of concerns, the former by involving the fate of mankind in the individual's fate by means of myth (as Drummond did in *Teares on the Death of Moeliades,* celebrating "A second Adons death"), the latter by using the death of the individual as the basis for speculations into metaphysics (as Donne and Herbert did). Campion chose instead to remain entirely within the realm of the particular and factual, by first stressing Prince Henry's individual virtues and exploits, and then exploring his meaning for the people close to him—father, mother, brother, sister—in personal rather than ideational terms. By opening out to Great Britain and the world at the end, the series achieves some universality of compass; but, even here, what is stressed is particular history (the East India venture, for instance), and the politically general has been reached by accretion rather than assimilation. The truly universal dimensions of Henry's death lie, for Campion, in the common emotions aroused by it. For Campion conceived of his song cycle as a meditative exercise, himself as priest (as the first six lines of the *Elegie* show), his purpose to move his audience to cleansing and even sanctifying grief by means of a spoken prelude and a body of song. The *Elegie,* by stressing Prince Henry's accomplishments and using the relation between Fate and Providence as a frame, is addressed to the audience's understanding. The seven songs that follow are to use this understanding as the basis of a cathartic act involving the emotions, at first indirectly by leading the audience to identify itself with those most deeply affected, then directly by addressing the people of England and Europe themselves as those most broadly affected by Henry's death.

ILLUSTRISSIMO,
POTENTISSIMOQUE PRIN-
CIPI, *FREDERICO* QUINTO, RHENI
COMITI PALATINO, DUCI BAVARIAE, &c.[1]

Cogimur; invitis (Clarissime) parce quaerelis
    Te salvo; laetis non sinet esse Deus:
Nec speratus Hymen procedit lumine claro;
    Principis extincti nubila fata vetant.
Illius inferias maesto iam Musica cantu   5
    Prosequitur, miseros haec Dea sola iuvat.
Illa suos tibi summittit (Dux inclite) quaestus,
    Fraternus fleto quem sociavit amor.
Sed nova gaudia, sed tam dulcia foedera rupit
    Fati infoelicis livor, et hora nocens.   10
Quod superest, nimios nobis omni arte dolores
    Est mollire animus, spes meliora dabit:
Cunctatosque olim cantabimus ipsi Hymenaeos,
    Laeta simul fas sit reddere vota Deo.

[1] "To the most illustrious and powerful Prince, Frederic the Fifth, Count Palatine of the Rhine, Duke of Bavaria, etc. We are hard-pressed; even though you are safe, pardon these unwelcome laments (most high); God does not permit them to be happy. Nor can the long-awaited Hymen proceed with a clear torch, for the fates of the dead prince forbid the wedding. Now Music pursues his funerals with mournful song, and that goddess helps only the unhappy. She presents her laments to you (noble Duke), whom fraternal love bound with weeping. But new joys, but so sweet a bond of friendship, did the envy of unhappy fate and the harmful moment break! What remains is the courage to soften excessive grief by all our art, and then hope will give us better things: and soon we ourselves shall sing your delayed wedding songs, as soon as it is meet to send happy thanks to God."

AN ELEGIE
upon the untimely death of
Prince *Henry*.

Reade, you that have some teares left yet unspent,
Now weepe your selves hart sicke, and nere repent:
For I will open to your free accesse
The sanctuary of all heavinesse,
Where men their fill may mourne, and never sinne: 5
And I their humble Priest thus first beginne.
  Fly from the Skies, yee blessed beames of light;
Rise up in horrid vapours, ugly night,
And fetter'd bring that ravenous monster Fate,
The fellon and the traytour to our state.   10
Law-Eloquence wee neede not to convince
His guilt; all know it, 'tis hee stole our Prince,
The Prince of men, the Prince of all that bore
Ever that princely name; O now no more
Shall his perfections, like the Sunne-beames, dare[2]   15
The purblinde world: in heav'n those glories are.
What could the greatest artist, Nature, adde
T' encrease his graces? devine forme hee had,
Striving in all his parts which should surpasse;
And like a well tun'd chime his carriage was   20
Full of coelestiall witchcraft, winning all
To admiration and love personall.
His Launce appear'd to the beholders eyes,
When his faîre hand advanc't it in the skyes,
Larger then truth, for well could hee it wield,   25
And make it promise honour in the field.
When Court and Musicke cal'd him, off fell armes,
And, as hee had beene shap't for loves alarmes,
In harmony hee spake, and trod the ground
In more proportion then the measur'd sound.   30
How fit for peace was hee, and rosie beds!
How fit to stand in troopes of iron heads,
When time had with his circles made complete
His charmed rounds! All things in time grow great.
  This feare, even like a commet that hangs high,   35

---

[2] stupefy.

And shootes his threatning flashes through the skye,
Held all the eyes of Christendome intent
Upon his youthfull hopes, casting th' event
Of what was in his power, not in his will:
For that was close conceal'd, and must lye still,   40
As deepely hid as that designe which late
With the French Lyon dyed.[3] O earthly state,
How doth thy greatnesse in a moment fall,
And feastes in highest pompe turne funerall!

But our young *Henry,* arm'd with all the arts   45
That sute with Empire, and the gaine of harts,
Bearing before him fortune, power, and love,
Appear'd first in perfection, fit to move
Fixt admiration; though his yeeres were greene,
Their fruit was yet mature: his care had beene   50
Survaying India, and implanting there
The knowledge of that God which hee did feare:
And ev'n now, though hee breathlesse lyes, his sayles
Are strugling with the windes, for our avayles
T' explore a passage hid from humane tract,   55
Will fame him in the enterprise or fact.[4]
O Spirit full of hope, why art thou fled
From deedes of honour? why's that vertue dead
Which dwelt so well in thee? a bowre more sweet,
If Paradise were found, it could not meete.   60
Curst then bee Fate that stole our blessing so,
And had for us now nothing left but woe,

[3] "The murder of Henry IV. of France by Ravaillac on the 4th of May, O. S. 1610, was a severe shock to the Prince, who had always had the highest esteem of the heroic qualities of that monarch, as the latter had a reciprocal regard for his Highness, and such a confidence in him, that one of our historians assures us, that he had seen papers, which make it more than probable, that the Prince was not only acquainted with the secret design of the King's vast preparations, made by him some time before his death, but likewise engaged in it" (Thomas Birch, *The Life of Henry Prince of Wales,* London, 1760, p. 189).

[4] "His Highness being convinced of how much importance the discovery of a North-West passage, formerly attempted in vain, would be, and being now resolved to employ for that purpose Captain Thomas Button. . . . The Captain accordingly set sail in April 1612 with two vessels, one called *the Resolution,* in which he sailed himself, and the other *the Discovery,* commanded by Capt. Ingram; being both victualled for eighteen months. They wintered on board the ships, and did not return till after the Prince's death, which prevented Capt. Button from making another voyage for the purpose of the discovery" (Birch, *Life,* p. 264).

Had not th' All-seeing providence yet kept
Another joy safe, that in silence slept:
And that same Royall workeman, who could frame   65
A Prince so worthy of immortall fame,
Lives; and long may hee live, to forme the other
His exprest image, and grace of his brother,
To whose eternall peace wee offer now
Guifts which hee lov'd, and fed: Musicks that flow   70
Out of a sowre and melancholike vayne,
Which best sort with the sorrowes wee sustaine.

1. *TO THE MOST SACRED*
King James.

O Griefe, how divers are thy shapes wherein men languish!
  The face sometime with teares thou fil'st,
  Sometime the hart thou kill'st
    With unseene anguish.
Sometime thou smil'st to view how Fate   5
  Playes with our humane state:
So farre from surety here
  Are all our earthly joyes,
That what our strong hope buildes, when least wee feare,
  A stronger power destroyes.   10

O Fate, why shouldst thou take from KINGS their joy and treasure?
  Their Image if men should deface,
  'Twere death, which thou dost race[5]
    Even at thy pleasure.
Wisedome of holy Kings yet knowes   15
  Both what it hath, and owes.
Heav'ns hostage, which you bredd
  And nurst with such choyce care,
Is ravisht now, great KING, and from us ledd
  When wee were least aware.   20

[5] rase, obliterate.

2. *TO THE MOST SACRED*
Queene *Anne.*

Tis now dead night, and not a light on earth
    Or starre in heaven doth shine:
Let now a mother mourne the noblest birth
    That ever was both mortall and divine.
    O sweetnesse peerelesse! more then humane grace!   5
    O flowry beauty!   O untimely death!
        Now, Musicke, fill this place[6]
        With thy most dolefull breath:
    O singing wayle a fate more truely funerall
    Then when with all his sonnes the sire of Troy[7] did fall. 10

Sleepe Joy, dye Mirth, and not a smile be seene,
    Or shew of harts content:
For never sorrow neerer touch't a QUEENE,
    Nor were there ever teares more duely spent.
    O deare remembrance, full of ruefull woe!   15
    O ceacelesse passion!   O unhumane hower!
        No pleasure now can grow,
        For wither'd is her flower.
    O anguish doe thy worst, and fury Tragicall,
    Since fate in taking one hath thus disorder'd all.   20

[6] There is an allusion to the music here, for the music is also to fill the space created by the rest in the middle of l. 6 (as indicated in the peculiar spacing of the line); in the next strophe, this same rest is used to comment on "ceacelesse."

[7] Priam; see *Aeneid* II. 469–558.

3. *TO THE MOST HIGH AND MIGHTY*
Prince Charles.

Fortune and Glory may be lost and woone,
But when the worke of Nature is undone
    That losse flyes past returning;
    No helpe is left but mourning.
What can to kinde youth more despightfull prove   5
    Then to be rob'd of one sole Brother?
             Father and Mother
Aske reverence, a Brother onely love.
Like age and birth, like thoughts and pleasures move:
    What gayne can he heape up, though showers of Crownes 10
        descend,
    Who for that good must change a brother and a friend?

Follow, O follow yet thy Brothers fame,
But not his fate: lets onely change the name,
    And finde his worth presented
    In thee, by him prevented.[8]   15
Or, past example of the dead, be great,
    Out of thy selfe begin thy storie:
             Vertue and glorie
Are eminent, being plac't in princely seate.
Oh, heaven, his age prolong with sacred heate,   20
    And on his honoured head let all the blessings light
    Which to his brothers life men wish't, and wisht them right.

[8] preceded.

4. *TO THE MOST PRINCELY AND VERTUOUS*
the Lady *Elizabeth.*

So parted you as if the world for ever
  Had lost with him her light:
Now could your teares hard flint to ruth excite,
    Yet may you never
  Your loves againe partake in humane sight: 5
O why should love[9] such two kinde harts dissever
As nature never knit more faire or firme together?

So loved you as sister should a brother,
  Not in a common straine,
For Princely blood doeth vulgar fire disdaine: 10
    But you each other
  On earth embrac't in a celestiall chaine.
Alasse for love, that heav'nly borne affection
To change should subject be, and suffer earths infection.

[9] Assumedly the god of Love is meant; see textual notes.

5. *TO THE MOST ILLUSTRIOUS AND MIGHTY*
Fredericke *the fift, Count Palatine of the Rhein.*

How like a golden dreame you met and parted,[10]
    That pleasing straight doth vanish:
    O, who can ever banish
The thought of one so princely and free harted!
But hee was pul'd up in his prime by fate,   5
And love for him must mourne, though all too late.
        Teares to the dead are due, let none forbid
        Sad harts to sigh: true griefe cannot be hid.

Yet the most bitter storme to height encreased
    By heav'n againe is ceased: 10
    O time, that all things movest,
In griefe and joy thou equall measure lovest:
Such the condition is of humane life,
Care must with pleasure mixe, and peace with strife:
        Thoughts with the dayes must change; as tapers waste, 15
        So must our griefes; day breakes when night is past.

[10] Though Henry and Frederic had corresponded since 1605, their per-
sonal acquaintance lasted only from Frederic's arrival on October 16 to
Henry's death on November 6, 1612.

6. To the Most Disconsolate
Great Brittaine.

When pale famine fed on thee
      With her insatiate jawes;
When civill broyles set murder free,
      Contemning all thy lawes;
When heav'n, enrag'd, consum'd thee so   5
With plagues, that none thy face could know,
        Yet in thy lookes affliction then shew'd lesse
        Then now for ones fall all thy parts expresse.

Now thy highest States[11] lament
      A sonne, and Brothers losse;   10
Thy nobles mourne in discontent,
      And rue this fatall crosse;
Thy Commons are with passion sad
To thinke how brave a Prince they had:
        If all thy rockes from white to blacke should turne, 15
        Yet couldst thou not in shew more amply mourne.

[11] rulers.

7. To the World.

O poore distracted world, partly a slave
    To Pagans sinnefull rage, partly obscur'd
With ignorance of all the meanes that save;
    And ev'n those parts of thee that live assur'd
Of heav'nly grace, Oh how they are devided   5
With doubts late by a Kingly penne decided![12]
    O happy world, if what the Sire begunne
    Had beene clos'd up by his religious Sonne!

Mourne all you soules opprest under the yoake
    Of Christian-hating Thrace: never appear'd   10
More likelyhood to have that blacke league broke,
    For such a heavenly prince might well be fear'd
Of earthly fiends.[13] Oh, how is Zeale inflamed
With power, when truth wanting defence is shamed!
    O princely soule, rest thou in peace, while wee   15
    In thine expect the hopes were ripe in thee.

A Table of all the Songs contayned in
this Booke.

FINIS.

[12] a reference to King James's reply to Cardinal Bellarmine, *Premonitions to all most mighty Monarchs, Kings, Free Princes, and States of Christendom,* 1609 (Bullen).

[13] Assumedly by "Thrace" is meant the Turkish Empire. Henry's interest in India and the East India Company (which was put under his protection in a charter of July 26, 1612) was at least partially motivated by a desire to break the Mohammedan hold on Asia and claim part of it for Christianity (see *Elegie,* ll. 51–52).

THE
THIRD
AND
FOURTH BOOKE
OF
AYRES:
Composed
BY
Thomas Campian.

So as they may be expressed by one *Voyce*, with a *Violl, Lute,* or *Orpharion.*

The Third and Fourth Booke of Ayres came forth from the presses without date, as had the first two books. But the dedicatory epistle to Sir Thomas Monson indicates a date of 1617, for on February 13 of that year Monson had attained the freedom to which the poem alludes. Since his trial for complicity in the Overbury murder case (see headnotes to *A Booke of Ayres* and *The Somerset Masque*) in December of 1615—a trial in which he had been scandalously treated by Coke and abused as a Papist—Monson had lain prisoner in the Tower. Even though no valid evidence had been brought against him, it took him over two years to obtain pardon and release; furthermore, his health had failed in January of 1616, after which time Campion had been allowed to attend him in his capacity as physician. Therefore, Campion celebrated his friend and patron's deliverance with no little bitterness at its delay and with great care to lift the burden of opprobrium from him. John Monson (1600–1683) was destined for a better fate than his father's; a valued financial advisor to Charles I, he acquired considerable land and wealth, and, even after the collapse of the Royalist cause, managed to live comfortably and long.

While Campion here followed his practice in *Two Bookes of Ayres* in addressing his two books to father and son respectively, the difference between the two is not the direct contrast of sacred and secular but rather a distinction in tone, between rather bitter and hard-headed songs on the one hand and lighter frothy ones on the other. Youth and age here signify innocence and experience. Surely one reason for the peculiar form of the distinction is that these two books are occasional in a way that none of the other songbooks are: in his epistle, Campion is at great pains to specify the way he feels about Monson and his relation to him in this book; hence, certain of the songs (for instance, "O griefe, o spight," a lament on the times) seem to allude directly to Monson's circumstances and experience. And, as in any good occasional verse that does not shy away from the particularity of the occasion, specificity of situation and complexity of tone result.

The curative function Campion assigns to *The Third Booke* determines its arrangement, for it takes Monson through a definite tonal progression from grief to lightheartedness. The first half is very dark: its dominant emotions are negative ones (as the reiterated word "distaste" implies), such as complaint, disappointment, anger, and cynical disenchantment. Suddenly with "Now winter nights" the tone rises to gay conviviality, a tone which is sustained in the rest of the volume, where if cynicism exists, it is the gay cynicism of the coquettes who sing "Silly boy," "If thou longst," or "So quicke, so hot, so mad," or where male disenchantment is spiced with comic acceptance.

The Third Booke carries the badge of achieved maturity: its lovers are experienced and, moreover, men of heightened ethical awareness. Its style is almost Baconian, since it is sprinkled much more heavily than any other volume with aphorisms compressing experience, such as "Friendship is the glasse of Truth," "Poorely hee lives, that can love none," or "Little knowes he how to love that never was deceived." Its characteristic devices are those that intensify the meanings or relations of individual weighty words, such as the repetition or variation of words ("simple" in iv, "good" in vi, "faith," "hope," and "love" in xxix) and antithesis, as in this complexly balanced line: "Bad with bad in ill sute well, but good with good live blessed." These songs, like many of those in *Two Bookes of Ayres,* are plain in style, dedicated to naming a situation and pronouncing a comprehensive judgment on it—as "Were my hart as some mens are" does supremely well. It is this sense of mature and sententious judgment that gives the dolefulness of much of *The Third Booke* its peculiar power.

If *The Fourth Booke* achieves a lighter tone than the third, it is partly because it is a retrospective volume, recapturing earlier concerns and earlier moods (as if Campion were re-examining his own youth through John Monson's). Two of the songs (xxii and xxiii) are revisions of material in *A Booke of Ayres* of 1601; at least four —vii, ix, xvii, and xviii—had been published by others as much as a decade previously; and several more—i, ii, vi, viii, xiii, and xix —seem like early work set forth anew. In the new songs of his mature manner, the serious, sententious mood of *The Third Booke* reappears only occasionally—in the third song's warning to youth, for instance, or in "Are you what your faire lookes expresse," Campion's sole attempt at philosophical love lyric. More frequently, these mature songs seem to be attempts at the Chaucerian manner to which he alludes in the preface: not only in the obscene songs he mentions directly, but in the songs of psychological cunning (such as "I must complain" and "Vaile, love, mine eyes") as well, and especially in songs like "Faine would I wed" and "Young and simple though I am," which use a naïve young singer for comic effect.

In this publication Campion returned to the solo accompanied song; his growing mastery of the form is attested by the fact that it was from this volume that most of the songs whose popularity survived the Restoration came.

A Table of all the Songs contayned in
the two Bookes following.

The Table of the first Booke.

The Table of the seconde Booke.

FINIS.

THE THIRD BOOKE

TO MY HONOURABLE FRIEND, Sr. THOMAS MOUNSON, *KNIGHT AND BARONET.*

Since now those clouds, that lately over-cast
Your Fame and Fortune, are disperst at last:
And now since all to you fayre greetings make,
Some out of love, and some for pitties sake:
Shall I but with a common stile salute   5
Your new enlargement?[1] or stand onely mute?
I, to whose trust and care you durst commit
Your pined health, when Arte despayr'd of it?
I, that in your affliction often view'd
In you the fruits of manly fortitude,   10
Patience, and even constancie of minde,
That Rocke-like stood, and scorn'd both wave and winde?
Should I, for all your ancient love to me,
Endow'd with waighty favours, silent be?
Your merits, and my gratitude, forbid   15
That eyther should in *Lethean* Gulfe lye hid.
But how shall I this worke of fame expresse?
How can I better, after pensivenesse,
Then with light straynes of Musicke, made to move
Sweetly with the wide-spreading plumes of love?   20
These youth-borne *Ayres,* then, prison'd in this Booke,
Which in your Bowres much of their beeing tooke,
Accept as a kinde offring from that hand
Which, joyn'd with heart, your vertue may command.
Who love a sure friend, as all good men doe,   25
Since such you are, let those affect[2] you to:
And may the joyes of that Crowne never end,
That innocence doth pitty, and defend.

Yours devoted,

THOMAS CAMPIAN.

[1] release from prison. [2] love.

I.

Oft have I sigh'd for him that heares me not,
Who absent hath both love and mee forgot.
Oh yet I languish still through his delay:
Dayes seeme as yeares, when wisht friends breake their day.[8]

Had hee but lov'd as common lovers use,
His faithlesse stay[4] some kindnesse would excuse:
O yet I languish still, still constant mourne
For him that can breake vowes, but not returne.

II.

Now let her change and spare not;
Since she proves strange[5] I care not:
Fain'd love charm'd so my delight
That still I doted on her sight.
But she is gone, new joies imbracing   5
And my desires disgracing.

When did I erre in blindnesse?
Or vexe her with unkindnesse?
If my cares serv'd her alone,
Why is shee thus untimely gone?   10
True love abides to th' houre of dying;
False love is ever flying.

False, then farewell for ever:
Once false proves faithfull never.
Hee that boasts now of thy love   15
Shall soone my present fortunes prove:
Were he as faire as bright *Adonis*,
Faith is not had where none is.

[8] break their appointments.   [4] absence.
[5] unfriendly.

Now let her change and spare not; Since she proves strange I care not: Fain'd love charm'd so __ my __ de · light That still I do · ted on her sight. But she is gone, new __ joies im · bra · cing And my de · sires dis · gra · cing.

III.

Were my hart as some mens are, thy errours[6] would not move me:
But thy faults I curious[7] finde, and speake because I love thee;
Patience is a thing divine and farre, I grant, above mee.

Foes sometimes befriend us more, our blacker deedes objecting,
Then th' obsequious bosome guest, with false respect affecting:
Friendship is the glasse of Truth, our hidden staines detecting.[8]

While I use of eyes enjoy, and inward light of reason,
Thy observer[9] will I be, and censor, but in season:
Hidden mischiefe to conceale in State and Love is treason.

IV.

Maydes are simple, some men say:
They, forsooth, will trust no men.
But, should they mens wils[10] obey,
Maides were very simple then.

Truth a rare flower now is growne,   5
Few men weare it in their hearts;
Lovers are more easily knowne
By their follies, then deserts.

Safer may we credit give
To a faithlesse wandring Jew   10
Then a young mans vowes beleeve
When he sweares his love is true.

Love they make a poore blinde childe,
But let none trust such as hee:
Rather then to be beguil'd,   15
Ever let me simple be.

[6] transgressions.   [7] strange, egregious.
[8] See Erasmus *Adagia* 476 E: *Non potes me simul et adulator uti, et amico* [You cannot use me as both flatterer and friend too].
[9] follower (not spy).
[10] desires.

V.

So tyr'd are all my thoughts, that sence and spirits faile;
Mourning I pine, and know not what I ayle.
O what can yeeld ease to a minde,
    Joy in nothing that can finde?

How are my powres fore-spoke?[11] what strange distaste[12] is this?   5
Hence, cruell hate of that which sweetest is:
Come, come delight, make my dull braine
    Feele once heate of joy againe.

The lovers teares are sweet, their mover[13] makes them so;
Proud of a wound the bleeding Souldiers grow: 10
Poore I alone, dreaming, endure
    Griefe that knowes nor cause, nor cure.

And whence can all this grow? even from an idle minde,
That no delight in any good can finde.
Action alone makes the soule blest: 15
    Vertue dyes with too much rest.

[11] bewitched.   [12] discomfort, as well as dislike.
[13] cause; i.e., the woman beloved.

VI.[14]

Why presumes thy pride on that, that must so private be
Scarce that it can good be cal'd, though it seemes best to
        thee,
Best of all that Nature fram'd, or curious eye can see?

Tis thy beauty, foolish Maid, that like a blossome growes,
Which who viewes no more enjoyes then on a bush a   5
        Rose;
That by manies handling fades, and thou art one of
        those.

If to one thou shalt prove true, and all beside reject,
Then art thou but one mans good, which yeelds a poore
        effect;[15]
For the common'st good by farre deserves the best
        respect.

But if for this goodnesse thou thy selfe wilt common[16]   10
        make,
Thou art then not good at all; so thou canst no way
        take
But to prove the meanest good, or else all good forsake.

Be not then of beauty proud, but so her colours[17] beare
That they prove not staines to her that them for grace
        should weare:
So shalt thou to all more fayre then thou wert borne   15
        appeare.

[14] Compare the third and fourth strophes to *"Ad Leam"* in *Epigrammatum Liber* II, 117, below. Compare also Sir Robert Ayton's "I doe confess th'art smooth." The song plays on the various senses of "good," such as *the valuable, morally upright,* and *chattel.*

[15] little gain.

[16] generally accessible, perhaps sexually so; see *Hamlet,* I, ii, 72–74.

[17] Beauty's livery, as well as complexion.

VII.[18]

Kinde are her answeres,
 But her performance keeps no day,
Breaks time, as dancers
 From their own Musicke when they stray:
 All her free favors   5
And smooth words wing my hopes in vaine.
O did ever voice so sweet but only fain?
 Can true love yeeld such delay,
 Converting joy to pain?

Lost is our freedome   10
 When we submit to women so:
Why doe wee neede them,
 When in their best they worke our woe?
 There is no wisedome
Can alter ends by Fate prefixt:[19]   15
O why is the good of man with evill mixt?
 Never were dayes yet cal'd two,
 But one night went betwixt.

[18] The setting of this song approaches the advanced *recitativo* style in its disjunctive phrasing (which blocks continuous melody), in its sudden skips, its tendency toward monotone, and its plain chordal accompaniment.
[19] predetermined.

Kinde are her an-sweres,   But   her per - for - mance keeps no   day,
Breaks time, as dan-cers   From their own Mu - sicke when they stray:

All   her free fa - vors And smooth words wing my   hopes   in vaine.

O   did e - ver voice   so sweet   but on - ly fain?

Can true love _ yeeld _ such de - lay, Con - ver - ting joy   to pain?

VIII.[20]

O griefe, O spight, to see poore Vertue scorn'd,
Truth far exil'd, False arte lov'd, Vice ador'd,
Free Justice sold, worst causes best adorn'd,
Right cast[21] by Powre, Pittie in vaine implor'd!
   O who in such an age could wish to live,   5
     When none can have or hold, but such as give?

O times! O men! to Nature rebels growne,
Poore in desert, in name rich, proud of shame,
Wise but in ill: your stiles[22] are not your owne,
Though dearely bought; honour is honest fame.   10
   Old Stories onely goodnesse now containe,
     And the true wisedome that is just, and plaine.

IX.

O never to be moved,
   O beauty unrelenting!
Hard hart, too dearely loved;
   Fond love, too late repenting!
Why did I dreame of too much blisse?   5
Deceitfull hope was cause of this.
   O heare mee speake this, and no more:
   Live you in joy, while I my woes deplore.

All comforts despayred
   Distaste[23] your bitter scorning;   10
Great sorrowes unrepayred
   Admit no meane in mourning:
Dye, wretch, since hope from thee is fled;
He that must dye is better dead.
   O deare delight, yet, ere I dye,   15
   Some pitty shew, though you reliefe deny.

[20] This song compresses a whole series of complaints common to the classical satirists; line 7 echoes Cicero's famous cry, *"O tempora! o mores!"* ("O times! o customs!"; see *In Catalinam* I. i. 2).

[21] overthrown.

[22] titles; one of the frequent allusions to the buying of knighthoods under James I; see Jonson, *Volpone*, IV, ii, 29–30.

[23] offend.

O nev-er to be mov-ed, O beau-ty un-re-len-ting!
Hard hart, too deare-ly lov-ed; Fond love, too late re-pen-ting!

Why did I dreame __ of too much __ blisse? De-ceit-full

hope was cause __ of this. O heare, o heare, o

heare mee speake, O heare mee speake this and no

more, this and no more, this and no' more: Live you in

joy,   while   I   my   woes,   my woes____ de · plore.

X.

Breake now my heart and dye! Oh no, she may relent.
Let my despaire prevayle! Oh stay, hope is not spent.
Should she now fixe one smile on thee, where were despaire?
    The losse is but easie which smiles can repayre.
    A stranger would please thee, if she were as fayre.   5

Her must I love or none, so sweet none breathes as shee;
The more is my despayre, alas, shee loves not mee:
But cannot time make way for love through ribs of steele?
    The Grecian, inchanted all parts but the heele,[24]
    At last a shaft daunted, which his hart did feele.   10

[24] Achilles, magically protected in all parts but the heel, which the arrow
of Paris pierced.

Breake now heart and dye! Oh no, oh no,
Let my de-spaire pre-vayle! Oh stay, oh stay,

no, she may re - lent,
stay, hope is not spent.

Should she now

fixe ____ one smile on thee, where were de - spaire?

The losse is but ea - sie which ___ smil can re - payre.
A stran - ger would please thee, if ___ she were as fayre.

XI.

If Love loves truth, then women doe not love;
Their passions all are but dissembled shewes;
Now kinde and free of favour[25] if they prove,
Their kindnes straight a tempest overthrowes.
    Then as a Sea-man the poore lover fares: 5
    The storme drownes him ere hee can drowne his cares.

But why accuse I women that deceive?
Blame then the Foxes for their subtile wile:
They first from Nature did their craft receive:
It is a womans nature to beguile.   10
    Yet some, I grant, in loving stedfast grow;
    But such by use[26] are made, not nature, so.

O why had Nature power at once to frame
Deceit and Beauty, traitors both to Love?
O would Deceit had dyed when Beauty came   15
With her divinenesse ev'ry heart to move!
    Yet doe we rather wish, what ere befall,
    To have fayre women false, then none at all.

[25] loving and generous.   [26] training.

XII.[27]

Now winter nights enlarge
    The number of their houres,
And clouds their stormes discharge
    Upon the ayrie towres;
Let now the chimneys blaze   5
    And cups o'erflow with wine,
Let well-tun'd words amaze
    With harmonie divine.
Now yellow waxen lights
    Shall waite on hunny Love,   10
While youthfull Revels, Masks, and Courtly sights,
    Sleepes leaden spels remove.

This time doth well dispence
    With[28] lovers long discourse;
Much speech hath some defence,   15
    Though beauty no remorse.
All doe not all things well:[29]
    Some measures comely tread,
Some knotted Ridles tell,
    Some Poems smoothly read.   20
The Summer hath his joyes,
    And Winter his delights;
Though Love and all his pleasures are but toyes,
    They shorten tedious nights.

[27] On this song, see Ing, *Elizabethan Lyrics,* pp. 159–60, and Yvor Winters, "The 16th Century Lyric in England: Part III," *Poetry: A Magazine of Verse,* LIV (1939), 37.
[28] dispense with: allow.   [29] See Virgil *Eclogue* VIII, l. 63.

XIII.

Awake, thou spring of speaking grace, mute rest becomes not
        thee;
The fayrest women, while they sleepe, and Pictures equall bee.[30]
    O come and dwell in[31] loves discourses,
      Old renuing, new creating.
    The words which thy rich tongue discourses   5
      Are not of the common rating.

Thy voyce is as an Eccho cleare which Musicke doth beget,
Thy speech is as an Oracle which none can counterfeit:
    For thou alone, without offending,
      Hast obtain'd power of enchanting;   10
    And I could heare thee without ending,
      Other comfort never wanting.

Some little reason brutish lives with humane glory share;
But language is our proper grace, from which they sever'd are.[32]
    As brutes in reason man surpasses,   15
      Men in speech excell each other:
    If speech be then the best of graces,
      Doe it not in slumber smother.

[30] See *Macbeth,* II, ii, 52–53: "the sleeping and the dead / Are but as
pictures."

[31] dwell upon.

[32] a common Renaissance sentence; see *Observations in the Art of English
Poesie,* first paragraph (below, p. 291).

XIV.

What is it that all men possesse,[33] among themselves conversing?[34]
Wealth or fame, or some such boast, scarce worthy the rehearsing?
Women onely are mens good, with them in love conversing.

If weary, they prepare us rest; if sicke, their hand attends us;
When with griefe our hearts are prest, their comfort best   5
       befriends us:
Sweet or sowre, they willing goe to share what fortune sends us.

What pretty babes with paine they beare, our name and form
       presenting!
What we get, how wise they keepe, by sparing, wants preventing;
Sorting all their houshold cares to our observ'd contenting.[35]

All this, of whose large use I sing, in two words is expressed: 10
Good wife is the good I praise, if by good men possessed;
Bad with bad in ill sute well, but good with good live blessed.

[33] hold to.   [34] living together in society.
[35] governing the performance of their household tasks according to whether they seem to please us or not.

XV.

Fire that must flame is with apt fuell fed,
Flowers that wil thrive in sunny soyle are bred;
How can a hart feele heate that no hope findes?
Or can hee love on whom no comfort shines?

Fayre, I confesse there's pleasure in your sight: 5
Sweet, you have powre, I grant, of all delight:
But what is all to mee, if I have none?
Churle[36] that you are, t' injoy such wealth alone.

Prayers move the heav'ns, but finde no grace with you;
Yet in your lookes a heavenly forme I view: 10
Then will I pray againe, hoping to finde,
As well as in your lookes, heav'n in your minde.

Saint of my heart, Queene of my life, and love,
O let my vowes thy loving spirit move:
Let me no longer mourne through thy disdaine,   15
But with one touch of grace cure all my paine.[37]

[36] miser.
[37] The strophe parodies litanies to the Virgin Mary and Saints.

XVI.

If thou longst so much to learne (sweet boy) what 'tis to love,
Doe but fixe thy thought on mee, and thou shalt quickly prove.[38]
       Little sute, at first, shal win
         Way to thy abasht desire,
       But then will I hedge thee in,   5
         Salamander-like, with fire.[39]

With thee dance I will, and sing, and thy fond dalliance beare;
Wee the grovy hils will climbe, and play the wantons[40] there;
       Other whiles wee'le gather flowres,
         Lying dalying on the grasse,   10
       And thus our delightfull howres
         Full of waking dreames shall passe.

When thy joyes were thus at height, my love should turne from
          thee;
Old acquaintance then should grow as strange as strange might be;
       Twenty rivals thou should'st finde   15
         Breaking all their hearts for mee,
       When to all Ile prove more kinde
         And more forward[41] then to thee.

Thus thy silly youth, enrag'd, would soone my love defie;
But, alas, poore soule, too late: clipt wings can never flye.   20
       Those sweet houres which wee had past,
         Cal'd to minde, thy heart would burne;
       And, could'st thou flye ne'er so fast,
         They would make thee straight returne.

[38] experience it.
[39] The salamander (because of its color) was supposed to be capable of living unharmed in the midst of fire.
[40] dally or behave loosely.   [41] generous.

XVII.[42]

Shall I come, sweet Love, to thee,
   When the ev'ning beames are set?
Shall I not excluded be?
    Will you finde no fained lett?
      Let me not, for pitty, more,   5
      Tell the long houres at your dore.

Who can tell what theefe or foe,
   In the covert of the night,
For his prey, will worke my woe,
    Or through wicked foule despight:[43]   10
      So may I dye unredrest,
      Ere my long love be possest.

But, to let such dangers passe,
   Which a lovers thoughts disdaine,
'Tis enough in such a place   15
    To attend loves joyes in vaine.
      Doe not mocke me in thy bed,
      While these cold nights freeze me dead.

[42] The setting reproduced for this song is a version for voice and bass viol (from British Museum Additional MS. 29481, fo. 20) in which the ornaments a performer might ordinarily have improvised on the bare melody have been written out. It is set one note higher than in the original printed edition, and contains some alterations of the original viol part (as well as textual variants). On this song, see Kastendieck, *England's Musical Poet,* pp. 92, 112–13, and Pattison, *Music and Poetry of the English Renaissance,* pp. 132–33.

[43] will work my woe either for booty (if a thief) or to satisfy his spite (if a foe).

From Add. MS. 29481 (fo. 20)

Shall I com sweet love to thee when the eve-ninge beames are sett Shall I not ex - - - clu-de - - d be wil you finde no fained lett let mee not for pit-tie a-ny more tell the longe howers tell the long howers at thy door.

XVIII.[44]

Thrice tosse these Oaken ashes in the ayre,
Thrice sit thou mute in this inchanted chayre;
Then thrice three times tye up this true loves knot,
And murmur soft, shee will, or shee will not.

Goe burne these poys'nous weedes in yon blew fire,   5
These Screech-owles fethers, and this prickling bryer,
This Cypresse gathered at a dead mans grave:
That all thy feares and cares an end may have.

Then come, you Fayries, dance with me a round,
Melt her hard hart with your melodious sound.   10
In vaine are all the charmes I can devise:
She hath an Arte to breake them with her eyes.

[44] Modeled on the "spells" in classical pastoral, e.g., Theocritus *Idyll* II
and Virgil *Eclogue* VIII. 64 ff.; from the latter come the details of the
ashes (l. 101), the love knot (77–78), and the poisonous weeds (95).

XIX.

Be thou then my beauty named,
Since thy will is to be mine:
   For by that am I enflamed,
Which on all alike doth shine.
      Others may the light admire,   5
      I onely truely feele the fire.

But, if lofty titles move thee,
Challenge[45] then a Sov'raignes place:
   Say I honour when I love thee,
Let me call thy kindnesse grace.   10
      State and Love things divers bee,
      Yet will we teach them to agree.

Or, if this be not sufficing,
Be thou stil'd my Goddesse then:
   I will love thee sacrificing,   15
In thine honour Hymnes Ile pen.
      To be thine, what canst thou more?[46]
      Ile love thee, serve thee, and adore.

[45] claim.   [46] what more can you want for yourself?

XX.[47]

    Fire, fire, fire, fire!
Loe here I burne in such desire
That all the teares that I can straine
Out of mine idle empty braine
Cannot allay my scorching paine.   5
        Come *Trent,* and *Humber,* and fayre *Thames,*
        Dread Ocean, haste with all thy streames:
        And, if you cannot quench my fire,
        O drowne both mee and my desire.

    Fire, fire, fire, fire!   10
There is no hell to my desire:
See, all the Rivers backward flye,
And th' Ocean doth his waves deny,
For feare my heate should drinke them dry.
        Come, heav'nly showres, then, pouring downe;   15
        Come, you that once the world did drowne:
        Some then you spar'd, but now save all,
        That else must burne, and with mee fall.

[47] Perhaps based on song xiv in Thomas Morley's *First Booke of Balletts to Five Voyces,* 1595:

        Fire! fire! my heart!
        O help! Ay me! I sit and cry me,
        And call for help, but none comes nigh me!

        O, I burn me! alas!
        I burn! Ay me! will none come quench me?
        Cast water on, alas, and drench me!

Fire, fire, fire, fire! Loe here I burne, I burne in such de-
sire, That all the teares that I can straine Out of mine
i-dle emp-ty braine Can-not al-lay my scor-ching paine.
Come *Trent*, and *Hum-ber*, and fayre *Thames*, Dread O-cean,

haste with all _____ thy ___ streames: And, if you can-
- not quench my fire, O ___ drowne both ___ mee, O ___
- drowne ___ both ___ mee and my _____ de - sire. -sire.

XXI.

O sweet delight, O more then humane blisse,
With her to live that ever loving is;
To heare her speake, whose words so well are plac't,
That she by them, as they in her are grac't;
    Those lookes to view, that feast the viewers eye;   5
    How blest is he that may so live and dye!

Such love as this the golden times did know,
When all did reape, yet none tooke care to sow:
Such love as this an endlesse Summer makes,
And all distaste[48] from fraile affection takes.   10
    So lov'd, so blest, in my belov'd am I;
    Which, till their eyes ake, let yron men[49] envy.

XXII.

Thus I resolve, and time hath taught me so:
Since she is fayre and ever kinde to me,
Though she be wilde and wanton-like in shew,
Those little staines in youth I will not see.
    That she be constant, heav'n I oft implore;   5
    If pray'rs prevaile not, I can doe no more.

Palme tree the more you presse, the more it growes:[50]
Leave it alone, it will not much exceede.[51]
Free beauty if you strive to yoke, you lose,
And for affection strange distaste you breede.   10
    What Nature hath not taught, no Arte can frame:
    Wilde borne be wilde still, though by force made tame.

[48] unpleasantness.
[49] men in this present Age of Iron (in contrast to his Golden Age, l. 7).
[50] See Pliny *Natural History* XIII. viii. 37, and Lyly, *Euphues: The Anatomy of Wit,* ed. Croll and Clemons, p. 19: "It is proper for the palm-tree to mount; the heavier you load it the higher it sprouteth."
[51] excel in height.

XXIII.

Come, O come, my lifes delight,
Let me not in langour pine:
    Love loves no delay: thy sight,
            O come, and take from mee   5
            The paine of being depriv'd of thee.

Thou all sweetnesse dost enclose,
Like a little world of blisse:
    Beauty guards thy lookes: the Rose
In them pure and eternall is.   10
            Come then, and make thy flight
            As swift to me as heav'nly light.

XXIV.

Could my heart more tongues imploy
Then it harbors thoughts of griefe,
    It is now so farre from joy
That it scarce could aske reliefe.
            Truest hearts by deedes unkinde   5
            To despayre are most enclin'd.

Happy mindes, that can redeeme
Their engagements[52] how they please,
    That no joyes or hopes esteeme
Halfe so pretious as their ease!   10
            Wisedome should prepare men so
            As if they did all foreknow.

Yet no Arte or Caution can
Growne affections easily change;
    Use is such a Lord of Man   15
That he brookes worst what is strange.
            Better never to be blest
            Then to loose all at the best.

[52] to redeem engagements: to cut loose from emotional involvements.

XXV.

Sleepe, angry beauty, sleep, and feare not me,
For who a sleeping Lyon dares provoke?
It shall suffice me here to sit and see
Those lips shut up that never kindely spoke.
     What sight can more content a lovers minde   5
     Then beauty seeming harmlesse, if not kinde?

My words have charm'd her, for secure[53] shee sleepes,
Though guilty much of wrong done to my love;
And in her slumber, see! shee close-ey'd weepes!
Dreames often more then waking passions move.   10
     Pleade, sleepe, my cause, and make her soft like thee,
     That shee in peace may wake and pitty mee.

[53] free from anxiety (as if she were actually sinless).

XXVI.

Silly boy, 'tis ful Moone yet, thy night as day shines
        clearely;[54]
Had thy youth but wit[55] to feare, thou couldst not love

Shortly wilt thou mourne when all thy pleasures are
        bereaved;[56]
Little knowes he how to love that never was deceived.

This is thy first mayden flame, that triumphes yet   5
        unstayned;
All is artlesse now you speake, not one word yet is
        fayned;
All is heav'n that you behold, and all your thoughts are
        blessed:
But no Spring can want[57] his Fall, each *Troylus* hath
        his *Cresseid*.

Thy well-order'd lockes ere long shall rudely hang
        neglected;
And thy lively pleasant cheare reade griefe on earth   10
        dejected.[58]
Much then wilt thou blame thy Saint, that made thy
        heart so holy,
And with sighs confesse, in love, that too much faith is
        folly.

Yet, be just and constant still; Love may beget a
        wonder,
Not unlike a Summers frost, or Winters fatall thunder:
Hee that holds his Sweet-hart true unto his day of   15
        dying
Lives, of all that ever breath'd, most worthy the envying.

[54] See Catullus VIII, ll. 3–4:

> *fulsere quondam candidi tibi soles,*
> *cum ventitabas quo puella ducebat*

[once the suns shone bright on you, when you used to go wherever your
mistress led you].

[55] intelligence.   [56] taken from you.   [57] lack.
[58] your face ("cheare"), hung low, will show all the signs of earthly grief.

XXVII.

Never love unlesse you can
Beare with all the faults of man:
Men sometimes will jealous bee
Though but little cause they see,
    And hang the head, as discontent,   5
    And speake what straight they will repent.

Men that but one Saint adore
Make a shew of love to more:
Beauty must be scorn'd in none,
Though but truely serv'd in one: 10
    For what is courtship, but disguise?
    True hearts may have dissembling eyes.[59]

Men, when their affaires require,
Must a while themselves retire:
Sometimes hunt, and sometimes hawke,   15
And not ever sit and talke.
    If these, and such like, you can beare,
    Then like, and love, and never feare.

[59] Lines 9–12 are indirect quotations of the man's excuses.

XXVIII.

So quicke,[60] so hot, so mad is thy fond sute,
So rude, so tedious growne, in urging mee,
That faine I would with losse make thy tongue mute,

  An houre with thee I care not[61] to converse, 5
  For I would not be counted too perverse.

But roofes too hot would prove for men all fire,[62]
And hils too high for my unused pace;
The grove is charg'd[63] with thornes and the bold bryer;
Gray Snakes the meadowes shrowde in every place: 10
  A yellow Frog, alas, will fright me so,
  As I should start and tremble as I goe.

Since then I can on earth no fit roome finde,
In heaven I am resolv'd with you to meete;
Till then, for Hopes sweet sake, rest your tir'd minde, 15
And not so much as see mee in the streete:
  A heavenly meeting one day wee shall have,
  But never, as you dreame, in bed, or grave.[64]

[60] lively and impatient. [61] I don't mind if I do.

[62] a rather obscure line; it could refer either to a meeting on the rooftop (probably in a banqueting house built on the roof of a manor, for such places were common trysting places) or to a meeting *under* any roof. If the former, rooftops already heated by the sun would become unbearable when heated further by the man's passion; if the latter, his passion would turn any room into an inferno. The woman is trying wittily to demolish any possible meeting place.

[63] loaded.

[64] in bed (as lovers), in the grave (as husband and wife at the end of a long happy marriage); "in grave" may also imply that his hot love would kill them both.

XXIX.[65]

Shall I then hope when faith is fled?
Can I seeke love when hope is gone?
 Or can I live when Love is dead?
Poorely hee lives, that can love none.
  Her vowes are broke, and I am free;   5
  Shee lost her faith in loosing mee.

When I compare mine owne events,[66]
When I weigh others like annoy,
 All doe but heape up discontents
That on a beauty build their joy.   10
  Thus I of all complaine, since shee
  All faith hath lost in loosing[67] mee.

So my deare freedome have I gain'd
Through her unkindnesse and disgrace;
 Yet could I ever live enchain'd,   15
As[68] shee my service did embrace.
  But shee is chang'd, and I am free:
  Faith failing her, Love dyed in mee.

[65] There is some witty play on the three theological virtues in this song.
[66] fate.
[67] "Loosing" is Campion's usual spelling of "losing," but here "loosing" or letting go may also apply.
[68] as long as.

THE FOURTH BOOKE

TO MY WORTHY FRIEND,
Mr. JOHN MOUNSON, Sonne and Heyre to
Sir Thomas Mounson, Knight and Baronet.

On you th' affections of your Fathers Friends,
With his Inheritance by right descends;
But you your gracefull youth so wisely guide,
That his[1] you hold, and purchase much beside.
Love is the fruit of Vertue, for whose sake   5
Men onely liking each to other take.
If sparkes of vertue shin'd not in you then,
So well how could you winne the hearts of men?
And, since that honour and well-suted Prayse
Is Vertues Golden Spurre, let mee now rayse   10
Unto an act mature[2] your tender age,
This halfe commending to your Patronage:
Which from your Noble Fathers, but one side,
Ordain'd to doe you honour, doth divide.
And so my love betwixt you both I part,   15
On each side placing you as neare my heart.

Yours ever,

THOMAS CAMPIAN.

[1] i.e., his inheritance and friends.
[2] i.e., by praising you let me spur you to mature acts of virtue.

To the READER.

The Apothecaries have Bookes of Gold, whose leaves being opened
are so light as that they are subject to be shaken with the least
breath, yet, rightly handled, they serve both for ornament and use;
~~such are light Ayres. But if any squeamish stomackes shall checke[8]~~
at two or three vaine Ditties in the end of this Booke, let them
powre off the clearest, and leave those as dregs in the bottome.
Howsoever, if they be but conferred with the *Canterbury Tales* of
that venerable Poet *Chaucer*, they will then appeare toothsome
enough. Some words are in these Bookes which have beene cloathed
in Musicke by others,[4] and I am content they then served their
turne: yet give mee now leave to make use of mine owne. Like-
wise you may finde here some three or four Songs that have beene
published before;[5] but for them, I referre you to the Players Bill,
that is stiled, *Newly revived, with Additions,*[6] for you shall finde all
of them reformed, eyther in Words or Notes. To be brief, all these
Songs are mine if you expresse them well, otherwise they are your
owne.[7] Farewell.

Yours as you are his,

THOMAS CAMPIAN.

[8] wince.   [4] Songs vii, ix, xvii, and xviii; see textual notes.

[5] Songs x (music only), xxii, and xxiii.

[6] a phrase all too frequently used in playbills for theatrical revivals and
title pages of later editions of plays.

[7] Bullen observes in his edition that Campion here echoes Martial *Epi-
grams* I. xxxviii:

> *Quem recitas meus est, o Fidentine, libellus:*
> *sed male cum recitas, incipit esse tuus*

[Fidentinus, the book you recite is mine: but when you recite it badly, it
begins to become your own].

I.

Leave prolonging thy distresse:
All delayes afflict the dying.
Many lost sighes long I spent, to her for mercy crying;
    But now, vaine mourning, cease:
    Ile dye, and mine owne griefes release.   5

Thus departing from this light
To those shades that end all sorrow,
Yet a small time of complaint, a little breath Ile borrow,
    To tell my once delight[8]
    I dye alone through her despight.   10

II.

Respect my faith, regard my service past;
The hope you wing'd[9] call home to you at last.
Great prise[10] it is that I in you shall gaine,
So great for you hath been my losse and paine.
    My wits I spent and time for you alone,   5
    Observing[11] you and loosing all for one.

Some rais'd to rich estates in this time are,
That held their hopes to mine inferiour farre:
Such scoffing mee, or pittying me, say thus,
Had hee not lov'd, he might have liv'd like us.   10
    O then, deare sweet, for love and pitties sake,
    My faith reward, and from me scandall take.[12]

[8] she who was once my only delight.
[9] engrafted wings on; the image comes from falconry.
[10] reward. [11] following (as a servant).
[12] Compare the second strophe with Sidney, *Astrophel and Stella,* cvii.

III.

Thou joy'st, fond boy, to be by many loved,
To have thy beauty of most dames approved.
For this dost thou thy native worth disguise

  Thy glasse thou councel'st more t' adorne thy skin, 5
  That first should schoole thee to be fayre within.

'Tis childish to be caught with Pearle, or Amber,
And woman-like too much to cloy[14] the chamber;
Youths should the Field affect,[15] heate their rough Steedes,
Their hardned nerves to fit for better deedes. 10
  Is't not more joy strong Holds to force with swords,
  Then womens weakenesse take with lookes or words?

Men that doe noble things all purchase glory:
One man for one brave Act hath prov'd a story:
But if that one tenne thousand Dames o'ercame, 15
Who would record it, if not to his shame?
  'Tis farre more conquest with one to live true
  Then every houre to triumph Lord of new.

IV.[16]

  Vaile, love, mine eyes, O hide from me
  The plagues that charge the curious[17] minde:
  If beauty private[18] will not be,
  Suffice it yet that she proves kinde.
    Who can usurp heav'ns light alone? 5
    Stars were not made to shine on one.

  Griefes past recure fooles try to heale,
  That greater harmes on lesse inflict;
  The pure offend by too much zeale,
  Affection should not be too strict. 10
    Hee that a true embrace will finde
    To beauties faults must still[19] be blinde.

---

[13] worship. [14] crowd. [15] love.
[16] Compare Herrick, "The Eclipse." [17] prying.
[18] true to one only. [19] always.

V.[20]

Ev'ry Dame affects good fame, what ere her doings be,
But true prayse is Vertues Bayes,[21] which none may weare
        but she.
Borrow'd guise fits not the wise, a simple look is best;
Native grace becomes a face, though ne'er so rudely drest.
    Now such new found toyes[22] are sold, these women to   5
        disguise,
    That, before the yeare growes old, the newest fashion dyes.

Dames of yore contended more in goodnesse to exceede
Then in pride to be envi'd for that which least they neede:
Little Lawne[23] then serv'd the Pawne,[24] if Pawne at all there
        were;
Home-spun thread, and houshold bread, then held out all   10
        the yeare.
    But th' attyres of women now weare out both house and
        land;
    That the wives in silkes may flow, at ebbe the Good-men
        stand.[25]

Once agen, *Astraea*,[26] then, from heav'n to earth descend,
And vouchsafe in their[27] behalfe these errours to amend:
Aid from heav'n must make all eev'n, things are so out of   15
        frame,
For let man strive all he can, hee needes must please his
        Dame.
    Happy man, content that gives, and what hee gives
        enjoyes;
    Happy Dame, content that lives, and breakes no sleepe for
        toyes.

[20] Compare Jonson, "Still to be neat," *Epicoene,* I, i.
[21] reward. [22] trifles. [23] fine linen.
[24] a corridor of fine shops built in the Royal Exchange in 1571, much frequented by women of fashion (Vivian's note).
[25] The line depends on a slight wordplay on "flow" (to circulate and to hang loosely): so that she may be swathed in silks and flow like the sea, her husband's fortunes must stand at ebb.
[26] the virgin goddess who presided over the Golden Age. [27] men's.

VI.

So sweet is thy discourse to me,
And so delightfull is thy sight,
   As I taste nothing right but thee.
O why invented Nature light?
     Was it alone for beauties sake,   5
     That her grac't words might better take?

No more can I old joyes recall:
They now to me become unknowne,
   Not seeming to have beene at all.
Alas, how soone is this love growne   10
     To such a spreading height in me
     As with it all must shadowed be!

VII.[28]

There is a Garden in her face,
Where Roses and white Lillies grow;
A heav'nly paradice is that place,
Wherein all pleasant fruits doe flow.[29]

Till Cherry ripe themselves doe cry.[30]

Those Cherries fayrely doe enclose
Of Orient Pearle a double row,
Which when her lovely laughter showes,
They looke like Rose-buds fill'd with snow.   10
Yet them nor Peere nor Prince can buy,
Till Cherry ripe themselves doe cry.

Her Eyes like Angels watch them still;
Her Browes like bended bowes doe stand,
Threatning with piercing frownes to kill   15
All that attempt with eye or hand
Those sacred Cherries to come nigh,
Till Cherry ripe themselves doe cry.

[28] The source of this song may be No. xvi of Thomas Morley's *First Booke of Balletts to Five Voyces* (1595):

> Lady, those cherries plenty,
> Which grow on your lips dainty,
>   Ere long will fade and languish.
> Then now, while yet they last them,
> O let me pull and taste them.

In turn, Campion's song probably inspired Herrick's "Cherrie-ripe." The music beneath the words "Cherry ripe" is taken from a London street seller's cry (and thus undercuts, with its earthy commercialism, the high Petrarchan style of the rest of the song).

[29] pour forth profusely.   [30] offer themselves for sale, as well as cry out.

ripe, Cher-ry ripe, Cher-ry ripe them-selves doe cry.

VIII.[31]

To his sweet Lute *Apollo* sung the motions of the Spheares,
The wondrous order of the Stars, whose course divides the
        yeares,
        And all the Mysteries above:
        But none of this could *Midas* move,
        Which purchast him his Asses eares.   5

Then *Pan* with his rude Pipe began the Country-wealth t' ad-
        vance,
To boast of Cattle, flockes of Sheepe, and Goates on hils that
        dance,
        With much more of this churlish kinde:
        That quite transported *Midas* minde,
        And held him rapt as in a trance.   10

This wrong the *God of Musicke* scorn'd from such a sottish
        Judge,
And bent his angry bow at *Pan,* which made the Piper trudge:
        Then *Midas* head he so did trim[32]
        That ev'ry age yet talkes of him
        And *Phoebus* right revenged grudge.   15

[31] See Ovid *Metamorphoses* XI. 146–93. By stressing the texts of Apollo's
and Pan's songs, Campion threw into relief the ancient Greek conflict be-
tween two different kinds of music: that of the lyre or stringed instruments
expressing the objective harmony of the universe, and that of the aulos or
wind instruments expressing human concerns and emotions. F. W. Sternfeld
(*Music in Shakespearean Tragedy* [London, 1963], pp. 227–29) adduces
many passages to show that Elizabethans often associated stringed instru-
ments with the spirit and the winds with the flesh.

[32] i.e., with the ears of an ass.

IX.

Young and simple though I am,
I have heard of *Cupids* name:
Guesse I can what thing it is
Men desire when they doe kisse.
   Smoake can never burne, they say,   5
   But the flames that follow may.

I am not so foule or fayre
To be proud, nor to despayre;
Yet my lips have oft observ'd,
Men that kisse them presse them hard,   10
   As glad lovers use to doe
   When their new met loves they wooe.

Faith, 'tis but a foolish minde,
Yet, me thinkes, a heate I finde,
Like thirst longing,[33] that doth bide   15
Ever on my weaker side,
   Where they say my heart doth move.
   Venus, grant it be not love.

If it be, alas, what then?
Were not women made for men?   20
As good 'twere a thing were past,
That must needes be done at last.
   Roses that are over-blowne
   Growe lesse sweet, then fall alone.

Yet nor Churle, nor silken Gull[34]   25
Shall my Mayden blossome pull:
Who shall not I soone can tell;
Who shall, would I could as well:
   This I know, who ere hee be,
   Love hee must, or flatter me.   30

[33] either thirst for drink, or any passionate desire.   [34] fop.

X.[35]

Love me or not, love her I must or dye;
Leave me or not, follow her needs must I.
O, that her grace would my wisht comforts give:

All my desire, all my delight should be   5
Her to enjoy, her to unite to mee:
Envy should cease, her would I love alone:
Who loves by lookes, is seldome true to one.

Could I enchant, and that it lawfull were,
Her would I charme softly that none should heare.   10
But love enforc'd rarely yeelds firme content;
So would I love that neyther should repent.

XI.

What meanes this folly, now to brave it so,
    And then to use submission?
Is that a friend that straight can play the foe?
    Who loves on such condition?

Though Bryers breede Roses, none the Bryer affect,[36]   5
    But with the flowre are pleased.
Love onely loves delight and soft respect:
    He must not be diseased.[37]

These thorny passions spring from barren breasts,
    Or such as neede much weeding.   10
Love onely loves delight and soft respect;[38]
    But sends them not home bleeding.

Command thy humour,[39] strive to give content,
    And shame not loves profession.
Of kindnesse never any could repent   15
    That made choyse with discretion.

[35] The first half of this song utilizes the music of "Follow your Saint,"
A Booke of Ayres, Part I, x.
[36] love; see note [2] to *The First Booke*, above.   [37] discomforted.
[38] See textual notes.   [39] restrain your natural bent.

XII.[40]

Deare, if I with guile would guild a true intent,
Heaping flattries that in heart were never meant,
    Easely could I then obtaine
      What now in vaine I force;[41]
    Fals-hood much doth gaine,   5
      Truth yet holds the better course.

Love forbid that through dissembling I should thrive,
Or, in praysing you, my selfe of truth deprive:
    Let not your high thoughts debase
      A simple truth in me;   10
    Great is beauties grace,
      Truth is yet as fayre as shee.

Prayse is but the winde of pride, if it exceedes;
Wealth, pris'd in it selfe, no outward value needes.
    Fayre you are, and passing fayre;   15
      You know it, and 'tis true:
    Yet let none despayre
      But to finde as fayre as you.

[40] Compare "Some can flatter" in Doubtful Poems, below.   [41] urge.

XIII.

O Love, where are thy Shafts, thy Quiver, and thy Bow?
Shall my wounds onely weepe, and hee ungaged[42] goe?
Be just, and strike him, to, that dares contemne thee so.

No eyes are like to thine, though men suppose thee blinde,
So fayre they levell[43] when the marke they list to finde: 5
Then strike, o strike the heart that beares the cruell minde.

Is my fond sight deceived? or doe I *Cupid* spye
Close ayming at his breast, by whom despis'd I dye?
Shoot home, sweet *Love,* and wound him, that hee may not
          flye!

O then we both will sit in some unhaunted shade,   10
And heale each others wound which *Love* hath justly made:
O hope, o thought too vaine, how quickly dost thou fade!

At large he wanders still, his heart is free from paine,
While secret sighes I spend, and teares, but all in vaine:
Yet, *Love,* thou know'st, by right I should not thus   15
          complaine.

[42] unbound.   [43] aim.

XIV.

Beauty is but a painted hell:
     Aye me, aye me,
Shee wounds them that admire it,
Shee kils them that desire it.
     Give her pride but fuell,   5
     No fire is more cruell.

Pittie from ev'ry heart is fled,
     Aye me, aye me;
Since false desire could borrow
Teares of dissembled sorrow,   10
     Constant vowes turne truthlesse,
     Love cruell, Beauty ruthlesse.

Sorrow can laugh, and Fury sing,
     Aye me, aye me;
My raving griefes discover   15
I liv'd too true a lover:
     The first step to madnesse
     Is the excesse of sadnesse.

XV.[44]

Are you what your faire lookes expresse?
    Oh then be kinde:
From law of Nature they digresse[45]
    Whose forme sutes not their minde:
Fairenesse seene in th' outward shape   5
Is but th' inward beauties Ape.[46]

Eyes that of earth are mortall made,
    What can they view?
All's but a colour or a shade,
    And neyther alwayes true.   10
Reasons sight, that is eterne,
Ev'n the substance can discerne.

Soule is the Man; for who will so
    The body name?
And to that power all grace we owe   15
    That deckes our living frame.
What, or how, had housen[47] bin,
But for them that dwell therein?

Love in the bosome is begot,
    Not in the eyes;   20
No beauty makes the eye more hot,
    Her flames the spright[48] surprise:
Let our loving mindes then meete,
For pure meetings are most sweet.

[44] This song depends heavily on the traditional *canzoni d'amore* of poets like Cavalcanti, Benivieni, and Spenser, especially Spenser's *An Hymne in Honour of Beautie*. Compare ll. 3–6 with Spenser's ll. 132–33:

> For of the soule the bodie forme doth take:
> For soule is forme, and doth the bodie make;

and ll. 15–18 with Spenser's ll. 117–19 (which themselves echo Benivieni):

> And [the soul] frames her house, in which she will be placed,
> Fit for her selfe, adorning it with spoyle
> Of th' heavenly riches, which she robd erewhyle.

[45] swerve. [46] mimic. [47] archaic plural of "house." [48] soul.

XVI.

Since she, ev'n shee, for whom I liv'd,
Sweet she by Fate from me is torne,
  Why am not I of sence depriv'd,
Forgetting I was ever borne?
        Why should I languish, hating light?   5
        Better to sleepe an endlesse night.

Be 't eyther true, or aptly fain'd,
That some of *Lethes* water write,
  'Tis their best med'cine that are pain'd
All thought to loose of past delight.   10
        O would my anguish vanish so!
        Happy are they that neyther know.

XVII.[49]

I must complain, yet doe enjoy my Love;
She is too faire, too rich in lovely parts:
Thence is my grief, for Nature, while she strove
~~With all her graces and divinest Arts~~

   To form her too too beautifull of hue,   5
   Shee had no leasure left to make her true.

Should I, agriev'd, then wish shee were lesse fayre?
That were repugnant to mine owne desires:
Shee is admir'd, new lovers still repayre;
That[50] kindles daily loves forgetfull fires.   10
   Rest, jealous thoughts, and thus resolve at last:
   Shee hath more beauty then becomes the chast.

[49] Compare *Epigrammatum Liber* II, 18 and 116, below. It is interesting to note that Campion's contemporaries perhaps found the cynicism of the second strophe hard to accept, and so composed many substitutes for it; see textual notes.

[50] i.e., jealousy of the new lovers.

I must com·plain, yet doe en·joy my Love;
Thence is my grief, for Na·ture,___ while she strove

She is too faire, too rich in love·ly parts:
With all her gra·ces and di·vin·est Arts

To form her too too beau·ti·full of hue,

Shee had no lea·sure left to make her true.

XVIII.

Think'st thou to seduce me then with words that have no meaning?
Parats[51] so can learne to prate, our speech by pieces gleaning:
Nurces teach their children so about the time of weaning.

Learne to speake first, then to wooe: to wooing much pertayneth:
Hee that courts us, wanting Arte, soone falters when he fayneth, 5
Lookes a-squint on his discourse,[52] and smiles when hee
                    complaineth.

Skilfull Anglers hide their hookes, fit baytes for every season;
But with crooked pins fish thou, as babes doe that want reason;
Gogions[53] onely can be caught with such poore trickes of treason.

Ruth[54] forgive me, if I err'd from humane hearts compassion   10
When I laught sometimes too much to see thy foolish fashion:
But, alas, who lesse could doe that found so good occasion?

[51] parrots.   [52] sneaks a look at his notes.
[53] gudgeons, a genus of small fish easily caught; hence, slang for gullible
persons (cf. the modern slang term "sucker," also the name of a fish).
[54] heavenly compassion.

XIX.

Her fayre inflaming eyes,
  Chiefe authors of my cares,
I prai'd in humblest wise
  With grace to view my teares:
    They beheld me broad awake,   5
    But, alasse, no ruth would take.

Her lips with kisses rich,
  And words of fayre delight,
I fayrely did beseech
  To pitty my sad plight: 10
    But a voyce from them brake forth
    As a whirle-winde from the North.

Then to her hands I fled,
  That can give heart and all;
To them I long did plead,
  And loud for pitty call: 15
    But, alas, they put mee off
    With a touch worse then a scoffe.

So backe I straight return'd,
  And at her breast I knock'd;   20
Where long in vaine I mourn'd,
  Her heart so fast was lock'd:
    Not a word could passage finde,
    For a Rocke inclos'd her minde.

Then downe my pray'rs made way   25
  To those most comely parts
That make her flye or stay,
  As they affect deserts:[55]
    But her angry feete, thus mov'd,[56]
    Fled with all the parts I lov'd.   30

Yet fled they not so fast
  As her enraged minde:
Still did I after haste,
  Still was I left behinde,
    Till I found 'twas to no end   35
    With a Spirit[57] to contend.

[55] according as they judge the object present as worthy of love or hate.
[56] passionately aroused (as well as in motion).
[57] a spirit because so elusive and because lacking a humanly warm body.

XX.

Turne all thy thoughts to eyes,
Turne all thy haires to eares,
Change all thy friends to spies,
And all thy joyes to feares:
    True Love will yet be free,   5
    In spite of Jealousie.

Turne darknesse into day,
Conjectures into truth,
Beleeve what th' envious say,
Let age interpret youth:[58]   10
    True love will yet be free,
    In spite of Jealousie.

Wrest every word and looke,
Racke ev'ry hidden thought,
Or fish with golden hooke,   15
True love cannot be caught:
    For that will still be free,
    In spite of Jealousie.

[58] adopt age's censorious view of youth.

XXI.

If any hath the heart to kill,
  Come rid me of this wofull paine.
For while I live I suffer still
  This cruell torment all in vaine:
    Yet none alive but one can guesse   5
    What is the cause of my distresse.

Thanks be to heav'n, no grievous smart,
  No maladies my limbes annoy;
I beare a sound and sprightfull heart,
  Yet live I quite depriv'd of joy: 10
    Since what I had, in vaine I crave,
    And what I had not, now I have.

A Love I had, so fayre, so sweet,
  As ever wanton eye did see.
Once by appointment wee did meete;   15
  Shee would, but ah, it would not be:
    She gave her heart, her hand shee gave;
    All did I give, shee nought could have.[59]

What Hagge did then my powers forespeake,[60]
  That never yet such taint did feele?   20
Now shee rejects me as one weake,[61]
  Yet am I all compos'd of steele.
    Ah, this is it my heart doth grieve:
    Now though shee sees, shee'le not believe!

[59] i.e., I gave her all I had. [60] enchant. [61] impotent.

XXII.[62]

Beauty, since you so much desire
To know the place of *Cupids* fire:
About you somewhere doth it rest,
Yet never harbour'd in your brest,
Nor gout-like in your heele or toe;   5
What foole would seeke Loves flame so low?
But a little higher, but a little higher,
There, there, o there lyes *Cupids* fire.

Thinke not, when *Cupid* most you scorne,
Men judge that you of Ice were borne;   10
For, though you cast love at your heele,
His fury yet sometime you feele;
And where-abouts if you would know,
I tell you still, not in your toe:
But a little higher, but a little higher,   15
There, there, o there lyes *Cupids* fire.

[62] a revision of "Mistris, since you so much desire," *A Booke of Ayres*,
Part I, xvi. Vivian has noted that its popularity is attested by its quotation in
Eastward Ho (1605), III, ii, 53–54. On the music of this song, with its
underlining of the sexual innuendos, see Kastendieck, *England's Musical
Poet*, pp. 114–15.

Beau-ty, since you so much de-sire To know the place of *Cu - pids*

fire: A-bout you some-where doth it rest, Yet ne-ver har-bour'd

in your brest, Nor __ gout-like in __ your __ heele __ or

toe: What foole would seeke Loves flame so low? But a lit-tle higher,

but a lit-tle higher, but a lit-tle __ higher, but a lit-tle

higher: There,　there, o　there,　lyes *Cu - pids* fire.

XXIII.[63]

Your faire lookes urge[64] my desire:
　Calme it, sweet, with love.
Stay, o why will you retire?
　Can you churlish prove?
If Love may perswade,　　　　　　　　　　　　5
　Loves pleasures, deare, deny not:
Here is a grove secur'd with shade;
　O then be wise, and flye not.

Harke, the Birds delighted sing,
　Yet our pleasure sleepes.　　　　　　　　　　10
Wealth to none can profit bring,
　Which the miser keepes:
O come, while we may,
　Let's chayne Love with embraces;
Wee have not all times time to stay,　　　　　15
　Nor safety in all places.

What ill finde you now in this?
　Or who can complaine?
There is nothing done amisse,
　That breedes no man payne.　　　　　　　　20
'Tis now flowry *May*,
　But ev'n in cold *December*,
When all these leaves are blowne away,
　This place shall I remember.

[63] a revision of "Your faire lookes enflame my desire," *A Booke of Ayres*,
Part I, xvii.
[64] incite.

XXIV.[65]

Faine would I wed a faire yong man that day and night
           could please mee,
When my mind or body grieved, that had the powre to ease
           mee.
Maids are full of longing thoughts that breed a bloudlesse
           sickenesse,
And that, oft I heare men say, is onely cur'd by quicknesse.[66]
Oft have I beene woo'd and prai'd, but never could be   5
           moved:
Many for a day or so I have most dearely loved,
But this foolish mind of mine straight loaths the thing resolved.
If to love be sinne in mee, that sinne is soone absolved.
Sure, I thinke I shall at last flye to some holy Order;
When I once am setled there, then can I flye no farther.   10
Yet I would not dye a maid, because I had a mother:
As I was by one brought forth, I would bring forth another.

FINIS.

[65] An amusing parody of this song was composed later in the 17th century;
see textual notes.
[66] liveliness, with an implication of the sensual.

OCCASIONAL POEMS

To. Campiani Epigramma de
instituto Authoris.[1]

Famam, posteritas quam dedit Orpheo,
Dolandi melius Musica dat sibi,
Fugaces reprimens archetypis sonos;
Quas et delitias praebuit auribus,
Ipsis conspicuas luminibus facit.

[1] prefixed to John Dowland's *The First Booke of Songs or Ayres of foure parts, with Tableture for the Lute,* 1597, the publication which inaugurated the solo ayre's rise over the madrigal. This book achieved more editions than any other Renaissance English music book; in it, and in his other publications, Dowland set many of Campion's texts to his own music. "An Epigram on the Author's Purpose, by Thomas Campion. The fame which posterity gave to Orpheus, the music of Dowland gives to him, capturing the fleeting sounds in their originals [i.e., in their musical notation]; and now his music makes those delights it offered to the ears visible to the eyes themselves."

In honour of the Author by *Tho: Campion*
Doctor in Physicke. To the Reader.[2]

Though neither thou doost keepe the Keyes of State,
Nor yet the counsels (Reader) what of that?
Though th' art no Law-pronouncer mark't by fate,
Nor field-commander (Reader) what of that?
Blanch[3] not this Booke; for if thou mind'st to be   5
Vertuous, and honest, it belongs to thee.
    Here is the Scoole of *Temperance,* and *Wit,*
Of *Justice,* and all formes that tend to it;
Here *Fortitude* doth teach to live and die,
Then, Reader, love this Booke, or rather buy.   10

EIUSDEM AD AUTHOREM.[4]

Personas propriis recte virtutibus ornas
    (Barnesi); liber hic vivet, habet Genium;
Personae virtus umbra est: hanc illa refulcit,
    Nec scio splendescat corpus, an umbra magis.

[2] prefixed to Barnabe Barnes's *Foure Bookes of Offices: Enabling Privat persons for the special service of all good Princes and Policies,* 1606. Barnes (ca. 1569–1609) was a small poet, known chiefly for two sonnet sequences, *Parthenophil and Parthenope* (1593) and *A Divine Centurie of Spirituall Sonnets* (1595). The *Foure Bookes of Offices* also contained poems by Campion's friends William Percy and Thomas Michelborne; for Campion's mockery of Barnes, see *Epigrammatum Liber* I, 17 and 143, and II, 80, below.

[3] blink, pass by without notice.

[4] "To the Author, from the Same. It is well that you adorn private men with their proper virtues, Barnes; this book lives, it has genius; virtue is the image of a person, this reflects that, nor do I know whether the body or the image shines more brightly."

To the Worthy Author.[5]

Musicks maister, and the offspring
　　Of rich *Musicks* Father,
Old *Alfonso's* Image living,[6]
　　These faire flowers you gather
Scatter through the *Brittish* soile;
　　Give thy fame free wing,
And gaine the merit of thy toyle:
　　Wee, whose loves affect to praise thee,
　　Beyond thine owne deserts can never raise thee.

By *T. Campion,* Doctor in Physicke.

[5] prefixed to *Ayres* (1609) by Alfonso Ferrabosco the Younger (ca. 1580–1628), composer of vocal and viol music, tutor to Prince Henry, later composer-in-ordinary to King Charles I, and Jonson's valued collaborator in the masques. This, his sole but distinguished book of ayres, contains settings of Jonson and Donne as well as of Campion himself; Campion's poem uses an interesting quantitative meter, much like the trochaic "Anacreonticks" in the *Observations*.

[6] Ferrabosco's father, Alfonso the Elder, had been a pioneer in bringing the new madrigal style from his native Italy to the court of Elizabeth; the English madrigal collections, especially Nicholas Yonge's *Musica Transalpina* (1588), were full of his compositions.

Incipit Thomas Campianus
Medicinae Doctor.[7]

In Peragrantissimi, Itinerosissimi,

Montiscandentissimique Peditis, Tho-
mae Coryati, viginti-hebdomadarium
Diarium, sex pedibus gradiens,
partim vero claudicans,
Encomiasticon.

Ad Venetos venit corio Coryatus ab uno
  Vectus, et, ut vectus, pene revectus erat.
Nave una Dracus sic totum circuit orbem,
  At rediens retulit te, Coryate, minus.
Illius undigenas tenet unica charta labores,
  Tota tuos sed vix bibliotheca capit.

Explicit Thomas Campianus.

[7] prefixed to *Coryats Crudities Hastily gobled up in five Moneths travells*
(1611), a very strange and amusing production. Thomas Coryate (ca.
1577–1617), from whom "The Traveller" in *The Caversham Entertain-*
ment may be drawn, was a learned and vivacious (but bumptious) mem-
ber of Prince Henry's retinue; in 1608 he embarked on a walking tour of the
Continent to Venice, and, upon his return, he hung up his famous shoes in
his parish church. When he published a voluminous and extravagantly writ-
ten account of his travels in 1611 (with an amusing engraved title page, re-
produced by William B. Hunter, Jr., in his edition of *The Complete Poetry of*
Ben Jonson, New York: Doubleday Anchor Books, 1963), the poets and wits,
apparently at the instigation of Jonson, deluged it with a flood of more than
fifty mock-complimentary poems, including songs, emblems, an egg-shaped
poem, mock-classical meters, and a poem in the Utopian tongue; Jonson,
Donne, Richard Corbet, John Hoskins, Inigo Jones, Michael Drayton, John
Davies of Hereford, and John Owen were among the contributors. Campion
in his poem imitates the comic form of the book—its lengthy prefaces al-
most dwarfing the bulky book itself—by making his title as long as his poem,
and puns on his metrical feet. "Here beginneth Thomas Campion, Doctor of
Medicine. Of the Twenty-week Journal of the Most Peregrinacious, Most
Itineritious, and Most Mountainscaling Footman, Thomas Coryate: An
Encomium, walking on six feet, partly, to be honest, limping. To the
Venetians came Coryate borne on a single hide [coracle-like], and, once
there, was almost borne back again on the same one. So Drake circled the
globe in one ship, but in returning brought back less than you, Coryate: one
chart holds his wave-borne labors, but a whole library scarcely holds yours!
Here endeth Thomas Campion."

Of this Ensuing Discourse.[8]

Markes that did limit *Lands* in former times
  None durst remove; so much the common good
Prevail'd with all men; 'twas the worst of crimes.
  The like in *Musicke* may be understood,
For *That* the treasure of the *Soule* is, next   5
  To the rich Store-house of *Divinity:*
Both comfort *Soules* that are with care perplext,
  And set the *Spirit Both* from passions free.
The Markes that limit *Musicke* heere are taught,
  So fixt of ould, which none by right can change,   10
Though *Use* much alteration hath wrought,
  To *Musickes Fathers* that would now seeme strange.
The best embrace, which herein you may finde,
  And th' *Author* praise for his good *Worke* and *Minde.*

THO: CAMPION.

[8] prefixed to *A Briefe Discourse of the true (but neglected) use of Charact'ring the Degrees by their Perfection, Imperfection, and Diminution in Measurable Musicke, against the Common Practise and Custome of these Times,* published in 1614 by Thomas Ravenscroft (ca. 1582–1635), one of the most popular musicians of his time, whose specialty was the editing of rounds and catches for convivial singing. In this treatise (which also contained prefatory poems by Dowland, Nathaniel Giles, and Martin Peerson) Ravenscroft tried to reinstitute the mediaeval time signatures in order to set the temporal "limits" of music for his contemporaries (see ll. 9–10).

MASQUES

THE
DISCRIPTION OF
A
MASKE,

Presented before the Kinges Majestie
at White-Hall, on Twelfth Night
last, in honour of the Lord HAYES, and
his Bride, Daughter and Heire to the
Honourable the Lord DENNYE, *their*
Marriage having been the same Day
at Court solemnized.

To this by occasion other small Poemes
are adjoyned.

Invented and set forth by THOMAS
CAMPION *Doctor of Phisicke.*

1607

James Hay or Hayes (d. 1636), first Earl of Carlisle and Baron Hay, was born at Pitscorthy in Fifeshire; he early became the favorite of James I, who knighted him and brought him to England with him. There seems to have been some difficulty in arranging the match with Honora Denny, whose father, Sir Edward Denny, had welcomed James to England in his capacity of High Sheriff of Hertfordshire; James had to create Denny a baron and grant his daughter Strixton Manor in 1604 in order to gain his consent. But these sacrifices must have seemed worth while to James, whose full intention—as it was lauded both by Campion and by Robert Wilkinson in the wedding sermon of January 6, 1607—was to strengthen the ties between his two kingdoms. Campion's masque, in response to this royal intention, is permeated with situations involving the uniting of opposites.

The Lord Hay's Masque uses myth as a base for many layers of meaning. On the most specific level, the device of Night and Apollo is courtly compliment: James, the "Phoebus" of this Western Isle, has sponsored the marriage, and by doing so has not only reconciled two kingdoms, but the principles of chastity and love besides. It also exploits the psychology of the bride and groom, who see in the masque a heightened image of their moment in time: the wedding day itself, betokening joy and fruitfulness with its scattered flowers; the coming of cool, chaste Night, which seems to destroy the aura of goodness around the wedding; and, finally, the transformation of night by the light of the occasion into a time of joy and fruitfulness. When Hesperus departs, the golden moment of the masque dissolves, and the bride will depart from the hall to begin that night which will be totally unlike any other. To this level belong all the transformations—the change of Night herself, the reduction of discord to concord by harmonious music, and the gradual changes of the Maskers from trees to leafy men to Knights of Apollo resplendent in crimson. On the most general level, Campion asks his audience to enter a "golden dreame" in which marriage is seen as the human analogue of cosmic creation, for his myth deals with the original opposition of principles in nature, female potential (the earth, dark, cold and wet, governed by Diana the moon) and male passion (the heavens, light, hot and dry, governed by Apollo the sun), the act of mutual love and grace by which they are reconciled, and the cosmic growth that results. Over this union rules the divine triad (and its self-multiple nine), the first union of the female-even and the male-odd.

Enid Welsford (*The Court Masque*, pp. 181–82) suggests that the plot of Campion's masque comes from Baïf's *Mascarade de M. le Duc de Longueville* of 1565 (in *Oeuvres*, ed. Charles Marty-Laveau, II [Paris, 1883], 331–42), wherein six maidens who had refused six knights were turned into trees, the knights into rocks, to recover their human shapes only when peace was concluded between France and Spain; at a sign from the King, the rocks and trees (which had opened the masquerade with a dance) resumed their true shapes and offered homage to him. The informing myth of male and female, however, had been with Campion since his *Umbra* of 1595.

The Lord Hay's Masque was presented in the Great Hall at Whitehall instead of the usual Banqueting House while the latter was undergoing reconstruction (see Reyher, *Les Masques anglais*, p. 341). The setting and costumes were assumedly the work of Inigo Jones, since the print of the Knight Masquer used as frontispiece to the original edition (reproduced as Plate I of the present edition) resembles several of his designs; moreover, Allardyce Nicoll (*Stuart Masques and the Renaissance Stage*, p. 58) attempts to link the scene to a design by Jones (No. 386, Plate XLIX in *Designs by Inigo Jones for Masques and Plays at Court: A Descriptive Catalog*, ed. Percy Simpson and C. F. Bell [Oxford, 1924]). Rudolf Brotanek (*Die Englischen Maskenspiele* [Vienna and Leipzig, 1902], p. 230) prints a conjectural diagram showing how the stage manager might have handled his task; this diagram has been reproduced on the following page.

Five pieces of music from the masque were appended to the original edition; the first two were the songs "Now hath Flora" and "Move now with measured sound," the three others being dances to which Campion wrote new texts; all five are transcribed by Andrew J. Sabol as Nos. 2, 3, 4, 5, and 6 of his *Songs and Dances for the Stuart Masque*. Another dance that may belong to this masque, "My Lord Hayis Currand," is preserved in the tablature book of John Skene (Advocates' MS. 5. 2. 15, fos. 119–22); and a set of three dances contained in a collection of instrumental music, British Museum Additional MS. 10444 (fos. 35 and 86), and entitled respectively "The Lord Hayes his first Masque," "The second," and "The third," may also belong here. Campion chose two collaborators in preparing the music. Thomas Giles was both organist of St. Paul's and a dancing master; it was in the latter capacity that he worked in Jonson's *Hymenaei*, *The Masque of Beauty*, *The Haddington Masque*, *The Masque of Queenes*, *Oberon*, and Campion's *Lords' Masque*. It was assumedly

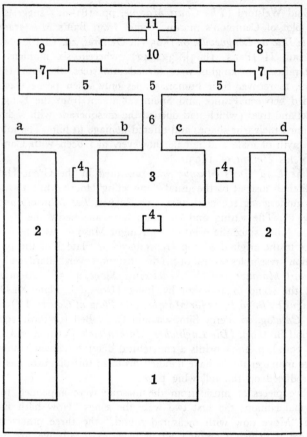

1	Cloth and chair of State	7	Ascents
2	Scaffolds and seats	8	Bower of Flora
3	Dancing place	9	House of Night
4	Musicians	10	Cliff and tree of Diana
5	Stage (a green valley)	11	Hill for the hoboyes
6	Descent	ab, cd	Skreene

Thomas Lupo the elder (d. 1628) who composed music for the
third and fifth songs; a violinist in the Kings Musicke, he set
the dance music of Jonson's *Love Freed from Ignorance and
Folly,* performed similar services for *Oberon* and Campion's *Lords'
Masque,* and produced many instrumental pieces.

The marginal glosses Campion prepared for his edition have been
incorporated into the notes.

To the most puisant and
Gratious James *King of great*
Britaine.

The disunited Scithians, when they sought
To gather strength by parties, and combine
That perfect league of freends which, once beeing wrought,
No turne of time or fortune could untwine,
This rite they held: a massie bowle was brought,
And ev'ry right arme shot his severall blood
Into the mazar[1] till 'twas fully fraught.
Then having stird it to an equall floud[2]
They quaft to th' union, which till death should last,
In spite of private foe, or forraine feare;
And this blood sacrament being knowne t' have past,
Their names grew dreadfull to all far and neere.
O then, great Monarch, with how wise a care
Do you these bloods devided mixe in one,
And with like consanguinities prepare
The high, and everliving Union
    Tweene Scots and English: who can wonder then
    If he that marries kingdomes, marries men?

An Epigram.

Merlin, the great King *Arthur* being slaine,
Foretould that he should come to life againe,
And long time after weild great Brittaines state
More powerfull ten-fould, and more fortunate.
    Prophet, 'tis true, and well we find the same,
    Save onely that thou didst mistake the name.

[1] bowl.   [2] i.e., mixed all the blood equally.

Ad Invictissimum,
Serenissimumque Iacobvm
Magnae Britanniae Regem.[3]

Angliae, et unanimis Scotiae pater, anne maritus
    Sis dubito, an neuter (Rex) vel uterque simul.
Uxores pariter binas sibi iungat ut unus,
    Credimus hoc, ipso te prohibente, nephas.
Atque maritali natas violare parentem
    Complexu, quis non cogitat esse scelus?
At tibi divinis successibus utraque nubit;
    Una tamen coniux, coniugis vnus amor.
Connubium O mirum! binas qui ducere, et unam
    Possis! tu solus sic, *Iacobe,* potes:
Divisas leviter terras componis in unam
    Atque unam aeternum nomine, reque facis:
Natisque, et nuptis, pater et vir factus utrisque es;
    Unitis coniux vere, et amore parens.

[3] To the most Invincible and Serene James, King of Great Britain. I wonder (O King) whether you are the father of England and united Scotland, or a husband, or neither, or both at once. For one man to marry two wives at once—that we believe, by your own prohibition, to be impiety. And for the parent to violate his daughter in marital embraces—who does not consider that a crime? But you, by divine succession, marry both; yet they are one wife, one conjugal love. O wonderful marriage, which can join two and one! You alone, James, can do this; easily you bring divided lands into one and make them eternally one in name and in fact. To both the children and the brides, you have become father and husband: truly a husband out of union and a father out of love.

To the Right Noble and Vertuous
Theophilus Howard, Lorde of
Walden, sonne and Heire to the right Hono-
rable the Earle of Suffolke.[4]

If to be sprong of high and princely blood,
If to inherite vertue, honour, grace,
If to be great in all things, and yet good,
If to be facill,[5] yet t' have power and place,
 If to be just and bountifull, may get
 The love of men, your right may chalenge it.

The course of forraine manners far and wide,
The courts, the countries, Citties, townes and state,
The blossome of your springing youth hath tried,
Honourd in ev'ry place and fortunate,
 Which now grown fairer doth adorne our Court
 With princelie revelling, and timely sport.

But if th' admired vertues of your youth
Breede such despairing to my daunted muse,
That it can scarcely utter naked truth,
How shall it mount, as ravisht spirits use,
 Under the burden of your riper dayes,
 Or hope to reach the so far distant bayes?

My slender Muse shall yet my love expresse,
And by the faire Thames side of you sheele sing;
The double streames shall beare her willing verse
Far hence with murmur of their ebbe and spring.
 But if you favour her light tunes, ere long
 Sheele strive to raise you with a loftier song.

[4] Here Campion makes his first bid for patronage to the powerful
Howards, protectors of his patron Monson (see headnote to *A Booke of Ayres,*
above); both *The Caversham Entertainment* for Lord Walden's brother-in-
law and *The Somerset Masque* for his sister's wedding fulfill Campion's
promise at the end of the poem.
[5] easy of access, affable.

To the Right Vertuous, and Hono-
rable, the Lord and Lady HAYES.

Should I presume to separate you now,
That were so lately joyn'de by holy vow,
For whome this golden dreame which I report
Begot so many waking eyes at Court,
And for whose grace so many nobles chang'd
Their names and habites, from themselves estrang'd?
Accept together, and together view
This little worke which all belongs to you,
And live together many blessed dayes,
To propagate the honour'd name of HAYES.

Epigramma.[6]

Haeredem (ut spes est) pariet nova nupta Scot' Anglum;
    Quem gignet posthac ille, Britannus erit:
Sic nova posteritas, ex regnis orta duobus,
    Utrinque egregios nobilitabit avos.

[6] Epigram. The hope is that the new bride will bring forth an Anglo-
Scottish heir; the one he begets later will be British: thus a new posterity,
born from the two kingdoms, will make the noble ancestors on both sides
famous.

THE

Description of a Maske presented
before the Kinges Majestie at White
Hall, on twelft night last, in honour
of the Lord HAYES, and his Bride, daugh-
ter and heire to the Honourable the Lord
DENNYE, *their mariage having been*
the same day at Court solemnized.

As in battailes, so in all other actions that are to bee reported,
the first, and most necessary part is the discription of the place, with
his oportunities, and properties, whether they be naturall or arti-
ficiall. The greate hall (wherein the Maske was presented) received
this division, and order: The upper part, where the cloth and chaire
of State[7] were plac't, had scaffoldes and seates on eyther side con-
tinued to the skreene;[8] right before it was made a partition for the
dauncing place; on the right hand whereof were consorted ten
Musitions, with Basse and Meane lutes, a Bandora, double Sack-
bott, and an Harpsicord, with two treble Violins;[9] on the other
side somewhat neerer the skreene were plac't 9 Violins and three
Lutes; and to answere both the Consorts (as it were in a triangle)
sixe Cornets, and sixe Chappell voyces, were seated almost right
against them, in a place raised higher in respect of the pearcing
sound of those Instruments; eighteen foote from the skreene, an
other Stage was raised higher by a yearde then that which was
prepared for dancing. This higher Stage was all enclosed with a
double vale, so artificially painted, that it seemed as if darke cloudes
had hung before it: within that shrowde was concealed a greene
valley, with greene trees round about it, and in the midst of them
nine golden trees of fifteene foote high, with armes and braunches
very glorious to behold. From the which grove toward the State
was made a broade descent[10] to the dauncing place, just in the

[7] the King's seat.   [8] the curtain before the stage.

[9] "Basse" and "Meane" lutes were lutes tuned low and high, respectively;
the "Bandora" or Pandora was a member of the cittern family (like the gui-
tar, with flat back instead of the lute's rounded back, and wire strings in-
stead of gut), small and low in range. The "Sack-bott" was a trombone,
a "double" or double-bass being the bass instrument of the family. The
"treble Violins" are the treble members of the violin family, i.e., modern
violins.

[10] apparently a ramp.

midst of it; on either hand were two ascents, like the sides of two hilles, drest with shrubbes and trees; that on the right hand leading to the bowre of Flora, the other to the house of Night; which bowre and house were plac't opposite at either end of the skreene, and betweene them both was raised a hill, hanging like a cliffe over the grove belowe, and on the top of it a goodly large tree was set, supposed to be the tree of Diana; behind the which toward the window was a small descent, with an other spreading hill that climed up to the toppe of the window,[11] with many trees on the height of it, whereby those that played on the Hoboyes at the Kings entrance into the hall were shadowed. The bowre of Flora was very spacious, garnisht with all kind of flowers, and flowrie branches with lights in them; the house of Night ample, and stately, with blacke pillors, whereon many starres of gold were fixt: within it, when it was emptie, appeared nothing but cloudes and starres, and on the top of it stood three Turrets underpropt with small blacke starred pillers, the middlemost being highest and greatest, the other two of equall proportion: about it were plac't on wyer artificiall Battes and Owles, continually moving: with many other inventions, the which for brevitie sake I passe by with silence.

Thus much for the place, and now from thence let us come to the persons.

The Maskers names were these (whom both for order and honour I mention in the first place).[12]

[11] There was a window set high in the farther wall, behind the stage in The Great Hall. "Hoboyes" are shawms, predecessors of the modern oboe.

[12] Theophilus Howard, Lord Walden (1584–1640): eldest son of the Earl of Suffolk and a prominent patron of music (see the fourth prefatory poem addressed to him); he danced in Campion's *Somerset Masque* as well as in Jonson's *Hymenaei* and *Haddington Masque;* John Dowland dedicated *A Pilgrimes Solace* to him in 1612.

Sir Thomas Howard (ca. 1580–1669): second son of Suffolk, later Earl of Berkshire; he danced in Jonson's *Hymenaei, Pleasure Reconciled to Virtue, For the Honour of Wales,* as well as in two other masques of Campion.

Sir Henry Carey, Master of the Jewel House: took part in *The Caversham Entertainment* and tilted at the Somerset wedding; Jonson's Epigram lxvi is addressed to him.

Sir Richard Preston (d. 1628): knighted at James I's coronation and made Gentleman of the Privy Chamber and instructor in arms to Prince Henry; tilted in *Prince Henry's Barriers* of 1610 and at the Somerset wedding.

Sir John Astley (or Ashley) of Maidenstone (d. 1639): Master of Queen Elizabeth's Jewels, knighted in 1603; served as Master of the Revels to both James I and Charles I, and as Gentleman of the Privy Chamber; he also danced in Jonson's *Hymenaei.*

1 Lord Walden.
2 Sir Thomas Howard.
3 Sir Henrie Carey, Master of the Jewell house.
4 Sir Richard Preston, ⎱ Gent. of the K. privie Chamber.
5 Sir John Ashley, ⎰
6 Sir Thomas Jarret, Pentioner.
7 Sir John Digby, one of the Kings Carvers.
8 Sir Thomas Badger, Master of the Kings Hariers.
9 Maister Goringe.

Their number Nine, the best and amplest of numbers,[13] *for as in Musicke seven notes containe all varietie, the eight being in nature the same with the first, so in numbring after the ninth we begin again, the tenth beeing as it were the Diappason*[14] *in Arithmetick. The number of 9 is famed by the Muses and Worthies, and it is of all the most apt for chaunge and diversitie of proportion. The chiefe habit which the Maskers did use is set forth to your view in the first leafe:*[15] *they presented in their fayned persons the Knights of* Apollo, *who is the father of heat and youth, and consequently of amorous affections.*

Sir Thomas Jarret (or Gerrard): knighted in 1603; tilted in the *Barriers* of 1606.

Sir John Digby (1580–1653): knighted in 1607, later Earl of Bristol (1622); as ambassador at Madrid, he conducted negotiations for the Spanish marriage; tilted in the *Barriers* of 1606.

Sir Thomas Badger (d. 1638): as Master of the Harriers, he is credited with creating the finest breed of bulldogs in England; tilted in the *Barriers* of 1606.

Master George Goring (ca. 1583–1663): the son of George Goring of Hurstpierpont, knighted 1608, made Gentleman of the Privy Chamber to Prince Henry in 1610, later Earl of Norwich; a favorite courtier and wit.

[13] Considered as the self-multiple of the divine number Three, 9 expresses the fullness of creation, as reflected in the planetary orbs, the Dionysian hierarchies, and the secular analogues Campion cites. As the number before 10, when numeration starts over again, it signifies traditionally the all-but-complete, the farthest reach of variety in the realm of becoming before the One, Being, rest, is attained. See Vincent F. Hopper, *Mediaeval Number Symbolism: Its Sources, Meaning, and Influence on Thought and Expression,* Columbia University Studies in English and Comparative Literature 132 (New York, 1938), pp. 10–11 and 149.

[14] octave. [15] See Plate I.

The Speakers were in number foure.

FLORA *the Queene of Flowers, attired in a changeable Taffatie*[16] *Gowne, with a large vale*[17] *embrodered with flowers, a Crowne of flowers, and white buskins painted with flowers.*

ZEPHYRUS *in a white loose robe of sky coloured Taffatie, with a mantle of white silke, prop't with wyre, stil*[18] *waving behind him as he moved; on his head hee wore a wreath of Palme deckt with Primmeroses and Violets; the hayre of his head and beard were flaxen, and his buskins white, and painted with flowers.*[19]

NIGHT *in a close robe of blacke silke and gold, a blacke mantle embrodered with starres, a crowne of starres on her head, her haire blacke and spangled with gold, her face blacke, her buskins blacke, and painted with starres; in her hand shee bore a blacke wand, wreathed with gold.*

HESPERUS *in a close robe of a deep crimson Taffatie mingled with skye colour, and over that a large loose robe of a lighter crimson taffatie; on his head he wore a wreathed band of gold, with a starre in the front thereof, his haire and beard red, and buskins yellow.*

These are the principall persons that beare sway in this invention; others that are but secunders to these, I will describe in their proper places, discoursing the Maske in order as it was performed.

As soone as the King was entred the great Hall, the Hoboyes (out of the wood on the top of the hil) entertained the time till his Majestie and his trayne were placed, and then after a little expectation the consort of ten began to play an Ayre, at the sound whereof the vale on the right hand[20] *was withdrawne, and the ascent of the hill with the bower of* Flora *were discovered, where* Flora *and* Zepherus *were busily plucking flowers from the Bower, and throwing them into two baskets, which two* Silvans[21] *held, who were attired in changeable Taffatie, with wreathes of flowers on their heads. As soone as the baskets were filled, they came downe in this order: First* Zepherus *and* Flora, *then the two* Silvans *with*

---

[16] taffeta so dyed as to seem various in color in different lights.

[17] veil.   [18] always.

[19] Nicoll (*Stuart Masques and the Renaissance Stage*, p. 165) notes Campion's indebtedness to Ripa's *Iconologia* and Cartari's *Le Imagini de gli dei de gli antichi* for this description of Zephirus. According to some mythographers, Zephirus was the husband of Flora; thus the masque might be said to open with a married couple on stage.

[20] the right half of the curtain.   [21] probably fauns or satyrs.

baskets after them; Foure Silvans *in greene taffatie and wreathes, two bearing meane Lutes, the third, a base Lute, and the fourth a deepe Bandora.*

  As soone as they came to the discent toward the dauncing place, the consort of tenne ceac't, and the foure Silvans *playd the same Ayre, to which* Zepherus *and the two other* Silvans *did sing these words in a base, Tenor, and treble voyce, and going up and downe as they song, they strowed flowers all about the place.*

Song   Now hath *Flora* rob'd[22] her bowers
        To befrend this place with flowers;
          Strowe aboute, strowe aboute,
        The Skye rayn'd never kindlyer Showers.
        Flowers with Bridalls well agree,
        Fresh as Brides, and Bridgromes be:
          Strowe aboute, strowe aboute,
        And mixe them with fit melodie.
          Earth hath no Princelier flowers
        Then Roses white, and Roses red,
        But they must still be mingled.
        And as a Rose new pluckt from *Venus* thorne,
        So doth a Bride her Bride-groomes bed adorne.

        Divers divers Flowers affect
        For some private deare respect;
          Strowe about, strowe about,
        Let every one his owne protect.
        But hees none of *Floras* friend
        That will not the Rose commend.
          Strow about, strow about,
        Let Princes Princely flowers defend.
          Roses, the Gardens pride,
        Are flowers for love and flowers for Kinges,
        In courts desir'd and Weddings.
        And as a Rose in *Venus* bosome worne,
        So doth a Bridegroome his Brides bed adorne.

[22] robbed.

The Musique ceaseth, and
Flora *speaks.*

FLORA. Flowers and good wishes *Flora* doth present,
Sweete flowers, the ceremonious ornament
Of maiden mariage, Beautie figuring,[23]
And blooming youth; which though we careles fling
About this sacred place, let none prophane
Thinke that these fruits from common hils are tane,
Or Vulgar vallies which do subject lie
To winters wrath and cold mortalitie.
But these are hallowed and immortall flowers
With *Floras* hands gather'd from *Floras* bowres.
Such are her presents, endles, as her love,
And such for ever may this nights joy prove.

ZEPH.[24] For ever endles may this nights joy prove,
So eccoes *Zephyrus* the friend of love,
Whose aide *Venus* implores when she doth bring
Into the naked world the greene-leav'd spring,
When of the Sunnes warme beames the Nets we weave
That can the stubborn'st heart with love deceive.
That Queene of beauty and desire, by me
Breaths gently forth this Bridall prophecie:
Faithfull and fruitfull shall these Bedmates prove,
Blest in their fortunes, honoured in their love.

FLOR. All grace this night, and, *Silvans,* so must you,
Off'ring your mariage song with changes new.

The song in forme of a Diaglogue.

CAN. Who is the happier of the two,
          A maide, or wife?
TEN. Which is more to be desired,
          Peace or strife?
CAN. What strife can be where two are one,
          Or what delight to pine alone?
BAS. None such true freendes, none so sweet life,
          As that betweene the man and wife.

[23] signifying.
[24] "*Zephirus.* The westerne wind, of all the most mild, and pleasant,
who with *Venus* the Queene of love is said to bring in the spring, when
naturall heate and appetite reviveth, and the glad earth begins to be beauti-
fied with flowers." (Campion)

TEN. A maide is free, a wife is tyed.

CAN. No maide but faine would be a Bride.

TEN. Why live so many single then?

Tis not, I hope, for want of men.

CAN. The bow and arrow both may fit,

And yet tis hard the marke to hit.

BAS. He levels faire that by his side

Laies at night his lovely Bride.[25]

CHO. Sing Io, Hymen: Io, Io, Hymen.

This song being ended the whole vale is sodainly drawne, the grove and trees of gold, and the hill with Dianas *tree, are at once discovered.*

Night *appeares in her house with her 9 houres, apparrelled in large robes of black taffatie, painted thicke with starres, their haires long, blacke, and spangled with gold, on their heads coronets of stars, and their faces blacke; every houre bore in his hand a blacke torch, painted with starres, and lighted.* Night *presently descending from her house spake as followeth.*

NIGHT. Vanish, darke vales;[26] let night in glory shine
As she doth burn in rage; come, leave our shrine,
You black-hair'd hours, and guide us with your lights:
Flora hath wakened wide our drowsy sprights.[27]
See where she triumphs, see her flowers are throwne,
And all about the seedes of malice sowne!
Despightfull *Flora,* ist not enough of griefe
That *Cynthia's* robd,[28] but thou must grace the theefe?
Or didst not hear Nights soveraigne Queen complaine
Hymen had stolne a Nimph out of her traine,
And matcht her here, plighted henceforth to be
Loves friend, and stranger to Virginitie?
And mak'st thou sport for this?

FLORA. Bee mild, sterne night;
Flora doth honour *Cinthia,* and her right.
Virginitie is a voluntary powre,
Free from constraint, even like an untoucht flower

[25] "Levels fair" contains wordplay: "aims well" and "lies down beautifully."

[26] mists, represented by the curtain. [27] spirits.

[28] "*Diana.* The Moone and Queen of Virginitie, is saide to be regent and Empresse of Night, and is therefore by Night defended, as in her quarrel for the losse of the Bride, her virgin." (Campion)

Meete to be gather'd when tis throughly blowne.[29]
The Nimph was *Cinthia* while she was her owne,
But now another claimes in her a right,
By fate reserv'd thereto, and wise foresight.

ZEPH. Can *Cynthia* one kind virgins losse bemone?
How if perhaps she brings her tenne for one?
Or can shee misse one in so full a traine?
Your Goddesse doth of too much store complaine.
If all her Nimphes would aske advise of me,
There should be fewer virgins then there be.
Nature ordaind not Men to live alone;
Where there are two, a Woman should be one.

NIGHT. Thou breath'st sweet poison, wanton *Zephyrus,*
But *Cynthia* must not be deluded thus.
Her holy Forrests are by theeves prophan'd,
Her Virgins frighted; and loe, where they stand
That late were *Phoebus* Knights, turnd now to trees
By *Cynthias* vengement for their injuries
In seeking to seduce her Nymphes with love:
Here they are fixt, and never may remove
But by *Dianaes* power that stucke them here.
Apollos love to them doth yet appeare,
In that his beames hath guilt them as they grow,
To make their miserie yeeld the greater show.
But they shall tremble when sad *Night* doth speake,
And at her stormy words their boughes shall breake.

Toward the end of this speech Hesperus *begins to descend by
the house of* Night, *and by that time the speech was finisht he was
readie to speake.*

HESP.[30] Hayle reverend angrie *Night,* haile Queene of
                      Flowers,
Mild spirited *Zephyrus,* haile, *Silvans* and *Howers.*
Hesperus brings peace, cease then your needlesse jarres[31]
Here in this little firmament of starres.
Cynthia is now by *Phoebus* pacified,

[29] bloomed.
[30] "*Hesperus.* The Evening starre foreshews that the wisht marriage
night is at hand, and for that cause is supposed to be the friend of Bride-
groomes and Brides." (Campion)
[31] causeless quarrels.

And well content her Nymph is made a Bride,
Since the faire match was by that *Phoebus* grac't
Which in this happie Westerne Ile is plac't
As he in heaven, one lampe enlightning all
That under his benigne aspect doth fall.[32]
Deepe Oracles he speakes, and he alone
For artes and wisedomes meete for *Phoebus* throne.
The Nymph is honour'd, and *Diana* pleas'd:
Night, be you then, and your blacke howers, appeas'd:
And friendly listen what your Queene by me
Farther commaunds: let this my credence[33] be,
View it, and know it for the highest gemme
That hung on her imperiall Diadem.

NIGHT. I know, and honour it, lovely *Hesperus,*
Speake then your message, both are welcome to us.

HESP. Your Soveraigne from the vertuous[34] gem she
      sends
Bids you take power to retransforme the frends
Of *Phoebus,* metamorphos'd here to trees,
And give them straight the shapes which they did leese.[35]
   This is her pleasure.

NIGHT. *Hesperus,* I obey,
Night must needs yeeld when *Phoebus* gets the day.

FLO. Honor'd be *Cynthia* for this generous deede.

ZEP. Pitie growes onely from celestiall seede.

NIGHT. If all seeme glad, why should we onely lowre?
Since t'expresse gladnes we have now most power.
Frolike, grac't Captives, we present you here
This glasse,[36] wherein your liberties appeare:
Cynthia is pacified, and now blithe *Night*
Begins to shake off melancholy quite.

ZEPH. Who shold grace mirth and revels but the night?
Next love she should be goddesse of delight.

NIGHT. Tis now a time when (*Zephyrus*) all with
      dancing

[32] a compliment to King James.
[33] credentials. [34] powerful. [35] lose.
[36] Apparently Diana's gem is meant.

Honor me, above day my state advancing.
Ile now be frolicke, all is full of hart,
And ev'n these trees for joy shall beare a part:
Zephyrus, they shall dance.

    ZEPH. Daunce, Goddesse? how?

    NIGHT. Seemes that so full of strangenes to you now?
Did not the Thracian harpe long since the same?[37]
And (if we ripp the ould records of fame)
Did not *Amphions* lyre the deafe stones call,
When they came dancing to the Theban wall?[38]
Can musicke then joye?[39] joy mountaines moves,
And why not trees? joyes powerfull when it loves.
Could the religious Oake speake Oracle
Like to the Gods? and the tree wounded tell
T'*AEneas* his sad storie?[40] have trees therefore
The instruments of speech and hearing more
Then th' ave of pacing? and to whom but Night
Belong enchantments? who can more affright
The eie with magick wonders? Night alone
Is fit for miracles, and this shalbe one
Apt for this Nuptiall dauncing jollitie.
Earth, then be soft and passable to free
These fettered roots! joy, trees! the time drawes neere
When in your better formes you shall appeare.
Dancing and musicke must prepare the way,
Ther's little tedious time in such delay.

    This spoken, the foure Silvans *played on their instruments the first straine of this song following, and at the repetition thereof the voices fell in with the instrumentes which were thus devided: a treble and a base were placed neere his Majestie, and an other treble and base neere the grove, that the words of the song might be heard of all, because the trees of gould instantly at the first sound of their voices began to move and dance according to the measure of the time which the musitians kept in singing, and the nature of the wordes which they delivered.*

[37] The harp of the Thracian poet Orpheus made the trees dance; see Ovid *Metamorphoses* X. 86 ff.

[38] See Ovid *Metamorphoses* VI. 176 ff.

[39] create joy or delight. The passage is obscure, and probably corrupt; the idea seems to be that music produces joy, which is capable of even greater miracles than music is.

[40] See *Aeneid* III. 24 ff.

Song.[41]

> Move now with measured sound,
> You charmed grove of gould,
> Trace forth[42] the sacred ground
> That shall your formes unfold.

Diana and the starry night for your *Apollos* sake
Endue your *Silvan* shapes with powre this strange delight to
    make.
Much joy must needs the place betide where trees for gladnes
    move:
A fairer sight was nere beheld, or more expressing love.

> Yet neerer *Phoebus* throne
> Mete on your winding waies,
> Your Brydall mirth make knowne
> In your high-graced *Hayes*.

Let Hymen lead your sliding rounds, and guide them with his
    light,
While we do Io Hymen sing in honour of this night,
Joyne three by three, for so the night by triple spel decrees
Now to release *Apollos* knights from these enchanted trees.

*This dancing song being ended, the goulden trees stood in rankes
three by three, and* Night *ascended up to the grove, and spake thus,
touching the first three severally with her wand.*

    NIGHT. By vertue of this wand, and touch devine,
These *Silvan* shadowes[43] back to earth resigne:
Your native formes resume, with habite faire,
While solemne musick shall enchant the aire.

Presently the Silvans *with their foure instruments and five voices
began to play and sing together the song following, at the begin-
ning whereof that part of the stage whereon the first trees stoode
began to yeeld, and the three formost trees gently to sincke, and this
was effected by an Ingin plac't under the stage. When the trees
had sunke a yarde they cleft in three parts, and the Maskers ap-*

---

[41] Andrew J. Sabol (*Songs and Dances for the Stuart Masque*, p. 163)
notes that the music to this song is the same as that of "The peacefull west-
erne winde," *Second Book of Ayres,* xii (see the transcription in this edition,
above). Both in turn are based on the well-known traditional melody "Wes-
tron Wynde"; the audience would therefore detect here a delicate musical
allusion to Zephirus and his power to revive natural heat.

[42] dance around.

[43] woodland images, i.e., the trees in which they are enclosed.

*peared out of the tops of them; the trees were sodainly convayed
away, and the first three Maskers were raysed againe by the Ingin.*[44]
*They appeared then in a false habit, yet very faire, and in forme not
much unlike their principall, and true robe. It was made of greene
taffatie cut into leaves, and laid upon cloth of silver, and their hats
were sutable to the same.*

Songe of transformation.

Night and *Diana* charge,
        And th'Earth obayes,
Opening large
        Her secret waies,
While *Apollos* charmed men
        Their formes receive againe.
Give gratious *Phoebus* honour then,
And so fall downe, and rest behinde the traine,
Give gratious *Phoebus* honour then,
And so fall, etc.

When those wordes were sung, the three maskers made an honour[45]
*to the King; and so falling backe the other six trees, three by three,
came forward, and when they were in their appointed places,* Night
spake againe thus:

NIGHT. Thus can celestials worke in humane fate,
Transforme and forme as they do love or hate;
Like touch, and change receive: the Gods agree
The best of numbers is contained in three.[46]

[44] "Either by the simplicity, negligence, or conspiracy of the painter,
the passing away of the trees was somewhat hazarded; the patterne of them
the same day having bene showne with much admiration, and the 9 trees
beeing left unsett together even to the same night" (Campion). Apparently
a stagehand had forgotten to reattach the trees to the engine after displaying
them to the nobility during the day.

[45] bow.

[46] Three is the best of numbers for at least two reasons: first, in imitation
of the Trinity, it is traditionally the number of perfection, as evidenced in
such diverse phenomena as the angelic hierarchies, the beginning, middle,
and end of a work, the dimensions of a solid object, and the resolution of
duality; secondly, it figures marriage, as combining the female or even 2 with
the male odd 1. See Hopper, *Mediaeval Number Symbolism,* p. 83.

The song of transformation againe.

Night and Diana, & c.

Then Night *toucht the second three trees and the stage suncke with them as before. And in breefe the second three did in all points as the first. Then* Night *spake againe.*

NIGHT. The last, and third of nine, touch, magick wand,
And give them back their formes at nights command.

Night *toucht the third 3 trees, and the same charme of* Night *and* Diana *was sung the third time; the last three trees were transformed, and the Maskers raisd. When presently the first Musique*[47] *began his full* Chorus.

Againe this song revive and sound it hie:
Long live *Apollo,* Brittaines glorious eye.

This Chorus *was in manner of an Eccho seconded by the Cornets, then by the consort of ten, then by the consort of twelve, and by a double* Chorus *of voices standing on either side, the one against the other, bearing five voices a peece, and sometime every* Chorus *was heard severally, sometime mixt, but in the end altogether: which kinde of harmony so distinguisht by the place, and by the severall*[48] *nature of instruments, and changeable conveyance*[49] *of the song, and performed by so many excellent masters as were actors in that musicke (their number in all amounting to fortie two voyces and instruments) could not but yeeld great satisfaction to the hearers.*

While this Chorus *was repeated twice over, the Nine maskers in their greene habitts solemnely descended to the dauncing place, in such order as they were to begin their daunce; and as soone as the* Chorus *ended, the violins, or consorte of twelve, began to play the second new daunce,*[50] *which was taken in form of an Eccho by the cornetts, and then catch't in like manner by the consort of ten; sometime they mingled two musickes together, sometime plaid all at once; which kind of ecchoing musicke rarely became their* Silvan

[47] i.e., the first consort or group of Silvans with four instruments and five voices.

[48] various.

[49] The melody kept shifting from choir to choir antiphonally.

[50] The "new" dances were those especially composed for the masque; toward the end of the masque, when the masquers danced with members of the audience in the "revels," standard dance tunes known to all would be used.

attire, and was so truely mixed together, that no daunce could ever bee better grac't then that, as (in such distraction[51] of musicke) it was performed by the maskers. After this daunce Night *descended from the grove, and addreste her speech to the maskers, as followeth.*

> NIGHT. *Phoebus* is pleas'd, and all rejoice to see
> His servants from their golden prison free.
> But yet since *Cinthia* hath so freendly smilde,
> And to you tree-borne Knights is reconcild,
> First, ere you any more worke undertake,
> About her tree solemne procession make,
> *Dianas* tree, the tree of Chastitie,
> That plac't alone on yonder hill you see.
> These greene leaved robes, wherein disguisde you made
> Stelths to her Nimphes through the thicke forrests shade,
> There to the goddesse offer thankfully,
> That she may not in vaine appeased be.
> The night shall guide you, and her howres attend you
> That no ill eyes, or spirits shall offend you.

At the end of this speech Night *began to leade the way alone, and after her an Houre with his torch, and after the Houre a masker; and so in order one by one, a torch-bearer and a masker, they march on towards* Dianas *tree. When the Maskers came by the house of* Night, *every one by his Houre received his helmet, and had his false robe pluckt off, and, bearing it in his hand, with a low honour offred it at the tree of Chastitie; and so in his glorious habit, with his Houre before him, march't to the bowre of* Flora. *The shape of their habit the picture before discovers; the stuffe was of Carnation satten layed thicke with broad silver lace, their helmets beeing made of the same stuffe.[52] So through the bowre of* Flora *they came, where they joyned, two torch-bearers and two Maskers; and when they past downe to the grove, the Houres parted on either side, and made way betweene them for the Maskers, who descended to the dauncing place in such order as they were to begin their third new dance. All this time of procession the sixe Cornets and sixe Chappell voices sung a sollemne motet[53] of sixe parts made upon these wordes.*

---

[51] variety.

[52] See Plate I.

[53] a polyphonic piece usually (but not here) set to a sacred text.

With spotles mindes now mount we to the tree
> Of single chastitie.
The roote is temperance grounded deepe,
Which the coldjewc't[54] earth doth steepe:
> Water it desires alone,
> Other drinke it thirsts for none:
Therewith the sober branches it doth feede,
> Which though they fruitlesse be,
Yet comely leaves they breede,
> To beautifie the tree.
Cynthia protectresse is, and for her sake
We this grave procession make.
Chast eies and eares, pure heartes and voices
Are graces wherein *Phoebe* most rejoyces.

The motet beeing ended, the Violins began the third new dance, which was lively performed by the Maskers, after which they tooke forth the Ladies, and danc't the measures[55] with them; which being finisht, the Maskers brought the Ladies back againe to their places; and Hesperus *with the rest descended from the grove into the dauncing place, and spake to the Maskers as followeth.*

HESPERUS. Knights of *Apollo,* proude of your new birth,
Pursue your triumphs still with joy and mirth:
Your changed fortunes, and redeemd estate,
Hesperus to your Soveraigne will relate.
Tis now high time he were far hence retir'd,
Th'ould Bridall friend that ushers Night desir'd,
Through the dimme evening shades then taking flight,
Gives place and honour to the nuptiall Night.
I, that wish't[56] evening starre, must now make way
To *Hymens* rights, much wrong'd by my delay.
But on Nights princely state you ought t'attend,
And t' honour your new reconciled frind.

NIGHT. *Hesperus,* as you with concord came, ev'n so
T'is meet that you with concord hence shold go.
Then joyne you, that in voice and art excell,
To give this starre a musicall farewell.

---

[54] cold-juiced, i.e., veined with water.

[55] The "measures" was probably a pavan, a slow and stately dance; for a thorough discussion of this term, see Otto Gombosi, "Some Musical Aspects of the English Court Masque," *Journal of the American Musicological Society,* I (1948), 3–19.

[56] desired, because he ushers in the wedding night.

A Diologue of foure voices, two Bases and two trebles.

1 Of all the starres which is the kindest
> To a loving Bride?

2 *Hesperus* when in the west
> He doth the day from night devide.

1 What message can be more respected
Then that which tells wish't joyes shalbe effected?

2 Do not Brides watch the evening starre?

1 O they can discerne it farre.

2 Love Bridegroomes revels?[57]

> 1 But for fashion.

2 And why?   1 They hinder wisht occasion.

2 Longing hearts and new delights
Love short dayes and long nights.

CHORUS.   *Hesperus,* since you all starres excell
> In Bridall kindnes, kindly farewell, farewell.

While these words of the Chorus (kindly farewell, farewell)
were in singing often repeated, Hesperus *tooke his leave severally*[58]
of Night, Flora, *and* Zephyrus, *the* Howers *and* Silvans; *and so
while the* Chorus *was sung over the second time, hee was got up to
the grove, where turning againe to the singers, and they to him,*
Hesperus *took a second farwel of them, and so past away by the
house of* Night. *Then* Night *spoke theis two lines, and therewith all
retired to the grove where they stoode before.*

NIGHT. Come, *Flora,* let us now withdraw our traine
That th' ecclipst revels maie shine forth againe.

*Now the Maskers began their lighter daunces as Currantoes,
Levaltas and galliards,*[59] *wherein when they had spent as much
time as they thought fit,* Night *spake thus from the grove, and in
her speech descended a little into the dauncing place.*

[57] entertainments consisting of dances between the wedding party and masked uninvited guests; the prototype of the court masque in England consisted of the arrival of the masquers, their performance of a "new" dance, and a lengthy "revels."

[58] successively.

[59] These are all fast social dances between the masquers and the ladies of the audience: the galliard (from *gaillard,* "young man") a moderately fast dance in triple time; the courante ("running") brisker and shorter, featuring a slide; the levalta (or "volta") of about the same speed as a courante, but featuring the "leap" its name implies at climactic moments. The volta had been a favorite dance at the court of Queen Elizabeth.

N. Here stay: Night leaden-eied and sprighted growes,
And her late houres begin to hang their browes.
Hymen long since the Bridall bed hath drest,
And longs to bring the turtles to their nest.
Then with one quick dence[60] sound up your delight,
And with one song weele bid you all god-Night.

*At the end of these words, the violins began the 4 new dance,
which was excellently discharged by the Maskers, and it ended with
a light change of musick and mesure. After the dance followed this
dialogue of 2 voices, a base and tenor sung by a* Silvan *and an*
Howre.

TEN. SILVAN. Tell me, gentle howre of night,
          Wherein dost thou most delight?
BAS. HOWRE. Not in sleepe. SIL. Wherein then?
HOWRE. In the frolicke vew of men.
SIL. Lovest thou musicke? HOWRE. O 'tis sweet.
SIL. Whats dauncing? HOWRE. Ev'n the mirth of feete.
SIL. Joy you in Fayries and in elves?
HOW. We are of that sort our selves.
     But, *Silvan*, say, whie do you love
     Onely to frequent the grove?
SIL. Life is fullest of content
    Where delight is innocent.
HOW. Pleasure must varie, not be long.
     Come then lets close, and end our song.
CHORUS. Yet ere we vanish from this princely sight,
      Let us bid *Phoebus* and his states[61] god-night.

This Chorus *was performed with severall Ecchoes of musicke and
voices, in manner as the great* Chorus *before. At the end whereof
the Maskers, putting off their visards and helmets, made a low hon-
our to the King, and attended his Majestie to the banquetting
place.*

[60] dance.
[61] King James and his nobles.

To the Reader.

Neither buskin now, nor bayes
Challenge I: a Ladies prayse
Shall content my proudest hope.
Their applause was all my scope,
And to their shrines properly
Revels dedicated be:
Whose soft eares none ought to pierce
But with smooth and gentle verse.
Let the tragicke Poeme swell,
Raysing raging feendes from hell;
And let Epicke Dactils range
Swelling seas and Countries strange:
Little roome small things containes;
Easy prayse quites easy paines.
Suffer them whose browes do sweat
To gaine honour by the great:[62]
Its enough if men me name
A Retailer of such fame.

Epigramma.[63]

Quid tu te numeris immisces? anne medentem
   Metra cathedratum ludicra scripta decent?
Musicus et medicus, celebris quoque, Phoebe, Poeta es,
   Et lepor aegrotos, arte rogante, iuvat.
Crede mihi, doctum qui carmen non sapit, idem
   Non habet ingenuum, nec genium medici.

FINIS.

[62] wholesale; see "Retailer" below.

[63] [Epigram. Why do you meddle with verses? Or do silly meters become an established physician? A musician and a physician, and also a celebrated poet are you, Phoebus; and pleasure helps the sick when the art requires it. Believe me, he who has no taste for learned verse, that man has neither the native bent nor the genius of a physician.]

[Songs used in the Maske][64]

III.

Shewes and nightly revels, signes of joy and peace.
Fill royall Britaines court while cruell warre farre off doth
    rage, for ever hence exiled.
Faire and princely branches with strong arms encrease
From that deepe rooted tree whose sacred strength and glory
    forren malice hath beguiled.
Our devided kingdomes now in frendly kindred meet
And old debate to love and kindnes turns, our power with
    double force uniting;
Truly reconciled, griefe appeares at last more sweet
Both to our selves and faithful friends, our undermining foes
    affrighting.[65]

IV.

    Triumph now with Joy and mirth;
        The God of peace hath blest our land:
    Wee enjoy the fruites of earth
        Through favour of his bounteous hand.
    We throgh his most loving grace
        A King and kingly seed beholde,
    Like a son with lesser stars,
        Or carefull shepheard to his fold:
    Triumph then, and yeelde him praise
    That gives us blest and joyfull dayes.

[64] Appended to this masque are five songs with their music; the first two, which (as Campion explains below) are the only ones that occurred in the masque itself, are "Now hath *Flora*" (p. 215) and "Move now" (p. 221).

[65] an allusion to the "Gunpowder Plot" of 1605 (see also *The First Booke of Ayres,* vi, above), a fitting contrast to the unity which the masque celebrates.

V.

Time, that leads the fatall round,
Hath made his center in our ground,
　　With swelling seas embraced;
And there at one stay he rests,
And with the fates keepes holy feasts,
　　With pomp and pastime graced.
Light Cupids there do daunce and Venus sweetly singes
With heavenly notes tun'd to sound of silver strings:
Their songs are al of joy, no signe of sorrow there,
But all as starres glistring faire and blith appeare.

　　These Songes were used in the Maske, whereof the first two
Ayres were made by M. *Campion*, the third and last by M. *Lupo*,
the fourth by M. *Tho. Giles;* and though the last three Ayres were
devised onely for dauncing, yet they are here set forth with words
that they may be sung to the Lute or Violl.[66]

[66] See headnote to this masque for information on the music and musicians.

A
RELATION
OF THE LATE ROY-
ALL ENTERTAINMENT
GIVEN BY THE RIGHT HONO-
RABLE THE LORD *KNOWLES*, AT

Cawsome-House neere *Redding:* to our most
Gracious Queene, Queene ANNE, *in her*
Progresse toward the *Bathe*, upon
the seven and eight and twentie
dayes of Aprill.

1613.

Whereunto is annexed the Description,
Speeches and Songs of the Lords Maske, presented
in the Banquetting-house on the Mariage night
of the High *and Mightie*, COUNT PALATINE,
and the Royally descended the Ladie
ELIZABETH.

Written by THOMAS CAMPIAN.

These two pieces were printed together in reverse chronological order, *The Lords' Masque* having been performed in February of 1613, *The Caversham Entertainment* the following April. Though the two have been treated chronologically for reasons of clarity below, the present text retains the printed order, for that arrangement seems designed to create a progression in tone from clowning in the country to stately action at court. These two tones (each of which rises, within its limitations, by deliberate modulations of style, one from rustic pretentiousness to the high style in verse, the other from mad babble to Latin verse) correspond to their respective occasions; the entertainment is designed to raise the spirits of a queen who has just lost her daughter to a husband, while the masque celebrates affairs of great estate.

The marriage of the Princess Elizabeth to Frederic, Elector Palatine, on February 14, 1613, was an event of great significance both for international politics and for the Protestant cause, as Campion showed fully at the end of the masque in the Latin verses of Sibilla, which connect fertility with political order while relating both to the Roman roots of European civilization. The occasion was also celebrated by Chapman's Lincoln's Inn and Middle Temple Masque on February 15, Beaumont's Inner Temple and Gray's Inn Masque on February 20, and several plays given in late February and early March. Campion's *Lords' Masque* was attended by the French, Venetian, and Dutch ambassadors, as well as Count Henry of Nassau, Frederic's uncle; the Spanish ambassador stayed away out of pique at the broken negotiations for a Spanish marriage. The masquers included the Earls of Montgomery and Salisbury and Lord Hay, all of whom had taken prominent parts in the wedding preparations and ceremony. For Hay, see the headnote to *The Lord Hay's Masque*. Philip Herbert (1584–1650), the younger brother of William, Earl of Pembroke, had been created Earl of Montgomery in 1605; he danced in Jonson's *Hymenaei, Haddington Masque, The Vision of Delight, Pleasure Reconciled to Virtue, For the Honour of Wales,* and *Loves Triumph,* and joined his brother as patron of Shakespeare's First Folio. William Cecil, second Earl of Salisbury, was the son of Elizabeth's and James I's secretary of state; born in 1591, he married Lady Catherine Howard in 1608, and succeeded to the title in 1612. Besides these men, it has been recorded that Anne Dudley, Elizabeth's lady of honor and beloved of Frederic's maître d'hôtel Schomberg, took the part of one of the transformed ladies.

John Chamberlain wrote of this masque to Sir Dudley Carleton, "that night was the lord's mask, whereof I hear no great commendation, save only for riches, their devices being long and tedious, and more like a play than a mask" (*The Court and Times of James I,* 2 vols. [London, 1848], I, 226). Among the expenses recorded for this performance were £66/13/4. to Campion, £50 to Inigo Jones, £30 or 40 each to the dancers Jerome Herne, Thomas Giles, Bochan, and Confess, £10 or 20 each to the musicians Giovanni Coperario, Robert Johnson, and Thomas Lupo, and £1 each to forty-two musicians and ten members of the King's violins (see Reyher, *Les Masques anglais,* p. 509). For Giles and Lupo, see notes to *The Lord Hay's Masque;* for Coperario, see the headnote to *Songs of Mourning.* Jerome Herne or Heron composed dances for Jonson's *Haddington Masque, Masque of Queenes,* and *Oberon.* Robert Johnson was one of the most prominent lutenists of the time; musician to Prince Henry and later to Charles, and member of Shakespeare's company, he composed music for *The Tempest* and plays by Middleton, Jonson, and Beaumont and Fletcher, as well as Jonson's *Oberon, Love Freed from Ignorance and Folly,* and Chapman's Lincoln Inn Masque; see John P. Cutts, "Robert Johnson: King's Musician," *Music and Letters,* XXXVI (1955), 110–25. Bochan and Confess, about whom little is known, were both involved in arranging the dances for Jonson's *Love Freed from Ignorance and Folly.*

Though none of the music was printed with the masque, there survive as many as nine pieces which can be assigned to it with varying degrees of certainty. "Wooe her, and win her" was printed at the end of *The Somerset Masque* in order to fill the empty pages. "Come away" is so similar metrically to the song beginning with the same words in *The Second Booke of Ayres* (xvii) that it seems almost certain to have utilized its setting. The others are instrumental dances: a set of three two-part dances entitled "The first," "The second," and "The third of the Lords" in British Museum Additional MS. 10444 (fos. 20–21 and 74–74ᵛ); another set of two dances, less certainly meant for Campion's masque (see John P. Cutts, "Jacobean Masque and Stage Music," *Music and Letters,* XXXV [1954], 194), later in the same MS. (fos. 26ᵛ and 78ᵛ); a piece in tablature entitled "Ladie Elizabeths Maske" in Advocates' MS. 5. 2. 15 (fo. 19); and a piece by Coperario entitled "Cuperaree or Grayes Inne" in Additional MS. 10444 and "The Lordes Maske" in *Parthenia In-Violata* published ca. 1625 (it is possible that the piece was used in both Campion's and Beaumont's masques).

Three of Inigo Jones's costume designs for *The Lords' Masque* have been preserved: Poetic Fury, reproduced as Plate III of the present edition, a knight masquer, and a page like a fiery spirit (see *Designs by Inigo Jones for Masques and Plays at Court*, Nos. 57 and 59, reproduced in Plate VI and Frontispiece, respectively). For further suggestions about the staging of this piece, see Nicoll, *Stuart Masques and the Renaissance Stage*, pp. 72–75.

Two months after the marriage, Queen Anne and King James bade farewell to Elizabeth and Frederic at Gravesend; and ten days later, on April 24, Queen Anne began her progress toward Bath, which she repeatedly visited for the gout. Of this progress John Chamberlain wrote, "The King brought her on her way to Hampton Court; her next move was to Windsor, then to Causham, a house of the Lord Knolles not far from Reading, where she was entertained with Revells, and a gallant mask performed by the Lord Chamberlain's four sons, the Earl of Dorset, the Lord North, Sir Henry Rich, and Sir Henry Carie, and at her parting presented with a dainty coverled or quilt, a rich carrquenet, and a curious cabinet, to the value in all of 1500 *l.*" (*Memorials of Affairs of State in the Reigns of Queen Elizabeth and King James I* collected from the papers of Sir Ralph Winwood by E. Sawyer, 3 vols. [London, 1725], III, 454). Her host, Sir William Knollys (1547–1632), was created Baron Knollys by James in 1603, Viscount Wallingford in 1616, and Earl of Banbury in 1626; both he and his second wife, Elizabeth Howard, enjoyed influence with the Queen, as he had with Queen Elizabeth (his mother's cousin), whom he had entertained at Caversham in August of 1601. Of the gentlemen masquers, Carie and two of Lord Chamberlain Suffolk's sons, Lord Walden and Sir Thomas Howard, had performed in *The Lord Hay's Masque;* the other two sons were Sir Charles Howard and Henry Howard. Richard Sackville (1589–1624), third Earl of Dorset, who had married Lady Anne Clifford, also tilted at the Somerset wedding in 1614; Dudley, Baron North (1581–1660), a musician and poet, was soon to retire from public affairs for reasons of health. Sir Henry Rich (1590–1649), second son of Penelope Rich and the most comely of King James I's favorites, later became infamous as Earl of Holland.

None of the designs or music for the entertainment at Caversham have survived.

A RELATION OF
THE LATE ROYALL
ENTERTAINMENT GIVEN BY
the Right Honorable, the Lord KNOWLES,
at *Cawsome*-House neere *Redding:* to our
most gracious Queen, Queene ANNE,
in her Progresse toward the Bathe
upon the seven and eight and
twentie dayes of Aprill.
1613.

*For as much as this late Entertainment hath beene much de-
sired in writing, both of such as were present at the performance
thereof, as also of many which are yet strangers both to the busines
and place, it shall be convenient, in this generall publication, a little
to touch at the description and situation of* Cawsome *seate. The
house is fairely built of bricke, mounted on the hill-side of a Parke
within view of* Redding, *they being severed about the space of two
miles. Before the Parke-gate, directly opposite to the House, a new
passage was forced through earable-land, that was lately paled in,*[1]
it being from the Parke about two flight-shots in length,[2] *at the
further end whereof, upon the Queenes approch, a* Cynick *ap-
peared out of a Bower, drest in a skin-coate, with Bases,*[3] *of greene*
Calico, *set thicke with leaves and boughes, his nakednesse being
also artificially shadowed with leaves; on his head he wore a false
haire, blacke and disordered, stucke carelessly with flowers.*

The speech of the Cynick *to the Queene and her Traine.*

CYNICK. Stay; whether you humane be or divine, here is no
passage; see you not the earth furrowed? the region solitarie? Cities
and Courts fit tumultuous multitudes: this is a place of silence;
heere a kingdome I enjoy without people; my selfe commands, my
selfe obeyes; Host, Cooke, and Guest my selfe; I reape without
sowing, owe all to Nature, to none other beholding: my skinne is

[1] i.e., some of the cultivated land before the park had been fenced in,
and a road had been made through it.

[2] A "flight" is a light arrow; Bullen, in his edition, calculates a flight-shot
as one fifth of a mile.

[3] A "skin-coate" is a close-fitting leather jerkin or jacket; "bases" are
short skirts hanging in tubular pleats resembling the bases of a suit of
armor.

my coate, my ornaments these boughes and flowers, this Bower my house, the earth my bed, herbes my food, water my drinke; I want no sleepe, nor health; I envie none, nor am envied, neither feare I, nor hope, nor joy, nor grieve. If this be happinesse, I have it; which you all that depend on others service or command want. Will you be happy? be private; turn Pallaces to Hermitages, noies to silence, outward felicitie to inward content.

A stranger on horse-back was purposely thrust into the troupe disguised, and wrapt in a cloake that he might passe unknowne, who at the conclusion of this speech beganne to discover himselfe as a fantastick Traveller[4] in a silken sute of strange Checker-worke, made up after the Italian cut, with an Italian hat,[5] a band of gold and silke, answering the colours of his sute, with a Courtly feather, long guilt spurres, and all things answerable.[6]

The Travellers *speech on horse-back.*

TRAVELL. Whither travels thy tongue, ill nurtur'd man? thy manners shew madnesse, thy nakednesse povertie, thy resolution folly. Since none will undertake thy presumption, let mee descend, that I may make thy ignorance know how much it hath injured sacred eares.

The Traveller then dismounts and gives his cloake and horse to his Foot-man; in the meane time the Cynick *speakes.*

CYN. Naked I am, and so is truth; plaine, and so is honestie; I feare no mans encounter, since my cause deserves neither excuse nor blame.

TRAV. Shall I now chide or pitie thee? thou art as miserable in life as foolish in thy opinion. Answere me: doest thou thinke that all happinesse consists in solitarinesse?

CYN. I doe.

TRAV. And are they unhappy that abide in societie?

CYN. They are.

TRAV. Doest thou esteeme it a good thing to live?

CYN. The best of things.

---

[4] The fantastic "Traveller," with his bumptuous pedantry, may be a private allusion to Thomas Coryate, who amused the court with accounts of his travels. See Campion's prefatory poem to *Coryats Crudities* in Occasional Poems, above, p. 198.

[5] probably a hat with a bag crown and a brim.   [6] alike.

TRAV. Hadst thou not a Father and Mother?

CYN. Yes.

TRAV. Did they not live in societie?

CYN. They did.

TRAV. And wert not thou one of their societie when they bred thee, instructing thee to goe, and speake?

CYN. True.

TRAV. Thy birth then and speech in spite of thy splene make thee sociable; goe, thou art but a vaine-glorious counterfait, and, wanting that which should make thee happie, contemnest the meanes; view but the heav'ns: is there not above us a Sunne and Moone, giving and receiving light? are there not millions of Starres that participate their glorious beames? is there any Element simple? is there not a mixture of all things? and wouldst thou only be singular? Action is the end of life, vertue the crowne of action, society the subject of vertue, friendship the band of societie, solitarinesse the breach. Thou art yet yong, and faire enough, wert thou not barbarous; thy soule, poore wretch, is farre out of tune, make it musicall; come follow me, and learn to live.

CYN. I am conquered by reason, and humbly aske pardon for my error; henceforth my heart shall honour greatnesse, and love societie; leade now, and I will follow, as good a fellow as the best.

The Traveller *and* Cynick *instantly mount on horse-backe, and hasten to the Parke-gate, where they are received by two Keepers, formally attired in green* Perpetuana,[7] *with jerkins and long hose,[8] all things else being in colour sutable, having either of them a horne hanging formally at their backes; and on their heads they had greene* Mommoth-caps,[9] *with greene feathers, the one of them in his hand bearing a hooke-bill, and the other a long pike-staffe, both painted greene: with them stood two* Robin-Hood-*men in sutes of greene striped with blacke, drest in doublets with great bellies*

[7] a glossy cloth like serge, noted for its durability.

[8] close-fitting jackets and close-fitting breeches joining the tight stockings at the knees.

[9] A Monmouth-cap (so called from the Welsh town where it was manufactured) is a round knitted cap with a high crown and no brim, frequently worn by soldiers and sailors.

*and wide sleeves, shaped fardingale-wise at the shoulders, without
wings;*[10] *their hose were round,*[11] *with long greene stockings; on
their heads they wore broad flat caps with greene feathers crosse
quite over them, carrying greene Bowes in their hands, and greene
Arrowes by their sides.*

*In this space Cornets at sundrie places intertaine the time, till
the Queene with her traine is entred into the Parke: and then one
of the Keepers presents her with this short speech.*

KEEPER. More then most welcome, renowned and gracious
Queene; since your presence vouchsafes to beautifie these woods,
whereof I am Keeper, be it your pleasure to accept such rude inter-
tainment as a rough Wood-man can yeeld. This is to us a high holy-
day, and henceforth yearly shall bee kept and celebrated with our
Countrie sports, in honour of so Royall a guest; come, friends and
fellowes, now prepare your voices, and present your joyes in a
Silvan dance.[12]

*Here standing on a smooth greene, and environed with the
Horse-men, they present a Song of five Parts, and withall a lively
Silvan-dance of sixe persons: the* Robin-Hood-*men faine two Tre-
bles, one of the Keepers with the* Cynick *sing two Countertenors,
the other Keeper the Base; but the Traveller being not able to sing,
gapes in silence, and expresseth his humour in Antike*[13] *gestures.*

A Song and Dance of sixe, two Keepers, two Robin-
hood-*men, the fantastick* Traveller, *and
the* Cynick.

I

Dance now and sing the joy and love we owe:
Let chearfull voices and glad gestures showe,
  The Queene of grace is shee whom we receive;
  Honour and State are her guides,
  Her presence they can never leave.
Then in a stately Silvan forme salute
  Her ever flowing grace.
Fill all the Woods with Ecchoed welcomes,

[10] Doublets are close-fitting waistcoats worn over the shirt; these have
"peascod bellies" produced by padding at the point of the waist. The
sleeves are puffed out, as if by hoops (as in a woman's farthingale), without
"wings" or ornamental flaps at the shoulders.

[11] i.e., their breeches were puffed out like pumpkins, as usual with an out-
fit of doublet and hose.

[12] country dance.   [13] grotesque.

And strew with flowers this place:
Let ev'ry bow and plant fresh blossomes yeeld,
   And all the aire refine.
Let pleasure strive to please our Goddesse,
   For shee is all divine.

2

Yet once againe, let us our measures move,
And with sweet notes record our joyfull love.
   An object more divine none ever had.
   Beautie, and heav'n-borne worth,
   Mixt in perfection never fade.
Then with a dance triumphant let us sing
   Her high advanced praise,
And ev'n to heav'n our gladsome welcomes
   With wings of musick raise;
Welcome, O welcome, ever-honoured Queene,
   To this now-blessed place,
That grove, that bowre, that house is happy
   Which you vouchsafe to grace.

This song being sung and danced twice over, they fall instantly into a kind of Curranta,[14] *with these wordes following.*

No longer delay her,
'Twere sinne now to stay her
   From her ease with tedious sport;
Then welcome still crying,
And swiftly hence flying,
   Let us to our homes resort.

In the end whereof the two Keepers carrie away the Cynick, *and the two* Robin-Hood-*men the Traveller; when presently Cornets begin againe to sound in severall places, and so continue with varietie, while the Queen passeth through a long smooth greene way, set on each side with Trees in equall distance; all this while her Majestie being carried in her Caroch.*[15]

But because some wet had fallen that day in the forenoone (though the Garden-walks were made artificially smooth and drie) yet all her foot-way was spred with broad cloth; and so soone as her Majestie with her traine were all entred into the Lower Garden, a Gardiner, with his Man and Boy, issued out of an Arbour to give

[14] couránte, a brisk dance which features a kind of running slide.
[15] carriage.

her Highnesse entertainment. The Gardener was suted in gray with a jerkin double jagged all about the wings and skirts;[16] *he had a paire of great slops with a cod-peece,*[17] *and buttoned Gamachios*[18] *all of the same stuffe; on his head he had a strawne hat, pibaldly drest with flowers,*[19] *and in his hand a silvered spade. His man was also suted in gray with a great buttoned flap on his jerkin, having large wings and skirts, with a paire of great slops and Gamachios of the same; on his head he had a strawne hat, and in his hand a silvered Mattox. The Gardiners Boy was in a prettie sute of flowrie stuffe, with a silvered Rake in his hand; when they approached neere the Queene, they all valed Bonet, and lowting low, the Gardner began after his anticke*[20] *fashion this speech.*

GARD. Most magnificent and peerelesse Diety, loe, I the surveyer of Lady *Floras* workes, welcome your grace with fragrant phrases into her Bowers, beseeching your greatnesse to beare with the late woodden[21] entertainment of the Wood-men; for Woods are more full of weeds then wits, but gardens are weeded, and Gardners witty, as may appeare by me. I have flowers for all fancies. Tyme for truth, Rosemary for remembrance, Roses for love, Hartsease for joy, and thousands more, which all harmoniously rejoyce at your presence; but my selfe, with these my Paradisians heere, will make you such musick as the wilde Wooddists shall bee ashamed to heare the report[22] of it. Come, sirs, prune your pipes, and tune your strings, and agree together like birds of a feather.

[16] a jacket, the borders of whose skirts and shoulder flaps are "double-jagged" or cut into double rows of scallops.

[17] "Slops" are wide knee breeches; "great slops" (in contrast to the more conservative "small slops") are voluminous, often distended by padding; a "cod-piece" is the front flap over the crotch.

[18] short gaiters.   [19] a straw hat ornamented with various flowers.

[20] grotesque, perhaps with some of the original sense of *antico,* "old-fashioned." The Gardiner's speech is full of the rhetorical schemes and sound effects (such as alliteration and rime) associated with Euphuism and related styles popular in the 1580s; contrast the Traveller's mock-scholastic style and the Cynick's curt Senecan.

[21] dull (with a pun).   [22] echo.

*A Song of a treble and base, sung by the Gardiners boy
and man, to musicke of Instruments, that was readie to second
them in the Arbour.*

I

Welcome to this flowrie place,
Faire Goddesse and sole Queene of grace:
   All eyes triumph in your sight,
Which through all this emptie space
Casts such glorious beames of light.

2

Paradise were meeter farre
To entertaine so bright a Starre:
   But why erres my folly so?
Paradise is where you are:
Heav'n above, and heav'n below.

3

Could our powers and wishes meete,
How well would they your graces greete.
   Yet accept of our desire:
Roses, of all flowers most sweete,
Spring out of the silly brier.

After this song, the Gardiner speakes againe.

GARD. Wonder not (great Goddesse) at the sweetnesse of our
Garden-aire (though passing sweet it be); *Flora* hath perfumed it
for you (*Flora* our mistresse, and your servant) who envites you
yet further into her Paradise; shee invisibly will leade your grace
the way, and we (as our duetie is) visibly stay behinde.

*From thence the Queene ascends by a few steps into the upper
Garden, at the end whereof, neere the house, this Song was sung
by an excellent counter-tenor voice, with rare varietie of division[23]
unto two unusuall instruments, all being concealed within the Ar-
bour.*

[23] variation of the theme.

1

O Joyes exceeding!
From love, from power of your wisht sight proceeding!
  As a faire morne shines divinely,
  Such is your view, appearing more divinely.

2

Your steppes ascending,
Raise high our thoughts for your content contending;
  All our hearts of this grace vaunting,
  Now leape as they were moved by inchaunting.

*So ended the entertainment without the House for that time;
and the Queenes pleasure being that night to suppe privately, The
Kings Violins attended her with their sollemnest musick, as an ex-
cellent consort in like manner did the next day at dinner.*

Supper being ended, her Majestie, accompanied with many *Lords and Ladies, came into the Hall, and rested Her selfe in Her Chaire of State, the Scaffoldes of the Hall being on all partes filled with beholders of worth; suddainely forth came the Traveller, Gardiner, Cynick, with the rest of their crue, and others furnished with their Instruments, and in maner following entertaine the time.*

TRAVELLER.

A hall, a hall for men of moment; Rationals and Irrationals, but not yet all of one breeding. For I an Academicke am, refined by travell, that have learn'd what to Courtship belongs, and so devine a presence as this; if we presse past good manners, laugh at our follies, for you cannot shew us more favour, then to laugh at us. If we prove ridiculous in your sights, we are gracious; and therefore wee beseech you to laugh at us. For mine owne part (I thank my Starres for it), I have beene laught at in most parts of Christendome.

GARDINER. I can neither bragge of my Travels, nor yet am ashamed of my profession; I make sweet walkes for faire Ladies; Flowers I prepare to adorne them; close Arbours I build wherein their Loves unseene may court them; and who can doe Ladies better service, or more acceptable? When I was a Child and lay in my Cradle (a very pretie Child) I remember well that Lady *Venus* appeared unto me, and setting a Silver Spade and Rake by my Pillow, bad me prove a Gardiner; I told my Mother of it (as became the duetie of a good Child) whereupon shee provided straight for mee two great Platters full of Pappe;[24] which having duetifully devoured, I grew to this portrature you see, sprung sodainely out of my Cabine, and fell to my profession.

TRAV. Verily by thy discourse thou hast Travelled much, and I am asham'd of my selfe that I come so farre behind thee, as not once to have yet mentioned *Venus* or *Cupid,* or any other of the gods to have appeared to mee. But I will henceforth boast truely, that I have now seene a Dietie as farre beyond theirs as the beautie of light is beyond darknesse, or this Feast, whereof we have had our share, is beyond thy Sallets.[25]

CYNICK. Sure I am, it hath stir'd up strange thoughts in me; never knew I the difference betweene Wine and Water before. *Bacchus* hath opened mine eyes; I now see braverie and admire it, beautie and adore it. I find my Armes naked, my discourse rude,

[24] thin cereal.
[25] salads.

but my heart soft as Waxe, ready to melt with the least beame of a faire eye; which (till this time) was as untractable as Iron.

GARD. I much joy in thy conversion; thou hast long beene a mad fellow, and now provest a good fellow; let us all therefore joyne together sociably in a Song, to the honour of good fellowship.

CYN. A very Musicall motion, and I agree to it.[26]

TRAV. Sing that sing can, for my part I will onely, while you sing, keepe time with my gestures, *A la mode de France.*[27]

A Song of three Voyces with divers Instruments.

1

Night as well as brightest day hath her delight.
Let us then with mirth and Musicke decke the night;
   Never did glad day such store
     Of joy to night bequeath:
   Her Starres then adore,
     Both in Heav'n and here beneath.

2

Love and beautie, mirth and Musicke, yeeld true joyes,
Though the *Cynickes* in their folly count them toyes.
   Raise your spirits nere so high,
     They will be apt to fall:
   None brave thoughts envie,
     Who had ere brave thought at all.

3

Joy is the sweete friend of life, the nurse of blood,
Patron of all health, and fountaine of all good:
   Never may joy hence depart,
     But all your thoughts attend;
   Nought can hurt the heart
     That retaines so sweete a friend.

At the end of this Song enters Silvanus, *shapt after the description of the ancient Writers.*[28] *His lower parts like a Goate, and*

[26] a musical pun: to agree was to harmonize.

[27] Assumedly, by "the French manner" pantomime is meant; dumb show was frequently used in the introductions of *ballets.*

[28] See, e.g., Virgil's Tenth *Eclogue,* ll. 24–25; Virgil is also perhaps responsible for the tradition that Silvanus rather than Phoebus was the lover of Cyparissus: see *Georgics* I. 20 and Natalis Comes, *Mythologiae,* V, x (p. 143 in the edition of Venice, 1568).

*his upper parts in an anticke habit of rich Taffatie, cut into Leaves;
and on his head he had a false Haire, with a wreath of long
Boughes and Lillies, that hung dangling about his necke; and in
his hand a Cypresse branch, in memorie of his love* Cyparissus. *The
Gardiner, espying him, speakes thus.*

GARD. Silence, sirs, here comes *Silvanus*, god of these Woods,
whose presence is rare, and importes some noveltie.

TRAV. Let us give place, for this place is fitter for Dieties then
us.

They all vanish and leave Silvanus *alone, who, comming
neerer to the State, and making a low Congee,*[29] *speakes.*

SILVANUS.

That health which harbours in the fresh-air'd groves,
Those pleasures which greene hill and valley moves,
Silvanus, the commander of them all,
Here offers to this State Emperiall;
Which as a homager he visites now,
And to a greater power his power doth bow.
With all, thus much his duetie signifies:
That there are certaine Semideities,
Belonging to his Silvan walkes, who come
Led with the Musicke of a Spritely drome,
To keepe the night awake and honour you
(Great Queene) to whom all Honours they hold due.[30]
So rest you full of joy, and wisht content,
Which though it be not given, 'tis fairely ment.

*At the end of this speech there is suddainly heard a great noise
of drums and phifes, and way being made, eight Pages first enter,
with greene torches in their hands lighted; their sutes were of*

[29] bow.
[30] See Ovid *Metamorphoses* I. 192–95:

> sunt mihi semidei, sunt, rustica numina, nymphae
> faunique satyrique et monticolae silvani;
> quos quoniam caeli nondum dignamur honore,
> quas dedimus, certe terras habitare sinamus

[I have semideities, I have rustic divinities, nymphs, fauns, and satyrs,
and mountain-dwelling silvan gods; since we do not yet deem them worthy
of the honor of heaven, let us at least permit them to inhabit the lands we
have given them].

greene Satten, with cloakes and caps of the same, richly and strangely set forth. Presently after them the eight Maskers came, in rich imbrodered sutes of greene Satten, with high hats of the same, and all their acoutrements answerable to such Noble and Princely personages as they concealed under their visards,[31] and so they instantly fell into a new dance, at the end whereof they tooke forth the Ladies, and danced with them; and so well was the Queene pleased with her intertainment, that shee vouchsafed to make her selfe the head of their Revels,[32] and graciously to adorne the place with her personall dancing: much of the night being thus spent with varietie of dances, the Maskers made a conclusion with a second new dance.

[31] The masquers were the Earl of Dorset, the Lord North, Sir Henry Rich, Sir Henry Carie, Theophilus Howard (Lord Walden), Sir Thomas Howard, Sir Charles Howard, and Henry Howard; for further information on them, see headnote.

[32] social dances between the masquers and the ladies of the audience.

At the Queenes parting on wednesday in the afternoone, *the Gardiner with his Man and Boy and three handsome Countrie Maides, the one bearing a rich bagge with linnen in it, the second a rich apron, and the third a rich mantle, appeare all out of an Arbour in the lower Garden; and meeting the Queene, the Gardiner presents this speech.*

GARDINER.

Stay, Goddesse, stay a little space,
Our poore Countrie love to grace;
Since we dare not too long stay you,
Accept at our hands, we pray you,
These meane presents, to expresse
Greater love then we professe,
Or can utter now for woe
Of your parting hast'ned so.
Gifts these are, such as were wrought
By their hands, that them have brought,
Home-bred things, which they presumed,
After I had them perfumed
With my flowrie incantation,
To give you in presentation
At your parting; come, feate[33] Lasses,
With fine cursies[34] and smooth faces,
Offer up your simple toyes
To the Mistris of our joyes;
While we the sad time prolong
With a mournefull parting song.

*A Song of three voices continuing while the presents
are delivered and received.*

I

Can you, the Author of our joy,
    So soone depart?
Will you revive, and straight destroy,
New mirth to teares convert?
    O that ever cause of gladnesse
    Should so swiftly turne to sadnesse!

[33] neat.   [34] curtsies.

2

Now as we droupe, so will these flowers,
  Bard of your sight,
Nothing availe them heav'nly showres
Without your heav'nly light.
    When the glorious Sunne forsakes us,
    Winter quickly over-takes us.

3

Yet shall our praiers your waies attend,
  When you are gone;
And we the tedious time will spend,
Remembring you alone.
    Welcome here shall you heare ever,
    But the word of parting never.

Thus ends this ample intertainment, which, as it was most nobly performed by the right honourable the Lord and Ladie of the house, and fortunately executed by all that any way were Actors in it, so was it as graciously received of her Majestie, and celebrated with her most royall applause.

THE DESCRIPTION,
SPEECHES, AND SONGS, OF
THE LORDS MASKE, PRESENTED IN
the Banquetting-house on the mariage night
of the high and mightie Count Palatine,
and the royally descended the Ladie
ELISABETH.

I have now taken occasion to satisfie many who long since were desirous that the Lords maske should be published, which, but for some private lets, had in due time come forth. The Scene *was divided into two parts from the roofe to the floore;[1] the lower part being first discovered (upon the sound of a double consort, exprest by severall instruments, plac't on either side of the roome), there appeared a Wood in prospective, the innermost part being of re-leave or whole round,[2] the rest painted. On the left hand from the seate was a Cave, and on the right a thicket, out of which came* Orpheus, *who was attired after the old Greeke manner, his haire curled and long; a lawrell wreath on his head; and in his hand hee bare a silver bird; about him tamely placed severall wild beasts; and upon the ceasing of the Consort* Orpheus *spake.*

ORPHEUS.

Agen, agen, fresh kindle *Phoebus* sounds,
T' exhale *Mania* from her earthie den;
Allay the furie that her sense confounds,[3]
And call her gently forth; sound, sound agen.

The Consorts both sound againe, and Mania *the Goddesse of madnesse appears wildly out of her cave. Her habit was confused and strange, but yet gracefull; shee as one amazed speaks.*

MANIA. What powerfull noise is this importunes me,
T' abandon darkenesse which my humour fits?
Joves hand in it I feele, and ever he
Must be obai'd, ev'n of the franticst wits.

ORPHEUS. *Mania!*

MANIA. Hah.

[1] i.e., divided in half horizontally.
[2] constructed either in relief or in the round.
[3] the fury that confuses her senses.

ORPHEUS. Braine-sick, why start'st thou so?
Approch yet nearer, and thou then shalt know
The will of *Jove,* which he will breath from me.

MANIA. Who art thou? if my dazeled eyes can see,
Thou art the sweet Enchanter heav'nly *Orpheus.*

ORPHEUS. The same, *Mania,* and *Jove* greets thee thus:
Though severall[4] power to thee, and charge he gave,
T' enclose in thy Dominions such as rave
Through blouds distemper, how durst thou attempt
T' imprison *Entheus,* whose rage is exempt
From vulgar censure? it is all divine,
Full of celestiall rapture, that can shine
Through darkest shadowes: therefore *Jove* by me
Commands thy power strait to set *Entheus* free.

MANIA. How can I? Franticks with him many more
In one cave are lockt up; ope once the dore,
All will flie out, and through the world disturbe
The peace of *Jove;* for what power then can curbe
Their rainelesse[5] furie?—

ORPHEUS.—Let not feare in vaine
Trouble thy crazed fancie; all againe,
Save *Entheus,* to thy safeguard shall retire;
For *Jove* into our musick will inspire
The power of passion, that their thoughts shall bend
To any forme or motion we intend.
Obey *Joves* will then; go, set *Entheus* free.

MANIA. I willing go, so *Jove* obey'd must bee.

ORPH. Let Musicke put on *Protean* changes now;
Wilde beasts it once tam'd, now let Franticks bow.

*At the sound of a strange musicke twelve Franticks enter, six
men and six women, all presented in sundry habits and humours:
there was the Lover, the Selfe-lover, the melancholicke-man full
of feare, the Schoole-man over-come with phantasie, the over-
watched[6] Usurer, with others that made an absolute medly of mad-
nesse; in middest of whom* Entheus *(or Poeticke furie) was hurried
forth, and tost up and downe, till by vertue of a new change in the
musicke, the Lunatickes fell into a madde measure, fitted to a loud*

---

[4] private.   [5] uncurbed.
[6] exhausted by watching over his treasure all night.

*phantasticke tune; but in the end thereof the musicke changed into
a very solemne ayre, which they softly played, while* Orpheus *spake.*

ORPH. Through these soft and calme sounds, *Mania,* passe
With thy Phantasticks hence; heere is no place
Longer for them or thee; *Entheus* alone
Must do *Joves* bidding now, all else be gone.

During this speech Mania *with her Franticks depart, leaving*
Entheus *behind them, who was attired in a close Curace of the An-
ticke fashion, Bases with labels, a Roabe fastned to his shoulders,
and hanging downe behind; on his head a wreath of Lawrell, out
of which grew a paire of wings; in the one hand he held a booke,
and in the other a pen.*[7]

ENTH. Divinest *Orpheus,* o how all from thee
Proceed with wondrous sweetnesse! Am I free?
Is my affliction vanisht?

ORPH.—Too too long,
Alas, good *Entheus,* hast thou brook't[8] this wrong;
What? number thee with madmen? o mad age,
Sencelesse of thee, and thy celestiall rage.
For thy excelling rapture, ev'n through things
That seems most light, is borne with sacred wings:
Nor are these Musicks, Showes, or Revels vaine,
When thou adorn'st them with thy *Phoebean* braine.
Th' are pallate sick[9] of much more vanitie,
That cannot taste them in their dignitie.
Jove therefore lets thy prison'd spright[10] obtaine
Her libertie and fiery scope againe:
And heere by me commands thee to create
Inventions rare, this night to celebrate,
Such as become a nuptiall by his will
Begun and ended.—

ENTH.—*Jove* I honor still,
And must obey. *Orpheus,* I feele the fires
Are reddy in my braine, which *Jove* enspires.

---

[7] See Plate III; the "Curace" is a cuirass, the "Bases with labels" are
skirts with strips of cloth attached. Nicoll (*Stuart Masques and the
Renaissance Stage,* p. 185) has shown that Campion's description of Poetic
Fury is derived from Cesare Ripa's *Iconologia* (ed. of Padua, 1618, p. 212);
the wings signify celerity of fancy.

[8] suffered.   [9] i.e., their palates have been cloyed.   [10] spirit.

Loe, through that vaile, I see *Prometheus* stand
Before those glorious lights, which his false hand
Stole out of heav'n, the dull earth to enflame
With the affects of Love, and honor'd Fame.
I view them plaine in pompe and majestie,
Such as being seene might hold rivalitie
With the best triumphes. *Orpheus,* give a call
With thy charm'd musicke, and discover all.

ORPH. Flie, cheerfull voices, through the ayre, and clear
These clouds, that yon hid beautie may appeare.

A Song.[11]

I

Come away; bring thy golden theft,
  Bring, bright *Prometheus,* all thy lights;
Thy fires from Heav'n bereft
  Shew now to humane sights.
Come quickly, come: thy stars to our stars straight present,
For pleasure, being too much defer'd, loseth her best content.
What fair dames wish should swift as their own thoughts
                appeare;
To loving and to longing harts every houre seemes a yeare.

2

See how faire: O how faire they shine;
  What yeelds more pompe beneath the skies?
Their birth is yet divine,
  And such their forme implies.
Large grow their beames, their nere approch afford[12] them so;
By nature sights that pleasing are, cannot too amply show.
O might these flames in humane shapes descend this place,
How lovely would their presence be, how full of grace!

   *In the end of the first part of this Song, the upper part of the
Scene was discovered by the sodaine fall of a curtaine; then in
clowdes of severall colours (the upper part of them being fierie, and
the middle heightned with silver) appeared eight Starres of extraor-
dinarie bignesse, which so were placed as that they seemed to be
fixed betweene the Firmament and the Earth; in the front of the
Scene stood* Prometheus, *attyred as one of the ancient Heroes.*

[11] See "Come away," *The Second Booke of Ayres,* xvii, above.   [12] enables.

ENTH. Patron of mankinde, powerfull and bounteous,
Rich in thy flames, reverend *Prometheus,*
In *Hymens* place aide us to solempnize
These royall Nuptials; fill the lookers eyes
With admiration of thy fire and light,
And from thy hand let wonders flow tonight.

PROM. *Entheus* and *Orpheus,* names both deare to me,
In equall ballance I your Third will be
In this nights honour. View these heav'n borne Starres,
Who by my stealth are become Sublunars;
How well their native beauties fit this place,
Which with a chorall dance they first shall grace;
Then shall their formes to humane figures turne,
And these bright fires within their bosomes burne.
Orpheus, apply thy musick, for it well
Helps to induce a Courtly miracle.

ORP. Sound, best of Musicks, raise yet higher our sprights,
While we admire *Prometheus* dancing lights.

A Song.

I

Advance your Chorall motions now,
   You musick-loving lights;
This night concludes the nuptiall vow,
   Make this the best of nights:
So bravely Crowne it with your beames,
   That it may live in fame,
As long as *Rhenus* or the *Thames*
   Are knowne by either name.[13]

2

Once move againe, yet nearer move
   Your formes at willing view;
Such faire effects of joy and love
   None can expresse but you:
Then revell midst your ayrie Bowres
   Till all the clouds doe sweat,
That pleasure may be powr'd in showres
   On this triumphant Seat.

[13] The device of the Gray's Inn and Inner Temple Masque later on February 20 was the marriage of the Thames to the Rhine.

3

Long since hath lovely *Flora* throwne
  Her Flowers and Garlands here;
Rich *Ceres* all her wealth hath showne,
  Prowde of her daintie cheare.[14]
Chang'd then to humane shape, descend,
  Clad in familiar weede,
That every eye may here commend
  The kinde delights you breede.

*According to the humour of this Song, the Starres mooved in
an exceeding strange and delightfull maner;[15] and I suppose fewe
have ever seene more neate artifice then Master Innigoe Jones
shewed in contriving their Motion, who in all the rest of the work-
manship which belong'd to the whole invention shewed extraordi-
narie industrie and skill; which if it be not as lively exprest in writ-
ing as it appeared in view, robbe not him of his due, but lay the
blame on my want of right apprehending his instructions for the
adoring of his Arte. But to returne to our purpose: about the end
of this Song, the Starres suddainely vanished, as if they had beene
drowned amongst the Cloudes, and the eight Maskers appeared in
their habits, which were infinitly rich, befitting States (such as in-
deede they all were),[16] as also a time so farre heightned the day
before[17] with all the richest shew of solemnitie that could be in-
vented. The ground[18] of their attires was massie Cloth of Silver,
embossed with flames of Embroidery; on their heads they had
Crownes, Flames made all of Gold-plate Enameled, and on the
top a Feather of Silke, representing a cloude of smoake. Upon their
new transformation, the whole Scaene being Cloudes dispersed,[19]
and there appeared an Element of artificiall fires, with severall
circles of lights, in continuall motion, representing the house of
Prometheus, who thus applies his speech to the Maskers.*

They are transformed.

[14] her beautiful countenance.

[15] Enid Welsford notes the resemblance of this device to a festival at
Florence in 1612 where four noblemen represented Galileo's four Medicean
stars (*The Court Masque*, p. 192).

[16] The masquers included the Earls of Montgomery and Salisbury and
the Lord Hay; see headnote.

[17] i.e., befitting the marriage ceremony earlier in the day.

[18] foundation.

[19] The curtain painted to resemble clouds was drawn up.

PROMETH. So pause awhile, and come, yee fierie spirits,
Breake forth the earth like sparks t'attend these Knights.

Sixteene Pages like fierie spirits, all their attires being alike
composed of flames, with fierie Wings and Bases,[20] *bearing in either*
hand a Torch of Virgine Waxe, come forth below dauncing a lively
measure; and the Daunce being ended, Prometheus *speakes to*
them from above.

The Torch-bearers Daunce.

PRO. Wait, spirits, wait, while through the clouds we pace,
And by descending gaine a hier place.

The Pages returne toward the Scaene, to give their attendance
to the Maskers with their lights: from the side of the Scaene ap-
peared a bright and transparant cloud, which reached from the
top of the heavens to the earth; on this cloud the Maskers led by
Prometheus *descended with the musicke of a full song; and at the*
end of their descent the cloud brake in twaine, and one part of it
(as with a winde) was blowne overthwart the Scaene.

While this cloud was vanishing, the wood being the underpart
of the Scaene was insensibly changed, and in place thereof appeared
foure Noble women-statues of silver, standing in severall nices,[21]
accompanied with ornaments of Architecture which filled all the
end of the house, and seemed to be all of gold-smithes work. The
first order consisted of Pillasters all of gold, set with Rubies, Sa-
phyrs, Emeralds, Opals, and such like. The Capitels were com-
posed,[22] *and of a new invention. Over this was a bastard order*
with Cartouses reversed,[23] *comming from the Capitels of every Pil-*
laster, which made the upper part rich and full of ornament. Over
every statue was placed a history in gold, which seemed to be of
base releave;[24] *the conceits which were figured in them were these.*
In the first was Prometheus, *embossing in clay the figure of a*
woman; in the second he was represented stealing fire from the
chariot-wheele of the Sunne; in the third he is exprest putting life
with this fire into his figure of clay; and in the fourth square, Ju-
piter, *enraged, turnes these new made women into statues. Above*
all, for finishing, ran a Cornish, which returned over every Pillas-
ter,[25] *seeming all of gold and richly carved.*

[20] shoulder flaps and skirts cut to resemble flames.
[21] niches. [22] the Roman composite order.
[23] a mixed order, featuring reversed scrollwork. [24] bas-relief.
[25] a cornice which touched the top of every pilaster.

A full Song.

Supported now by Clouds descend,
Divine *Prometheus, Hymens* friend:
Leade downe the new transformed fires,
And fill their breasts with loves desires;
That they may revell with delight,
And celebrate this nuptiall night,
So celebrate this nuptiall night,
    That all which see may stay:
They never viewed so faire a sight,
    Even on the cleerest day.

ENTHEUS. See, see, *Prometheus:* four of these first dames
Which thou long since out of thy purchac't[26] flames
Did'st forge with heav'nly fire, as they were then
By *Jove* transformed to Statues, so agen
They suddenly appeare by his command
At thy arrivall. Loe, how fixt they stand;
So did *Joves* wrath too long, but now at last
It by degrees relents, and he hath plac't
These Statues, that we might his ayde implore,
First for the life of these, and then for more.

PROM. *Entheus,* thy councels are divine and just;
Let *Orpheus* decke thy Hymne, since pray we must.

The first Invocation in a full Song.

Powerfull *Jove,* that of bright starres
Now hast made men fit for warres,
Thy power in these Statues prove,
And make them women fit for love.

ORPHEUS. See, *Jove* is pleas'd; Statues have life and move:
Go, new-borne men, and entertaine with love
These new-borne women; though your number yet
Exceedes their's double, they are arm'd with wit
To beare your best encounters. Court them faire:
When words and Musicke speake, let none despaire.

[26] captured.

The Song.[27]

1

Wooe her, and win her, he that can:
   Each woman hath two lovers,
So shee must take and leave a man,
   Till time more grace discovers;
This doth *Jove* to shew that want
   Makes beautie most respected;
If faire women were more skant,
   They would be more affected.[28]

2

Courtship and Musicke suite with love,
   They both are workes of passion;
Happie is he whose words can move,
   Yet sweete notes helpe perswasion.
Mixe your words with Musicke then,
   That they the more may enter;
Bold assaults are fit for men,
   That on strange beauties venture.

*While this Song is sung, and the Maskers court the fowre
new transformed Ladies, foure other Statues appeare in their places.*

PROMET. Cease, cease your woing strife; see, *Jove* intends
To fill your number up, and make all friends.
Orpheus and *Entheus,* joyne your skils once more,
And with a Hymne the Dietie implore.

The second Invocation to the tune of the first.

Powerfull *Jove,* that hast given fower,
Raise this number but once more,
That, complete, their numerous feet[29]
May aptly in just measures meet.

[27] On this song, which was printed with its music at the end of *The
Somerset Masque,* see Frederick W. Sternfeld, "A Song for Campion's *Lord's
Masque,*" *Journal of the Warburg and Courtauld Institutes,* XX (1957),
373–75.
[28] desired.
[29] rhythmically moving feet.

*The other foure statues are transformed into women, in the
time of this invocation.*

ENTH. The number's now complete, thankes be to *Jove:*
No man needs fear a Rivall in his love;
For, all are sped,[30] and now begins delight
To fill with glorie this triumphant night.

*The Maskers, having every one entertained his Lady, begin
their first new entring dance;[31] after it, while they breath, the time
is entertained with a dialogue song.*

> Breath you now, while Io Hymen
>   To the Bride we sing:
> O how many joyes, and honors,
>   From this match will spring!
> Ever firme the league will prove,
> Where only goodnesse causeth love.
> Some for profit seeke
> What their fancies most disleeke:
> These love for vertues sake alone:
> Beautie and youth unite them both in one.

CHORUS.

> Live with thy Bridegroome happy, sacred Bride;
> How blest is he that is for love envi'd.

The Maskers second dance.

> Breath againe, while we with musicke
>   Fill the emptie space:
> O but do not in your dances
>   Your selves only grace.
> Ev'ry one fetch out your *Pheare,*[32]
> Whom chiefely you will honor heere.
> Sights most pleasure breed,
> When their numbers most exceed:
> Chuse then, for choice to all is free;
> Taken or left, none discontent must bee.

[30] taken care of.
[31] the first dance composed especially for this masque, marking the
masquers' entry from the stage down into the dancing area of the room.
[32] companion.

CHORUS.

Now in thy Revels frolicke-faire delight,
To heap Joy on this ever honored night.

*The Maskers during this Dialogue take out others to daunce
with them, men women, and women men; and first of all the
Princely Bridegroome and Bride were drawne into these solemne
Revels,*[33] *which continued a long space, but in the end were broken
off with this short Song.*

A Song.

Cease, cease you Revels, rest a space;
New pleasures presse into this place,
Full of beautie and of grace.

*The whole scaene was now againe changed, and became a
prospective with Porticoes on each side, which seemed to go in a
great way; in the middle was erected an Obeliske, all of silver, and
in it lights of severall colours; on the side of this Obeliske, standing
on Pedestals, were the statues of the Bridegroome and Bride, all of
gold in gratious postures. This Obeliske was of that height, that the
toppe thereof touched the highest cloudes, and yet* Sybilla *did draw
it forth with a threed of gold. The grave* Sage *was in a Roabe of
gold tuckt up before to her girdle, a Kirtle*[34] *gathered full, and of
silver; with a vaile on her head, being bare-neckt, and bearing in
her hand a scrole of Parchment.*[35]

ENTHEUS. Make cleare the passage to *Sibilla's* sight,
Who with her Trophee[36] comes, to crowne this night;
And, as her selfe with Musicke shall be led,
So shall shee pull on with a golden thread
A high vast *Obeliske,* dedicate to fame,
Which immortalitie it selfe did frame.
Raise high your voices now; like Trumpets fill
The roome with sounds of Triumph, sweete and shrill.

[33] social dances between masquers and audience. [34] skirt.
[35] In Ripa's *Iconologia* (ed. of Padua, 1618, pp. 224–25) a gold-clad
figure with an obelisk or pyramid represents "The Glory of Princes."
[36] monument, i.e., the obelisk.

A SONG.

Come triumphing, come with state,
    Old *Sibilla,* reverend Dame;
Thou keep'st the secret key of fate,
    Preventing[37] swiftest fame.
This night breath onely words of joy,
And speake them plaine, now be not coy.

SIB.[38]

Debetur alto iure Principium Iovi,
Votis det ipse vim meis, dictis fidem.
Utrinque decoris splendet egregium Iubar;
Medio triumphus mole stat dignus sua,
Caelumque summo Capite dilectum petit.
Quam pulchra pulchro sponsa respondet viro!
Quam plena numinis! Patrem vultu exprimit,
Parens futura masculae prolis, Parens
Regum, imperatorum. Additur Germaniae
Robur Britannicum: ecquid esse par potest?
Utramque iunget una mens gentem, fides,
Deique Cultus unus, et simplex amor.
Idem erit utrique hostis, sodalis idem, idem
Votum periclitantium, atque eadem manus.
Favebit illis Pax, favebit bellica
Fortuna, semper aderit Adiutor Deus.
Sic, sic Sibilla; vocibus nec his deest
Pondus, nec hoc inane monumentum trahit.
Et aureum est, et quale nec flammas timet,
Nec fulgura, ipsi quippe sacratur Jovi.

[37] anticipating.

[38] [The beginning is owing rightly to lofty Jove; let him give force to my prayers, truth to my words. The excelling light of glory shines out on both sides: in the midst of the structure, the trophy worthy of it stands and seeks delightful heaven with its summit. How the beautiful bride responds to the handsome husband! How full of power! She expresses her father in her face, the future mother of male progeny, the mother of kings, of emperors. Let the British strength be added to the German: can anything equal it? One mind, one faith, will join two peoples, and one religion, and simple love. Both will have the same enemy, the same ally, the same prayer for those in danger, and the same strength. Peace will favor them, and the fortune of war will favor them; always God the helper will be at their side. Thus, thus, Sibyl; nor is weight lacking to these words, nor is this monument she draws empty. It is of gold, and such as fears no flames, nor thunderbolts: for it is consecrated to Jove himself.]

PRO. The good old *Sage* is silenc't; her free tongue,
That made such melodie, is now unstrung:
Then grace her Trophee with a dance triumphant;
Where *Orpheus* is, none can fit musick want.

A Song and dance triumphant of the Maskers.

I

Dance, dance, and visit now the shadowes of our joy,
All in height, and pleasing state, your changed formes imploy.
And as the bird of *Jove* salutes, with loftie wing, the morn,
So mount, so flie, these Trophees to adorne.
Grace them with all the sounds and motions of delight,
Since all the earth cannot expresse a lovelier sight.
View them with triumph, and in shades the truth adore:
No pompe or sacrifice can please *Ioves* greatnesse more.

2

Turne, turne, and honor now the life these figures beare;
Loe, how heav'nly natures farre above all art appeare;
Let their aspects revive in you the fire that shin'd so late,
Still mount and still retaine your heavenly state.
Gods were with dance, and with musick serv'd of old,
Those happy daies deriv'd their glorious stile from gold:[39]
This pair, by *Hymen* joyn'd, grace you with measures then,
Since they are both divine, and you are more then men.

ORPH. Let here *Sybilla's* Trophee stand,
Leade her now by either hand,
That shee may approch yet nearer,
And the Bride and Bridegroome heare her
Blesse them in her native tongue,
Wherein old prophesies shee sung,
Which time to light hath brought:
Shee speakes that which *Jove* hath taught:
Well may he inspire her now,
To make a joyfull and true vow.

SYB.[40] Sponsam sponse toro tene pudicam,

[39] i.e., the Golden Age.
[40] [Husband, hold your chaste wife fast by the marriage bed; wife, hold your chaste husband fast by the marriage bed. It is not a single night alone which is given over to the happy, but this one night will reward you perpetually with many descendants and with equal love. Sibyl speaks happy and true words; from on high Jupiter himself assents to her speech.]

Sponsum sponsa tene toro pudicum.
Non haec unica nox datur beatis,
At vos perpetuo haec beabit una
Prole multiplici, parique amore.
Laeta, ac vera refert Sybilla; ab alto
Ipse Iuppiter annuit loquenti.

PRO. So be it ever, joy and peace,
And mutuall love give you increase,
That your posteritie may grow
In fame, as long as Seas doe flow.

ENTH. Live you long to see your joyes,
In faire Nymphs and Princely Boyes;
Breeding like the Garden flowers,
Which kinde heav'n drawes with her warme showers.

ORPH. Enough of blessing, though too much
Never can be said to such;
But night doth wast, and *Hymen* chides,
Kinde to Bridegroomes and to Brides.
Then, singing, the last dance induce,[41]
So let good night prevent excuse.

The Song.

No longer wrong the night
Of her *Hymenaean* right;
A thousand *Cupids* call away,
Fearing the approching day;
The Cocks alreadie crow:
Dance then and goe.

*The last new Dance of the Maskers, which concludes
all with a lively straine at their go-
ing out.*

[41] lead in.

THE
DESCRIPTION
of a Maske:
Presented in the
Banqueting roome at *Whitehall*, on
Saint Stephens night last, At the Mariage of
the Right Honourable the Earle of
Somerset: And the right noble
the Lady FRANCES
Howard.

Written by *Thomas Campion.*

Whereunto are annexed divers choyse *Ayres* composed
for this Maske that may be Sung with a single voyce
to the Lute or Base-Viall.

1614

The sordid background of this fine masque is very circum-
stantially recorded in *The Murder of Sir Thomas Overbury* by
William McElwee (New York, 1952). The political context is the
effort of the Howards, under Northampton, to gain influence over
Robert Carr (later Earl of Somerset), the successor to James Hay
as King James's favorite; to this end, they encouraged Carr's
passion for Frances Howard, Countess of Essex, and finally even
managed to annul her earlier marriage to Essex in order to pave
the way for a new one to Carr. When Overbury, Carr's "Governor"
(as Queen Anne called him), opposed the match bitterly, the
favorite, abetted by the Countess and Northampton, got him im-
prisoned on a bald pretext in the Tower where, from April to
September 1613, he was subjected to numerous attempts on his
life by the Countess' poisons. She finally succeeded with sublimate
of mercury, and Overbury died on September 15; the annulment
was granted on September 25, and, after Carr had been made
Earl of Somerset to equal his wife's rank, the wedding took place
on December 26. It was celebrated on a grand scale by Campion's
masque on the wedding night, Jonson's *Irish Masque* (a deliberate
burlesque of Campion's masque, in dialect) on December 29,
Middleton's *Masque of Cupid* and another on January 4, and
The Masque of Flowers by Gray's Inn on the 6th. "The whole
occasion" of Campion's masque, as McElwee writes (p. 147),
"was ostentatiously a Howard triumph. Of the twelve noble gentle-
men who volunteered to take part in the mask, four were Howards
and another, the new Earl of Salisbury, was married to a Howard"
(see the list of masquers at the end of the masque). Three of the
masquers, Dorset, Pembroke, and Montgomery, had originally
opposed both Carr and the Howards; and (by a curious irony)
Montgomery, Hay, Walden, and Sir Thomas Howard had all
danced in Jonson's *Hymenaei* celebrating the Countess' first mar-
riage in 1606.

The occasion was not without irony for Campion himself; for
both he and his patron Sir Thomas Monson were implicated in
the case later opened after Carr's fall from favor in 1615. Monson,
as Keeper of the Armoury at the Tower, was the prime instrument
in replacing the incorruptible Lieutenant of the Tower, Sir
William Waad, by the Howards' tool, Sir Jervis Elwes; and
Campion had collected Elwes' bribe of £1400 in person. Campion
was cleared of knowledge of the purpose in hand in 1615 (his

deposition of October 26 is reproduced as the frontispiece of Vivian's edition), Monson much later in 1617.

The Somerset Masque is notable both for its extensive anti-masque, all in pantomime, which Campion may have drawn from the *Ballet of the Winds* performed at Florence in 1608 (see Enid Welsford, *The Court Masque,* pp. 114 and 197) and for its realism. This quality shows itself not only in the avoidance of myth in the main masque but also in its closeness to the actual situation; for the device of the twelve knights enchanted by the evil illusions of Rumor and freed by the sufferance of the Queen (who had originally opposed the Somerset match) seems deliberately designed as a tactful attempt to lift opprobrium from the Countess' remarriage. Campion seems to have had the wedding of Peleus and the sea nymph Thetis, as celebrated by Catullus, frequently in mind during the composition of this masque; perhaps it suggested to him both the number symbolism of the earthly tetrad transcended by the divine triad and the imagery of land and water, for Abraham Fraunce had noted that this wedding signified "the generation of things, for πηλος is slyme, and *Thetis* water, whereof all things are made, yet by an efficient; and therfore all the gods were at that wedding, except Discord, the only cause of dissolution" (*The Third Part of the Countesse of Pembrokes Yvychurch,* 1592, p. 5ᵛ).

Since Inigo Jones had left for Italy in February of 1613 and did not return until 1615, Campion had to avail himself of the not entirely satisfactory services of Constantine de Servi (1554–1622), a wandering Florentine architect and designer who had been granted a yearly pension of £200 by Prince Henry in 1612. None of Servi's designs have survived. On the other hand, we have more music for this masque than for any other. Of the five songs appended to the original edition, the four belonging to this masque have been transcribed on the pages following the text (the fifth, "Wooe her, and win her," "A Song, made by *Th. Campion,* and sung in the Lords Maske at the *Count Palatines Marriage,* we have here added, to fill up these emptie Pages"). Beyond these, we have three dance tunes. There is a two-part arrangement of "The Saylers Masque" in British Museum Additional MS. 10444, fos. 27ᵛ–28 and 79ᵛ which, Sabol suggests (*Songs and Dances for the Stuart Masque,* p. 169), belongs either here or in Jonson's *Neptunes Triumph;* he transcribes it as No. 45 of his collection. No. 63 of his collection, labeled "Squiers Masque" on fos. 48ᵛ, 98ᵛ of the same source, can be more confidently assigned to this masque, either as a dance or as entry music. Finally, a piece entitled

"Sommersets Maske" survives in tablature on fos. 27–28 of Advocates' MS. 5. 2. 15 (Skene). For Giovanni Coperario, Campion's major collaborator among the "severall Authors," see the headnote to *Songs of Mourning*. Nicholas Lanier (1588–1666) here made the debut of a long career as composer for the masque, a career which included work in *stylo recitativo* for Jonson's *Lovers Made Men, The Gypsies Metamorphosed, The Masque of Augurs,* and, perhaps, Aurelian Townshend's *Tempe Restored;* Sabol (p. 13) finds Lanier's setting of "Bring away" a very impressive experiment in the declamatory style; see McD. Emslie, "Nicholas Lanier's Innovations in English Song," *Music and Letters,* XLI (1960), 13–27. Lanier's fellow singer Allen received the praise of Ben Jonson for his work in *The Masque of Queenes:* "that most excellent *tenor* voyce, and exact Singer (her Ma:ties servant, mr. Jo. Allin)" (*Works,* ed. C. H. Herford and Percy and Evelyn Simpson, VII [Oxford, 1941], 315).

Pulchro pulchra datur, sociali foedere amanti
Tandem nubit amans; ecquid amabilius?

Verae ut supersint nuptiae
Praeite duplici face:
Praetendat alteram necesse
Hymen, alteram par est Amor.

Uni ego mallem placuisse docto,
Candido, et fastu sine iudicanti,
Millium quam millibus imperitorum
Inque videntum.[1]

[1] The three prefatory epigrams read as follows:

"The beautiful is given to the beautiful, at last the lover weds the beloved with social bonds: what could be lovelier?"

"That true marriages may endure, you must lead the wedding procession with two torches: Hymen must hold one torch, and it is best that Love hold the other."

"I should prefer to please one man who is learned, candid, and judicious without arrogance, than thousands upon thousands of the ignorant and envious."

The third epigram was probably provoked by Jonson's burlesque of this masque in his *Irish Masque.*

The description of a Masque, Pre-
sented in the Banqueting roome at *Whitehall*,
On St. *Stephens* night last: At the Mariage
of the right Honourable the Earle of
Somerset, & the right noble the
Lady *Frances Howard*.

*In ancient times, when any man sought to shadowe or heighten
his Invention, he had store of feyned persons readie for his purpose,
as* Satyres, Nymphes, *and their like: such were then in request and
beliefe among the vulgar. But in our dayes, although they have not
utterly lost their use, yet finde they so litle credit, that our moderne
writers have rather transfered their fictions to the persons of En-
chaunters and Commaunders of Spirits, as that excellent Poet* Tor-
quato Tasso *hath done,*[2] *and many others.*

*In imitation of them (having a presentation in hand for Per-
sons of high State) I grounded my whole Invention upon Inchaunt-
ments and several transformations. The work-manship whereof was
undertaken by M.* Constantine, *an Italian, Architect to our late
Prince* Henry; *but he, being too much of him selfe, and no way to
be drawne to impart his intentions, fayled so farre in the assurance
he gave, that the mayne invention, even at the last cast, was of
force drawne into a farre narrower compasse then was from the be-
ginning intended. The description whereof, as it was performed, I
will as briefely as I can deliver. The place wherein the Maske was
presented, being the Banquetting house at White Hall, the upper
part, where the State*[3] *is placed, was Theatred with Pillars, Scaf-
folds, and all things answerable*[4] *to the sides of the Roome. At the
lower end of the Hall, before the Sceane, was made an Arch Try-
umphall, passing beautifull, which enclosed the whole Workes. The
Sceane it selfe (the Curtaine being drawne) was in this manner
divided.*

*On the upper part there was formed a Skye with Clowdes very
arteficially shadowed. On either side of the Sceane belowe was set
a high Promontory, and on either of them stood three large pillars
of golde; the one Promontory was bounded with a Rocke standing
in the Sea, the other with a Wood. In the midst betwene them*

[2] for instance, in the enchantments of Ismeno and Armida in *Geru-
salemme Liberata*.

[3] the canopied throne set at one end of the hall.   [4] accordant.

apeared a Sea in perspective with ships, some cunningly painted, some arteficially sayling. On the front of the Sceane, on either side, was a beautifull garden, with sixe seates a peece to receave the Maskers; behinde them the mayne Land, and in the middest a paire of stayres made exceeding curiously in the form of a Schalop shell.[5] *And in this manner was the eye first of all entertayned. After the King, Queene, and Prince were placed, and preparation was made for the beginning of the Maske, there entred foure Squires, who as soone as they approached neare the Presence, humbly bowing themselves, spake as followeth.*

THE FIRST SQUIRE.

That fruite that neither dreads the *Syrian* heats,
Nor the sharp frosts which churlish *Boreas* threats,
The fruite of *Peace* and *Joy* our wishes bring
To this high State, in a Perpetuall Spring.
Then pardon (Sacred Majestie) our griefe
Unseasonably that presseth for reliefe.
The ground[6] whereof (if your blest eares can spare
A short space of Attention) we'le declare.

Great Honors Herrald, *Fame,* having Proclaym'd
This Nuptiall feast, and with it all enflam'd,
From every quarter of the earth[7] three Knights
(In Courtship seene,[8] as well as Martiall fights)
Assembled in the Continent, and there
Decreed this night A solemne Service here.
For which, by sixe and sixe embarqu'd they were
In several Keeles;[9] their Sayles for *Britaine* bent.
But (they that never favour'd good intent)
Deformed *Errour,* that enchaunting fiend,
And wing-tongu'd *Rumor,* his infernall freind,

[5] scallop shell, on which Venus floated to land at her birth.
[6] basis.
[7] The persistence of the tetrad in this masque stems from the traditional Pythagorean and Christian symbolism of the number 4 as the pattern of the cosmos, the mundane sphere (hence of the microcosm); this mundane tetrad is superseded by the divine triads of the Destinies and Harmony which disperse the antimasque. See Hopper, *Mediaeval Number Symbolism,* pp. 83–84. Jonson burlesqued Campion's lines in ll. 95–98 of *The Irish Masque:*

> DERMOCK: For all tey have no goot vindsh to blow tem heter, nor elementsh to presherve 'hem.
> DONNELL: Nor all te foure cornersh o' te world, to creepe out on.

[8] experienced.   [9] different ships.

With *Curiositie* and *Credulitie,*
Both Sorceresses, all in hate agree
Our purpose to divert; in vaine they strive,
For we in spight of them came neere t' arive,[10]
When sodainly (as Heaven and hell had met)
A storme confus'd against our Tackle beat,
Severing the Ships; but after what befell
Let these relate, my tongu's too weake to tell.[11]

THE SECOND SQUIRE.

A strange and sad Ostent[12] our Knights distrest;
For while the Tempests fierye rage increast,
About our Deckes and Hatches, loe, appeare
Serpents, as *Lerna* had been pour'd out there,[13]
Crawling about us; which feare to eschew,[14]
The Knights the Tackle climb'd, and hung in view,
When violently a flash of lightning came,
And from our sights did beare them in the flame.
Which past, no Serpent there was to be seene,
And all was husht, as storme had never beene.

THE THIRD SQUIRE.

At Sea, their mischeifes grewe, but ours at Land;
For being by chance arriv'd, while our Knights stand
To view their storme-tost friends on two Cliffes neere,
Thence, loe, they vanish'd, and sixe Pillars were
Fixt in their footsteps; Pillars all of golde,
Faire to our eyes, but wofull to beholde.

THE FOURTH SQUIRE.

Thus with prodigious hate and crueltie,
Our good Knights for their love afflicted be;
But, o, protect us now, Majesticke Grace,
For see, those curst Enchanters presse in place
That our past sorrowes wrought: these, these alone
Turne all the world into confusion.

[10] were about to arrive.
[11] In ll. 29–49 of Jonson's *Irish Masque* the four footmen quarrel about which is to speak first.
[12] sight.
[13] Lerna is the marsh in Argolis where the huge serpent Hydra lived.
[14] in order to avoid that fearsome sight.

Towards the end of this speech, two Enchanters, and two En-chanteresses appeare: Error *first, in a skin coate[15] scaled like a Serpent, and an antick habit[16] painted with Snakes, a haire of curled Snakes, and a deformed visard.[17] With him* Rumor *in a skin coate full of winged Tongues, and over it an antick robe; on his head a Cap like a tongue, with a large paire of wings to it.*

Curiosity *in a skin coate full of eyes, and an antick habit over it, a fantastick Cap full of Eyes.*

Credulity *in the like habit painted with eares, and an antick Cap full of eares.*

When they had whispered a while as if they had rejoyced at the wrongs which they had done to the Knights, the Musick and their Daunce began: strait forth rusht the foure Windes confusedly, The Eastern Winde in a skin coate of the colour of the Sun-rising, with a yellow haire, and wings both on his shoulders and feete.

The Westerne Winde in a skin coate of darke crimson, with crimson haire and wings.

The Southerne Winde in a darke russet skin coate, haire and wings sutable.

The Northern Winde in a grisled[18] skin coate, with haire and wings accordingly.

After them in confusion came the foure Elements: Earth, *in a skin coate of grasse greene, a mantle painted full of trees, plants and flowers, and on his head an oke growing.*

Water, *in a skin coate waved,[19] with a mantle full of fishes, on his head a Dolphin.*

Ayre, *in a skye-coloured skin coate, with a mantle painted with Fowle, and on his head an Eagle.*

Fire, *in a skin coate and a mantle painted with flames: on his head a cap of flames, with a Salamander in the midst thereof.*

Then entred the foure parts of the earth in a confused measure.[20]

Europe *in the habit of an Empresse, with an Emperiall Crowne on her head.*

Asia *in a Persian Ladies habit, with a Crowne on her head.* Africa *like a Queene of the Moores, with a crown.*

[15] a tight-fitting leather jerkin or jacket.   [16] a grotesque costume.
[17] ugly mask.   [18] gray.   [19] painted so as to look like waves.

[20] For Campion's slight indebtedness to Ripa's *Iconologia* for his description of the continents, see Nicoll, *Stuart Masques and the Renaissance Stage,* p. 192 and Fig. 164. Campion's other personifications here are totally independent of Ripa.

America *in a skin coate of the colour of the juyce of Mulberies, on her head large round brims of many coloured feathers, and in the midst of it a small Crowne.*

All these having daunced together in a strange kind of confusion, past away, by foure and foure.

At which time, Eternity *appeared in a long blew Taffata robe, painted with Starres, and on her head a Crowne.*

Next, came the three Destinies, in long robes of white Taffata like aged women, with Garlands of Narcissus *Flowers on their heads; and in their left hands they caried distaffes according to the descriptions of* Plato *and* Catullus,[21] *but in their right hands they carried altogether a Tree of Golde.*

After them, came Harmony with nine Musitians more, in long Taffata robes and caps of Tinsell, with Garlands guilt, playing and singing this Song.

CHORUS.

Vanish, vanish hence, confusion;
Dimme not *Hymens* goulden light
    With false illusion.
The Fates shall doe him right,
And faire Eternitie,
    Who passe through all enchantements free.

ETERNITIE SINGES ALONE.

Bring away this Sacred Tree,
The Tree of Grace and Bountie,
    Set it in Bel-Annas eye,
For she, she, only she
    Can all Knotted spels unty.
Pull'd from the Stocke, let her blest Hands convay
    To any suppliant Hand, a bough,
    And let that Hand advance it now
Against a Charme, that Charme shall fade away.

Toward the end of this Song the three destinies set the Tree of Golde before the Queene.

CHORUS.

Since Knightly valour rescues Dames distressed,
    By Vertuous Dames let charm'd Knights be released.

[21] See Plato. *Republic* X. 14–16 (617 d) and Catullus LXIV. 304 ff. The golden tree is apparently original with Campion.

After this Chorus, one of the Squires speakes.

Since Knights by valour rescue Dames distrest,
Let them be by the Queene of Dames releast:
So sing the Destinyes, who never erre,
Fixing this Tree of Grace and Bountie heere,
From which, for our enchaunted Knights we crave
A branche, pull'd by your Sacred Hand, to have;
That we may beare it as the Fates direct,
And manifest your glory in th' effect.[22]
In vertues favour then, and Pittie now
(Great Queene), vouchsafe us a divine touch't bough.

At the end of this speech, the Queene puld a branch from the Tree and gave it to a Nobleman, who delivered it to one of the Squires.

A Song while the Squires descend with the bough toward the Scene.

Goe, happy man, like th' Evening Starre,
Whose beames to Bride-groomes well-come are:
May neither Hagge nor Feind withstand
The pow're of thy Victorious Hand.
    The Uncharm'd Knights surrender now,
    By vertue[23] of thy raised Bough.

Away, Enchauntements, Vanish quite,
No more delay our longing sight:
'Tis fruitelesse to contend with Fate,
Who gives us pow're against your hate.
    Brave Knights, in Courtly pompe appeare,
    For now are you long-look't for heere.

Then out of the ayre a cloude descends, discovering sixe of the Knights alike, in strange and sumptuous atires, and withall on either side of the Cloud, on the two Promontories, the other sixe Maskers are sodainly transformed out of the pillars of golde; at which time, while they all come forward to the dancing-place, this Chorus is sung, and on the sodaine the whole Sceane is changed: for whereas before all seemed to be done at the sea and sea coast, now the Promontories are sodainly remooved, and London with the Thames is very arteficially presented in their place.

[22] act.
[23] power.

The Squire lifts up the Bough.

CHORUS.

Vertue and Grace, in spight of Charmes,
Have now redeem'd our men at Armes.
Ther's no inchauntement can withstand,
Where Fate directs the happy hand.

The Maskers first Daunce.

*The third Song of three partes, with a Chorus of
five partes, sung after the first Daunce.*

While dancing rests, fit place to musicke graunting,
Good spels the Fates shall breath, al envy daunting,
Kind eares with Joy enchaunting,   chaunting.[24]

CHORUS.
Io, Io Hymen.

Like lookes, like hearts, like loves are linck't together:
So must the Fates be pleas'd, so come they hether,
To make this Joy persever   ever.

CHORUS.
Io, Io Hymen.

Love decks the spring, her buds to th' ayre exposing:
Such fire here in these bridall Breasts reposing
We leave with charmes enclosing,   closing.

CHORUS.
Io, Io Hymen.

The Maskers second Daunce.

*The fourth Song, a Dialogue of three, with a
Chorus after the second Daunce.*

1 Let us now sing of Loves delight,
   For he alone is Lord to night.

2 Some friendship betweene man and man prefer,
   But I th' affection betweene man and wife.

3 What good can be in life,
   Whereof no fruites appeare?

[24] singing.

1 Set is that Tree in ill houre,
   That yeilds neither fruite nor flowre.

2 How can man Perpetuall be,
   But in his owne Posteritie?

CHORUS.

That pleasure is of all most bountifull and kinde,
That fades not straight, but leaves a living Joy behinde.

After this Dialogue the Maskers daunce with the Ladies, wherein spending as much time as they held fitting, they returned to the seates provided for them.

Straight in the Thames appeared foure Barges with skippers in them, and withall this song was sung.

Come a shore, come, merrie mates,
With your nimble heeles and pates:[25]
Summon ev'ry man his Knight,
Enough honour'd is this night.
Now, let your Sea-borne Goddesse[26] come,
Quench these lights, and make all dombe.
Some sleepe; others let her call:
And so Godnight to all, godnight to all.

At the conclusion of this song arrived twelve skippers in red capps, with short cassocks and long slopps,[27] wide at the knees, of white canvas striped with crimson, white gloves and Pomps,[28] and red stockins: these twelve daunced a brave and lively daunce, shouting and tryumphing after their manner.

After this followed the Maskers last daunce, wherewith they retyred.

At the Embarking of the Knights, the Squires approach the state, and speake.

THE FIRST SQUIRE.

All that was ever ask't, by vow of *Jove*,
To blesse a state with Plentie, Honor, Love,
Power, Triumph, private pleasure, publique peace,
Sweete springs, and *Autumn's* filld with due increase,
All these, and what good els thought can supplie,
Ever attend your Triple Majestie.

[25] heads, hence wit. [26] Venus.
[27] short tunics and long knee breeches. [28] pumps.

THE SECOND SQUIRE.

All blessings which the *Fates,* Propheticke, Sung,
At *Peleus* Nuptialls,[29] and what ever tongue
Can figure more, this night, and aye, betide
The honour'd Bride-groome and the honourd Bride.

ALL THE SQUIRES TOGETHER.

Thus speakes in us th' affection of our Knights,
Wishing your health, and Miriads of goodnights.

*The Squires speeches being ended, this Song is Sung while the
Boates passe way.*

> Hast aboord, hast now away:
> Hymen frownes at your delay.
> Hymen doth long nights affect;[30]
> Yeild him then his due respect.
> The Sea-borne Goddesse straight will come,
> Quench these lights, and make all dombe.
> Some Sleepe; others she will call:
> And so godnight to all, godnight to all.

FINIS.

[29] See Catullus LXIV. 327 ff., whence Campion had drawn his description of the Destinies; their chief prophecy was the birth of a son, Achilles.
[30] desire.

AYRES,
Made by severall Authors:
And
Sung in the Maske at the Marriage of the
Right Honourable ROBERT, Earle of *Somerset,*
and the Right Noble the lady FRANCES
HOWARD.

Set forth for the Lute and Base Violl, and may be ex-
prest by a single voyce, to eyther of those Instruments.

I.

Canto

The first Song: made and exprest by Mr. Nicholas Lanier.

Bring a - way, bring a - way this sa - cred Tree,

the tree of grace and boun - tie, Set it in *Bel - An - nae's*

eye, for shee, ___ she one - ly, she one - ly, she can all knot - ted

spels un - tie. Pull'd from this stocke, let her blest

hand con - vey   To a - ny   sup - pliant hand_____ a

bough,   And   let   that   hand ad - vance   it now

A - gainst a charme, that   charme _____   shall fade   a - way.

II.

Canto.

These three Songs following were composed by Mr. Coprario, and sung by Mr. John Allen, and Mr. Lanier.

Goe hap·py man like th'Eve·ning Starre, . Whose
May nei·ther Hag nor Fiend with·stand The

beams to Bride·groomes wel·come are. Th'un·char·med Knights
power of thy— vic·tor·ious hand.

sur·ren·der now, By ver·tue — of ———— thy rai·sed Bow.

III.

While daunc - ing rests, fit place to Mu - sicke graun -
ting, Good spels the Fates shall breathe, __ all __ En - vy __
__ daun - ting, Kind eares with joy en - chant - ting.
I - o   I - o   I - o   I - o   I - o   Hy - men, ___ I - o Hy - men. - men.

IV.

Canto

Come _ a - shore, come, _ mer-ry Mates, With _ your _ nim - ble

heeles and pates, Sum-mon eve - ry man his Knight, E - nough ____

ho - nour'd is this night. Now _ let your sea - borne

God - desse come, Quench these _ lights and make all dombe.

Some sleepe, oth-ers let __ her call, And so good night, good __

night to all, good night, good night, good night, good night to all.

The Names of the Maskers.[31]

1 The Duke of *Lennox.*

2 The Earle of *Pembrooke.*

3 The Earle of *Dorset.*

4 The Earle of *Salisburie.*

5 The Earle of *Mountgomerie.*

6 The Lord *Walden.*

7 The Lord *Scroope.*

8 The Lord *North.*

9 The Lord *Hayes.*

10 Sir *Thomas Howard.*

11 Sir *Henry Howard.*

12 Sir *Charles Howard.*

FINIS.

[31] Nine of the twelve masquers had danced in earlier productions by Campion: for Walden and Hay, see notes to *The Lord Hay's Masque;* for Dorset, Salisbury, Montgomery, North, and the three Howards, see notes to *The Caversham Entertainment* and *Lords' Masque.* Lodovic Stuart (1574–1624), second Duke of Lennox and later Duke of Richmond, had come to England with James I; he tilted in the *Barriers* of 1606, *Prince Henry's Barriers* of 1610, and danced in Jonson's *Haddington Masque.* William, Earl of Pembroke (1580–1630) is well known as Ben Jonson's patron, to whom both *Catiline* and the *Epigrams* were dedicated; he also danced in *The Haddington Masque.* Emanuel, Lord Scroope, later Earl of Sunderland, was Lord President of the King's Council in the North in 1618–19; he tilted at the *Challenge at Tilt* later in 1614.

TREATISES

OBSERVATIONS
in the Art of English Poesie.

By *Thomas Campion.*

Wherein it is demonstra-
tively prooved, and by example
confirmed, that the English toong
will receive eight severall kinds of num-
bers, proper to it selfe, which are all
in this booke set forth, and were
never before this time by any
man attempted.

1602

"These my late observations in English Poesy," as Campion
calls them, may have been written down some time before their
publication in 1602, perhaps, as G. B. Harrison proposes, as early
as 1591 ("Books and Readers, 1591-4," *The Library,* Fourth
Series, VIII [1927], 279-80). Whatever its date of composition,
the *Observations* forms the last and most persuasive of the arguments
for classical meters (based on time-value instead of accent) in
English. The movement, which paralleled and received some im-
petus from the efforts of Tolomei in Italy and Baïf in France,
began with the Humanist Ascham's plea for quantitative meters
and quotation of a few examples by himself and Thomas Watson
in both *Toxophilus* (1545) and *The Scholemaster* (1570). Its
great exemplar was Sir Philip Sidney who, encouraged by the rules
and arguments of Thomas Drant, produced many fine poems in a
variety of classical meters in his original *Arcadia* as well as a
persuasive argument for them as more easily set to music than
accentual rimes (see *The Poems of Sir Philip Sidney,* ed. William
A. Ringler, Jr. [Oxford, 1962], pp. 389-93). He also, apparently,
led both Edmund Spenser and Gabriel Harvey to try similar
experiments (in their *Correspondence* of 1579), and his example
led William Webbe to include a section on classical meters in
A Discourse of English Poetry (1586). Chief among the poems in
these meters—most of them in hexameters—are Richard Stany-
hurst's *The First Four Bookes of Virgil his Aeneis* (1582), Abraham
Fraunce's *Amyntas* (1587), his *Countesse of Pembrokes Emanuel*
(1591) and *Amyntas Dale* (1592), a few songs set by William
Byrd in *Psalms, Sonets, and Songs* (1588), Richard Barnfield's
Hellens Rape (1594), and the anonymous *First Booke of the
Preservation of King Henry VII* (1599); the last of them, several
elegies on Sidney in Francis Davison's *Poetical Rhapsody,* appeared
in the same year as Campion's treatise.

It is apparent, then, that the *Observations,* rooted in 16th-cen-
tury Humanism and arising directly from Sidney (whose experi-
ments Campion was imitating in 1591), was resurrecting an old
debate which had lain dormant since late in the 1530s. Campion
seems to have realized this fact (for he himself had bid farewell
to quantitative metrics the year before in the Preface to *A Booke
of Ayres*), but at the same time to have been motivated by the
desire to make a last attempt, and one more sensible than the
others. Therefore he immediately discards the hexameter and its
companion, the dactyl, as unsuitable to the English tongue, and

accepts the iambic base of the language. Therefore, too, he bases quantity on accent (as Sidney, Drant, and Webbe did not), so that his quantitative verse follows, in the main, the normal auditory patterns of English speech. His only departures from those patterns arise from his rule of position which, as G. R. Willcock is quick to observe ("Passing Pitefull Hexameters: A Study of Quantity and Accent in English Renaissance Verse," *MLR,* XXIX [1934], 15–16), often thwarts accent. Nevertheless, even here he is less extreme than many of his contemporaries, since he avoids the easy refuge (taken by Drant, Sidney, Spenser, and especially Stanyhurst) of tampering with orthography for quantity, of, for instance, merely doubling a consonant to produce a long syllable. Campion's examples are unusually easy to scan without wrenching, for he has helped the English reader by repeated or assonant words in corresponding positions of different lines, repeated use (in his trochaic meters) of the naturally trochaic adverbs ending in "ly," and other devices (see Kastendieck, *England's Musical Poet,* p. 87). Throughout his treatise he is careful to repudiate the romantic or retrospective classicism of his predecessors, and to insist on making classical virtues native to England by illustrative poems fitting to the English tongue, drawing on English subject matter, and using native English names. His main accomplishment, as he sees it, is that he has produced eight new and interesting meters for English poets to use.

Samuel Daniel answered Campion in *A Defence of Ryme* (ca. 1603), and literary history has unanimously awarded the palm to Daniel. His main point, aside from an eloquent defense of the English accentual tradition, is that Campion's new meters are really variations of the old iambic pentameter line, "apparelled in forraine Titles." He asserts, for example, that Campion's Elegaics in Chapter 7 are "no other then our old accustomed measure of five feet: if there be any difference, it must be made in the reading" (*A Defence of Ryme* in *Elizabethan Critical Essays,* ed. G. Gregory Smith, 2 vols. [Oxford, 1904], II, 377). On the other hand, Catherine Ing finds in the even-numbered lines of the Elegaic "Constant to none" "a kind of 'hinged' line of two phrases" (*Elizabethan Lyrics,* p. 102) with a falling trochaic effect like that which Ovid prescribed for this meter: *sex mihi surgat opus numeris, in quinque residat* ("in six measures let my work rise, and fall again in five": *Amores* I. i. 27). Many of Campion's classical experiments are, in fact, quite successful— notably "Rose-cheekt *Lawra,*" "Raving warre," "Constant to none," and "Follow, followe." And his insistent drive for metrical variety, coupled with his liberal use of assonance and other sound effects to shore up correct scansion, is responsible in no small measure for the unique sounds of *A Booke of Ayres* and its successors.

To the Right Noble and
worthily honourd, the Lord
*Buckhurst, Lord high Treasurer
of England.*[1]

In two things (right honorable) it is generally agreed that man
excels all other creatures, in reason and speech: and in them by
how much one man surpasseth an other, by so much the neerer he
aspires to a celestiall essence.

Poesy in all kind of speaking is the chiefe beginner, and main-
tayner of eloquence, not only helping the eare with the ac-
quaintance of sweet numbers,[2] but also raysing the minde to a
more high and lofty conceite.[3] For this end have I studyed to
induce a true forme of versefying into our language: for the vulgar
and unarteficiall custome of riming hath, I know, deter'd many
excellent wits from the exercise of English Poesy. The observations
which I have gathered for this purpose I humbly present to your
Lordship, as to the noblest judge of Poesy, and the most honorable
protector of all industrious learning; which if your Honour shall
vouchsafe to receive, who both in your publick and private Poemes
have so devinely crowned your fame, what man will dare to re-
pine? or not strive to imitate them? Wherefore with all humility I
subject my selfe and them to your gratious favour, beseeching you
in the noblenes of your mind to take in worth so simple a present,
which by some worke drawne from my more serious studies I will
hereafter endevour to excuse.

Your Lordships humbly devoted

THOMAS CAMPION.

[1] Thomas Sackville (1536–1608), created Baron Buckhurst and later
Earl of Dorset, author of the *Induction* to *A Mirrour for Magistrates*
(1563) and collaborator with Thomas Norton on *Gorboduc* (1561); his
private poems referred to below have not been recovered. Since *Gorboduc*
was the first regular English tragedy (and praised as such early by Sidney)
and in blank verse, Campion's appeal to its author would hold good on
at least two grounds: classicism and the cultivation of unrimed verse.

[2] metrical feet. [3] thought.

The Writer to his Booke.[4]

Whether thus hasts my little booke so fast?
To Paules Churchyard.[5] What? in those cels to stand,
With one leafe like a riders cloke put up
To catch a termer?[6] or lye mustie there
With rimes a terme set out, or two before?
Some will redeeme me. Fewe. Yes, reade me too.
Fewer. Nay love me. Now thou dot'st, I see.
Will not our English *Athens* arte defend?
Perhaps. Will lofty courtly wits not ayme
Still at perfection? If I graunt?[7] I flye.
Whether? To Pawles. Alas, poore Booke, I rue
Thy rash selfe-love; goe, spread thy pap'ry wings:
Thy lightnes can not helpe, or hurt my fame.

Observations in the Art
of English Poesy, by *Thomas Campion.*

The first Chapter, intreating of numbers in generall.

There is no writing too breefe, that without obscuritie comprehends the intent of the writer. These my late observations in English Poesy I have thus briefely gathered, that they might prove the lesse troublesome in perusing, and the more apt to be retayn'd in memorie. And I will first generally handle the nature of Numbers. Number is *discreta quantitas,*[8] so that when we speake simply of number, we intend only the dissever'd quantity; but when we speake of a Poeme written in number, we consider not only the distinct number of the sillables, but also their value, which is contained in the length or shortnes of their sound. As in Musick

[4] As Bullen observes in his edition, this dialogue poem is based on the opening lines of Persius' first satire. J. V. Cunningham has pointed out to me the close resemblance of Jonson's *Epigrammes* III, ll. 7–9, to these opening lines.

[5] the bookstall district of London.

[6] a man who comes up from the country to London for the legal term.

[7] i.e., say then that I grant that one point?

[8] "measured quantity"; see Scaliger, *Poetice* IV, 1 and 45 (noted by Smith, *Elizabethan Critical Essays,* II, 454).

we do not say a straine of so many notes, but so many sem'briefes (though sometimes there are no more notes then sem'briefes),[9] so in a verse the numeration of the sillables is not so much to be observed, as their waite and due proportion. In joyning of words to harmony there is nothing more offensive to the eare then to place a long sillable with a short note, or a short sillable with a long note, though in the last the vowell often beares it out. The world is made by Simmetry and proportion, and is in that respect compared to Musick, and Musick to Poetry: for *Terence* saith, speaking of Poets, *artem qui tractant musicam*,[10] confounding musick and Poesy together. What musick can there be where there is no proportion observed? Learning first flourished in *Greece,* from thence it was derived unto the *Romaines,* both diligent observers of the number and quantity of sillables, not in their verses only but likewise in their prose. Learning, after the declining of the *Romaine* Empire and the pollution of their language through the conquest of the *Barbarians,* lay most pitifully deformed till the time of *Erasmus, Rewcline,*[11] Sir *Thomas More,* and other learned men of that age, who brought the Latine toong againe to light, redeeming it with much labour out of the hands of the illiterate Monks and Friers: as a scoffing booke, entituled *Epistolae obscurorum virorum,*[12] may sufficiently testifie. In those lack-learning times, and in barbarized *Italy,* began that vulgar and easie kind of Poesie which is now in use throughout most parts of Christendome, which we abusively call Rime and Meeter, or *Rithmus* and *Metrum,* of which I will now discourse.

The second Chapter, declaring the unaptnesse of Rime in Poesie.

I am not ignorant that whosoever shall by way of reprehension examine the imperfections of Rime must encounter with many glorious enemies, and those very expert and ready at their weapon, that can, if neede be, extempore (as they say) rime a man to

[9] whole notes; a metrical foot was to equal a whole note in time value.

[10] "who labor in the art of music": *Phormio,* Prologue, l. 17.

[11] Johann Reuchlin (1455–1522), German humanist especially noted for his revival of Hebrew studies, cabalistic explorations (whence Campion may have derived some of his number symbolism in the masques), and his mockery of the friars.

[12] "Letters of Obscure Men," a series of satirical letters composed mainly by Ulrich von Hutten and published in two parts in 1515 and 1516; written in dog Latin, these letters were aimed chiefly at the barbarism, pedantry, and pomposity of mediaeval theologians and friars.

death.[13] Besides there is growne a kind of prescription in the use of Rime, to forestall the right of true numbers, as also the consent of many nations, against all which it may seeme a thing almost impossible and vaine to contend. All this and more can not yet deterre me from a lawful defence of perfection, or make me any whit the sooner adheare to that which is lame and unbeseeming. For custome, I alleage that ill uses are to be abolisht, and that things naturally imperfect can not be perfected by use. Old customes, if they be better, why should they not be recald, as the yet florishing custome of numerous poesy used among the *Romanes* and *Grecians?* But the unaptnes of our toongs and the difficultie of imitation dishartens us; againe, the facilitie and popularitie of Rime creates as many Poets as a hot sommer flies. But let me now examine the nature of that which we call Rime. By Rime is understoode that which ends in the like sound, so that verses in such maner composed yeeld but a continual repetition of that Rhetoricall figure which we tearme *similiter desinentia,* and that, being but *figura verbi,* ought (as *Tully* and all other Rhetoritians have judicially observ'd)[14] sparingly to be us'd, least it should offend the eare with tedious affectation. Such was that absurd following of the letter amongst our English so much of late affected, but now hist out of Paules Church-yard:[15] which foolish figurative repetition crept also into the Latine toong, as it is manifest in the booke of P[s] cald *proelia porcorum,* and another pamphlet all of F[s] which I have seene imprinted;[16] but I will leave these follies to their owne ruine, and returne to the matter intended. The eare is a rationall sence and a chiefe judge of proportion; but in our kind of riming what proportion is there kept, where there remaines such a confusd inequalitie of sillables?

[13] See Sidney, *The Defence of Poesie* (in *Works,* ed. A. Feuillerat [London, 1912–1926] III, 46): "I will not wish unto you . . . to be rimed to death as is said to be done in *Ireland.*"

[14] For "similar ending" of rime as a "figure of words" or verbal ornament to be sparingly used, see Cicero *De Oratore* III. 54 and Quintilian *Institutia Oratoria* IX. 3 (Smith's note); compare Sidney, *Defence of Poesie,* p. 42.

[15] Alliteration or "following the letter," so fashionable in the work of poets like Gascoigne in the 1570s, had been laughed off the bookstalls by Sidney; see *Defence of Poesie,* p. 42, and *Astrophel and Stella,* xv.

[16] *Pugna porcorum per P. Porcium poetam* [The Battle of the Pigs by P. Porcius, poet], a burlesque in which each word begins with *p,* was published by Joannes Leo Placentius in 1530; its illustrious ancestor (unfortunately serious) was Hucbald of St. Amand's *Ecloga de Calvis* (9th century), a poem praising baldness, written entirely in words beginning with *c.* The pamphlet all of *f*s I cannot identify.

Iambick and *Trochaick* feete, which are oppos'd by nature, are by all Rimers confounded; nay, oftentimes they place instead of an *Iambick* the foot *Pyrrychius,* consisting of two short sillables, curtalling their verse,[17] which they supply in reading with a ridiculous and unapt drawing of their speech. As for example:

> Was it my desteny, or dismall chaunce?

In this verse the two last sillables of the word *Desteny,* being both short, and standing for a whole foote in the verse, cause the line to fall out shorter then it ought by nature. The like impure errors have in time of rudenesse bene used in the Latine toong, as the *Carmina proverbialia* can witnesse, and many other such reverend bables.[18] But the noble *Grecians* and *Romaines,* whose skilfull monuments outlive barbarisme, tyed themselves to the strict observation of poeticall numbers, so abandoning the childish titillation of riming that it was imputed a great error to *Ovid* for setting forth this one riming verse.

> *Quot caelum stellas tot habet tua Roma puellas.*[19]

For the establishing of this argument, what better confirmation can be had then that of Sir *Thomas Moore* in his booke of Epigrams, where he makes two sundry Epitaphs upon the death of a singing-man at *Westminster,* the one in learned numbers and dislik't, the other in rude rime and highly extold: so that he concludes, *tales lactucas talia labra petunt,* like lips, like lettuce.[20] But there is yet another fault in Rime altogether intollerable, which is, that it inforceth a man oftentimes to abjure his matter and extend a short conceit beyond all bounds of arte: for in *Quatorzens*[21] me thinks the Poet handles his subject as tyrannically as *Procrustes*

[17] shortening the time value of the line: the line contains the requisite number of syllables, but its time value is thrown off by the substitution of a short syllable for a long.

[18] "Proverbial Poems," a set of riming Latin proverbs intended for young scholars (thus a "reverend" bauble or toy).

[19] "As many stars as has the sky, so many girls has your Rome": *Ars Amatoria* I. 59.

[20] See More's *Latin Epigrams* (ed. L. Bradner and C. A. Lynch [Chicago, 1953]) 141 and 142; the second of these is in rimed Leonine verses. Epigram 143 contains the comment Campion quotes and translates.

[21] the fourteen-line sonnet; Ben Jonson repeated the analogy between the sonnet and the bed of Procrustes to William Drummond in 1619 (see *Works,* ed. Herford and Simpson, I, 133–34); as Herford and Simpson note, the analogy was first attributed to Claudio Tolomei by Stefano Guazzo in his *Dialoghi Piacevole* (1587), p. 197.

the thiefe his prisoners, whom when he had taken, he used to cast
upon a bed, which if they were too short to fill, he would stretch
them longer, if too long, he would cut them shorter. Bring before
me now any the most selfe-lov'd Rimer, and let me see if without
blushing he be able to reade his lame halting rimes. Is there not a
curse of Nature laid upon such rude Poesie, when the Writer is
himself asham'd of it, and the hearers in contempt call it Riming
and Ballating? What Devine in his Sermon, or grave Counseller in
his Oration, will alleage the testimonie of a rime? But the devinity
of the *Romaines* and *Gretians* was all written in verse: and
Aristotle, Galene, and the bookes of all the excellent Philosophers
are full of the testimonies of the old Poets. By them was laid the
foundation of all humane wisedome, and from them the knowledge
of all antiquitie is derived. I will propound but one question, and
so conclude this point. If the *Italians, Frenchmen* and *Spanyards,*
that with commendation have written in Rime, were demaunded
whether they had rather the bookes they have publisht (if their
toong would bear it) should remaine as they are in Rime, or be
translated into the auncient numbers of the *Greekes* and *Ro-
maines,* would they not answere, into numbers? What honour were
it then for our English language to be the first that after so many
yeares of barbarisme could second the perfection of the industrious
Greekes and *Romaines?* which how it may be effected I will now
proceede to demonstrate.

The third Chapter: of our English numbers in generall.

There are but three feete, which generally distinguish the
Greeke and Latine verses, the *Dactil,* consisting of one long sil-
lable and two short, as $\bar{v}\breve{i}\breve{v}ere$; the *Trochy,* of one long and one
short, as $\bar{v}\breve{i}ta$; and the *Iambick* of one short and one long, as
$\breve{a}\bar{m}or$. The *Spondee* of two long, the *Tribrach* of three short, the
Anapaestick of two short and a long, are but as servants to the
first. Divers other feete I know are by the Grammarians cited, but
to little purpose. The *Heroical* verse that is distinguisht by the
Dactile hath bene oftentimes attempted in our English toong, but
with passing pitifull successe: and no wonder, seeing it is an at-
tempt altogether against the nature of our language. For both the
concurse of our monasillables make our verses unapt to slide,[22]

[22] i.e., to allow an even flow of alternating vowels and consonants, thus
avoiding the hiatus or "gaping" effect so disliked by rhetoricians since
Isocrates.

and also, if we examine our polysillables, we shall find few of them, by reason of their heavinesse, willing to serve in place of a *Dactile*. Thence it is, that the writers of English heroicks do so often repeate *Amyntas, Olympus, Avernus, Erinnis,* and such like borrowed words, to supply the defect of our hardly intreated *Dactile*. I could in this place set downe many ridiculous kinds of *Dactils* which they use, but that is not my purpose here to incite men to laughter. If we therefore reject the *Dactil* as unfit for our use (which of necessity we are enforst to do), there remayne only the *Iambick* foote, of which the *Iambick* verse is fram'd, and the *Trochee,* from which the *Trochaick* numbers have their originall. Let us now then examine the property of these two feete, and try if they consent with the nature of English sillables. And first for the *Iambicks,* they fall out so naturally in our toong, that, if we examine our owne writers, we shall find they unawares hit oftentimes upon the true *Iambick* numbers, but alwayes ayme at them as far as their eare without the guidance of arte can attain unto, as it shall hereafter more evidently appeare. The *Trochaick* foote, which is but an *Iambick* turn'd over and over, must of force in like manner accord in proportion with our British sillables, and so produce an English *Trochaicall* verse. Then, having these two principall kinds of verses, we may easily out of them derive other formes, as the Latines and Greekes before us have done: whereof I will make plaine demonstration, beginning at the *Iambick* verse.

The fourth Chapter, of the Iambick verse.

I have observed, and so may any one that is either practis'd in singing, or hath a naturall eare able to time a song, that the Latine verses of sixe feete, as the *Heroick* and *Iambick,* or of five feete, as the *Trochaick,* are in nature all of the same length of sound with our English verses of five feete; for either of them being tim'd with the hand, *quinque perficiunt tempora,*[23] they fill up the quantity (as it were) of five sem'briefs; as for example, if any man will prove to time these verses with his hand.

A pure *Iambick.*
Suis et ipsa Roma viribus ruit.

A licentiate *Iambick.*
Ducunt volentes fata, nolentes trahunt.

[23] The phrase is translated in the clause following.

An *Heroick* verse.
Tytere, tu patulae recubans sub tegmine fagi.

A *Trochaick* verse.
Nox est perpetua una dormienda.[24]

English *Iambicks* pure.
The more secure, the more the stroke we feele
Of unprevented harms; so gloomy stormes
Appeare the sterner if the day be cleere.

Th' English *Iambick* licentiate
Harke how these winds do murmur at thy flight.

The English *Trochee.*
Still where Envy leaves, remorse doth enter.

The cause why these verses differing in feete yeeld the same
length of sound, is by reason of some rests which either the
necessity of the numbers or the heavines of the sillables do beget.
For we find in musick that oftentimes the straines of a song cannot
be reduct to true number without some rests prefixt in the beginning
and middle, as also at the close if need requires. Besides, our English
monasillables enforce many breathings which no doubt greatly
lengthen a verse, so that it is no wonder if for these reasons our
English verses of five feete hold pace with the *Latines* of sixe. The
pure *Iambick* in English needes small demonstration, because it
consists simply of *Iambick* feete; but our *Iambick licentiate* offers
itselfe to a farther consideration; for in the third and fift place we
must of force hold the *Iambick* foote, in the first, second, and
fourth place we may use a *Spondee* or *Iambick* and sometime a
Tribrack or *Dactile,* but rarely an *Anapestick* foote, and that in
the second or fourth place. But why an *Iambick* in the third place?
I answere, that the forepart of the verse may the gentlier slide into
his *Dimeter;* as, for example sake, devide this verse: *Harke how
these winds do murmure at thy flight. Harke how these winds,*
there the voice naturally affects a rest; then *murmur at thy flight,*
that is of itselfe a perfect number, as I will declare in the next
Chapter; and therefore the other odde sillable betweene them ought
to be short, least the verse should hang too much betweene the

[24] "and Rome through her own strength is falling" (Horace *Epode* xvi,
l. 2), "the fates lead the willing, and drag the unwilling" (Seneca *Epistle*
CVII. 11), "you, Tityrus, lying in the shade of the spreading beech-tree"
(Virgil *Eclogue* I, l. 1), "we must sleep one perpetual night" (Catullus
Carmina V, l. 6). For Campion's version of Catullus V see *A Booke
of Ayres,* Part I, i, above.

naturall pause of the verse and the *Dimeter* following; the which *Dimeter,* though it be naturally *Trochaical,* yet it seemes to have his originall out of the *Iambick* verse. But the better to confirme and expresse these rules, I will set downe a short Poeme in *Licentiate Iambicks,* which may give more light to them that shall hereafter imitate these numbers.

> Goe, numbers, boldly passe, stay not for ayde
> Of shifting rime, that easie flatterer
> Whose witchcraft can the ruder eares beguile.
> Let your smooth feete, enur'd to purer arte,
> True measures tread. What if your pace be slow,
> And hops not like the Grecian elegies?
> It is yet gracefull, and well fits the state
> Of words ill-breathed, and not shap't to runne.
> Goe then, but slowly, till your steps be firme;
> Tell them that pitty or perversely skorne
> Poore English Poesie as the slave to rime,
> You are those loftie numbers that revive
> Triumphs of Princes, and sterne tragedies:
> And learne henceforth t' attend those happy sprights
> Whose bounding fury height and waight affects.
> Assist their labour, and sit close to them,
> Never to part away till for desert
> Their browes with great *Apollos* bayes are hid.
> He first taught number, and true harmonye;
> Nor is the lawrell his for rime bequeath'd.
> Call him with numerous accents paisd[25] by arte,
> He'le turne his glory from the sunny clymes,
> The North-bred wits alone to patronise.
> Let France their *Bartas,* Italy *Tasso* prayse;[26]
> *Phaebus* shuns none, but in their flight from him.

Though, as I said before, the naturall breathing place of our English *Iambick* verse is in the last sillable of the second foote, as our *Trochy* after the manner of the Latine *Heroick* and *Iambick* rests naturally in the first of the third foote, yet no man is tyed altogether to observe this rule, but he may alter it, after the judgment of his eare, which Poets, Orators, and Musitions of all men ought to have most excellent. Againe, though I said peremtorily before that the third and fift place of our licentiate *Iambick* must

[25] weighed.
[26] Guillaume Salluste du Bartas and Torquato Tasso, famous 16th-century epic poets.

always hold an *Iambick* foote, yet I will shew you example in both places where a *Tribrack* may be very formally[27] taken, and first in the third place,

Some trade in *Barbary,* some in *Turky* trade.

An other example.

Men that do fall to misery, quickly fall.

If you doubt whether the first of *misery* be naturally short or no, you may judge it by the easie sliding of these two verses following:

The first.

Whome misery can not alter, time devours.

The second.

What more unhappy life, what misery more?

Example of the *Tribrack* in the fift place, as you may perceive in the last foote of the fourth verse:

Some from the starry throne his fame derives,
Some from the mynes beneath, from trees or herbs:
Each hath his glory, each his sundry gift,
Renown'd in ev'ry art there lives not any.

To proceede farther, I see no reason why the English *Iambick* in his first place may not as well borrow a foote of the *Trochy,* as our *Trochy* or the Latine *Hendicasillable* may in the like case make bold with the *Iambick;* but it must be done ever with this caveat, which is, that a *Sponde, Dactile,* or *Tribrack* do supply the next place: for an *Iambick* beginning with a single short sillable, and the other ending before with the like, would too much drinke up the verse if they came immediately together.

The example of the *Sponde* after the *Trochy.*

As the faire sonne the lightsome heav'n adorns.

The example of the *Dactil.*

Noble, ingenious, and discreetly wise.

The example of the *Tribrack.*

Beawty to jelosie brings joy, sorrow, feare.

[27] according to the rules of art.

Though I have set downe these second licenses as good and ayreable enough,[28] yet for the most part my first rules are generall.

These are those numbers which Nature in our English destinates to the Tragick and Heroick Poeme: for the subject of them both being all one, I see no impediment why one verse may not serve for them both, as it appeares more plainely in the old comparison of the two Greeke writers, when they say, *Homerus est Sophocles heroicus,* and againe, *Sophocles est Homerus tragicus,*[29] intimating that both *Sophocles* and *Homer* are the same in height and subject, and differ onely in the kinde of their numbers.

The *Iambick* verse in like manner being yet made a little more licentiate,[30] that it may thereby the neerer imitate our common talke, will excellently serve for Comedies; and then may we use a *Sponde* in the fift place, and in the third place any foote except a *Trochy,* which never enters into our *Iambick* verse but in the first place, and then with his caveat of the other feete which must of necessitie follow.

The fifth Chapter, of the Iambick Dimeter, or English march.

The *Dimeter* (so called in the former Chapter) I intend next of all to handle, because it seems to be a part of the *Iambick,* which is our most naturall and auncient English verse. We may terme this our English march, because the verse answers our warlick forme of march in similitude of number. But call it what you please, for I will not wrangle about names, only intending to set down the nature of it and true structure. It consists of two feete and one odde sillable. The first foote may be made either a *Trochy,* or a *Spondee,* or an *Iambick,* at the pleasure of the composer, though most naturally that place affects[31] a *Trochy* or *Spondee;* yet, by the example of *Catullus* in his *Hendicasillables,* I adde in the first place sometimes an *Iambick* foote. In the second place we must ever insert a *Trochy* or *Tribrack,* and so leave the last sillable (as in the end of a verse it is alwaies held) common.[32] Of this kinde I will subscribe three examples, the first being a peece of a *Chorus* in a Tragedy.

[28] singable enough.
[29] "Homer is the epic Sophocles" and "Sophocles is the tragic Homer."
[30] licensed, allowed as free from rules.
[31] desires.   [32] either long or short.

Raving warre, begot
In the thirstye sands
Of the *Lybian* Iles,
Wasts our emptye fields;[33]
What the greedye rage
Of fell wintrye stormes
Could not turne to spoile,
Fierce *Bellona* now
Hath laid desolate,
Voyd of fruit, or hope.
Th' eger thriftye hinde,
Whose rude toyle reviv'd
Our skie-blasted earth,
Himselfe is but earth,
Left a skorne to fate
Through seditious armes:
And that soile, alive
Which he duly nurst,
Which him duly fed,
Dead his body feeds:
Yet not all the glebe[34]
His tuffe hands manur'd
Now one turfe affords
His poore funerall.
Thus still needy lives,
Thus still needy dyes
Th' unknowne multitude.

An example *Lyrical*.

Greatest in thy wars,
Greater in thy peace,
Dread *Elizabeth;*
Our muse only Truth,
Figments cannot use,
Thy ritch name to deck
That it selfe adornes:
But should now this age
Let all poesye fayne,
Fayning poesye could
Nothing faine at all
Worthy halfe thy fame.

[33] See *Ad Thamesin,* ll. 102 ff., below.   [34] soil.

An example *Epigrammaticall.*

Kind in every kinde,
This, deare Ned, resolve,
Never of thy prayse
Be too prodigall;
He that prayseth all
Can praise truly none.

The sixt Chapter, of the English Trochaick verse.

Next in course to be intreated of is the English *Trochaick,* being a verse simple, and of it selfe depending.[35] It consists, as the Latine *Trochaick,* of five feete, the first whereof may be a *Trochy,* a *Spondee,* or an *Iambick,* the other foure of necessity all *Trochyes;* still holding this rule authenticall, that the last sillable of a verse is alwayes common.[36] The spirit of this verse most of all delights in *Epigrams,* but it may be diversly used, as shall hereafter be declared. I have written divers light Poems in this kinde, which for the better satisfaction of the reader I thought convenient here in way of example to publish. In which, though sometimes under a knowne name I have shadowed a fain'd conceit, yet it is done without reference or offence to any person, and only to make the stile appeare the more English.

The first *Epigramme.*

Lockly spits apace, the rhewme he cals it,
But no drop (though often urgd) he straineth
From his thirstie jawes; yet all the morning
And all day he spits, in ev'ry corner;
At his meales he spits, at ev'ry meeting;
At the barre he spits before the Fathers;
In the Court he spits before the Graces;
In the Church he spits, thus all prophaning
With that rude disease, that empty spitting:
Yet no cost he spares, he sees the Doctors,
Keepes a strickt diet, precisely useth
Drinks and bathes drying, yet all prevailes not.
'Tis not *China (Lockly), Salsa Guacum,*

[35] i.e., composed of only one kind of line (simple, as against compound), and therefore self-contained.
[36] either long or short.

Nor dry *Sassafras* can helpe, or ease thee;[37]
'Tis no humor hurts, it is thy humor.[38]

The second *Epigramme*.

Cease, fond wretch, to love, so oft deluded,
Still made ritch with hopes, still unrelieved.
Now fly her delaies; she that debateth
Feeles not true desire; he that, deferred,
Others times attends, his owne betrayeth:
Learne t'affect[39] thy selfe, thy cheekes deformed
With pale care revive by timely pleasure,
Or with skarlet heate them, or by paintings
Make thee lovely; for such arte she useth
Whome in vayne so long thy folly loved.

The third *Epigramme*.[40]

Kate can fancy only berdles husbands,
Thats the cause she shakes off ev'ry suter,
Thats the cause she lives so stale a virgin,
For, before her heart can heate her answer,
Her smooth youths she finds all hugely berded.

The fourth *Epigramme*.

All in sattin *Oteny* will be suted,
Beaten sattin (as by chaunce he cals it);[41]
Oteny sure will have the bastinado.

The fift *Epigramme*.

Tosts as snakes or as the mortall *Henbane*
Hunks detests when huffcap ale[42] he tipples,
Yet the bread he graunts the fumes abateth:
Therefore apt in ale, true, and he graunts it;
But it drinks up ale, that *Hunks* detesteth.

[37] China or cinchona is the modern quinine, *salsa guacum* a salt made from the resin of the guaiac tree; these, along with sassafras, dieting, and mercury to induce spitting, were common cures for syphilis (not, as Lockly pretends, for throat congestion).

[38] i.e., the cause is none of your bodily fluids (humors), but only your insistence (humor) on wenching.

[39] love.

[40] Compare the Latin poem *"In Laurentiam"* in *Epigrammatum Liber* I, 56, below.

[41] "beaten sattin" was heavily embroidered satin (with a pun on "beaten" which comes out in "bastinado").

[42] strong ale.

The sixt *Epigramme.*

What though *Harry* braggs, let him be noble;
Noble *Harry* hath not halfe a noble.[43]

The seaventh *Epigramme.*

Phoebe all the rights *Elisa* claymeth,
Mighty rivall, in this only diff'ring
That shees only true, thou only fayned.[44]

The eight *Epigramme.*[45]

Barnzy stiffly vowes that hees no Cuckold,
Yet the vulgar ev'rywhere salutes him
With strange signes of hornes, from ev'ry corner;
Wheresoere he commes, a sundry Cucco
Still frequents his eares; yet hees no Cuccold.
But this *Barnzy* knowes that his *Matilda,*
Skorning him, with *Harvy* playes the wanton.
Knowes it? nay desires it, and by prayers
Dayly begs of heav'n, that it for ever
May stand firme for him; yet hees no Cuccold.
And tis true, for *Harvy* keeps *Matilda,*
Fosters *Barnzy,* and relieves his houshold,
Buyes the Cradle, and begets the children,
Payes the Nurces, ev'ry charge defraying,
And thus truly playes *Matildas* husband:
So that *Barnzy* now becomes a cypher,
And himselfe th' adultrer of *Matilda.*
Mock not him with hornes, the case is alterd;
Harvy beares the wrong, he proves the Cuccold.

The ninth *Epigramme.*

Buffe loves fat vians, fat ale, fat all things,
Keepes fat whores, fat offices, yet all men
Him fat only wish to feast the gallous.

[43] a gold coin worth about ten shillings.
[44] See "Greatest in thy wars," p. 302, above.
[45] This epigram may allude to Barnabe Barnes and Gabriel Harvey;
Campion mocked the former in *Epigrammatum Liber* I, 17, *"In Barnum";*
see also Epigram 143, *"In Crispinum,"* of the same book, below.

The tenth *Epigramme*.

Smith, by sute divorst, the knowne adultres
Freshly weds againe; what ayles the mad-cap
By this fury? euen so theeves by frailty
Of their hemp reserv'd,[46] againe the dismall
Tree embrace, againe the fatall halter.

The eleventh *Epigramme*.

His late losse the Wiveless *Higs* in order
Ev'rywere bewailes to friends, to strangers;
Tels them how by night a yongster armed
Saught his Wife (as hand in hand he held her)
With drawne sword to force; she cryed; he mainely
Roring ran for ayde, but (ah) returning
Fled was with the prize the beawty-forcer,
Whome in vaine he seeks, he threats, he followes.
Chang'd is *Hellen, Hellen* hugs the stranger,
Safe as *Paris* in the Greeke triumphing.
Therewith his reports to teares he turneth,
Peirst through with the lovely Dames remembrance;
Straight he sighes, he raves, his haire he teareth,
Forcing pitty still by fresh lamenting.
Cease, unworthy, worthy of thy fortunes,
Thou that couldst so faire a prize deliver,
For feare unregarded, undefended,
Hadst no heart I thinke, I know no liver.[47]

The twelfth *Epigramme*.

Why droopst thou, *Trefeild?* Will *Hurst* the Banker
Make dice of thy bones? By heav'n he can not.
Can not? whats the reason? Ile declare it:
Th' ar all growne so pockie, and so rotten.

The seaventh Chapter, of the English Elegeick *verse*.

The *Elegeick* verses challenge[48] the next place, as being of
all compound[49] verses the simplest. They are deriv'd out of our
owne naturall numbers as neere the imitation of the *Greekes* and

[46] i.e., saved from hanging because the rope broke.
[47] courage, whose seat was supposed to be the liver.
[48] claim.   [49] made of different kinds of lines.

Latines as our heavy sillables will permit. The first verse is a meere licentiate *Iambick;* the second is fram'd of two united *Dimeters.* In the first *Dimeter* we are tyed to make the first foote either a *Trochy* or a *Spondee,* the second a *Trochy,* and the odde sillable of it alwaies long. The second *Dimeter* consists of two *Trochyes* (because it requires more swiftnes then the first) and an odde sillable, which, being last, is ever common. I will give you example both of *Elegye* and *Epigramme,* in this kinde.

An *Elegye.*

Constant to none, but ever false to me,
    Traiter still to love through thy faint desires,
Not hope of pittie now nor vaine redresse
    Turns my griefs to teares, and renu'd laments.
Too well thy empty vowes, and hollow thoughts
    Witnes both thy wrongs, and remorseles hart.
Rue not my sorrow, but blush at my name;
    Let thy bloudy cheeks guilty thoughts betray.
My flames did truly burne, thine made a shew,
    As fires painted are which no heate retayne,
Or as the glossy *Pirop*[50] faines to blaze,
    But, toucht, cold appeares, and an earthy stone.
True cullours deck thy cheeks, false foiles thy brest,
    Frailer then thy light beawty is thy minde.
None canst thou long refuse, nor long affect,
    But turn'st feare with hopes, sorrow with delight,
Delaying, and deluding ev'ry way
    Those whose eyes are once with thy beawty chain'd.
Thrice happy man that entring first thy love
    Can so guide the straight raynes of his desires,
That both he can regard thee, and refraine:
    If grac't, firme he stands, if not, easely falls.

Example of *Epigrams,* in *Elegeick* verse.

The first *Epigramme.*

Arthure brooks only those that brooke not him,
    Those he most regards, and devoutly serves:
But them that grace him his great brav'ry skornes,

---

[50] red bronze; see Ovid *Metamorphoses* II. 2: *clara micante auro flammasque imitante pyropo* [bright with glittering gold and red bronze that simulates flames].

Counting kindnesse all duty, not desert:
Arthure wants forty pounds, tyres ev'ry friend,
But finds none that holds twenty due for him.

The second *Epigramme*.[51]

If fancy can not erre which vertue guides,
In thee, *Laura,* then fancy can not erre.

The third *Epigramme*.

Drue feasts no Puritans; the churles, he saith,
Thanke no men, but eate, praise God, and depart.

The fourth *Epigramme*.[52]

A wiseman wary lives, yet most secure,
Sorrowes move not him greatly, nor delights.
Fortune and death he skorning, only makes
Th'earth his sober Inne, but still heav'n his home.

The fift *Epigramme*.

Thou telst me, *Barnzy, Dawson* hath a wife:
Thine he hath, I graunt; *Dawson* hath a wife.

The sixt *Epigramme*.

Drue gives thee money, yet thou thankst not him,
But thankst God for him, like a godly man.
Suppose, rude Puritan, thou begst of him,
And he saith God help, who's the godly man?

The seaventh *Epigramme*.

All wonders *Barnzy* speakes, all grosely faind:
Speake some wonder once, *Barnzy,* speake the truth.

The eight *Epigramme*.

None then should through thy beawty, *Lawra,* pine,
Might sweet words alone ease a love-sick heart:
But your sweet words alone, that quit so well
Hope of friendly deeds, kill the love-sick heart.

---

[51] This epigram can be read two ways: "if amorous fancy, guided by virtue, can never err, your fancy will never err, Laura"; or "if amorous fancy can never err when guided by the virtue of the beloved, no such fancy will ever come *your* way, Laura."

[52] Compare "The man of life upright" in *A Booke of Ayres,* Part I, xviii, above.

The ninth *Epigramme*.[53]

At all thou frankly throwst, while, *Frank,* thy wife
Bars not *Luke* the mayn; *Oteny,* barre the bye.

The eight Chapter, of Ditties *and* Odes.

To descend orderly from the more simple numbers to them that
are more compounded, it is now time to handle such verses as
are fit for *Ditties* or *Odes,* which we may call *Lyricall,* because
they are apt to be soong to an instrument, if they were adorn'd
with convenient notes. Of that kind I will demonstrate three in this
Chapter, and in the first we will proceede after the manner of the
Saphick, which is a *Trochaicall* verse as well as the *Hendicasil-
lable* in Latine. The first three verses therefore in our English
Saphick are meerely those *Trochaicks* which I handled in the
sixt Chapter, excepting only that the first foote of either of them
must ever of necessity be a *Spondee,* to make the number more
grave. The fourth and last closing verse is compounded of three
Trochyes together, to give a more smooth farewell, as you may
easily observe in this Poeme made upon a Triumph at *Whitehall,*
whose glory was dasht with an unwelcome showre, hindring the
people from the desired sight of her Majestie.[54]

The English *Sapphick.*

Faiths pure shield, the Christian *Diana,*
Englands glory crownd with all devinenesse,
Live long with triumphs to blesse thy people
    At thy sight triumphing.
Loe, they sound; the Knights in order armed
Entring threat the list, adrest to combat
For their courtly loves; he, hees the wonder
    Whome *Eliza* graceth.

[53] The epigram uses gaming terms in *double entendre.* "Main" and
"bye" refer to the main and byplay (or side bets) in dice games; to "bar
the dice" was to declare the throw void. Compare Drayton, "As love
and I," *Idea,* 59, l. 11.

[54] The incident referred to is probably one of the Accession Day Tilts
held at the Tiltyard at Whitehall yearly during Elizabeth's reign on 17 No-
vember. Although there is no extant record of a Tilt dispersed by rain, the
Tilt for 1599 is listed for 19 November only, perhaps because such an
incident forced postponement (see E. K. Chambers, *The Elizabethan Stage,*
4 vols. [Oxford, 1923], IV, 112). The "vulgar heaps" were the commoners
admitted to the stands for twelvepence.

Their plum'd pomp the vulgar heaps detaineth,
And rough steeds; let us the still devices
Close observe, the speeches and the musicks
   Peacefull arms adorning.
But whence showres so fast this angry tempest,
Clowding dimme the place? Behold, *Eliza*
This day shines not here; this heard, the launces
   And thick heads do vanish.

The second kinde consists of *Dimeter*, whose first foote may either be a *Sponde* or a *Trochy*. The two verses following are both of them *Trochaical*, and consist of foure feete, the first of either of them being a *Spondee* or *Trochy,* the other three only *Trochyes.* The fourth and last verse is made of two *Trochyes.* The number is voluble, and fit to expresse any amorous conceit.

The Example.

 Rose-cheekt *Lawra,* come,
Sing thou smoothly with thy beawties
Silent musick, either other
   Sweetely gracing.
 Lovely formes do flowe
From concent devinely framed;
Heav'n is musick, and thy beawties
   Birth is heavenly.
 These dull notes we sing
Discords neede for helps to grace them;
Only beawty purely loving
   Knowes no discord:
 But still mooves delight,
Like cleare springs renu'd by flowing,
Ever perfect, ever in them-
   selves eternall.

The third kind begins as the second kind ended, with a verse consisting of two *Trochy* feete, and then as the second kind had in the middle two *Trochaick* verses of foure feete, so this hath three of the same nature, and ends in a *Dimeter* as the second began. The *Dimeter* may allow in the first place a *Trochy* or a *Spondee,* but no *Iambick.*

The Example.

Just beguiler,
Kindest love, yet only chastest,
Royall in thy smooth denyals,
Frowning or demurely smiling,
Still my pure delight.

Let me view thee
With thoughts and with eyes affected,
And if then the flames do murmur,
Quench them with thy vertue, charme them
With thy stormy browes.

Heav'n so cheerefull
Laughs not ever, hory winter
Knowes his season, even the freshest
Sommer mornes from angry thunder
Jet[55] not still secure.

The ninth Chapter, of the Anacreontick *Verse.*

If any shall demaund the reason why this number, being in it selfe simple, is plac't after so many compounded numbers, I answere, because I hold it a number too licentiate for a higher place, and in respect of the rest imperfect; yet is it passing gracefull in our English toong, and will excellently fit the subject of a *Madrigall*, or any other lofty or tragicall matter. It consists of two feete: the first may be either a *Sponde* or *Trochy*, the other must ever represent the nature of a *Trochy*, as for example:[56]

Follow, followe,
Though with mischiefe
Arm'd, like whirlewind,
Now she flyes thee;
Time can conquer
Loves unkindnes;
Love can alter
Times disgraces;
Till death faint not

[55] strut.
[56] Catherine Ing (*Elizabethan Lyrics*, p. 105) observes that "echoes at the ends of lines almost supply the place of rime" in this poem.

Then, but followe.
Could I catch that
Nimble trayter,
Skornefull *Lawra,*
Swift foote *Lawra,*
Soone then would I
Seeke avengement.[57]
Whats th' avengement?
Even submissely
Prostrate then to
Beg for mercye.

Thus have I briefely described eight several kinds of English num-
bers simple or compound. The first was our *Iambick* pure and
licentiate. The second, that which I call our *Dimeter,* being de-
rived either from the end of our *Iambick,* or from the beginning of
our *Trochaick.* The third which I delivered was our English
Trochaick verse. The fourth our English *Elegeick.* The fift, sixt,
and seaventh were our English *Sapphick* and two other *Lyricall*
numbers, the one beginning with that verse which I call our
Dimeter, the other ending with the same. The eight and last was
a kind of *Anacreontick* verse, handled in this Chapter. These
numbers which by my long observation I have found agreeable
with the nature of our sillables, I have set forth for the benefit of
our language, which I presume the learned will not only imitate,
but also polish and amplifie with their owne inventions. Some eares
accustomed altogether to the fatnes of rime may perhaps except
against the cadences of these numbers; but let any man judicially
examine them, and he shall finde they close of themselves so
perfectly that the help of rime were not only in them superfluous,
but also absurd. Moreover, that they agree with the nature of our
English it is manifest, because they entertaine so willingly our owne
British names, which the writers in English Heroicks could never
aspire unto, and even our Rimers themselves have rather delighted
in borrowed names then in their owne, though much more apt
and necessary. But it is now time that I proceede to the censure[58]
of our sillables, and that I set such lawes upon them as by imita-
tion, reason, or experience I can confirme. Yet before I enter into
that discourse, I will briefely recite and dispose in order all such
feete as are necessary for composition of the verses before de-
scribed. They are six in number, three whereof consist of two
sillables, and as many of three.

[57] vengeance.   [58] examination.

Feete of two sillables.

Iambick: revénge.
Trochaick: as   Beáwtie.
Sponde: constant

Feete of three sillables.

Tribrack: miserie.
Anapestick: as   miseries.
Dactile: Destenie.

The tenth Chapter, of the quantity of English sillables.

The *Greekes* in the quantity of their sillables were farre more licentious then the *Latines,* as *Martiall* in his Epigramme of *Earinon* witnesseth, saying, *Musas qui colimus severiores.*[59] But the English may very well challenge much more licence then either of them, by reason it stands chiefely upon monasillables, which, in expressing with the voyce, are of a heavy cariage, and for that cause the *Dactil, Trybrack,* and *Anapestick* are not greatly mist in our verses. But above all the accent of our words is diligently to be observ'd, for chiefely by the accent in any language the true value of the sillables is to be measured. Neither can I remember any impediment except position that can alter the accent of any sillable in our English verse. For though we accent the second of *Trumpington* short, yet is it naturally long, and so of necessity must be held of every composer.[60] Wherefore the first rule that is to be observed is the nature of the accent, which we must ever follow.

The next rule is position, which makes every sillable long, whether the position happens in one or in two words, according to the manner of the *Latines,* wherein is to be noted that *h* is no letter.

[59] "We who cultivate severer Muses," Martial *Epigrams* IX. xi. 17.
[60] To this treatment of "Trumpington" compare Gabriel Harvey on the analogous "carpenter": "You shall never have my subscription or consent (though you should charge me wyth the authoritie of five hundreth Maister Drants) to make your Carpénter our Carpénter, an inch longer, or bigger, than God and his English people have made him" (*Variorum Spenser,* IX, *Prose Works,* ed. R. Gottfried [London, 1949], 473-74).

Position is when a vowell comes before two consonants, either in one or two words. In one, as in *best*, *e* before *st* makes the word *best* long by position. In two words, as in *setled love*, *e* before *d* in the last sillable of the first and *l* in the beginning of the second makes *led* in *setlēd* long by position.

A vowell before a vowell is alwaies short, as *flĭīng*, *dĭīng*, *gŏīng*, unlesse the accent alter it, as in *dĕnĭing*.

The diphthong in the midst of a word is alwaies long, as *plāiing*, *decēiving*.

The *Synalaephas* or *Elisions* in our toong are either necessary to avoid the hollownes and gaping in our verse, as *to* and *the*, *t'inchaunt*, *th'inchaunter*, or may be usd at pleasure, as for *let us* to say *let's*; for *we will*, *wee'l*; for *every*, *ev'ry*; for *they are*, *th'ar*; for *he is*, *hee's*; for *admired*, *admir'd*; and such like.

Also, because our English Orthography (as the French) differs from our common pronunciation, we must esteeme our sillables as we speake, not as we write,[61] for the sound of them in a verse is to be valued, and not their letters, as for *follow* we pronounce *follo*; for *perfect*, *perfet*; for *little*, *littel*; for *love-sick*, *love-sik*; for *honour*, *honor*; for *money*, *mony*; for *dangerous*, *dangerus*; for *raunsome*, *raunsum*; for *though*, *tho*; and their like.

Derivatives hold the quantities of their primatives, as *dĕvōut*, *dĕvoutĕlĭe*; *prŏphāne*, *prŏphānelĭe*; and so do the compositives, as *dĕsērv'd*, *undĕsērv'd*.

In words of two sillables, if the last have a full and rising accent that sticks long upon the voyce, the first sillable is always short, unlesse position, or the diphthong, doth make it long, as *dĕsīre*, *prĕserve*, *dĕfine*, *prŏphāne*, *rĕgard*, *mănūre*, and such like.

If the like dissillables at the beginning have double consonants of the same kind, we may use the first sillable as common,[62] but more naturally short, because in their pronunciation we touch but one of those double letters, as *ătēnd*, *ăpēare*, *ŏpōse*. The like we may say when silent and melting consonants meete together, as *ădrēst*, *rĕdrēst*, *ŏprēst*, *rĕprēst*, *rĕtriv'd*, and such like.

Words of two sillables that in their last sillable mayntayne a flat

---

[61] Baïf was moved by this fact to compose a phonetic alphabet to aid himself in composing *vers mesuré*.

[62] either long or short.

or falling accent,[63] ought to hold their first sillable long, as *rigor, glorie, spirit, furie, labour,* and the like; *any, many, prety, holy,* and their like are excepted.

One observation which leades me to judge of the difference of these dissillables whereof I last spake, I take from the originall monasillable; which if it be grave, as *shade,* I hold that the first of *shadie* must be long; so *true, trulie; have, having; tire, tiring.*

Words of three sillables for the most part are derived from words of two sillables, and from them take the quantity of their first sillable, as *florish, florishing* long; *holie, holines* short; but *mi* in *miser* being long hinders not the first of *misery* to be short, because the sound of the *i* is a little altred.

De, di, and *pro* in trisillables (the second being short) are long, as *desolate, diligent, prodigall.*

Re is ever short, as *remedie, reference, redolent, reverend.* Likewise the first of these trisillables is short, as the first of *benefit, generall, hideous, memorie, numerous, penetrate, seperat, timerous, variant, various;* and so may we esteeme of all that yeeld the like quicknes of sound.

In words of three sillables the quantity of the middle sillable is lightly taken from the last sillable of the originall dissillable, as the last of *devine,* ending in a grave or long accent, makes the second of *devining* also long; so *espie, espiing; denie, deniing;* contrarywise it falles out if the last of the dissillable beares a flat or falling accent, as *glorie, gloriing; envie, enviing;* and so forth.

Words of more sillables are eyther borrowed and hold their owne nature, or are likewise deriv'd and so follow the quantity of their primatives, or are knowne by their proper accents, or may be easily censured by a judiciall eare.

All words of two or more sillables ending with a falling accent in *y* or *ye,* as *fairelie, demurelie, beawtie, pittie,* or in *ue,* as

---

[63] Campion is writing of the pronunciation of the individual word rather than scansion, and he sees the accent of the individual syllable as a matter of pitch reinforcing stress. Though his terminology is sometimes confusing, it appears that a syllable is either "grave" or stressed, "flat" or unstressed; either "rising" or high in pitch, or "falling" or low in pitch.

vertue, rescue, or in ow, as follow, hollow, or in e, as parle,
Daphne, or in a, as Manna, are naturally short in their last sil-
lables; neither let any man cavill at this licentiate abbreviating of
sillables, contrary to the custome of the *Latines*, which made all
their last sillables that ended in u long, but let him consider that
our verse of five feete, and for the most part but of ten sillables,
must equall theirs of sixe feete and of many sillables, and there-
fore may with sufficient reason adventure upon this allowance. Be-
sides, every man may observe what an infinite number of sillables
both among the *Greekes* and *Romaines* are held as common. But
words of two sillables ending with a rising accent in y or ye, as
denye, descrye, or in *ue*, as *ensue*, or in *ee*, as *foresee*, or in *oe*, as
forgoe, are long in their last sillables, unlesse a vowell begins the
next word.

All monasillables that end in a grave accent are ever long, as
wrath, hath, these, those, tooth, sooth, through, day, play, feate,
speede, strife, flow, grow, shew.

The like rule is to be observed in the last of dissillables bearing
a grave rising sound, as *devine, delaie, retire, refuse, manure*, or
a grave falling sound, as *fortune, pleasure, rampire*.

All such as have a double consonant lengthning them, as warre,
barre, starre, furre, murre, appeare to me rather long then any way
short.

There are of these kinds other, but of a lighter sound, that, if
the word following do begin with a vowell, are short, as *doth,
though, thou, now, they, two, too, flye, dye, true, due, see, are, far,
you, thee*, and the like.

These monasillables are alwayes short, as a, the, thi, she, we, be,
he, no, to, go, so, do, and the like.

But if i or y are joyn'd at the beginning of a word with any
vowell, it is not then held as a vowell, but as a consonant, as
jelosy, jewce, jade, joy, Judas, ye, yet, yel, youth, yoke. The like
is to be observ'd in w, as *winde, wide, wood*; and in all words that
begin with va, ve, vi, vo, or vu, as *vacant, vew, vine, voide*, and
vulture.[64]

---

[64] The rules in this paragraph were necessitated by the practice in Renais-
sance orthography of using i and j, u and v interchangeably to denote
vowels or consonants. In the present edition v has been substituted for
consonantal u, j for consonantal i.

All Monasillables or Polysillables that end in single consonants, either written or sounded with single consonants, having a sharp lively accent and standing without position of the word following, are short in their last sillable, as *scăb, flĕd, pārtĕd, Gŏd, ŏf, ĭf, bāndŏg, ănguĭsh, sĭck, quĭck, rīvăl, wĭll, peōplĕ, sīmplĕ, cŏme, sŏme, hĭm, thĕm, frŏm, sūmmŏn, thĕn, prŏp, prōspĕr, hōnoŭr, lāboŭr, thĭs, hĭs, spēchĕs, gōddĕsse, pērfĕct, bŭt, whăt, thăt,* and their like.

The last sillable of all words in the plurall number that have two or more vowels before *s* are long, as *vertūes, dutīes, miserīes, fellōwes.*

These rules concerning the quantity of our English sillables I have disposed as they came next into my memory; others more methodicall, time and practise may produce. In the meane season, as the Grammarians leave many sillables to the authority of Poets, so do I likewise leave many to their judgements; and withall thus conclude, that there is no Art begun and perfected at one enterprise.

FINIS.

A NEW WAY
OF MAKING FOWRE
parts in *Counter-point*, by a
most familiar, and infallible
RULE.

Secondly, a necessary discourse of *Keyes*,
and their proper *Closes*.

Thirdly, the allowed passages of all *Concords*
perfect, or imperfect, are declared.

*Also by way of Preface, the nature of the Scale is
expressed, with a briefe Method teaching to Sing.*

By THO: CAMPION

Campion's only work on musical theory appeared without date; Vivian dates it 1617, M. C. Boyd, 1613 (in *Elizabethan Music and Musical Criticism*, 2d ed. [Philadelphia, 1962]), both without giving evidence for their conclusions. The dedication to Prince Charles indicates a terminal date of 1616, for in that year he was invested as Prince of Wales, and thenceforth would have been addressed as such. The question of dating is complicated by the intimate relation of this treatise with Giovanni Coperario's manuscript *Rules how to Compose*, which Manfred Bukofzer in his facsimile edition (Los Angeles, 1952, p. 2) dates between 1610 and 1614. For Coperario not only duplicates two of Campion's examples but also uses the same wording in a passage on cadences. Bukofzer is unable to ascertain whether Coperario copied Campion or vice versa. But the fact that Charles was Coperario's pupil makes it less likely that Campion would have presented him with a volume containing examples filched from his master and more likely that Campion had begun it for Coperario's use in instructing Charles and that Coperario took parts of it for the instruction of John Egerton, first Earl of Bridgewater, who owned the manuscript of the *Rules*. 1613 or 1614 seem the most likely dates for both treatises.

A New Way is really a collection of separate little treatises on the scale, counterpoint, tonality, and the concords. But three of them, at least, find a point of unity in an overriding concern for harmonic sequence, and, beneath that, in a baroque concept of music as simultaneously vertical and linear, as the motion of chords.

In the brief "Preface" on the scale, Campion seeks to simplify the "Gam" or "Gamut," the scale established on the basis of the hexachord by Guido of Arezzo in the eleventh century and still in use in Campion's time. In it, there were seven hexachords in a single scale from *G* to *e″*, the notes of the whole scale being indicated by capital letters, the six notes of each individual hexachord being indicated by the vocables *ut, re, mi, fa, sol, la*. The scale appears thus, reading from bottom to top (modern equivalents in right-hand column):

E						la	(Ela)	e″
D					la	sol	(Delasol)	d″
C					sol	fa	(Cesolfa)	c″
B					fa	mi	(Befami)	b′
A				la	mi	re	(Alamire)	a′
G				sol	re	ut	(Gesolreut)	g′
F				fa	ut		(Fefaut)	f′
E			la	mi			(Elami)	e′
D		la	sol	re			(Delasolre)	d′
C		sol	fa	ut			(Cesolfaut)	c′
B		fa	mi				(Befami)	b
A	la	mi	re				(Alamire)	a
G	sol	re	ut				(Gesolreut)	g
F	fa	ut					(Fefaut)	f
E	la	mi					(Elami)	e
D	sol	re					(Desolre)	d
C	fa	ut					(Cefaut)	c
B	mi						(Bemi)	B
A	re						(Are)	A
G	ut						(Gamut)	G

In this system, as Campion observes, the same note, *d*, could be called either *re* or *sol*, according to which hexachord it was considered to belong to. His intention is to simplify by replacing the hexachord with a tetrachord modeled on the Greek system and prefiguring the modern octave system. His chief problem in doing so is to explain the positions of the semitones, which in the hexachord were always in the same position, between *mi* and *fa*.

The main treatise on counterpoint, in which Campion took such pride, is designed to teach the beginner how to compose note-against-note counterpoint in four parts by means of a simple table which ensures both contrary motion and perfect triads. The really crucial innovation in this treatise, however, is Campion's insistence on making the Bass, instead of the Tenor, the foundation of the other parts. Kastendieck points out that "by drawing attention to a formal bass as the foundation of everything, Campion thus chains the other parts to a movement in accordance with a definite scheme of intervals (of the third, fifth, and eighth) reckoned from the bass. Thus the idea of chord progressions based on a succession of bass notes is established" (*England's Musical Poet,* p. 178). Since this is basically the system of modern contrapuntal harmonic technique, Kastendieck uses it to prove his thesis that Campion was the first English theorist to think in vertical harmonic terms instead of linear polyphonic terms (as Thomas Morley, who still worked from the Tenor, did); Bukofzer also advances this thesis.

The brief discourse on keys presents Campion's attempt to solve the confusions (which also plagued Morley) resulting from the coexistence, in his time, of both the mediaeval modes and some sense of the modern keys as the possible bases of tonality. He tries to guide the musician toward consistency by establishing the cadences proper to the different keys.

Campion's final treatise on concords is, as he admits, a summary of Calvisius' rules. Sethus Calvisius, born Seth Kalwitz (1556–1615), Thuringian mathematician, astronomer, and musician, served as musical director of St. Thomas Church, Leipzig, for most of his life. His compositions include instrumental *bicinia,* hymns, and psalm-settings. His theoretical works are *MELOPOEIA sive Melodiae condendae ratio* (1592), *Compendium musicae pro incipiendis* (1594), expanded in its third edition into the *Musicae artis praecepta* . . . (1612), *Exercitationes musicae duae* . . . (1600), and *Exercitatio tertia* (1611). Campion takes nearly all his examples from *MELOPOEIA,* and translates part of its text.

Campion's (with the possible exception of Coperario's) is the only Renaissance English treatise of interest to the historian of music theory, all the others being either mediaeval survivals—Butler's *Principles of Musicke* (1636), Ravenscroft's *Briefe Discourse* (1614), and Dowland's translation (1609) of Ornithoparcus' *Micrologus,* originally written in 1517—or interesting for their lively testimony about contemporary practice rather than for their theoretical innovations, as is Thomas Morley's *Plaine and Easie Introduction to Practicall Musicke* (1597). Only in Campion do we find any theoretical reflections of the great changes music was undergoing at this time. Bukofzer, who finds Campion in some respects "ahead of his time by more than a century," concludes that "His ideas are so highly original and radical that one is tempted to assume that only a musical amateur, such as Campion was, would rush in where theorists fear to tread, not fully realizing the revolutionary effect the ideas could have" (p. 19). It was perhaps for this reason that Campion's treatise was incorporated into the Restoration vade mecum, John Playford's *Introduction to the Skill of Musick,* in 1660, there to remain, with some alterations, through the various editions until it was replaced in 1694 by a new section on descant written by the giant of the English baroque, Henry Purcell.

The musical examples have not been altered save for transposition into modern clefs and correction of a few obvious errors.

TO THE FLOWRE
OF PRINCES, CHARLES,
PRINCE OF GREAT
BRITTAINE.

The first inventor of Musicke (most sacred Prince) was by olde records *Apollo,* a King, who, for the benefit which Mortalls received from his so divine invention, was by them made a God. *David* a Prophet, and a King, excelled all men in the same excellent Art. What then can more adorne the greatnesse of a Prince, then the knowledge thereof? But why should I, being by profession a Physition, offer a worke of Musicke to his Highnesse? *Galene* either first, or next the first of Physitions, became so expert a Musition, that he could not containe himselfe, but needes he must apply all the proportions of Musicke to the uncertaine motions of the pulse.[1] Such far-fetcht Doctrine dare not I attempt, contenting my selfe onely with a poore, and easie invention, yet new and certaine, by which the skill of Musicke shall be redeemed from much darknesse, wherein envious antiquitie of purpose did involve it. To your gratious hands most humbly I present it, which if your Clemency will vouchsafe favourably to behold, I have then attained to the full estimate of all my labour. Be all your daies ever musicall (most mighty Prince) and a sweet harmony guide the events of all your royall actions. So zealously wisheth

Your Highnesse
most humble servant,
THO: CAMPION.

THE PREFACE

There is nothing doth trouble, and disgrace our Traditionall Musition more then the ambiguity of the termes of Musicke, if he cannot rightly distinguish them, for they make him uncapable of any rationall discourse in the art hee professeth. As if wee say a

[1] in the *De Pulsum Differentiis.*

lesser Third consists of a Tone, and a Semi-tone; here by a Tone
is ment a perfect Second, or as they name it a whole note. But if
wee aske in what Tone is this or that song made, then by Tone
we intend the key which guides and ends the whole song. Like-
wise the word *Note* is sometime used properly, as when in respect
of the forme of it, we name it a round or square Note; in regard
of the place we say, a Note in rule or a Note in space; so for the
time, we call a Briefe or Sembriefe a long Note, a Crotchet or
Quaver a short note.[2] Sometime the word *Note* is otherwise to be
understood, as when it is *signum pro signato,* the signe for the
thing signified: so we say a Sharpe, or flat Note, meaning by the
word Note, the sound it signifies; also we terme a Note high, or
low, in respect of the sound. The word *Note* simply produced
hath yet another signification, as when we say this is a sweet
Note, or the Note I like but not the words, wee then meane by
this word Note, the whole tune, putting the part for the whole:
but this word *Note,* with addition, is yet far otherwise to be
understood; as when we say a whole Note, or a halfe Note, we
meane a perfect or imperfect Second, which are not Notes, but the
severall distances betweene two Notes, the one being double as
much as the other; and although this kinde of calling them a whole
and a halfe Note, came in first by abusion, yet custome hath made
that speech now passable. In my discourse of Musicke, I have
therefore strived to be plaine in my tearmes, without nice and
unprofitable distinctions, as that is of *tonus maior,* and *tonus
minor,* and such like, whereof there can be made no use.

In like manner there can be no greater hinderance to him that
desires to become a Musition, then the want of the true under-
standing of the Scale, which proceeds from the errour of the com-
mon Teacher, who can doe nothing without the olde *Gam-ut*[3] in
which there is but one Cliffe, and one Note, and yet in the same
Cliffe he wil sing *re* and *sol.* It is most true that the first inven-
tion of the *gam-ut* was a good invention; but then the distance of
Musicke was cancelled within the number of twenty Notes, so
were the six Notes properly invented to helpe youth in vowelling;
but the liberty of the latter age hath given Musicke more space
both above and below, altering thereby the former naming of the

[2] The white mensural notation used in the Renaissance consisted of the
following: Long (quadruple the value of a modern whole note), Brief
(double whole note), Semibrief (whole note), Minim (half note), Crotchet
(quarter note), Quaver (eighth note), and Semiquaver (sixteenth note).

[3] For instance, Thomas Morley began *A Plaine and Easie Introduction
to Practicall Musicke* (1597) by having his pupil memorize the Gam.

Notes, the curious observing whereof hath bred much unneces-
sary difficultie to the learner, for the Scale may be more easily and
plainely exprest by foure Notes, then by sixe, which is done by
leaving out *Ut* and *Re.*

The substance of all Musicke, and the true knowledge of the
scale, consists in the observations of the halfe note, which is ex-
pressed either by *Mi Fa,* or *La Fa,* and they being knowne in
their right places, the other Notes are easily applyed unto them.

To illustrate this I will take the common key which we call
Gam-ut, both sharpe in *Bemi* and flat, as also flat in *Elami,* and
shew how with ease they may be expressed by these foure Notes,
which are *Sol, La, Mi, Fa.*

I shall neede no more then one eight for all, and that I have
chosen to be in the Base, because all the upper eights depend upon
the lowest eight, and are the same with it in nature; then thus first
in the sharpe:

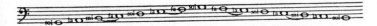

First observe the places of the halfe Notes, which are marked
with a halfe circle, and remember that if the lowest be *Mi Fa,*
the upper halfe Note is *La Fa,* and contrariwise if the lowest halfe
Note be *La Fa,* the upper must be *Mi Fa.*

It will give great light to the understanding of the Scale, if you
trye it on a Lute, or Voyall,[4] for there you shall plainely perceive
that there goe two frets to the raising of a whole Note, but one to
a halfe Note, as on the Lute in this manner the former eight may
be expressed.

Here you may discerne that between *A.* and *C.* and *C.* and *E.*
is interposed a fret, which makes it double as much as *E.* and *F.*
which is markt for the halfe Note, so the whole Note you see con-
taines in it the space of two halfe Notes, as *A.C.* being the whole
Note, containes in it these two halfe Notes, *A.B.* and *B.C.*

Now for the naming of the Notes, let this be a generall rule:
above *Fa,* ever to sing *Sol,* and to sing *Sol* ever under *La.*

4 viola da gamba, which could use tablature like the lute's.

Here in the flat *Gam-ut,* you may finde *La Fa* below, and *Mi Fa* above; which on the Lute take their places thus:

The lower halfe Note is betweene *C.* and *D.,* the higher betweene *E.* and *A.;* but next let us examine this Key as it is flat in *Elami,* which being properly to be set in *Are,* so is it to be sung with ease, *La,* instead of *Re,* being the right limits of this eight.

Mi Fa here holds his place below, and *La Fa* above but yet removed a Note lower. The same on the Lute.

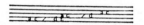

You shall here finde the upper halfe note placed a fret lower then it was in the example of the flat *Gam-ut* which was set downe next before, by reason of the flat in *Elami,* which makes that whole Note but halfe so much as it was being sharpe.

This is an easie way for him that would eyther with ayde of a teacher, or by his owne industrie learne to sing; and if hee shall well beare in minde the placing of the halfe Notes, it will helpe him much in the knowledge of the cords, which have all their variety from the halfe Note.

OF COUNTERPOINT.

The parts of Musicke are in all but foure, howsoever some skil-full Musitions have composed songs of twenty, thirty, and forty parts: for be the parts never so many, they are but one of these foure in nature. The names of those foure parts are these. The *Base* which is the lowest part and foundation of the whole song: The *Tenor,* placed next above the *Base;* next above the *Tenor* the *Meane* or *Counter-Tenor,* and in the highest place the *Treble.* These foure parts by the learned are said to resemble the foure Elements; the Base expresseth the true nature of the earth, who being the gravest and lowest of all the Elements, is as a founda-tion to the rest. The Tenor is likened to the water, the Meane to the Aire, and the Treble to the Fire. Moreover, by how much the water is more light then the earth, by so much is the Aire lighter then the water, and Fire then Aire. They have also in their native property every one place above the other, the lighter upper-most, the waightiest in the bottome. Having now demonstrated that there are in all but foure parts, and that the Base is the foundation of the other three,[5] I assume that the true sight and judgement of the upper three must proceed from the lowest, which is the Base, and also I conclude that every part in nature doth affect his proper and naturall place as the elements doe.

True it is that the auncient Musitions, who entended their Musicke onely for the Church, tooke their sight from the Tenor, which was rather done out of necessity then any respect to the true nature of Musicke: for it was usuall with them to have a Tenor as a Theame, to which they were compelled to adapt their other parts. But I will plainely convince by demonstration that contrary to some opinions the Base containes in it both the Aire and true judgement of the Key, expressing how any man at the first sight may view in it all the other parts in their originall es-sence.

In respect of the variety in Musicke which is attained to by farther proceeding in the Arte, as when Notes are shifted out of their native places, the Base above the Tenor, or the Tenor above the Meane, and the Meane above the Treble, this kinde of Counterpoint, which I promise, may appeare simple and onely fit

[5] As Bukofzer notes (p. 18), this passage echoes Zarlino, *Istituti Har-moniche* (Venice, 1558), III, 58, p. 239, where the bass is called *fondamento dell' harmonia.*

for young beginners (as indeede chiefly it is); yet the right specula-
tion may give much satisfaction, even to the most skilfull, laying
open unto them, how manifest and certaine are the first grounds
of Counterpoint.

First, it is in this case requisite that a formall Base, or at least
part thereof be framed, the Notes rising and falling according to
the nature of that part, not so much by degrees as by leaps of a
third, fourth, or fift, or eight, a sixt being seldome, a seaventh
never used, and neyther of both without the discretion of a skil-
full Composer. Next wee must consider whether the Base doth rise
or fall, for in that consists the mistery. That rising or that falling
doth never exceed a fourth, for a fourth above is the same that a
fift is underneath, and a fourth underneath is as a fift above;
for example, if a Base shall rise thus:

The first rising is said to be by degrees, because there is no
Note betweene the two Notes; the second rising is by leaps, for *G.*
skips over *A.* to *B.*, and so leaps into a third; the third example
also leaps two Notes into a fourth. Now for this fourth if the Base
had descended from *G.* above to *C.* underneath, that descending fift
in sight and use had beene all one with the fourth, as here you may
discerne, for they both begin and end in the same keys, thus:

This rule likewise holds if the Notes descend a second, third, or
fourth; for the fift ascending is all one with the fourth descending,
example of the first Notes.

The third two Notes, which make the distance of a fourth, are
all one with this fift following.

But let us make our approach yet neerer. If the Base shall ascend either a second, third, or fourth, that part which stands in the third or tenth above the Base shall fall into an eight, that which is a fift shall passe into a third, and that which is an eight shall remove into a fift.

But that all this may appeare more plaine and easie, I have drawne it all into these six figures.[6]

8	3	5
3	5	8

Though you finde here onely mentioned and figured a third, fift and eight, yet not onely these single concords are ment, but by them also their compounds,[7] as a tenth, a twelfth, a fifteenth, and so upward, and also the unison as well as the eight.

This being graunted, I will give you example of those figures prefixed. When the Base riseth, beginning from the lowest figure, and rising to the upper, as if the Base should rise a second, in this manner.

Then if you will beginne with your third, you must set your Note in *Alamire*, which is a third to *Ffaut*, and so looke upward, and that cord which you see next above it use, and that is an eight in *Gsolreut.*

After that, if you will take a fift to the first Note, you must looke upward and take the third you finde there for the second Note. Lastly if you take an eight for the first Note, you must take for the second Note the corde above it, which is the fift.

---

[6] The object is to preserve the triad while allowing contrary motion between parts. If the Bass rises, the student must read the table from the bottom up: the part (whether Tenor, Mean, or Treble) which is in the third above the first Bass note must go to the eighth above the next Bass note; the part in the fifth must go to the third; the part in the eighth must go to the fifth. On the other hand, if the Bass descends, the student must read downward: the part in the eighth goes to the third; the part in the third goes to the fifth; and the part in the fifth goes to the eighth.

[7] the intervals larger than an octave interval.

Example of all the three parts added to the Base.

What parts arise out of the rising of the second, the same answere in the rising of the third and fourth, thus:

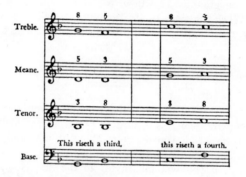

Albeit any man by the rising of parts, might of himselfe conceive the same reason in the falling of them, yet, that nothing may be thought obscure, I will also illustrate the descending Notes by example.

If the Base descends or falls a second, third, or fourth, or riseth a fift (which is all one as if it had fallen a fourth, as hath beene shewed before) then looke upon the sixe figures, where in the first place you shall finde the eight which descends into the third, in the second place the third descending into the fift, and in the third and last place the fift which hath under it an eight.

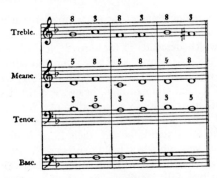

Thus much for the rising and falling of the Base in severall;
now I will give you a briefe example of both of them mixed to-
gether in the plainest fashion; let this straine serve for the Base.

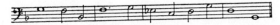

The first two Notes fall a second; the second and third Notes
fall a fift, which you must call rising a forth; the third and forth
Notes rise a fift, which you must name the fourth falling; the
fourth and fift Notes rise a second; the fift and sixt notes fall a
third; the sixt and seaventh Notes also fall a third; the seaventh
and eight rise a second; the eight and ninth Notes rise a fourth,
the ninth and tenth fall a fourth; the tenth and eleventh Notes fall
a fift, which you must reckon rising a fourth.

Being thus prepared, you may chuse whether you will begin
with an eight, a fift, or a third; for as soone as you have taken
any one of them, all the other Notes follow necessarily without
respect of the rest of the parts; and every one, orderly without
mixing, keeps his proper place above the other, as here you may
easily discerne.

Let us examine onely one of the parts, and let that be the Tenor, because it stands next to the Base. The first Note in *B*. is a third to the Base, which descends to the second Note of the Base: now looke among the sixe figures, and when you have found the third in the upper place, you shall finde under it a fift; then take that fift which is *C*.: next from *F*. to *B*. below, is a fift descending, for which say ascending, and so you shall looke for the fift in the lowest row of the figures, above which stands a third which is to be taken; that third stands in *D*.: then from *B*. to *F*. the Base rises a fift, but you must say falling, because a fift rising and a fourth falling is all one, as hath beene often declared before; now a third when the Base falls requires a fift to follow it. But what needes farther demonstration when as he that knowes his Cords cannot but conceive the necessitie of consequence in all these with helpe of those sixe figures?

But let them that have not proceeded so farre take this note with them concerning the placing of the parts: if the upper part or Treble be an eight, the Meane must take the next Cord under it, which is a fift, and the Tenor the next Cord under that, which is a third. But if the Treble be a third, then the Meane must take the eight, and the Tenor the fift. Againe, if the uppermost part stands in the fift or twelfe (for in respect of the learners ease, in the simple Concord I conclude all his compounds), then the Meane must be a tenth, and the Tenor a fift. Moreover, all these Cords are to be seene in the Base, and such Cords as stand above the Notes of the Base are easily knowne, but such as in sight are found under it, trouble the young beginner; let him therefore know that a third under the Base is a sixt above it, and if it be a greater third, it yeelds the lesser sixt above; if the lesser third, the greater sixt. A fourth underneath the Base is a fift above, and a fift under the Base is a fourth above it. A sixt beneath the Base is a third above; and, if it be the lesser sixt, then is the third above the greater third; and if the greater sixt underneath, then is it the lesser third above; and thus far have I digressed for the Schollers sake.

If I should discover no more then this already deciphered of Counter-point, wherein the native order of foure parts with use of the Concords is demonstratively expressed, might I be mine owne Judge, I had effected more in Counterpoint then any man before me hath ever attempted; but I will yet proceed a little farther. And that you may perceive how cunning and how certaine nature is in all her operations, know that what Cords have held good in this ascending and descending of the Base answere in the contrary by the very same rule, though not so formally as the other, yet so, that much use is and may be made of this sort of Counter-point.[8] To keepe the figures in your memorie, I will here place them againe, and under them plaine examples.

8	3	5
3	5	8

In these last examples you may see what variety nature offers of her selfe; for if in the first Rule the Notes follow not in expected formality,[9] this second way, being quite contrary to the other, affords us sufficient supply: the first and last two Notes rising and falling by degrees, are not so formall as the rest, yet thus they may be mollified, by breaking two of the first Notes.

[8] Here Campion merely asserts that the rules for rising and falling may be reversed, as in the examples that follow.

[9] "But in descanting you must not only seek true chords but formality also, that is to make your descant carry some form of relation to the plainsong" (Thomas Morley, *A Plaine and Easie Introduction to Practicall Musicke,* ed. R. Alec Harman [New York, 1952], p. 149). Therefore Campion here is seeking means to allow close imitation of the Bass in the upper parts. In the example which follows, he makes a stepwise motion common to all parts by "breaking," a form of division which consists of dividing a single long note into several short ones, in this case by filling in the interval between the first and second notes.

How both the waies may be mixed together, you may perceive by the next example, wherein the blacke Notes distinguish the second way from the first.

In this example the fift and sixt Notes of the three upper parts are after the second way, for from the fourth Note of the Base, which is in from *G.* and goeth to *B.*, is a third rising; so that, according to the first rule, the eight should passe into a fift, the fift into a third, the third into an eight: but here contrariwise the eight goes into a third, the fift into an eight, and the third into a fift; and by these Notes you may censure the rest of that kinde.

Though I may now seeme to have finished all that belongs to this sort of Counterpoint, yet there remaines one scruple, that is, how the sixt may take place here, which I will also declare. Know that whensoever a sixt is requisite, as in *B.* or in *E.* or *A.*, the key being in *Gamut,* you may take the sixt in stead of the fift, and use the same Cord following which you would have taken if the former cord had beene a fift. Example:

The sixt in both places (the Base rising) passes into a third, as it should have done if the sixt had beene a fift. Moreover if the Base shall use a sharpe, as in *F.* sharpe, then must we take the sixt of necessity, but the eight to the Base may not be used, so that exception is to be taken against our rule of Counterpoint. To which I answere thus, first, such Bases are not true Bases, for where a sixt is to be taken, either in *F.* sharpe, or in *E.* sharpe, or in *B.* or in *A.*, the true Base is a third lower, *F.* sharpe in *D.*, *E.* in *C.*, *B.* in *G.*, *A.* in *F.*, as for example.

In the first Base two sixes are to be taken, by reason of the imperfection of the Base, wanting due latitude, the one in *E.* the other in *F.* sharpe; but in the second Base the sixes are removed away and the Musicke is fuller.

Neverthelesse, if any be pleased to use the Base sharpe, then, in stead of the eight, to the Base hee may take the third to the Base, in this manner.

Here the Treble in the third Note, when it should have past into the sharpe eight in *F.*, takes for it a third to the Base in *A.*, which causeth the Base and Treble to rise two thirds, whereof we will speake hereafter.

Note also that when the Base stands in *E.* flat, and the part that is an eight to it must passe into a sharpe or greater third, that this passage from the flat to the sharpe would be unformall; and therefore it may be thus with small alteration avoided, by removing the latter part of the Note into the third above, which, though it meets in unison with the upper part, yet it is right good, because it jumps not with the whole, but onely with the last halfe of it. Example:

For the second example looke hereafter in the rule of thirds, but for the first example here: if in the Meane part the third Note that is divided had stood still a Minum (as by rule it should), and so had past into *F.* sharpe, as it must of force be made sharpe at a close, it had beene then passing unformall.

But if the same Base had beene set in the sharpe key, the rest of the parts would have falne out formall of themselves without any helpe, as thus:

But if the third Note of the Base in *E.* flat had been put in his place of perfection, that is in *C.* a third lower, then the other parts would have answered fitly, in this manner.

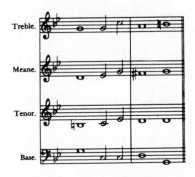

When the Base shall stand still in one key, as above it doth in the third Note, then the other parts may remove at their pleasure.

Moreover it is to be observed that, in composing of the Base, you may break it at your pleasure, without altering any of the other parts: as for example.

One other observation more I will handle that doth arise out of this example, which according to the first rule may hold thus:

Herein are two errours, first in the second Notes of the Base and Treble, where the third to the Base ought to have beene sharpe, secondly in the second and third Notes of the same parts, where the third, being a lesser third, holds[10] while the Base falls into a fift which is unelegant; but if the upper third had beene the greater third, the fift had fitly followed, as you may see in the third and fourth Notes of the Tenor and the Base.

But that scruple may be taken away by making the second Note of the Treble sharpe, and, in stead of a fift, by removing the third Note into a sixt. Example:

There may yet be more variety afforded the Base, by ordering the fourth Notes of the upper parts according to the second rule, thus:

[10] that is, the note is repeated.

But that I may (as neere as I can) leave nothing untoucht concerning this kinde of Counterpoint, let us now consider how two thirds, being taken together betweene the Treble and the Base, may stand with our Rule. For sixes are not in this case to be mentioned, being distances so large that they can produce no formality. Besides, the sixt is of it selfe very imperfect, being compounded of a third, which is an imperfect Concord, and of a fourth, which is a Discord: and this the cause is, that the sixes produce so many fourths in the inner parts. As for the third, it, being the least distance of any Concord, is therefore easily to be reduced into good order. For if the Base and Treble doe rise together in thirds, then the first Note of the Treble is regular with the other part, but the second of it is irregular; for, by rule, in stead of the rising third, it should fall into the eight. In like sort, if the Base and Treble doe fall two thirds, the first Note of the Treble is irregular, and is to be brought into rule by being put into the eight, but the second Note is of it selfe regular. Yet, whether those thirds be reduced into eights or no, you shall by supposition thereof finde out the other parts, which never vary from the rule but in the sharpe Base. But let mee explaine my selfe by example.

The first two Notes of the Treble are both thirds to the Base; but, in the second stroke,[11] the first Note of the Treble is a third, and the second, which was before a third, is made an eight, onely to shew how you may finde out the right parts which are to be used when you take two thirds betweene the Treble and the Base. For according to the former rule, if the Base descends, the third then in the Treble is to passe into the eight, and the meane must first take an eight, then a fift, and the Tenor a fift, then a third; and these are also the right and proper parts if you returne the eight of the Treble into a third againe, as may appeare in the first example of the Base falling, and consequently in all the rest.

But let us proceed yet farther, and suppose that the Base shall use a sharpe, what is then to be done? as if thus:

[11] bar.

If you call to minde the rule before delivered concerning the sharpe Base, you shall here by helpe thereof see the right parts, though you cannot bring them under the rule: for if the first Note of the Base had been flat, the Meane part should have taken that, and so have descended to the fift; but being sharpe you take for it (according to the former observation) the third to the Base, and so rise up into the fift. The Tenor that should take a fift, and so fall by degrees into a third, is heere forced, by reason of the sharpe Base, for a fift to take a sixt and so leap downeward into the third. And so much for the thirds.

Lastly, in favour of young beginners let me also adde this, that the Base intends a close as often as it riseth a fift, third, or second, and then immediately either falls a fift, or riseth a fourth. In like manner, if the Base falls a fourth or second, and after falls a fift, the Base insinuates a close; and in all these cases the part must hold, that in holding can use the fourth or eleventh, and so passe eyther into the third or tenth.[12]

[12] Compare Coperario, *Rules how to Compose,* fo. 4: "The Bass meanes to make a close when he rises a 5, 2, or 3, and then falls a 5, or rises a 4. Likewise if the Bass fall a 4, or 2, and then fall a 5, he meanes to use a close, then that part must hold, which in holding can use the 11, or 4 with the Bass in the next note rising, or falling, and then you must use either the 3, or 10." As Bukofzer notes (p. 18), the first five measures of Coperario's example of this rule duplicate measures 2, 6, 8, 10, and 4, respectively, of Campion's example on this page.

In the examples before set downe I left out the closes, of purpose that the Cords might the better appeare in their proper places, but this short admonition will direct any young beginner to helpe that want at his pleasure. And thus I end my treatise of Counterpoint both briefe and certaine, such as will open an easie way to them that without helpe of a skilfull Teacher endeavour to acquire the first grounds of this Arte.

A shorte Hymne, Composed after this forme of Counterpoint, to shew how well it will become any Divine, *or grave* Subject.

In this Aire the last Note onely is, for sweetnesse sake, altered from the rule; in the last Note of the Treble, where the eight, being a perfect Concord, and better befitting an outward part at the Close, is taken for a third; and in the Tenor, in stead of the fift, that third is taken descending; for in a middle part, imperfection is not so manifest as in the Treble, at a close which is the perfection of a song.

OF THE TONES OF MUSICKE.

Of all things that belong to the making up of a Musition, the most necessary and usefull for him is the true knowledge of the Key, or Moode, or Tone, for all signifie the same thing, with the closes belonging unto it; for there is no tune that can have any grace or sweetnesse, unlesse it be bounded within a proper key, without running into strange keyes which have no affinity with the aire of the song. I have therefore thought good in an easie and briefe discourse to endeavour to expresse that which many in large and obscure volumes have made fearefull to the idle Reader.

The first thing to be herein considered is the eight which is equally divided into a fourth, and a fift as thus:

Here you see the fourth in the upper place, and the fift in the lower place, which is called *Modus authentus:*[13] but contrary thus:

This is called *Modus plagalii;*[14] but howsoever the fourth in the eight is placed, wee must have our eye on the fift, for that onely discovers the key, and all the closes pertaining properly thereunto. This fift is also divided into two thirds; sometimes the lesser third hath the upper place, and the greater third supports it below; sometimes the greater third is higher, and the lesser third rests in the lowest place, as for example:

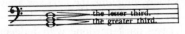

---

[13] The twelve Church modes were divided into two types according to the positions of the fourth and fifth in each: in the six "authentic" modes supposedly established by St. Ambrose (Dorian, Phrygian, Lydian, Mixolydian, Aeolian, and Ionian), the fourth was above the center tone and the fifth below it.

[14] In the six "plagal" (or collateral) modes supposedly added by St. Gregory (Hypodorian, Hypophrygian, etc.), the fifth was above the center tone and the fourth below it.

The lowest Note of this fift beares the name of the Key; as, if the eight be from *G.* to *G.*, the fift from *G.* beneath to *D.* above, *G.*, being the lowest Note of the fift, showes that *G.* is the key; and if one should demaund in what key your song is set, you must answere in *Gamut,* or *Gsolreut,* that is in *G.*

If the compasse of your song shall fall out thus:

Respect not the fourth below, but looke to your fift above, and the lowest Note of that fift assume for your key, which is *C.*; then divide that fift into his two thirds, and so you shall finde out all the closes that belong to that key.

The maine and fundamentall close is in the key it selfe, the second is in the upper Note of the fift, the third is in the upper Note of the lowest third, if it be the lesser third; as for example, if the key be in *G.* with *B.* flat, you may close in these three places.

The first close is that which maintaines the aire of the key, and may be used often, the second is next to be preferd, and the last, last.

But if the key should be in *G.* with *B.* sharpe, then the last close being to be made in the greater or sharpe third is unproper, and therfore for variety sometime the next key above is joyned with it, which is *A.*, and sometimes the fourth key, which is *C.*; but these changes of keyes must be done with judgement; yet have I aptly closed in the upper Note of the lowest third of the key, the key being in *F.* and the upper Note of the third standing in *A.* as you may perceive in this Aire:[15]

[15] Here Campion quotes his own song "Fire that must flame," *The Third Booke of Ayres,* xv, in its entirety.

In this aire the first close is in the upper note of the fift, which from *F.* is *C.*; the second close is in the upper Note of the great third, which from *F.* is *A.*

But the last and finall close is in the key it selfe, which is *F.* as it must ever be; wheresoever your key shall stand, either in *G.* or *C.* or *F.* or elsewhere, the same rule of the fift is perpetuall, being divided into thirds, which can be but two waies, that is, eyther when the upper third is lesse by halfe a Note then the lower, or when the lower third contains the halfe Note, which is *Mi Fa,* or *La Fa.*

If the lower third contains the halfe Note it hath it eyther above as *La Mi Fa, La Mi* being the whole Note, and *Mi Fa* but halfe so much, that is the halfe Note; or else when the halfe Note is underneath, as in *Mi Fa Sol: Mi Fa* is the halfe Note, and *Fa Sol* is the whole Note; but whether the halfe Note be uppermost or lowermost, if the lowest third of the fift be the lesser third, that key yeelds familiarly three closes; example of the halfe Note, standing in the upper place was shewed before, now I will set downe the other.

But for the other keyes that divide the fift, so that it hath the lesse third above, and the greater underneath, they can challenge but two proper closes, one in the lowest Note of the fift which is the fundamentall key, and the other in the uppermost Note of the same wherin also you may close at pleasure. True it is that the key next above hath a great affinity with the right key, and may therefore as I said before be used, as also the fourth key above the finall key.

Examples of both in two beginnings of Songs.[16]

In the first example *A.* is mixt with *G.*, and in the second *C.* is joyned with *G.*, as you may understand by the second closes of both.

To make the key knowne is most necessary in the beginning of a song, and it is best exprest by the often using of his proper fift, and fourth, and thirds, rising or falling.

There is a tune ordinarily used, or rather abused, in our Churches, which is begun in one key and ended in another, quite contrary to nature; which errour crept in first through the ignorance of some parish Clarks, who understood better how to use the keyes of their Church-doores, then the keyes of Musicke, at which I doe not much mervaile; but that the same should passe in the booke of Psalmes set forth in foure parts, and authorised by so many Musitions, makes mee much amazed. This is the tune.[17]

[16] The "two beginnings of Songs" are, respectively, those of "Turne all thy thoughts," *The Fourth Booke of Ayres,* xx, and "Young and simple though I am," *The Fourth Booke,* ix.

[17] The tune is the second of the traditional ten psalm tones and designated for use with Psalms 10, 13, 17, etc. The "booke of Psalmes . . . authorised by so many Musitions" is *The Whole Booke of Psalmes: With Their Wonted Tunes, as they are sung in Churches, composed into foure parts. . . . Compiled by Sondry Authors* (among whom were Richard Alison, Michael Cavendish, John Dowland, Giles Farnaby, Edward Johnson, and George Kirbye) issued by Thomas East in 1592. The four-part setting of this tune that Campion criticizes is Psalm 10 as set by George Kirbye.

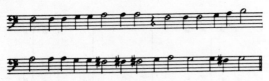

If one should request me to make a Base to the first halfe of his aire, I am perswaded that I ought to make it in this manner:

Now if this be the right Base (as without doubt it is), what a strange unaireable[18] change must the key then make from *F*. with the first third sharp to *G*. with *B*. flat.

But they have found a shift for it, and beginne the tune upon the upper Note of the fift, making the third to it flat; which is as absurd as the other. For first they erre in rising from a flat third into the unison, or eight, which is condemned by the best Musitions; next the third to the fift is the third which makes the cadence of the key, and therefore affects to be sharpe by nature, as indeed the authour of the aire at the first intended it should be. I will therefore so set it downe in foure parts according to the former Rule of Counterpoint.

[18] unsingable.

This was the Authors meaning, and thus it is lawfull to beginne a song in the fift, so that you maintaine the aire of the song, joyning to it the proper parts; but for such dissonant and extravagant errors as I have justly reprehended, I heartily wish they should be remedied, especially in devine service, which is devoted to the great authour of all harmony. And briefly thus for the Tones.

OF THE TAKING OF ALL CONCORDS, PERFECT AND IMPERFECT.

Of all the latter writers in Musicke whom I have knowne, the best and most learned is *Zethus Calvisius,* a Germane; who, out of the choisest Authors, hath drawne into a perspicuous method the right and elegant manner of taking all Concords, perfect and imperfect, to whom I would referre our Musitions, but that his booke is scarce any where extant, and besides it is written in Latine, which language few or none of them understand. I am therefore content for their sakes to become a Translator; yet so, that somewhat I wil adde, and somewhat I will alter.[19]

The consecution of perfect concords among themselves is easie; for who knowes not that two eights or two fifts are not to be taken rising or falling together, but a fift may eyther way passe into an eight, or an eight into a fift, yet most conveniently when the one of them moves by degrees, and the other by leaps; for when both skip together the passage is lesse pleasant. The waies by degrees are these.

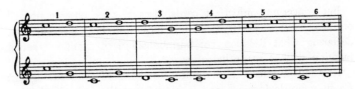

[19] Campion translates part of *"Caput Decimum: De Progressu Consonantiarum imperfectarum"* from Calvisius' *MELOPOEIA sive melodiae condendae ratio* (Erfurt, 1592). Campion's prefatory remarks on perfect and imperfect concords are his own, but his comment on relation not harmonical and his example at the foot of page 350 come from Calvisius, Sig. E 8ᵛ. *"Of the lesser or imperfect third"* is a translation of Calvisius' *"Regula quarta, De Semiditono"* (Sigs. E 6–E 7) and uses Calvisius' examples on page 351, at the head of page 352, and as the first two examples on page 353; the third example on page 353 is original, as is the discussion and quotation of his own "short aire" on page 352. The other three chapters with their examples are taken from Calvisius in their entirety: *"Of the greater or perfect Third"* from *"Regula quinta, De Ditono"* (Sigs. E 7–E 8ᵛ), including the first two examples on page 354; *"Of the lesser Sixt"* from *"Regula sexta, De sexta minore"* (Sigs. E 8ᵛ–F 1ᵛ), including the third example on page 354 and the second and third on page 355; and *"Of the greater Sixt"* from *"Regula septima"* (Sigs. F 1ᵛ–F 2), including the last example on page 355 and the one on page 356.

The fourth way is onely excepted against, where the fift riseth into the eight, and in few parts it cannot well be admitted, but in songs of many voices it is oftentimes necessary.

The passage also of perfect Concords into imperfect, eyther rising or falling, by degrees or leaps, is easie, and so an unison may passe into a lesser third, or a greater third; also into the lesser sixt, but seldome into the greater sixt. A fift passeth into the greater sixt, and into the lesser sixt, as also into the greater or lesser third; and so you must judge of their eights; for *de octavis idem est iudicium*,[20] and therefore when you reade an unison, or a fift, or a third, or a sixt, know that by the simple Concords the Compounds also are meant.

Note here that it is not good to fall with the Base being sharpe in *F.* from an eight unto a sixt.[21]

But concerning imperfect cords, because they observe not all one way in their passages, we will speake of them severally, first declaring what Relation not harmonicall doth signifie, whereof mention will be made hereafter.

Relation or reference, or respect not harmonicall is *Mi* against *Fa* in a crosse forme,[22] and it is in foure Notes, when the one being considered crosse with the other doth produce in the Musicke a strange discord. Example will yeeld it more plaine.

[20] "the same judgment holds for octaves"; Calvisius quotes this rule on Sig. C 2ᵛ of *MELOPOEIA*.

[21] Bukofzer notes (p. 18) that Coperario says the same on fo. 3ᵛ of *Rules how to Compose* and duplicates Campion's first example on page 350 in his last two examples.

[22] i.e., cross part, from the first note of the upper part to the second of the lower, etc.

The first Note of the upper part is in *Elami* sharpe, which being considered, or referred to the second Note of the lower part, which is *Elami,* made flat by the cromaticke flat signe, begets a false second, which is a harsh discorde; and though these Notes sound not both together, yet in few parts they leave an offence in the eare. The second example is the same descending; the third is from *Elami* sharpe in the first Note of the lower part, to the second note in the upper part, it being flat by reason of the flat signe; and so betweene them they mixe in the Musicke a false fift; the same doth the fourth example, but the fift example yeelds a false fourth, and the sixt a false fift.

There are two kindes of imperfect concords, thirds or sixes, and the sixes wholy participate of the nature of the thirds; for to the lesser third, which consists but of a whole Note and halfe, adde a fourth, and you have the lesser sixt; in like manner to the greater third that consists of two whole Notes, adde a fourth, and it makes up the greater sixt; so that all the difference is stil in the halfe note according to that only saying, *Mi et Fa sunt tota Musica.*[23] Of these foure we wil now discourse, proceeding in order from the lesse to the greater.

Of the lesser or imperfect third.

The lesser third passeth into an unison, first by degrees when both parts meete, then by leaps ascending or descending when one of the parts stand still; but when both the parts leap or fall together, the passage is not allowed.

Secondly, the lesser third passeth into a fift, first in degrees when they are seperated by contrary motions, then by leaps when the lower part riseth by degrees, and the upper part descends by degrees, and thus the lesser tenth may passe into a fift. Lastly, both parts leaping, the lesser third may passe into a fift, so that the upper part doth descend by leap the distance of a lesser third. Any other way the passage of a lesser third into a fift, is disallowed.

[23] "*Mi* and *Fa* comprise all of music"; in the hexachord, the semitones always occurred between *Mi* and *Fa,* and if the student remembered that fact he had little to worry about.

In the last disallowance, which is when the upper part stands, and the lower part falls from a lesser third to a fift, many have been deceived, their eares not finding the absurdity of it: but as this way is immusicall, so is the fall of the greater third in the former manner, into a fift, passing harmonious; in so much that it is elegantly and with much grace taken in one part of a short aire foure times, whereas, had the fift beene halfe so often taken with the lesser third falling, it would have yeelded a most unpleasing harmony.[24]

He that will be diligent to know, and carefull to observe the true allowances, may be bolde in his composition, and shall prove quickly ready in his sight, doing that safely and resolutely which others attempt tymerously and uncertainely. But now let us procede in the passages of the lesser third.

Thirdly, the lesser third passeth into an eight, the lower part

[24] The "short aire" Campion quotes partly is his own three-part song "A secret love or two I must confesse," *The Second Booke* xix.

descending by degrees, and the upper part by leaps; but very seldome when the upper part riseth by degrees, and the lower part falls by a leap.

Fourthly, the lesser third passeth into other Concords, as when it is continued as in degrees it may be, but not in leaps. Also it may passe into the greater third, both by degrees and leaps, as also into the lesser sixt if one of the parts stand still. Into the great sixt it sometime passeth, but very rarely.

Lastly, adde unto the rest this passage of the lesser third into the lesser sixt, as when the lower part riseth by degrees, and the upper part by leaps.

Of the greater or perfect Third.

The greater or perfect third, being to passe into perfect Concords, first takes the unison, when the parts ascend together, the higher by degree, the lower by leap; or when they meete together in a contrary motion, or when one of the parts stand still. Secondly it passeth into a fift when one of the parts rests, as hath beene declared before; or else when the parts ascend or descend together one by degrees, the other by leaps; and so the greater tenth may passe into a fift; seldome when both parts leape together, or when they seperate themselves by degrees; and this is in regard of the relation not harmonicall which falls in betweene the parts. Thirdly, the greater third passeth into the eight by contrary motions, the upper part ascending by degree.

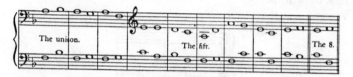

The greater third may also passe into other Concords; and first into a lesser third, when the parts ascend or descend by degrees, or by the lesser leaps. Secondly it is continued, but rarely, because it falls into Relation not harmonicall, thereby making the harmony lesse pleasing. Thirdly, into a lesser sixt, when the parts part asunder, the one by degree, the other by leap. Fourthly, into a greater sixt, one of the parts standing, or else the upper part falling by degree, and the lower by leap.

Of the lesser Sixt.

The lesser sixt regularly goes into the fift, one of the parts holding his place. Rarely into an eight, and first when the parts ascend or descend together, and one of them proceeds by the halfe Note, the other by leap.

Howsoever the waies of rising and falling from the lesser sixt into the eight in the former example may passe, I am sure that if the Base be sharpe in *Ffaut,* it is not tollerable to rise from a sixt to an eight.

Lastly, the lesser sixt may passe into an eight in Crotchets, for they are easily tollerated.

It passeth likewise into other Concords, as into a greater sixt the parts rising or falling by degrees, as also into a greater or lesser third, the one part proceeding by degree, the other by leap; or when one of the parts stands. It selfe it cannot follow, by reason of the falling in of the Relation not harmonicall.

Of the greater Sixt.

The greater sixt in proceeding affects[25] the eight; but it will hardly passe into the fift, unlesse it be in binding wise,[26] or when way is prepared for a close.

Finally, the greater sixt may in degrees be continued, or passe into a lesser sixt, as also into a greater third, or a lesser third.

[25] prefers.   [26] in a tie for suspension.

These are the principall observations belonging to the passages of Concords, perfect and imperfect, in few parts; and yet in those few, for fuge and formality sake,[27] some dispensation may be graunted. But in many parts, necessity enforcing, if any thing be committed contrary to rule, it may the more easily be excused, because the multitude of parts will drowne any small inconvenience.

FINIS.

[27] for the sake of close imitation of voices.

SELECTIONS
FROM
THE LATIN POEMS

From the Middle Ages until the Restoration, much of the literary work produced by Englishmen was in Latin. Bacon usually published his treatises in Latin; the Latin poems of Campion, Crashaw, Cowley, Milton, and others were as well known as their English poems; the Latin epigrams of John Owen went through innumerable editions in England and on the Continent, while John Barclay's Latin romance *Argenis* rivaled Sidney's *Arcadia* in popularity.

Campion's Latin poetry, which comprises about one third of his total output, appeared in two volumes, his second and final publications. *Thomae Campiani Poemata* (1595) contained the minor epic *Ad Thamesin; Fragmentum Umbrae,* the first half of a long Ovidian poem; sixteen elegies; and one hundred twenty-nine epigrams. *Tho. Campiani Epigrammatum Libri II,* etc. (1619), contained the finished *Umbra;* thirteen elegies, of which eleven were revisions of earlier pieces, two new; and four hundred fifty-three epigrams—two hundred twenty-five new ones in *Liber Primus;* eighty-eight revisions of the 1595 epigrams, and one hundred forty new ones in *Liber Secundus.*

Campion's Latin Poetry, then, represents mainly his early work in either its original or revised form. This early work frequently reveals unsuspected aspects of Campion as a poet; it reveals a decorative poet, a poet guilty of surprising structural weaknesses; it reveals a poet working in both the epic and the erotic Ovidian traditions, with a strong sense of the meaning of myth.

Ad Thamesin, which bears the distinction of being the first Latin poem totally devoted to the defeat of the Armada seven years since (see Bradner, *Musae Anglicanae,* pp. 53–54), is a curious piece of work. It might best be classified as an epic fragment, derived ultimately from the infernal council of Tasso's *Gerusalemme Liberata,* Book IV (as was William Alabaster's incomplete epic *Elisaeis,* ca. 1590); and, like its progenitor, it possesses many features unusual in traditional epic poetry. While its matter and narrative manner (beginning *in medias res* with the epic question of *cause* immediately referred to the supernatural) are quite traditional, its Latin style is more Ovidian than Virgilian, there is but one attempt at the large epic simile, and most of the poem is taken up with descriptive work, especially in those static absolutes defining rather than presenting action, the allegorical houses so dear to Spenser—the House of Dis, the House of Avarice, the Fountain of Envy. So intent was Campion on these descriptive pieces that he left a scant eighteen lines for the defeat itself, and then broke that

off for an apostrophe to Elizabeth. Campion here deserves much
more than Tasso the accusation of having composed a set of scenes
or madrigals rather than a whole poem. Yet it must be alleged that
the purpose of the poem is not to present the defeat of the
Armada but to place it in its proper epic frame by relating it to the
broadest of human concerns.

Umbra is a much better poem. It has a clear structure of two
parts, female and male, with cross relations: the story of the
reluctant female Iole embraced in sleep by Phoebus, their love
issuing in an ironic birth; and the story of their passionate son
Melampus, loved by the god of sleep, all his passion issuing in
living death. The poem belongs to the genre of Ovidian poem or
erotic epyllion whose vogue in the 1590s was inaugurated in 1589
by Lodge's *Scillaes Metamorphosis* and was continued, after Cam-
pion's contribution, by Marlowe's *Hero and Leander,* Heywood's
Oenone and Paris, and Drayton's *Endimion and Phoebe,* among
others. Campion captures the Ovidian style quite successfully with
his self-observing declamations, his turns on words with their
resultant wit, his sound effects (tending, however, to heavy allitera-
tion), and, especially, the sense he gives of the mordancy of a
transformation by which a person becomes reduced to the static
representation of a single personal desire. But the most interesting
thing about this poem is the archetypal quality of its myth. The
myth bears some resemblance to Spenser's tale of Amoret and
Belphoebe in Book III of *The Faerie Queene:* Iole's conception
in sleep resembles Chrysogone's, the resulting children are in each
case figures of Amor, and the setting, the valley where Cybele gives
the flowers their forms, is redolent of the Garden of Adonis.
Campion used his light and dark imagery to infuse this myth
with suggestions of cosmic archetypes, of the paradoxical relations
between the cold, dark, wet female center of earth with its un-
awakened potentiality and the hot, light, dry male inseminating
principle in the skies, of the tensions between them and the neces-
sity of their eventual conjunction, of their reluctance or eagerness
to join and the fecundity or barrenness which may result. By means
of such imagery and symbolism, the figures of the myth act out the
timeless processes of great creating nature.

In the first elegy of the 1595 set, Campion announces himself
as the first English elegist, relates himself to a long British erotic
tradition stemming from Chaucer, and links Ovidian grace to the
peace of Elizabeth. Some of the thirteen poems in Campion's
collection mock Love and other lovers, others are frankly erotic;
but most of them, addressed to the wanton Mellea and the cold

Caspia, capture the Ovidian tone of passion mingled with ironic self-observation. These poems establish Campion's as one of the authentic voices of an English tradition that includes the formal elegies of Marlowe, Jonson, Donne, and Carew as well as erotic epyllia like *Venus and Adonis, Ovids Banquet of Sence,* and *Hero and Leander.*

Though the overriding Ovidian tone of Campion's Latin work enters the epigrams in several love poems to Mellea, Caspia, and others, the master of the collection as a whole is, of course, Martial. The bulk of the poems are topical: there are complimentary pieces to James, Anne, and Charles; elegiac pieces on Sidney, Prince Henry, Henri of Navarre, and private friends; poems addressed to great and obscure friends like William Strachey, Nicholas Hornsey, James Thurbarne, Thomas Smith, George Gervis, Edmund Bracy, John Stanford, and the residents of Gray's Inn; and poems on a variety of subjects such as tobacco, *aurum potabile,* London citizens, honor, wrath, physicians, poetasters, pocket watches, bald men, the tarantella, and the death of a dog. These epigrams, which at their first appearance in 1595 rode on the tide of the new vogue of brevity, exhibit a side of Campion already quite familiar in the *Observations* and the epigrammatic ayres. Therefore there have been selected for this edition a mere handful of forty-nine of the four hundred fifty-three. Two considerations besides intrinsic worth have governed the selection: direct bearing on Campion's English poems which either translate the Latin poems or develop their ideas differently, and illustration of Campion's wide literary acquaintance (which included Spenser, Davies, Nashe, Chapman, and Bacon, in addition to many minor figures).

AD THAMESIN.

ARGUMENTUM.

Totum hoc poema gratulationem in se habet ad Thamesin de Hyspanorum fuga, in qua adumbrantur causae quibus adducti Hyspani expeditionem in Angliam fecerint. Eae autem sunt, avaritia, crudelitas, superbia, atque invidia. Deinde facta Apostrophe ad Reginam pastoraliter desinit.

Nympha potens Thamesis soli cessura Dianae,
Caeruleum caput effer aquis, charchesia late
Quae modo constiterant signis horrenda cruentis,
Ecce tuos trepide liquere fugacia portus.
Non tulit Hispanos crudelia signa sequentes   5
Neptunus pater, et multum indignantia spumis
Aequora, non deus aetherea qui fulminat arce,
Nubila qui solvit, ventorumque assidet alis.
Ille suos cultus, sua templa, suosque Britannos
Proteget, ultricemque suam victricibus armis.   10
Nec Romana feret purgatis Orgia fanis
Reffluere, aut vetitas fieri libamen ad aras.
O pietas odiosa deo, scelerataque sacra,
Quae magis inficiunt (damnosa piacula) sontes.
    Est locus Hesperiis, Diti sacer, abditus undis,   15
Quem pius occuluit Nereus, hominumque misertus
Oceanus, quemque ipse deis metuendus Apollo
Luminis inditio quod detegit omnia, sensit

TO THE THAMES.

ARGUMENT.

This whole poem congratulates the Thames for the rout of the Spaniards. In it are outlined the reasons for which the Spaniards were led to make an expedition against England. These are greed, cruelty, pride, and envy. Then an apostrophe to the queen ends the work like a bucolic.

Powerful nymph of the Thames, second only to Diana,[1] raise your dark head from the waters; see how far and wide the fleet which had just stood firm with bloody standards has left your harbors in panic like a runaway. Father Neptune did not endure the Spaniards following   5 their cruel standards and the seas raging wide with foam, nor did the god of heaven who thunders in his citadel, who looses the clouds and rides on the wings of the winds. He protects his cults, his temples, and his Britons—and his avenger—with victorious arms. Nor will he allow the Ro-   10 man Orgies to flow back into the cleansed shrines, or a sacrifice to be made at forbidden altars. O piety hateful to the god, and scandalous rituals (destructive sacraments) which the wicked corrupt even more.

    There is a place in the west sacred to Dis,[2] hidden in   15 the waves, which the blessed Nereus and Oceanus, taking pity on men, concealed; and Apollo himself (to be feared by the gods because he revealed all by the disclosure of his

---

[1] "Elisabethae": Campion's gloss.

[2] "Americae poetica descriptio" [poetic description of America]: Campion's gloss.

Ignotis sub aquis melius potuisse latere.
At pater umbrarum cui nox parit horrida natos   20
Terribiles, nigro vultus signante corymbo,
Ille per obscuras petit antra immania silvas
Aurea, silvarum Stygiae sub tegmine nymphae
Atra tenebrosis spectant in fontibus ora.
Eumenides regem comitantur, et ortus Echidna   25
Cerberus, et quae monstra tulit furialis origo,
Quos caput horrendum quatiens sic alloquitur Dis:
    Paci inimica cohors, nunc iras sumite pleno
Pectore, nunc totas penitus diffundite vires,
Exululate sacros, et quos horrere susurros   30
Ipse velim, collecta simul conflate venena,
Tabe Promethea riguus quas Caucasus herbas,
Tantaleaeve ferunt limphae, Phlegetonve, Acheronve,
Laetificas armate manus, Anioque, Tyburque
Sentiat infusum virus, Duriusque, Tagusque,   35
Diraque Avernales exuscitet unda furores,
Irarumque minas, avidique incendia belli.
    Dixit, et effugiunt quassantes ore colubros
Anguicomae, Ditem dolor excitat, evolat antro,
Et vagus excurrit sinuosi margine ponti   40
Atra velut nubes ventis agitata; senemque
Oceanum vocat, et rauco clamore remugit.
Constiterant fluctus, egere silentia venti;
Cyaneis os tollit aquis venerabile numen
Aequoreum, madidasque comas a fronte removit,   45
Ismarias superare nives albedine visas.
Quamvis nulla senis subiit reverentia Ditem,
Sic tamen affatur, mollitque astutia vultum:
O qui luctantes civiliaque arma gerentes
Imperio fluctus componis, et aequora late   50
Fusa, et sidentes ruptis de montibus amnes,
Cur invisa iacet? cur haec vacat insula cultu?
Pondere terra gemit, foeto maturuit alvo
Resplendens aurum; ferit hoc mortalia sydus
Pectora, tu solus prohibes quod amabilis auri   55
Suadet amor facinus; non has Romanus ad oras,

light) realized that it was a better hiding place there be-
neath the unknown waters. But the father of the shades, 20
to whom gloomy night bore terrible children (a black
garland marking their faces), sought huge golden caves
through the dim forests there, where the Stygian nymphs
under the shade of the forests look at their black faces in
the shadowy streams. The Eumenides accompany their 25
king and Cerberus, spawn of Echidna, and those monsters
which the stock of furies bore. Shaking his awful head, Dis
addresses them thus:

"Company hostile to peace, now bring forth the wrath
from full hearts, now pour out all the violence deep
within, howl out the accursed words and hisses I myself 30
would cringe from, blow poisons concentrated in one, the
herbs from Promethean slime which watery Caucasus or
the streams of Tantalus bear or Phlegethon or Acheron.
Arm your joyous bands, let Anio[3] and Tiber experience
the injected poison, and Durius and Tagus,[4] and let the 35
dreadful wave start to consume the furies of Avernus and
the threats of wrath and the fires of ravenous war."

He spoke, and shaking the snakes from their faces, the
Gorgons fled; anguish seized Dis, he flew out of the cave
and aimlessly darted along the edge of the billowy sea like 40
a black cloud driven by the winds; and he called the
ancient Oceanus and bellowed with a raucous shout. The
waves stood still and the winds drove on in silence; the
venerable spirit of the waters lifted his face from the Cya-
nean[5] sea and brushed from his brow the dripping hair, 45
whiter than Ismarian snows.[6] Although the old man ap-
proached Dis with no reverence, still Dis addressed him
thus, and shrewdly softened his expression: "O thou who
hold sway over the waves (struggling and waging civil 50
wars), and the seas spread far and wide, and the streams
falling from the clefts in mountains: why does this island
remain unseen? why does this island lack civilization? The
earth groans with its weight, with shining gold ripened in
its fertile womb; this star strikes mortal hearts, but you 55
alone keep them away because the love of luring gold en-
courages crime; not a Roman has reached these shores, no

[3] a tributary of the Tiber. [4] the rivers Duero and Tajo in Spain.
[5] The Cyaneae are islands at the entrance of the Euxine Sea.
[6] Ismarus is a river in Thrace.

Non venit Hispanus castris assuetus et armis,
Nec quisquam Italiae, tua monstra natantia terrent.
Esto precor facilis, quosque ingens gloria Martis
Extulit Hesperios, animis rebusque potentes   60
Excipe, conde sinu, nostroque in littore siste.
Quem contra Oceanus: Tibi, Dis, patet orcus, et omnis
Vis terrena, nocensque aegris mortalibus aurum,
Verum siquid habent, et habent tua munera pulchri.
Sunt Angli, sunt Troiana de gente Britanni,   65
Qui pacem, numenque colunt, et templa fatigant.
Sin longa spectes serie numerosa trophaea,
Has etiam spectes immensae molis arenas.
Ingemuit, traxitque imo suspiria corde
Tartareus, spumaque oris barbam albicat atra.   70
Aggressumque tuas, decus o regina Britannum,
Virtutes narrare, fremens occoepit acutis
Obturbare senem stridoribus, et ferus ira
Concussit piceos scabra rubigine dentes.
Ardebant oculi, vultu pax exulat omnis,   75
Excidit obsequium et meditata precamina, diras
Evomit atque minas quales irata Medea.
Et tibi, ait, quoniam levis est mea visa potestas,
Rumpam fundamenta maris quae tegmine nostras
Obfuscant aedes; post imas quaere sub umbras   80
In fluctus requiem, sedemque cadentibus undis.
Horruit Oceanus (vitium formido senile est)
Sed quid non ausit demens furor, et mala praeceps
In sua; vix motum longa mulcedine Ditem
Leniit, et malus impetratis rebus abivit.   85
Carbasa tenduntur subito venientibus Euris,
Et ruit aequoreos male gratum pondus in armos.
Cogitat Oceanus rapido nunc mergere ponto,
Nunc gravibus scopulis, in acutaque figere saxa.
Cauta iram cohibet mens, at vindicta dolentem   90
Oblectat, sensitque animo te, Drace, futurum
Exitio Hispanis, clarumque insignibus ausis
Frobucerum, pariterque novis successibus oras
Ampla reportantem ad patrias spolia auripotentem
Candisium, audaces animos fortuna secundat.   95
    Excipit Hesperios Dis quem tegit aurea palla,
Corporis et tenebrae vestis fulgore coruscant.

Spaniard accustomed to armed camp, no one from Italy, because they fear your swimming monsters. Be gentle, I pray, receive, hide in your bosom, and plant on our shore the Hesperians[7] powerful in spirit and wealth, whom the 60 great glory of war has exalted." Oceanus answered: "To you, Dis, Orcus lies open and all earthly power, and gold harming weak mortals; but whatever they have, the fair have also your favors. These are the English, they are Brit- 65 ons from the Trojan race, who cherish peace and worship the spirit and frequent temples. And if you should see many triumphs in long array, you will also see these sands the field of a mighty struggle." Dis groaned and sighed from the depths of his heart, and black foam flecked the beard on his cheeks. Raging, he began to trouble the old man 70 with shrill shrieks as Oceanus started to tell of your vir- tues, O queen pride of Britain, and wild with rage, Dis gnashed his teeth, black with scaly rust. His eyes flashed, all peace was banished from his expression. He forgot about complaisance and contrived entreaties, and he spewed forth dire threats just like the enraged Medea. 75 And he said, "Since my power seems trivial to you, I shall break the foundations of the sea which darken our house with their shade; afterwards you may seek for peace in the depths of the shades and for a home on the falling 80 waves." Oceanus shrank back (fear is a fault of old age) but what Oceanus did not dare, mad fury, subsiding into the depths of its own evils, dared, and softened the angry Dis scarcely affected by such extensive soothing; and the evil one, having accomplished his purpose, went off. Sud- 85 denly the sails were filled by the freshening East Wind and the unwelcome burden fell into the arms of the sea. Oceanus planned now to sink the fleet in the swift current, now on the hazardous shoals, and to impale it on the sharp rocks. But his clever wit marshaled his wrath, and vengeance diverted his pain; he realized that you, Drake, 90 would bring destruction to the Spaniards, and noble Frobisher of outstanding daring, and likewise the wealthy Cavendish bringing back rich spoils to his native shores from new successes; for fortune favors bold hearts. 95

Dis received the Hesperians wearing a golden cloak, and the shadows gleamed with the splendor of his body and

[7] the Spaniards, whose struggle with the British over America is predicted in ll. 67–68 below.

Vix hunc credideris caecas habitare cavernas,
Squallentemque situ Stygiis sordere sub umbris.
O quam splendescit Venus aurea! suavis in auro est   100
Gratia, multus honos, absque auro gratia nulla est.

   Propter Avarities stat inhospita, lumine laeta
Sollicito; mirum, hoc laetatur in hospite, nullum
Quae colit hospitium. Libica est procul invia Syrtis
Per vada, stant tacitae longa insuetudine silvae,   105
Semper et obdormit tranquilla in montibus Eccho,
Dissimilisque sui, non est qui suscitet illam.
Moenibus obsepta est sublimibus aerea turris,
Mulciber hanc vario torquens errore viarum
Aeternum statuit non expugnabile tectum.   110
Haec domus, hic misera insomnis noctesque diesque
Thesaurum observat caeca tellure sepultum.
Et quia causa deest, fingit sibi monstra timenda,
Formidatque animo quas non praesenserat umbras.
Turribus aeriis tuta est si credere posset,   115
Tuta loco, extructisque ingens super aequor arenis.
Alta per exiguam clauduntur moenia portam,
Hanc sola ingreditur, nunquam egreditur nisi Plutus
Evocet, eximium hunc spretis habet omnibus unum.

   Proxima purpurea succedit cuspide Caedes   120
Suspitiose oculos obliquans, atque cruentum
Vix animo halato cor in ilia gurgitat atra,
Atra aestu, rabieque insana fellis adusti.

   Ultima subsequitur manifesta Superbia curru;
Fastiditque solum, sellam haud dignatur eburnam   125
Qua vehitur, quam traxit avis Iunonia pompam
Pennarum expandens, gemmasque elata recludens.
Agmina conveniunt, dextras utrinque dederunt,
Dis ait: Hesperii satis est dextraeque moraeque,
Mensa diesque vocant, periit pars optima lucis.   130
Applaudunt regi umbrarum portuque recedunt.

   Ecce fatigatos laevo curvamine coeli
Lentus agens Hyperion equos, curruque reclinans
Viderat Hesperios, et quis novus incola terras

his vestments. Scarcely would you have believed that he inhabited the dark caves, and that wallowing in mold he groveled beneath the Stygian shades. O how golden Venus shone! there is sweet grace in gold, much honor; and apart from gold, there is no grace.

Nearby stands inhospitable Greed, rejoicing in the flickering light; strange that she who cherishes no friendship rejoices in this friend. Impassable Syrtes is far off through th eLibyan sea;[8] there the forests stand silent through long disuse, and always peaceful Echo sleeps in the mountains unlike herself, where there is none to arouse her. A bronze tower there is hedged by high battlements, for Vulcan, ringing this with a maze of paths, made a shelter never to be captured. Here in this house the sleepless wretch watches night and day over her treasure buried in the dark earth. And for no reason she fashions monsters for herself to fear, and dreads in her heart shadows which she has not known. She is safe in the bronze towers if she could have trust, safe in this place above the great plain with heaps of sand. The high walls are sealed by a narrow gate which she alone enters, never does she go out unless Plutus[9] summons her, for this one is the exception to all who have been scorned.

Next Slaughter follows with his crimson blade, casting his eyes suspiciously, and he steeps his bloody heart in the black entrails when life is scarcely gone, in the black tide and boiling fury of brown bile.

Last follows Pride displayed in her chariot; she shrinks from the ground and does not deem worthy the ivory chair in which she rides, a chair which Juno's bird draws, opening her fan of feathers to proudly disclose her jewels.[10] The lines meet, they exchange handclasps. Dis says: "Hesperians, this is pledge of friendship enough, and enough delay, the day's banquet table calls, the best part of the day has passed away." They applaud the king of the shades and leave the harbor.

Lo, Hyperion slowly driving his weary horses down the left vault of heaven and reclining in his chariot saw the Hesperians, and he wondered what new colonist had come

[8] *"Avaritiae domus"* [The House of Avarice]: Campion's gloss.
[9] the god of riches.
[10] Compare Spenser's Lucifera, *The Faerie Queene,* I, iv, 17.

Venit in ignotas miratur; eoque morantes   135
Cursores animat, Tethidosque hortatur ad undas.
Interea ingentem vino cratera propinant,
Indulgentque epulis Dis cum regaliter usis
Hospitibus, donec gelidis stipata tenebris
Induxit somnos nox, atque papavera sparsit.   140
   Postera deformes roseo velamine texit
Umbras aurora, et simulatis fronte capillis.
Concurrunt stygiae feriuntes tympana nymphae,
Et recinunt miserum clamoso gutture carmen.
Ducentesque choros dominum, regemque requirunt.   145
Turba petit silvas somno experrecta madentes
Rore levi suavesque expirans gramen odores.
Valle sub obscura liquidis argenteus undis
Fons erat, Invidiae sacer, hunc, Narcisse, petisses
Tutus, in adversam quia nulla repercutitur lux   150
Seu lucis radius speciem, sed quicquid in orbe
Est usquam limphis manifesto cernitur illis.
Fons mundi speculum est, sed qui speculatur in illo
Morbum oculis haurit macidum, et lethale venenum.
Huc divertentes cum Dite Hyspana iuventus   155
Immisere oculos avide putealibus undis,
Et sub aqua mirantur aquas, urbesque, domosque,
Agnovere suos portus, nemora, arvaque et aurei
Lucida signa Tagi: longe omnibus eminet una
Cuncta mari tellus, celeberrima rupibus albis.   160
Hanc spectant, et agros, urbes, vada, flumina, fontes
Laudant inviti; hac una regione morantur;
Quaeque vident cupiunt, atque invidere videndo.
Paulatim increvit pulmonibus ardor anhelis,
Lividus ora color, macies cariosa medullas   165
Occupat; illi acres pugnant superare dolores;
Iamque odio locus est, nec iam discedere possunt.
Sic miseri cum flamma aedes circumflua vastat,
Excussi somnis media sub nocte paventes
Corpora proriperent, obsistit at obvius ignis;   170
Cernentesque adversa oculos, et cassa moventes
Effugia exurit feralis taeda lacertos.
   Postquam irretitas acies, et vulneris aestu

into unknown lands; he goaded on his coursers lingering   135
there and urged them on to the waves of Tethys. Mean-
while they brought on a huge bowl of wine, and Dis and
his royally treated guests enjoyed the feast until the night
filled with icy shadows brought sleep and scattered the   140
poppies.

The next dawn wove shapeless shadows with its rosy veil
and the mock hair on its brow.[11] The Stygian nymphs
gathered beating their timbrels and sang out a sad song
with their mournful voices. Leading the dance, they sought   145
out their master and king. The throng roused from sleep
sought the forests dripping with light dew and the grass
breathing sweet aromas. At the foot of a dim vale was a
spring silvery with crystal water, sacred to Envy;[12] you
would have sought this in safety, Narcissus, because no
light or beam of light was reflected on the facing features,   150
but whatever is anywhere in the world is clearly seen in
these waters. The spring is the mirror of the world, but
whoever looks in it drinks in a wasting illness with his eyes
and deadly poison. Turning to this with Dis, the Spanish   155
youth greedily flooded their eyes with the waters of the
spring. And beneath the water they marveled at waters
and cities and houses, they recognized their own harbors
and groves, fields, and the shining landmarks of the golden
Tagus: far above all rose one land entirely on the sea, most
famous for its white cliffs. They looked at this and, un-   160
asked, praised its fields, cities, fords, rivers, springs; they
lingered in this one region; what they saw they desired,
and they grew envious by seeing. Little by little yearning
grew in their panting breasts, a leaden hue stole over their   165
faces, a rotting decay seized their bones; they strove to
overcome their sharp pains; already there was room for
hatred, nor could they now go away. Thus it is when fire
surrounds a house and destroys it. Aroused from sleep at
nearly midnight, quaking with fear, the wretches rush out,   170
but the fire ahead stops them; and like a funeral torch it
consumes the eyes as they look at what is ahead, and the
arms that devise futile ways of escape.

After he realized that their intention was ensnared and

---

[11] i.e., a mist.
[12] *"Fons Invidiae sacer"* [The Fountain dedicated to Envy]: Campion's
gloss. The description is based on Ovid's pool of Narcissus, *Metamorphoses*
III. 407–12.

Senserat arderi et frangi iuvenilia corda
Dis, arrisit aquis, laetusque silentia rupit.   175
Spectatae satis, o iuvenes, nimiumque recedant
Coelestes lymphae, mens est et numen in illis.
Ecce ferunt violas, detexaque lilia nymphae,
Ecce struunt in serta rosas fontemque coronant.
Nondum extrema gravis diverberat ora loquentis   180
Imber, et obducto recidentia nubila coelo.
Tristis hiems, et nox nullo suadente resurgit
Vespere, terrarumque orbem intempesta recondit.
Per iuga dissiliunt fluctus, volvuntur et imas
In valles, teretesque trahunt de montibus ornos.   185
Intremuere omnes, Dis autem interritus umbras
Increpat, et facilem concussit arundine terram,
Terra tremit, nigrasque aditum patefecit ad arces.
   At dirupta iam ruituris subvolat Auster
Nube, pruinosisque cadentes sustinet alis.   190
Taenarium nemus umbriferum, tacitaeque cavernas
Noctis, et aeternum quibus obdormire sepulchris
Adsuevit Morphei pater, haec praetervolat aestu
Fulmineo, donec portas prope sensit opacas
Stantem Hecaten, mediis qua circumcingitur umbris.   195
Desilit hic terramque vagis amplectitur ulnis.
Laeta viro occurrit Plutonia, dumque stupescit
Haud expectatos comites, fugit imbrifer Auster.
Et numerosa horret niveis concussa capillis
Styria, luctificique fluunt cum grandine nimbi.   200
   Delitias facit hospitibus, stygiosque lepores
Dis; et in obscuros Trivia comitante recessus
Monstrat iter. Stant mensae epulis vinoque repletae,
Aureo et effulgent operosa cubilia tecto.
Accubuere, canente suam accumbentibus Orpheo   205
Euridicen, quaeque olim inter Rhodopeia saxa
Fudit ad umbrosas quercus, tenuesque miricas.
Quin etiam immites Thressas flevisset, et Hebro
Dimersum caput et cytheram, si non dea mater,
Flens dea Calliope nati compresserat ora.   210
Conticuit, subitoque oritur miserabile murmur,

burned with the fire of the wound, and that the youthful
spirits were broken, Dis smiled on the waters and gladly   175
broke the silence. "O youths, let the holy waters, observed
long enough, recede; there is reason and divine will in
them. See the nymphs bring violets and lilies they have
made, see how they arrange the roses in garlands and
crown the spring." A heavy rain slashed down before he   180
finished speaking and the lowering clouds blotted out the
sky. A gloomy storm and an unseasonable night unher-
alded by the evening arose, and buried the whole world.
The floods leapt over the ridges and churned in the deep
valleys and uprooted the smooth mountain ash trees. All   185
trembled, but Dis, unfrightened, reproved the shades and
smote the yielding earth with his rod. The earth shook
and opened a path to the black citadels.

But when the cloud burst the South Wind flew upon
those rushing forth and supported them as they fell with
his frosty wings. The rainy grove of Taenarus,[13] the caves   190
of silent night, and the tombs in which the father of
Morpheus was wont to sleep forever, these Dis flew past
on a tide of lightning until he realized that Hecate was
standing near the dusky doors where she was surrounded   195
by the shades. Here he sped down and embraced the
earth with his waving arms. Joyously Plutonia came to
meet her husband, and while she stood amazed at his un-
expected companions, the rain-filled South Wind fled and
countless icicles bristled like white hair, and the baleful   200
clouds teemed with hail.

She made dainties for the guests and Dis performed the
Stygian courtesies; in the dark recesses with Trivia as his
companion he pointed out the way. The tables stood
loaded with food and wine and the embroidered couches
gleamed with a gold cover. They reclined at the table
while Orpheus was singing to them of his Eurydice who   205
once among the rocks of Rhodope glided through the
shady oaks and pliant tamarisks. Indeed he would have
lamented the cruel Thracians and the life drowned in the
Hebrus[14] and his lyre, if his weeping mother Calliope had   210
not silenced the lips of her son. He grew silent, and sud-

[13] a mountain in Laconia, beneath which was the entrance to the infernal
regions.

[14] the river Hebrus in Thrace.

Quale sepulturis cum naenia flebilis inter
Affines canitur resono plangore gementes.
Lugentque Hesperii nequaquam in vatis honorem,
Pestiferi sed enim torquentur imagine fontis,   215
Visorumque memor furit aegris dira cupido
Pectoribus, totasque aedes singultibus implent.
Nec sua turpari moesto convivia luctu
Sustinet ulterius Cereris gener, atque ita fatur:
   Ite leves umbrae, celsas ad sydera pinus   220
Extruite, et fluidas lato super aequore turres.
Vosque nisi hospitii pigeat fortassis Iberi
Exhilerate animos, neu quem simulachra dolorem
Vana ferant. Nam quae niveis fonte insula saxis
Emicuit spectans Helecen gelidumque Booten   225
Insula, dives opum, sedes veneranda Britannis,
Ingentes diffisa suis horrere carinas
Discet, et Hispano tandem succumbere ferro.
   Cincta sub haec aderat torto caput angue Megaera,
Horrida tela, ignes, et ahenea monstra ministrans.   230
Ergo incenduntur furiis, Stygiasque ad arenas
Armati incedunt, nigros ubi cernere manes
Littoribus tot erat, quot apes praesepia circum,
Aut aestate solent turmatim irrepere sulcis
Formicae; cursansque ignito horrenda flagello   235
Undique Tysiphone cessantes verberat umbras.
Iam sed in immensum ceu turres seu iuga Pindi
Increvere rates, quas est mirata iuventus
Hesperia, et Stygio faciunt vota impia regi.
   Incubuere omnes, et olenti littore classem   240
Diducunt mare per gelidum. Cynosuris euntes
Respicit, aspectu sed dedignante Calistho.
Iamque fremens, ut erat vultu illaetabilis ursa
Unguibus immites nimbos concussit, et auras
Nubibus infestat, pugnamque Aquilonibus Austros   245
Adversum instituit, veteresque resuscitat iras.
   At tu nympharum Thamesis pulcherrima limphis
Alta tuis, procul ut vidisti hostilia signa,
Tu dea flumineam spaciosa gurgite frontem

denly a plaintive murmur arose just as when a mournful
dirge at a funeral is sung in the midst of relatives groaning
with re-echoing wails. The Hesperians were mourning not
out of respect for the bard but because they were indeed
wracked by the image of the noxious fountain. Mindful of   215
the visions seen there, a fierce desire burned in their sick
hearts, and they filled the whole palace with their sobs.
The son-in-law of Ceres did not let his banquet be further
defiled by the mournful lament and said these words:

"Go, light shades, raise the soaring masts to the skies   220
and the floating towers on the broad sea. Unless perhaps
you are ashamed of the Spanish friendship, lift up your
hearts and do not let empty images bring any pain. For
the island which sparkled with white rocks in the spring
looking toward the Great Bear and frosty Boötes, rich in   225
wealth, the adored seat of the British, despairing of its own
men, will learn to tremble at the huge ships and at last to
yield to the Spanish steel."

After this, Megaera[15] was at hand, her head wreathed
by a twisted snake, tending her awful weapons, fires and   230
brazen monsters. So they were aroused by the Furies and
in arms went out upon the Stygian sands where they could
see as many black shades on the shores as there are bees
around the hives or as there are ants in squadrons creeping
along the trails in summer; and running hither and thither   235
on all sides, the fearsome Tisiphone with her fiery scourge
lashed the loitering shades. But now the vessels grow to a
great size like towers or the heights of Pindus.[16] The Hes-
perian youth marveled at them and made shameless prom-
ises to the Stygian king.

All lay on, and from the noisome shore they launched   240
the fleet upon the icy sea. The Small Bear watched them
but Callisto[17] spurned the sight. Now growling, unhappy
as he was in appearance, the bear smote the raging storm
clouds with his claws, spotted the breezes with clouds,
started a fight between the North Winds and the South   245
Winds, and revived the old angers.

But you, Thames, fairest of nymphs, deep in your clear
waters, as you saw the enemy standards far off, you,
goddess, concealed the source of the river in a wide eddy

[15] one of the Furies, as is Tisiphone (line 236, below).
[16] Mezzara, a mountain in Thrace. [17] Callisto, Ursa Major.

Celata, aequoreas turbasti fluctibus undas.   250
Donec Ibera cohors ventorum pulsa furore,
Et virtute virum, per Hybernica saxa refugit.
Illic dira fames Scythicas illapsa per auras,
Et Lybico vesana sitis de pulvere nata,
Tum Phlegetonteae pestes, rabidique furores,   255
Ingratusque sibi dolor, et sua funera Erinnis
Exornans, nigra Hyspanos sub tartara mittunt.
Sic o sic pereant advorsis undique fatis,
Ira Calisthoniae trepidisque impendeat ursae,
Sive bibant Tyberim, vel aquas torrentis Iberi,   260
Sive Aurora novo, sero vel sole recedens
Hesperus illustret gentes, umbrasque repellat.
Sic pereat, quicunque tuas fleturus in oras
Vela inimica dabit, Brutique nepotibus, et diis
O vetus hospitium, sanctumque Britannia nomen.   265
    Tuque viresce diu dea ceu Daphneia laurus.
Tu dea, tu foelix Anglorum numen Elisa.
Non aconitum in te virus, non ensis acumen,
Nec magicum vim carmen habet, nec flamma calorem.
Scilicet integrum divina potentia pectus   270
Firmat et humano dedit inviolabile ferro.
Ergo diu vigeas, procul hinc fuge, pigra senectus,
Ismarioque cuba glaciali frigida saxo,
Vel steriles inter quas alluit Ister arenas,
I fuge, coelestes animas tentare nefandum est.   275
Fallor? an excessit tardo per inane volatu?
Ecce autem rigidam trahit inter nubila pallam,
Et tremit, et cani recidunt horrore capilli.
At te diva rosis ambit formosa iuventa,
Atque Heliconiacas aspergit floribus undas,   280
O diva, o miseris spes Elisabetha Britannis
Una, senectutem superes, pulsisque superstes
Hostibus, innumeros gemines virtutibus annos.

and confused the waters of the sea with your waves, until   250
the Iberian company, driven back by the fury of the
winds and the courage of the men, escaped through the
Hibernian rocks. There keen hunger gliding over the
Scythian breezes and wild thirst sprung from the Lybian
dust, then the diseases of Phlegethon and raving madness,   255
unwelcome pain, and Erinnys lauding her own death sent
the Spaniards down under black Tartarus. Thus indeed
may they perish with the fates opposing on all sides, may
the wrath of Callisto and the restless bear threaten whether
they drink of the Tiber or the waters of the raging Ebro.[18]   260
May Aurora with the new sun or Hesperus setting with
the late sun shed light on these people and drive away the
shadows. So let perish whoever, soon to weep, will set sail
against your shores, heirs of Brutus, long friends of the   265
gods, sacred name, Britain.

Long may you thrive, goddess, like the laurel of Daphne.
You; goddess, propitious spirit of the English, Elizabeth,
Aconite has no poison against you, the sword no blade, the
spell no magic power, and the flame no heat. To be sure
divine power strengthens your pure heart and renders it   270
inviolable to human sword. Long may you flourish. Fly far
from here, dull old age, and rest freezing on the glacial
Ismarian rock or among the barren sands washed by the
Danube. Go, fly away, it is wicked to tempt celestial spirits.   275
Am I mistaken? Or did he leave on a slow flight through
the void? But see how he draws his stiff cape among the
clouds and trembles, and how his white hair recoils with a
shudder. But, divine one, handsome youth encircles you
with roses and sprinkles Helicon's waves with flowers. O   280
goddess Elizabeth, sole hope of wretched Britons, may
you conquer old age, and may you witness your enemies
laid low, and may you redouble countless years by your
vigor.

[18] a river in Spain.

UMBRA.

Foemineos dea quae nigro sub Limine manes
Occludis, coelo ostentans, iterumque reducens
Umbriferum per iter: quanquam crudelis amanti,
Sis mihi tu facilis; quanquam non aequa resumis
Formosarum animas festina morte peremptas.   5
Abreptas solus resonante reducere plectro
Threicius potuit, lucique ostendere amores;
Non potuit tamen; ad tristes devolvitur umbras
Quicquid formosum est, et non inamabile natum.
O Sacra Persephone, liceat tua regna canenti,   10
Lucifugasque umbras, aperire abscondita terris
Iura, tenebrarumque arcana adoperta silentum.
Respice qui viridi radiancia tempora lauro
Comprimis; insidias, et furtivos Hymenaeos,
Et Nympham canimus, sed quae tibi prodita somno   15
Nupsit; facta parens, etiam sibi credita virgo.
   Est in visceribus terrae nulli obvia vallis,
Concava, picta rosis, variaque ab imagine florum;
Fontibus irrorata, et fluminibus lapidosis:
Mille specus subter latitant, totidemque virenti   20
Stant textae myrto casulae, quibus anxia turba
Nympharum flores pingunt, mireque colorant.
Nec minus intenta est operi Berecynthia mater,
Instituens natos frutices quo syderis ortu
Aerio credant capita inconstantia coelo.   25
Admonet immaturae hyemis, gelidaeque pruinae,

SHADOW.

Goddess who confine the shades of women beneath the
black threshold, and reveal them to the heaven only to
withdraw them again along the shadowy path: although
you are cruel to a lover, may you be gentle to me; even
though you unjustly take back the souls of the beautiful   5
claimed by a swift death. The Thracian[1] alone could
bring back his departed loves by the music of his lyre and
show them to the light; yet he could not prevail; whatever
is beautiful and can be loved is swept back to the sad
shades. O holy Persephone, may your realms, the shades   10
which flee the light of day, reveal to the poet the oaths
hidden in the earth and the buried secrets of the silent
shadows. You who bind your radiant temples with the
green laurel, pay attention; we sing of treachery, a stealthy
marriage, and a nymph pledged to you but wed in her   15
sleep, and made a mother even as she believed herself a
maid.

There is in the bowels of the earth a vale open to no one,
recessed, adorned with roses and by flowers of various
shapes, watered by springs and rocky streams: a thousand   20
caves lurk below, and there are as many bowers woven of
living myrtle for which the industrious throng of nymphs
fashion colored flowers in wondrous ways. No less does the
Berecynthian mother[2] attend the work, planting her seed-
ling shrubs at whatever season they may trust their bob-   25
bing heads to the air of heaven. She gives warning of the

[1] Orpheus, who momentarily won back his wife Eurydice from Pluto
and Persephone, gods of the underworld.
[2] Cybele, the mother of the gods.

Imbriferumque Austrorum, horrendisonumque Aquilonum;
Grandine concussam Rhodopen, Taurumque nivalem,
Concretosque gelu prohibet transcendere montes.
Tantum qui placido suspiras ore, Favoni,   30
Arboreos tibi commendat dea sedula foetus.
Fraga, rosas, violasque iubet latitare sub umbris.
Forma rosis animos maiores indidit, ausis
Tollere purpureos vultus, et despicere infra
Pallentes odio violas, tectasque pudore.   35
Diva rosas leviter castigat, et admonet aevi
Labilis; aspiceres foliis prodire ruborem,
Et suspendentes ora annutantia flores.
  Accelerant Nymphae properata ex ordine matri
Pensa ostentantes, quarum pulcherrima Iole   40
Asportat gremio texturas millecolores.
Hanc olim ambierat furtim speciosus Apollo;
Muneribus tentans, et qua suasisse loquela
Posset; saepe adhibet placidam vim, saepe et amantum
Blanditias cupidus, sed non cupiente puella.   45
Brachia circumdat collo, simul illa repellit;
Instat hic, illa fugit; duplicant fastidia flammas;
Ardet non minus ac rutilo Semeleia proles
Cum curru exciderat, totumque incenderat orbem.
Spes sed ut illusas vidit deus, et nihil horum   50
Virginis aversam potuisse inflectere mentem,
Dira subinde vovet pervertens fasque nefasque;
Illicitumque parat spreto medicamen amori,
Lactucas humectantes gelidumque papaver,
Cyrceiaeque simul stringit terrestria mala   55
Mandragorae, condens sudatos pixide rores.
  Nox erat, incedit nullo cum murmure Phaebus,
Nulli conspiciendus adit spelaea puellae;
Illa toro leviter roseo suffulta iacebat,
Sola struens flores varia quos finxerat arte.   60
Candida lucebat fax, hanc primum inficit atra
Nube; deinde linit medicati aspergine succi
Pulvillosque leves et picti strata cubilis;

early storm, the chilling frost, the rainy season of the
South Winds, the shrieking blast of the North Winds; she
prevents Rhodope pelted with hail, snowy Taurus,[3] and
the mountains stiff with ice from crossing over. To you,
West Wind, who breathe only gentle breezes, the careful   30
goddess entrusts the seedling trees. She commands the
strawberries, roses, and violets to hide in the shadows.
Beauty instills greater courage in the roses which dare to
raise their shining faces and look down from above with
scorn on the fading violets covered with shame. The god-   35
dess mildly reproves the roses and reminds them of time
slipping by; you might see redness appear on the leaves
and the flowers hanging down their nodding faces.

The Nymphs rush up in hasty disorder to show their
weaving to their mother; Iole, the fairest of them, carries   40
webs of a thousand colors in her arms. Once the handsome
Apollo secretly courted her, tempting her with gifts and
with whatever sweet talk he was able to use to persuade
her. Often in his desire he used gentle force, and often
the blandishments of lovers, but the maid was not willing.   45
He put his arms around her neck, at once she pushed him
away; he pressed his suit, she fled; her disdain doubled
the flames; he burned no less than when Semele's son[4]
had fallen from the golden chariot and set the whole world
on fire. As the god saw that his hopes had vanished and   50
none of his ploys could change the stubborn mind of the
maid, perverting right and wrong, forthwith he made
dreadful vows; he prepared an illicit drug for his slighted
love; he pressed together dank lettuce leaves and chilling
poppy and ground apples of Circe's mandrake, secreting   55
the pressed juices in a flask.

It was night; with no sound Phoebus advanced; visible
to no one he entered the cavern of the maid; she had
heaped up flowers which she had fashioned by her unique
and diverse skill and was lying gently supported on her rosy   60
couch. A shining torch was gleaming, and he shrouded it
at once with a black cloud; then he sprinkled her down
cushions and the covers of her ornate bed with drops of

[3] mountains in Thrace and Lycia, respectively.
[4] Bacchus was the son of Semele, but the reference seems to be to
Phaëthon, son of the Sun and Clymene.

Terque soporiferas demulcet pollice cordas
Plectripotens, nectitque Hecateio carmine somnos.   65
Virgineos oculos vapor implicat, excipit artus
Alta quies, et membra toro collapsa recumbunt.
Vidit et obstupuit deus; inter spemque metumque
Accedit, refugitque iterum; suspirat ab imo
Pectore; nec pietas, nec siderea ora puellae   70
Plura sinunt; sed amor, sed ineffraenata libido
Quid castum in terris intentatumve relinquit?
Oscula non referenda serit, tangitque, premitque;
Illa (quod in somnis solet) ambigua edidit ore
Murmura, ploranti similis nec digna ferenti;   75
Saepe manu urgentem quamvis sopita repellit.
Nequidquam, raptor crebris amplexibus haeret,
Vimque per insidias fert, indulgetque furori.
Nec satis est spectare oculis, tetigisse, fruique;
Ingratum est quicquid sceleris latet. Illaque turpe   80
Quod patitur vitium quia non sensisse videtur,
Maestus abit (revocante die) spoliumque pudoris
Tanquam invitus habet; semper sibi quod petat ultra
Invenit ingeniosus amor, crescitque favendo.

   Tandem discusso nova nupta sopore resurgit,   85
Illam sed neque turba vocat, neque clari Hymenaei
Illius ante fores iuvenum non inclita pompa
Conspicitur, placide charis commista puellis.
Omnia muta tacent, pariter tacuisset Iole,
Verum nescio quae morborum insignia terrent;   90
Nec valet a stomacho, nec non tremulum omnia frigus
Membra quatit: cubito incumbens sic anxia secum:
Numquid et hoc morbi est? nam quae mutatio sanas
Attentat vires? nec enim satis illa placebant,
Postrema quae nocte timens insomnia vidi.   95
Quos ego praeterii fluctus! quae praelia sensi
In somnis! quantis, o dii, transfixa sub hastis
Occubui! vereor diros ne iratus Apollo
In me condiderit parientia spicula morbos.
Sed nec Apollineas pestes, nec respicit iras   100
Hic in corde pudor meus; hoc solamen, Iole,
Semper habes, moriare licet, moriere pudica.
Assurgit, cingitque operi se. Candida fecit
Lilia, quae gustare cupit, quia candida fecit:
Quidque oculi cernunt animus desiderat; aegrum   105
Pectus ferre moras nescit, votisve carere.

the drugged juices; thrice he sweetly played the chords of
a lullaby on his lyre and wove a web of sleep with a spell   65
of Hecate. Mist shrouded the eyes of the girl; a deep sleep
settled on her limbs and her whole body lay inert on the
couch. The god watched in amazement; between hope
and fear, he drew near and drew back again; he heaved a
deep sigh; neither his honor nor the angelic face of the   70
girl allowed much more, but what in the world does love,
unbridled lust, leave pure and untouched? He showered
unrequited kisses on her, and touched and pressed; she, as
she was wont in sleep, murmured wordless sounds, as if   75
she wept and could not bear her plight; often she pushed
away his pawing hand even though she was drugged. To
no avail; her ravisher clung to frequent embraces and
treacherously plied his force and indulged his madness; it
was not enough to gaze with his eyes, to have touched,
to enjoy; whatever sin lurked unfulfilled was disagreeable.   80
Because she seemed not to have felt the ravishment she
suffered shamefully, he went away sadly when day sum-
moned him anew, and carried the plume of her chastity
although he had been unbidden; crafty love has always
found still more than it sought for itself, and has always
grown greater with favor.

At last, sleep dispelled, the new bride rose, but no train   85
called her forth, nor was a glorious procession of youths,
peacefully mingled with the dear girls, to be spied before
the doors of that famous god of marriage. All remained
silent; Iole also would have been silent but some signs of
distress frightened her; either nausea or a slight chill   90
shook her whole body: lying on her bed she worried
thus: "What is this illness? what change saps my robust
health? Indeed there was no pleasure in those things which
I saw as I lay awake in fear last night. What waves I   95
passed over! What struggles I experienced in my dreams!
O gods, pierced by what great lances did I lie prostrate! I
fear that Apollo in anger buried in me his darts which
foster dread diseases. But here in my heart, my honor has
regard for neither the plagues nor the wrath of Apollo;   100
you always have this consolation, Iole, you may die, but
you will die chaste." She rose and bent to her work. She
made lilies white and wished to enjoy them since she made
them white: what the eyes see, the soul desires; she did not   105
know that her tortured heart carried obstacles and was re-

Singula quae gravidae possunt ignara ferebat;
Torpores lassata graves, fastidia, bilem;
Luminaque in morbum veniunt, putat illa fuisse
Obtutu nimio; causas ita nectit inanes.   110
Sed simul atque impleri uterum, sensitque moveri
Vivum aliquid, potuitque manu deprendere motus,
Exanimata metu nemorum petit avia tecta
Tristis, ut expleret miserando pectora planctu.

  Crudeles, ait, et genus implacabile, Divi,   115
Quas tandem aerumnas animique et corporis hausi
Immerita? assurgunt etiam nova monstra; tumere
Coepit uter nobis; iam virgo puerpera fiam;
Nec dubitat natura suas pervertere leges
Quo magis excrucier possimque horrenda videri,   120
Demque pudicitiae, sceleris sed nomine, poenas.
Quo fugiam? quae nunc umbrae? quae nubila frontem,
Vel tumulum hunc defuncti animi tectura cupressus?
Quam bene cum tenebris mihi convenit! horreo Solem;
Iam culpa possum, sed non caruisse timore;   125
Frangitur ingenuus pudor, et succumbit in ipsa
Suspicione mali, scelerisque ab imagine currit;
Ceu visis fugiunt procul a pallentibus umbris.
Infoelix partus, nisi quid monstrosius illo est,
Absque tuo genitore venis, nomenque paternum   130
Si quis quaerat habes nullum; patrem assere primum,
Post tibi succedam gravis atque miserrima mater.

  Talia iactantem venti laeva arbitra risit
Invida populea latitans sub cortice Nais;
Laetaque per sentes repit, tenuesque myricas;   135
Sed simul explicuit se, proditione superba,
Praecipitique gradu loca nota perambulat, omnes
Suscipiens nymphas, referensque audita; nec illa
Per se magna satis, reddit maiora loquendo;
Et partes miserantis agit, vultusque stupentes   140
Effingit, monstrumque horret, crimenque veretur.
Inde per alternos rumores fama vagatur,
Flebiliorque deae tandem florentia tecta
Pervenit; illa novo temere conterrita monstro
Exiliit, natamque animo indignata requirit.   145

leased from her vows of virginity. Unknowingly she bore
each distress which pregnant women can; exhausted she
withstood heavy sluggishness, squeamishness, melancholy;
her eyes grew dull; she thought it was because of too much   110
contemplation; so she invented groundless reasons. But as
her womb began to fill, and she realized that something
living moved and that she could feel the movements with
her hand, she was overcome by fear and sought the track-
less cover of the groves in sorrow to appease her heart with
pitiable wails.

"O cruel gods," she said, "implacable race, pray what   115
suffering of mind and body have I endured, undeserved?
Even new monsters rise, my womb begins to swell; now I,
a maid, shall be a mother; nature does not hesitate to per-
vert her laws so that I may be tortured the more and can   120
become an object of loathing and may pay the penalty for
my chastity in the name of sin. Whither shall I flee? What
shadows now, what clouds hide my brow? or what cypress
will cover the grave of my dead soul? How well the shades
suit me! I shrink from the Sun; now I can be free from
guilt but I could not be free from fear; my natural honor   125
is destroyed and sinks in the very suspicion of evil, and runs
from the shape of sin; or rather, they flee far from the pale
shades they have seen. Luckless offspring, unless there is
something more monstrous than he, you come from your
creator, and if anyone asks the name of your ancestors, you   130
have none; claim a father first; afterwards I shall follow
you, your sad most wretched mother."

The hateful Nais, hiding beneath the bark of a poplar,
laughed at her casting such foolish thoughts on the wind;
happily she crept through the brambles and pliant tama-   135
risks; but once she was in the open, proud in her treach-
ery, with headlong stride she passed through the familiar
places, overtaking all the nymphs and repeating what she
had heard; nor were the things great enough in them-
selves, she made them greater by her words; and she
played the role of one who sympathized, and assumed   140
stunned expressions and shrank from what was seen and
feared a crime. Thence through varying tales, Rumor
wandered, and at last more tearfully reached the flowering
bower of the goddess; she, rashly horrified by this strange
vision, leapt forth and, with anger in her heart, sought her   145

Sed procul ut matrem approperantem vidit Iole
Concidit exanimis, gemitus timor exprimit altos,
Exortosque utero creat ingeminatque dolores.
Continuo silva effulsit velut aurea, et omne
Per nemus auditur suave et mirabile murmur.   150
Diva pedem, perculsa soni novitate, repressit,
Interea sine ploratu parit, ipsaque tellus
Effudit molles puero incunabula flores.
Occurrit natae Berecynthia, prima nepotem
Suscipit, ille niger totus, ni candida solis   155
Haeserat effigies sub pectore, patris imago.

Sed non ambiguo iam personat omnia cantu
Phoebus, et ardentes incendit lumine silvas;
Dum sua furta canens miseram solatur Iolen.
Obstupuit dea, nunc lucos, nunc humida natae   160
Lumina suspiciens, vultusque pudore solutos.
Proditor, exclamat, non haec, si Iupiter aequus,
Probra mihi vel tecta diu, vel inulta relinquam.
Quo fugis? infestum caput inter nubila, Phoebe,
Nequicquam involvis; scelus et tua facta patebunt,   165
Nec mihi surripiet fuga te. Sequar ocior Euris,
Maternusque dolor vires dabit, iraque iusta.
Nec mora, per nubes summi ad fastigia coeli
Contendit; nymphae tristi exanimaeque sorori
Circumfusae acres tentant lenire dolores,   170
Et placidis dictis tristes subducere curas.
Illa immota sedet, tacitoque incensa furore
Ardet, et ingenti curarum fluctuat aestu.

Foelices quibus est concessum, ait, intemerata
Virginitate frui! mea iam defloruit aetas   175
Immature; heu maternos sensisse dolores,
Gaudia non potui; sed me nec gaudia tangunt;
Nec duri, si non infamia iuncta, dolores.
Nox et somne, meo pars insidiata pudori,
Hos mihi pro meritis partus, haec pulchra dedistis   180
Pignora, formosique patris referentia vultus?
Nempe ego, Phoebe, tuos amplexus dura refugi,
Et simplex, tali quam posses prole beare.

daughter. But as Iole saw her mother approaching far off, she sank down exhausted, and fear brought forth deep groans, and from her womb she began and redoubled pangs of labor. At once the forest shimmered as it were with a golden glow and through the whole grove a sweet 150 marvelous noise was heard. The goddess stopped, stunned by the strange sound. Meanwhile with no cry, Iole bore the child, and earth itself as a cradle put forth sweet flowers for the boy. Berecynthia ran to her daughter; first she lifted her grandson. He was completely black, except for the white shape of the Sun that had clung beneath his 155 heart, the shape of his father.

But now Phoebus made everything resound with his clear song and enflamed the glowing woodlands with his light; while singing his secret loves he consoled the wretched Iole. The goddess was amazed, now looking at 160 the groves, now at the moist eyes of her daughter, and her face flooded with shame. "You are the traitor," she shouted, "not she; if Jupiter is just, I shall leave such a disgrace neither long concealed nor unavenged. Whither do you flee? in vain do you shroud your wicked head among the clouds, Phoebus; your crime and your deeds will be re- 165 vealed, nor will flight steal you away from me, I shall follow more keenly than the East Winds, and a mother's grief and righteous wrath will give me strength." She did not delay, she sped through the clouds to the heights of heaven on high; the Nymphs pressed round their sad and listless sister and tried to lighten her keen woes, and with 170 gentle words to relieve her painful sorrow. She remained unmoved and enflamed by silent rage, she burned, and tossed on a vast tide of griefs.

"Blessed ones," she said, "to whom the right has been given to enjoy unstained virginity: now my life has with- 175 ered prematurely, alas to have felt the pangs of childbirth. I was not capable of joy; but neither did joys affect me; nor would my pains have been harsh if infamy had not been attendant. Night and sleep, the henchmen who plot- ted against my honor, have you given me this child for my merits, this beautiful reward, recalling the face of his hand- 180 some father? Indeed Phoebus, I steadfastly recoiled from your embraces. I was indeed an innocent whom you could bless with such an offspring. Would that I might have

Atque utinam caruisse tuo, speciose, liceret
Munere! quantumvis indocta et stulta putarer,   185
Non tamen infamis, turpique cupidine laesa,
Cogerer ad nigros animam demittere manes.
Sic effata, aliquid vultu letale minanti,
Deficit, excipiunt Nymphae, manibusque levatam
Celsa ferunt intecta deae stratisque reponunt.   190

    Cuncta Iovi interea narraverat ordine Phoebus,
Factaque lascivis praetexuit impia verbis;
Addiderat Cycnumque, et terga natantia tauri,
Furtivumque aurum, et duplicatae praemia noctis.
Iupiter officii tanti memor irrita risit.   195
Vota deae, iustumque odium in ludibria vertit.
Illa sed ingenti luctu confusa recedit,
Conqueriturque fidem divum; saevoque ululatu
Indefessa diu languentes suscitat iras;
At nulla in terris tanti vis nata doloris   200
Quam non longa dies per amica oblivia solvat.

    Iamque puer, tacite praeter labentibus annis,
Paulatim induerat iuveniles corpore vultus;
Cui quamvis nullo variantur membra colore,
Multus inest tamen ore lepos, tinctosque per artus   205
Splendescit mira novitate illecta venustas.
Si niger esset Amor, vel si modo candidus ille,
Iurares in utroque deum; non dulcior illo
Ipsa Venus, Charitesque, et florida turba sororum.
Huic olim nymphae nomen fecere Melampo,   210
Lucentesque comis gemmas, laterique pharetram
Aptarunt, qualem cuperet gestare Cupido.
Ille levem tenera sectatur arundine praedam
Aurorae ut primo rarescit lumine coelum;
Mox fervente aestu viridantes occupat umbras,   215
Aut ab euntis aquae traducit murmure somnum.

    Tempus erat placidis quo cuncta animalia terris
Solverat alta quies, solita cum Morpheus arte
(Somnia vera illi nullo mandante deorum)
Florigeram penetrat vallem, sopitaque ludit   220
Pectora nympharum, portentaque inania fingit,

been free of your favor, handsome one, however unsophisti- 185
cated and foolish I might be thought! Then, for all that, I
would not have to consign my soul to the black shades in
disgrace and torn by shameful lust!" Having said these
words, her face foreshadowing death, she fainted. The
Nymphs took her and quickly bore their burden in their
arms to the lofty open courts of the goddess, and laid it on 190
the coverlets.

Meanwhile Phoebus had told Jupiter everything in
order, and cloaked his wicked deeds with roguish words;
he had added allusions to the swan and the back of the bull
swimming and stealthy gold and the values of a double
night.[5] Jupiter, mindful of such great obligations, laughed 195
at these vanities. He changed the vows of the goddess and
her righteous hatred into mere trifles. But she withdrew dis-
turbed by the mighty struggle, and deplored the faith of
the gods; unwearied by her savage howl, for a long time she
kept aflame her powerless wrath; but there is no passion 200
born of such great grief on earth which a long time may
not dispel with kind forgetfulness.

Now little by little, over the silently gliding years, the
boy's body had donned the appearance of young man-
hood; although his limbs were marked by no color, still
there was much grace in his face, and a charm drawn out 205
by his wonderful strangeness shone through his dusky
veins. If cupid were black, or if only the boy were white,
you would swear the god was in both: no sweeter than he
was Venus herself, the Graces, or the blooming throng of
sisters. At some time the Nymphs gave him the name 210
Melampus and placed shining jewels in his hair, and they
fit a quiver to his side such as Cupid liked to wear. He
pursued his graceful prey with his slender shafts as the sky
grew thin at the first light of dawn; and soon in the burn-
ing heat he took to the leafy shades, or was lulled to sleep 215
by the murmur of a running stream.

There was a time when a deep sleep had released all the
animals on the peaceful earth, and Morpheus with his
usual skill (since none of the gods demanded true dreams
of him) entered the flowery vale and played on the sleep- 220
ing breasts of the Nymphs and fashioned meaningless

[5] In exculpation of his deed, Apollo reminds Jove of his own affairs
(in which Apollo aided him) with Leda, Europa, Danaë, and Alcmena.

Horribilesque metus; mox laetis tristia mutat,
Inducitque leves choreas, convivia, lusus,
Secretosque toros, simulataque gaudia amoris;
Saepe alias Satyro informi per devia turpes   225
Tradit in amplexus, alias tibi, pulcher Adoni,
Aut, Hyacynthe, tibi per dulcia vincula nectit.
Sic deus effigies varias imitatus, opaca
Dum loca percurrit, sopitum forte Melampum
Cernit odorato densoque in flore iacentem: 230
Accedit prope, spectanti dat Cynthia lumen.
Et quid, ait, mira nostram dulcedine mentem
Percellit? meve illudis, formose Cupido?
Sideream nigra frontem cur inficis umbra?
Iam placet iste color? vilescunt lilia? sordent   235
Materni flores? sed ubi nunc arcus et auro
Picta pharetra tibi? cui tu, lascive, sororum
Hac struis arte malum? tua quem nova captat imago?
At si non amor es, quis es? an furtiva propago
Atrigenae noctis? num crescit gratia tanta   240
E tenebris, iucunde, tibi? tam vividus unde
Ridet in ore lepos? tale et sine lumine lumen?
Ut decet atra manus, somno quoque mollior ipso,
Qui te sed leviter tangi sinit, aptus amori!
O utinam quae forma tuos succenderet ignes   245
Cognorim! puer illa foret, seu foemina, seu vir;
Quam cupide species pro te mutarer in omnes!
Utcunque experiar, spes nulla sequetur inertes!
Induit ex illo facies sibi mille decoras;
Versat et aetates sexumque, cuilibet aptans   250
Ornatus varios; nequicquam, immobilis haeret
Spiritus, et placido pueri mens dedita somno est.
Iamque fatigatus frustratum deflet amorem
Morpheus, indulgens animo pronoque furori.

     Luce sub obscura procul hinc telluris in imo   255
Persephones patet atra domus, sed pervia nulli;
Quam prope secretus, muro circundatus aereo,
Est hortus, cuius summum provecta cacumen
Haud superare die potuit Iovis ales in uno.
Immensis intus spaciis se extendit ab omni   260
Parte, nec Elisiis dignatur cedere campis,
Finibus haud minor, at laetarum errore viarum

omens and horrible fears; soon (in their dreams) sorrow
changed to joy and he led the graceful dances, feasts and
games, secret trysts and pretended delights of love; often he
foolishly surrendered some to a shapeless satyr for his dis-   225
gusting embraces, others he bound to you, beautiful Adonis,
or to you, Hyacinthus, by sweet ties. Thus the god, assum-
ing varied shapes while he traversed the shadowy realms,
spied by chance the sleeping Melampus lying in the deep   230
fragrant flowers: he drew near, Cynthia gave him light to
see. "Ah, what," he said, "dismays my mind with a strange
sweetness? Do you make sport of me, beautiful Cupid?
Why do you veil your heavenly brow with a black shadow?
Does that color please you now? Are the lilies becoming   235
worthless?[6] Are your mother's flowers despised? but where
now are your bow and the quiver decorated with gold?
for which of the sisters do you plot evil with this ruse, you
rogue? whom does your new guise enthrall? But if you are
not Love, who are you? some secret offspring of black-   240
faced night? surely such great grace does not grow in you
from the shades, fair one, does it? whence does charm so
lively smile in your face? such light yet without light? How
comely is a black hand, even softer than sleep itself, which
allows you to be touched but lightly, suited for love! O   245
would that I might know what beauty enkindles your
flames! it might be a boy or a woman or a man; how
eagerly I would be changed into all shapes for you! How-
ever I try, no hope will follow my feeble efforts!" He
assumed thereafter a thousand shapely guises; he changed   250
his age and sex, suiting varied adornments to whatever role
he wished; in vain, the spirit remained motionless and the
boy was devoted to peaceful slumber. Then, worn out,
Morpheus bewailed his spurned love, indulging his heart
and defeated madness.

Under the glimmering light far from here in the depths   255
of the earth the black house of Persephone stands open,
but none may enter; near it, surrounded by a wall of
bronze, is a secret garden whose highest peak the eagle of
Jupiter borne aloft could scarcely surmount in one day.
Within it stretch great distances in all directions; nor is   260
it inferior to the Elysian fields, by no means smaller in area
and far more beautiful in the maze of glad paths and in

[6] See l. 104.

Deliciisque loco longe iucundior omni.
Et merito, his umbrae nam diversantur in hortis
Quot nunc pulchrarum sunt, saeclo quotve fuere   265
Primo, quotve aliis posthac visentur in annis.
Vallem vulgus amat, quarum peragendaque sylvis
Fabula sit, liquidis spectant in fontibus ora,
Aut varias nectunt vivo de flore corollas;
At quibus urbanae debetur turgida vitae   270
Mollities, studiis aliis, alioque nitori
Assuescunt animos, nil simplicitatis habentes.
Altior, et longe secretior heroinis
Contingit sedes, Parnasso suavior ipso;
Gemmarum locus, atque oculorum lumine lucet.   275
Non huc fas cuiquam magnum penetrare deorum;
Soli sed Morpheo, cui nil sua fata negarunt,
Concessum est, pedibus quamvis incedere lotis:
Illum durus amor, sibi nil spondente salutis
Arte sua, tandem his languentem compulit hortis,   280
Tot puero ex formis ut fingat amabile spectrum.
   Primo fons aditu stat molli fultus arena,
Intranti, gradibus variisque sedilibus aptus.
Hic se cum redeunt, labem si traxerat ullam
Vita, lavant, purae remeantque penatibus umbrae.   285
Morpheus hac utrumque pedem ter mersit in unda,
Et toties mistis siccat cum floribus herbis;
Inde vias licitas terit, et velatus opaca
Nube, lubens saturat iucundis lumina formis.
Aspicit has tacita sua mutua fata sub umbra   290
Narrantes, choreis certantes mollibus illas
Quas olim didicere, vel ignes voce canentes
Quales senserunt dum lubrica vita manebat.
Sed deus obliquo species sibi lumine notas
Praeterit, Antiopam Nycteida, Deiphilemque,   295
Tyndaridemque Helenam, desponsatamque priori
Hermionem, calido dotatam sanguine nuptam;

the delights of the whole place. And rightly so, for in these
gardens are dispersed the shades of the beautiful women,   265
as many as there are now, as many as there have been since
the beginning of time, and as many as will come afterwards
in other years. The throng loves the valley, in the glades of
which their story must be brought to an end; they look at
their faces in the clear springs or weave multicolored neck-
laces of live flowers; but those for whom the lush volup-   270
tuousness of formal living is necessary accustom their
minds (which scorn simplicity) to other pursuits and other
elegances. Higher and far more withdrawn, the home of
the heroines is next, sweeter than Parnassus itself; it is a
place of jewels and glows with the sparkle of their facets.   275
No one of the mighty gods is permitted to enter here; but
the right is conceded to Morpheus alone, to whom his
fates deny nothing, to approach albeit with purified feet.
Cruel love at length drove him languishing to these
gardens, although his skill assured him of no safety, to   280
fashion a lovable specter for the boy from so many beau-
ties.

At the outermost entrance stood a fountain raised on
the shifting sand, fitted with steps and many benches for
any who entered. When they returned here, if life had
left any stain, they washed, and their pure shades went   285
back to their native homes. Thrice Morpheus dipped each
foot in this wave and thrice he dried them with grass
mingled with flowers; then he trod the paths permitted,
and veiled by a dark cloud, gladly he sated his eyes with
delightful beauties. He saw some discussing their mutual
fates beneath the quiet shade, others competing in pleasant   290
dances which they learned at some time, or singing of what
great passions they had experienced while fleeting life re-
mained. But the god passed by the familiar faces with only
a fleeting glance, Antiope, the daughter of Nycteus,[7] Dei-
phile, and Helen, the child of Tyndareus,[8] and Her-   295
mione, betrothed to one before but the dowered bride
of one of passionate blood;[9] he was indifferent to Argia[10]

[7] Antiope the daughter of Nycteus was wife of Lycus, king of Thebes,
and mother of Amphion.

[8] Helen of Troy, though begotten by Jove, was nominally the daughter
of Tyndareus, Leda's husband.

[9] Hermione the daughter of Menelaus and Helen was wife of Orestes.

[10] Argia was the daughter of Adrastus and wife of Oedipus' son Polynices
(one of the seven against Thebes).

Argiam, et Rhodopen, victoris et Hippodamiam
Expositam thalamis, pomis captasque puellas;
Roxanamque, Hieramque, ut cognita sydera spectans   300
Negligit, innumerasque pari candore micantes.
Hinc dorsum sublime petit per amoena roseta
Evectus, picta et multo viridaria flore.
Undanti circum locus est velut insula valle
Inclusus, formis aptus privusque Britannis,   305
Densis effulgens tanquam via lactea stellis.
Prima suo celerem tenuit Rosamunda decore
Ingenti, cui Shora comes rutilantibus ibat
Admiranda oculis, gravis utraque conscia sortis.
Inde Geraldinam coelesti suspicit ore   310
Fulgentem, Aliciamque caput diademate cinctam,
Casti constantisque animi lucente trophaeo.
Nec tamen his contentus abit deus, altius ardet
Accelerare pedem, fulgor procul advocat ingens
Apparens oculis, maioraque sidera spondet.   315
Emicat e viridi myrteto stella Britanna,
Penelope, Astrophili quae vultu incendet amores
Olim, et voce ducem dulci incantabit Hybernum.
Constitit eximiae captus dulcedine formae
Morpheus, atque uno miratur corpore nasci   320
Tot veneres, memori quas omnes mente recondit.
Proxima Franciscae divina occurrit imago,
Eiaculans oculis radios, roseisque labellis
Suave rubens, magni senis excipienda cubili

and Rhodope[11] and Hippodamia[12] shown in the victor's
bridal chambers and the maids captured by apples; and
Roxana[13] and Hiera[14] and countless others who sparkled   300
with equal splendor, he passed by as one looking at famil-
iar constellations. Hence through the lovely rose garden
he went forth and sought the highest ridge, and the or-
chard adorned with many flowers. This place was secluded
like an island in the sea of the valley, fit and proper for the
beauties of Britain, resplendent with myriad stars, as it   305
were like the milky way. First Rosamund[15] stayed his
speed with her great charm together with her companion
Shore,[16] remarkable for her sparkling eyes, each aware of
her sad lot. Then he spied Geraldine,[17] her heavenly face   310
aglow, and Alice[18] wearing a tiara on her head, a shining
reward for a chaste and steadfast spirit. Still not satisfied
with these, the god went on; he burned to hasten higher;
far off a mighty glow appeared before his eyes and sum-
moned him and promised greater stars. The star of   315
Britain twinkled from the green myrtle grove, Penelope[19]
who once enflamed the love of Astrophil with her face and
will enchant the Hibernian chief with her sweet voice.
Morpheus stopped, smitten by the charm of too much   320
beauty, and he marveled that so many passions sprang
from one body, all of which he hid in his heart's memory.
Next the divine shade of Frances[20] came to meet him, her
eyes flashing rays of light and her rosy lips sweetly glow-

11 By Rhodope, Procne is assumedly meant; she was called Rhodope after
the mountain range which dominates Thrace, the home of her husband.

12 Hippodamia was the daughter of Oenomaus, king of Elis; Pelops won
her hand by winning a chariot race with her father.

13 Roxana was the Persian wife of Alexander the Great; William Ala-
baster wrote a Latin tragedy about her, ca. 1592.

14 Hero, the heroine of Marlowe's and Chapman's *Hero and Leander*.

15 Rosamund Clifford, mistress of Henry II and a famous romantic
heroine; see *The Second Booke of Ayres,* vii.

16 Jane Shore, Edward IV's mistress, celebrated in the *Mirrour for Magis-
trates* and often coupled with Rosamund (e.g., in the first thirty lines of
Daniel's *Complaynt of Rosamond,* 1592).

17 Surrey's "Geraldine," Elizabeth Fitzgerald.

18 Vivian suggests Alice Spencer of Althorpe, who married Thomas Eger-
ton, Baron Ellesmere.

19 Sidney's "Stella," Penelope Rich; the next line alludes to her marriage
in 1605 to Charles Blount, Lord Mountjoy, who was Lord Lieutenant of
Ireland.

20 Frances Howard, daughter of Thomas, Viscount Howard of Bindon
(Vivian); not to be confused with Lady Somerset.

Mollis odoriferis prope Catherina sedebat   325
Fulta rosis, tacitam minitantur lumina fraudem,
Chara futura viro, toto spectabilis orbe.
Coniugibus laetae minus huic speciosa Brigetta
Succedit, radiis et pulchris Lucia fervens.
Formam forma parit, nova spectantemque voluptas   330
Decipit oblitum veteris, placidaeque figurae.
Utque satur conviva deus rediturus, apricam
Planiciem duo forte inter nemora aurea septam
Cernit, et in medio spaciantem, corpore celso,
Egregiam speciem, magnae similemque Dianae.   335
Nube sed admota propius dum singula spectat;
Digna sorore Iovis visa est, aut coniuge; sola
Maiestate levis superans decora omnia formae,
Haec comitata suis loca iam secreta pererrat,
Conscia fatorum, dicetur et Anna Britanna   340
Olim, fortunae summa ad fastigia surgens.
Altera subsequitur foelix, et amabilis umbra,
Cui Rheni imperium, et nomen debetur Elizae.
Morpheus hic haeret; capiunt hae denique formae
Formarum artificem, nec se iam proripit ultra.   345
Gratia, nec venus ulla fugit, congesta sed unam
Aptat in effigiem, Policleto doctior ipso.
Sic redit ornatus, tenero metuendus amico,
Cuius in amplexus ruit, haud renuente puello.
Quo non insignis trahis exuperantia formae   350
Humanum genus? hac fruitur; Iunonis ut umbra

ing, to be taken to the marriage bed of an ancient
noble;[21] nearby, gentle Catherine[22] sat resting on fra- 325
grant roses; her eyes threatened silent treachery, about to
be dear to a husband, admirable to the whole world.
After this woman less fortunate in her husbands came
lovely Bridget,[23] and Lucia,[24] burning with beams of
beauty. Beauty equaled beauty, a new pleasure made him 330
forgetful of the old gentle faces even as he looked. As
the god, having feasted enough, was about to go back, by
chance he saw a sunny plain hedged in between two groves
and, strolling in the midst, an outstanding vision of beauty,
with a tall frame, very like the great Diana.[25] But, as the 335
cloud grew nearer, as he gazed at each feature, she seemed
worthy to be sister or wife of Jupiter; she alone surpassed
all the glories of airy beauty in her splendor; escorted by
her attendants, she wandered through these haunts, now
secret. Aware of her destiny, at some time she would be
called Anne of Britain,[26] rising to the highest pinnacle of 340
fortune. A second blessed and lovable shade followed close
behind; to her sway over the Rhine was due, and the name
Eliza.[27] Here Morpheus stopped; at last these beauties
captivated the sculptor of beauties, nor did he now press 345
on farther. Neither the massed loveliness nor any charm
escaped, but more elegantly than Polyclitus himself,[28] he
fashioned all into one image. Thus adorned he returned, a
thing of awe to his innocent friend Melampus, into whose
arms he rushed without the boy's refusal. Where has not
this excess of remarkable beauty led the human race? 350
Morpheus enjoyed him; as Ixion by the shade of Juno,[29]

[21] a reference to Frances Howard's marriage to Lord Hertford in 1600, when he was sixty-one years old.

[22] Vivian suggests Catherine Parr, the sixth wife of Henry VIII (he was the third of her four husbands).

[23] Vivian suggests Bridget Fitzgerald, who married, first, the Earl of Tyrconnel, then the Viscount Kingsland.

[24] Lucy, Countess of Bedford, to whom both Donne and Jonson addressed poems (Bullen).

[25] Queen Elizabeth.

[26] Queen Anne, for whose recreation Campion wrote *The Caversham Entertainment*.

[27] Elizabeth, Queen of Bohemia, for whose marriage Campion wrote *The Lords' Masque*.

[28] Polyclitus was the famous Greek sculptor who laid down rules for human proportions.

[29] Ixion, the lover of Juno, embraced a cloud resembling her instead of the goddess herself.

Ixion, falso delusus amore Melampus.
Sed patris adventu, somno iam luce fugato,
Gaudia vanescunt; atque experrectus amata
Spectra puer quaerit nequicquam, brachia nudum   355
Aera circundant, nil praeter lumina cernunt.
Saepe repercussis coelo connivet ocellis,
Amissi cupidus visi, dulcisque soporis;
Et caput inclinat, sed acutas undique spinas
Curae supponunt tristes, arcentque quietem.   360
Nusquam quod petit apparet, nec praemia noctis
Permittit constare dies, ut inania tollit.
Saevit at introrsum furor, et sub pectore flammas
Exacuit, subditque novas; inimica dolori
Lux est, oblectat nox, et loca lumine cassa.   365
Silvarum deserta subit, clausosque recessus
Insanus puer, et dubio marcescit amore;
Sperat et in tenebris aliquid, terraque soporem
Porrectus varie captat; tum murmure leni
Somne, veni, spirat; prodi, o lepidissime divum;   370
Et mihi redde meam, prope sponsam dixerat amens;
Redde mihi quaecunque fuit, vel virgo, vel umbra,
Qualiscunque meo placuit, semperque placebit
Infoelici animo; veri, vel ficti Hymenaei
Quid refert? vitae domina est mens unica nostrae,   375
Sed non talis erat quem vidi vultus inanis.
Quod sensi corpus certe fuit, oscula labris
Fixa meis haerent, si quid discriminis hoc est,
Nunc frigent, eadem cum praebuit illa calebant.
Illa, quid illa? miser quod amo iam nescio quid sit: 380
Hoc tantum scio, conceptu formosius omni est.
Terra sive lates, suspensa vel aere pendes,
Vel coelum, quod credo magis, speciosa petisti;
Pulchra redi, et rursus te amplexibus insere nostris.
Pollicita es longum, nec me mens fallit, amorem.   385
Dic ubi pacta fides nunc? nondum oblita recentis
Esse potes voti cum me fugis, et revocari
A charo non laetaris, quem spernis, amante.
Sic varias longo perdit sermone querelas,
Atque eadem repetit, nec desinit; igne liquescit   390
Totus, et ardenti cedit vis victa dolori.

Melampus was deceived by this false love. But at the arrival
of his father [Apollo], when sleep was routed by light, his
joys vanished; and as he awakened, the boy sought his be-
loved visions in vain; his arms clasped empty air, his eyes   355
saw nothing left. Often with his eyes rolled back, he blinked
at the heavens, desiring his lost apparition and sweet slum-
ber; and he bowed his head, but on all sides sad cares
implanted sharp thorns and warded off rest. Nowhere did   360
what he sought appear, nor did the day allow gifts of night
to last, as it took away the hollow dreams. But madness
raged within him and fanned the flames deep in his breast,
and set new fires; light is hostile to grief, night and places   365
free of light divert it. The maddened boy plunged into the
wastelands of the forests and the remote recesses, and pined
away with perplexed love; he hoped for something in the
shadows, and offered rest by many lands, he eagerly pur-
sued it; then with a soft murmur he breathed, "Sleep,
come. Come forth most charmming of the gods and re-   370
turn to me my"—he had almost said senselessly, my wife—
"return to me whatever she was, whether maiden or shade,
whatever pleased and will always please my hapless heart;
what does it matter whether a real or imagined marriage?[30]
The mistress of our life is our intellect alone, but it was not   375
such a visionary face which I saw. The body which I felt
was surely real, the kisses planted on my lips cling there, if
that is any proof. Now they are cold; when she offered
them, they were warm. She—what is she? Wretch that I
am, I know not what it is I love: I know only this, it is   380
more lovely than any mere idea. Whether you hide in the
earth or hang suspended in the air or gloriously have sought
heaven, which I rather believe, return in beauty and once
more enfold yourself in my embrace. You promised a long
love, and my mind does not deceive me. Tell me where   385
now is the plighted troth? You could not have forgotten
your recent vows when you escaped me, and you are not
glad to be called back by a dear lover whom you spurn."
Thus he squandered many complaints in long harangue,
and said them all again, nor did he cease; he was com-
pletely wasted away with passion, and conquered strength   390
yielded to burning grief. But while he kept searching for the

[30] Compare Iole at l. 89.

Mente sed ereptam vigili dum quaeritat umbram,
Umbrae fit similis; tenui de corpore sanguis
Effluit, et paulatim excussus spiritus omnis
Deserit exanimum pectus, motusque recedit;   395
Optatumque diu fert mors, sed sera, soporem.
Corpus at inventum terrae mandare parabant
Lugentes nymphae, flores, herbasque ferentes
Funereas plenis calathis; quae vidit Apollo
Omnia, et iratus puero hunc invidit honorem.   400
Utque erat in manibus nympharum non grave pondus,
Labitur, obscuram sensim resolutus in umbram;
Et fugit aspectum solis, fugietque per omne
Tempus perpetuo damnatus luminis exul.

purloined shade with wakeful mind, he became like a
shade; the blood left his slender body and, little by little,
all his battered spirit abandoned his lifeless breast and   395
movement ceased; death brought his long chosen sleep, but
too late. The mourning Nymphs were ready to commit the
body found to the earth, bringing flowers and funereal
herbs in full baskets; Apollo saw all this, and angered at the   400
boy, he begrudged the honor. As he was not a heavy weight
in the hands of the Nymphs, he floated off, gradually re-
leased in the dark shade; he fled the sight of the sun and
will flee throughout all time, forever condemned to exile
from the light.

ELEGIARUM LIBER

ELEGEIA I (1595).

Ite procul tetrici, moneo, procul ite severi,
    Ludit censuras pagina nostra graves.
Ite senes nisi forte aliquis torpente medulla
    Carminibus flammas credit inesse meis.
Aptior ad teneros lusus florentior aetas,   5
    Vel iuvenis, vel me docta puella legat.
Et vatem celebrent Bruti de nomine primum
    Qui molles elegos et sua furta canat.
Probro nec semper fax sit tua, Phoebe, remota,
    Fervet ab innato flamma calore magis.   10
Nobis egelidas Neptunus molliit auras
    Qui fovet amplexu litora lata suo.
Et nos Phoebus amat: quantumque hieme abdicat, ardens
    Tanto plus facili conspicit ore pater.
Quid sacras memorem nymphis habitantibus undas,   15
    Sive tuas Thamesis, sive, Sabrina, tuas?
Mille etiam Charites silvis, totidemque Napaeae,
    Tot Veneres, tot eunt Indigenaeque deae.
Ut taceam musas, toto quas orbe silentes
    Chaucerus mira fecerat arte loqui.   20
Ille Palaemonios varie depinxit amores,
    Infidamque viro Chressida Dardanio.

ELEGY I (1595).

Go far away, gloomy men; I warn you, go far off, stern
men, our page makes sport of serious judgments. Go, old
men, unless by chance someone with sluggish marrow be-
lieves there are flames in my songs. A more vigorous age
better suited to gentle sports or a youth or a clever girl   5
should read me. And let the British celebrate by name the
first poet to sing sweet elegies and his own intrigues.
Apollo, may your torch not always be far from me, a sin-
ner; rather may the flame glow with inborn heat.[1] Nep-   10
tune softens the icy breezes for us just as he fondles the far
flung shores in his embrace.[2] And Phoebus loves us: the
farther he withdraws in winter, the more kindly the father
looks down, glowing.[3] What shall I recall of the nymphs   15
inhabiting the sacred waves or yours, O Thames, or yours,
O Severn? There live a thousand woodland graces and as
many nymphs of the dells, as many Venuses and as many
native goddesses. Let me not neglect the muses, silent the
world over, whom Chaucer by his rare skill made speak.   20
He painted the loves of Palaemon in varied hues, and
Cressida who betrayed her Dardanian husband. As he

[1] *"Arguuntur enim Septentrionales quantum a sole absunt tantum abesse
ab humanitate et litteris"* [The Northern climes are accused of being as
far from politeness and letters as they are from the sun]; Campion's mar-
ginal gloss.

[2] *"Aer insularum iuxta Philosophos perpetuo aestu maris calescit"* [Ac-
cording to the Philosophers the air of islands is warmed by the perpetual
heaving of the sea]; Campion's gloss.

[3] *"Aestate"* [In summer]; Campion's gloss.

Prodigiosa illo dictante canebat arator
   Ludicra, decertans cum molitore faber.
Sic peregrinantum ritus perstringit aniles,   25
   Rivalemque dei devovet usque papam.
Quis deus, o vates magnis erepte tenebris,
   Admovit capiti lumina tanta tuo?
Fabula nec vulgi, nec te Romana fefellit
   Pompa, nec Ausonii picta theatra lupi.   30
Imperio titubante novos sibi finxit honores
   Quae mundi dominos callida Roma tenet.
Iuris sola sui gentes procul Anglia ridet
   Tendentes Latio libera colla iugo.
Sacra libertate dea regnante potimur,   35
   Quae dare iam nobis otia sola potest.
Omnia nunc pacem, montesque urbesque fatentur,
   Cum Venere et nudo qui pede saltat Amor.
Pacis amans deus est, quamvis fera bella Cupido
   Corde gerens nostro semper ad arma vocat.   40
Alme puer, teneris adsit tua gratia musis,
   Paces sive deae, seu tua bella canunt.

spoke, the plowman told his marvelous jokes, the miller vy-
ing with the carpenter.[4] Thus he touched upon the silly   25
rituals of the pilgrims and even cursed the rival bishop of
god. What god, O seer rescued from the great shadows,
put such eyes in your head? Neither a story of the rabble
nor Roman pomp escaped you, nor the painted theaters
of the Ausonian wolf.[5] As the empire wavered, he fash-   30
ioned for himself new dignitaries that crafty Rome made
masters of the world. Only England far away smiles on the
peoples of its realm, keeping their necks free of the Latin
yoke. We obtain sacred freedom with a goddess as queen   35
who alone can now give us repose. Now all places, moun-
tains and cities, acknowledge peace with Venus and Cu-
pid, who dances with bare feet. The god is lover of peace,
however much Cupid wages cruel wars in our heart and
always calls us to arms. Sweet boy, may your grace be   40
propitious to our slender muses, whether they sing of the
peace of our goddess or of your wars.

[4] The Chaucerian allusions are to "The Knight's Tale"; *Troilus and Criseyde;* the apocryphal "Plowman's Tale," satirizing the clergy; and "The Miller's Prologue and Tale."

[5] the Italian Pope.

ELEGIA I (1619).

Ver anni Lunaeque fuit, pars verna diei;
   Verque erat aetatis dulce, Sybilla, tuae.
Carpentem vernos niveo te pollice flores
   Ut vidi, dixi, tu dea Veris eris.
Et vocalis, eris, blanditaque reddidit Eccho;   5
   Allusit votis mimica nympha meis.
Vixdum nata mihi simulat suspira, formam
   Quae dum specto tuam plurima cudit Amor.
Si taceo, tacet illa; tacentem spiritus urit:
   Si loquor, offendor garrulitate deae.   10
Veris amica Venus fetas quoque sanguine venas
   Incendit flammis insidiosa suis.
Nec minus hac immitis Amor sua spicula nostro
   Pectore crudeli fixit acuta manu.
Heu miser, exclamo, causa non laedor ab una;   15
   Una, Eccho resonat; quam, rogo, diva, refers?
Anne Sybillam? illam, respondit. Sentio vatem
   Mox ego veridicam, fatidicamque nimis:
Nam perii, et verno quae coepit tempore flamma,
   Iam mihi non ullo frigore ponet hyems.   20

ELEGY I (1619).[6]

It was the spring of the year and of the moon, the spring-time of the day; and it was the sweet spring of your life, Sybilla. As I saw you picking the spring flowers with your snowy fingertips I said, "The goddess of spring will be you." And the vocal, flattering Echo returned, "Will be you." The mimicking nymph made sport of my vows. She copied the sighs, scarcely born in my heart, which Love fashioned in abundance while I beheld your beauty. If I was silent, she was silent; my spirit burned within me while I was silent; if I spoke, I was vexed by the chatter-box goddess. Venus, the mistress of spring, also treacher-ously fired the blood of my young veins with her flames. No less than she did relentless Love plunge sharp darts into my breast with his cruel hand. "Alas, wretch that I am, not for one cause do I suffer, one alone." "One alone" Echo rebounded; "whom do you mean, goddess?" I asked, "Sy-billa, is it she?" "She," she answered. Soon I realized her voice of truth was the voice of doom as well. For I am lost, and now the winter cannot quench with all its cold the flame that began in the springtime.

[6] The poem depends on echo effects in the Latin (ll. 4–5, 15–16, and 17) which are reflected in the various repetitions of the word *"Ver"* [spring].

EPIGRAMMATUM LIBER PRIMUS

17. *In Barnum.*

In vinum solui cupis Aufilena quod haurit,
   Basia sic faelix, dum bibit illa, dabis;
Forsitan attinges quoque cor; sed (Barne) matella
   Exceptus tandem, qualis amator eris!

34. *De Epigrammate.*

Sicut et acre piper, mordax epigramma palato
   Non omni gratum est: utile nemo negat.

FIRST BOOK OF EPIGRAMS

17. *On Barnes.*[1]

You want to be dissolved in the wine which Aufilena drinks; thus you will happily kiss her while she is drinking; perhaps you will touch her heart too; but, Barnes, after you are caught in the chamber pot, what a lover you will be!

34. *Concerning the Epigram.*

Like sharp pepper, the biting epigram is not pleasing to every taste: no one says it's not useful.

[1] This epigram mocks Barnabe Barnes's Sonnet lxiii in *Parthenophil and Parthenope* (1593), in which the lover wishes to be transformed into wine,
> which down her throat doth trickle,
> To kiss her lips, and lie next at her heart,
> Run through her veins, and pass by Pleasures part.

Barnes's lines were also ridiculed by Nashe in *Have with you to Saffron-Walden* (*Works,* ed. R. B. McKerrow, 5 vols. [London, 1904–1910], III, 103) and Marston in *The Scourge of Villainy,* VIII, ll. 126–27. See Campion's prefatory poems to Barnes's *Four Bookes of Offices* (p. 196), and Epigrams 143 and II, 80, below.

45. *Ad Castricum.*

Acceptum pro me perhibes te, Castrice, ludis
    Admissum; pro te captus at eiicior:
Esse mei similem non est tibi causa dolendi,
    Sed me tam similem poenitet esse tui.

46. *Ad Rob. Caraeum Equitem Auratum nobilissimum.*

Olim te duro cernebam tempore Martis,
    In se cum fureret Gallia, qualis eras.
Teque, Caraee, diu florentem vidimus aula,
    Dux, idem et princeps, dum tua cura fuit.
Unus erat vitae tenor, et prudentia iuncta.
    Cum gravitate tibi sic quasi nata foret:
Nec mutavit honos, nec te variabilis aetas;
    Qui novit iuvenem, noscet itemque senem.

56. *In Laurentiam.*

Imberbi, si cui, Laurentia nubere vovit;
    Invenit multos haec sibi fama procos;
Impubes omnes, mora quos in amore pilosos
    Reddidit; ignoto sic perit illa viro.

45. *To Castricus.*[2]

You swear that you were received and admitted to the
games instead of me, Castricus; I was seized and thrown
out for you: you have no reason to grieve that you are my
double, but I grieve because I'm yours.

46. *To Robert Carey, Most Noble and Illustrious Knight.*[3]

At one time during that difficult period when France was
raging with civil war, I used to observe what kind of a
man you were.[4] For a long time, Carey, I, your com-
mander, and your prince,[5] watched you flourishing at
court while that was your concern. There was a single de-
sign to your life, and prudence as well. This was, as it were,
born in you along with severity: nor did political prestige
nor increasing maturity change you; whoever knew you as
a boy will recognize you likewise in your old age.

56. *On Laurentia.*[6]

Laurentia swore she'd marry a beardless man if anyone;
this story gained many suitors for her; time made all
these lads hairy during the courtship; so she is dying and
she has never known a man.

[2] Vivian suggests that "Castricus" was some person whose name in En-
glish contained the syllable *Camp*, thus allowing the confusion with Cam-
pion.

[3] Sir Robert Carey (ca. 1560–1639), knighted for his part in Essex's
expedition to Normandy in 1591 and created Earl of Monmouth in 1626,
was famous as both soldier and courtier (and rather infamous for his haste
to ingratiate himself with James while Elizabeth was on her deathbed):
while he was involved in foreign expeditions and border defense under
Elizabeth, his later fortunes depended on Prince Charles, whose Master of
Robes he became in 1611.

[4] Vivian takes this to be a reference to Essex's siege of Rouen in 1591,
and further assumes—from this epigram, II, 9 and II, 80—that Campion
saw service in this campaign (Introduction, xxxiii–iv).

[5] the Earl of Essex and Prince Charles.

[6] Compare the epigram "*Kate* can fancy only berdles husbands" in the
Observations (p. 304).

58. *In Nervam.*

Dissecto Nervae capite, haud (chirurge) cerebrum
    Conspicis; eia, alibi quaere; ubi? ventriculo.

69. *Ad Guil. Camdenum.*

Legi operosum iamdudum, Camdene, volumen,
    Quo gens descripta et terra Britanna tibi est,
Ingenii foelicis opus solidique laboris:
    Verborum et rerum splendor utrinque nitet.
Lectorem utque pium decet, hoc tibi reddo merenti,
    Per te quod patriam tam bene nosco meam.

73. *In Ligonem.*

Invideat quamvis sua verba Latina Britannis
    Causidicis, docto nunc Ligo fertur equo.
Et medici partes agit undique notus; Alenum
    Scenarum melius vix puto posse decus.

95. *In Morachum.*

Mors nox perpetua est; mori proinde
Non suadet sibi nyctalops Morachus,
In solis titubans ne eat tenebris.

58. *On Nerva.*

When Nerva's head is opened, you see no brain at all, surgeon; oh well, look somewhere else; where? in his stomach.

69. *To William Camden.*[7]

I had read your painstaking tome long ago, Camden, in which you described the people and land of Britain, a work of fruitful genius and solid labor: the shining splendor of the writing equals the splendor of the deeds. As befits a devoted reader, I pay you this compliment you deserve, for through you I know my own country so well.

73. *On Ligo.*

However much he may begrudge their Latin words to the British advocates, now Ligo rides an educated horse. Known everywhere, he even plays the role of a doctor. I think that Alenus[8] can scarcely achieve more glory on the stage.

95. *On Morachus.*

Death is perpetual night;[9] hence the half-blind Morachus doesn't plead for death lest he should go reeling among the forsaken shadows.

[7] Complimenting the historian William Camden (1551–1623); his *Britannia,* originally published in 1586, had appeared in translation in 1610; compare Jonson's *Epigram* xiv. Camden indicated reciprocal respect when, in his *Remaines* (1605), he named Campion among the major English poets along with Sidney, Spenser, Shakespeare, Drayton, and others.

[8] Edward Alleyn (1566–1626), the famous actor and producer. "Ligo" has not been identified.

[9] See Catullus V, l. 6, *"nox est perpetua una dormienda,"* adapted in *A Booke of Ayres,* Part I, i, l. 6.

96. *In obitum Hen. Mag. Brit. Principis.*

Grandior et primis fatis post terga relictis,
  Concipiens animo iam nova regna suo,
Princeps corripitur vulgari febre Britannus;
  Hinc lapso ut coepit vivere flore perit.
Sic moriemur? ad haec ludibria nascimur? et spes
  Fortunaeque hominum tam cito corruerint?

97. *De Fran. Draco.*

Nomine Dracus erat signatus ut incolat undas;
  Dracum namque anatem lingua Britanna vocat.

98. *In obitum Iacobi Huissii.*

Heu non maturo mihi fato, dulcis Huissi,
  Occidis, heu, annis digne Mathusaliis;
Occidis ex morbo quem fraus et avara Synerti
  Saevitia ingenuit; cui mala multa viro
Det Deus; et, lachrymis quotquot tua funera flerunt
  In diras versis, ira odioque necent.

118. *In Nervam.*

Et miser atque vorax optat sibi Nerva podagram,
  Solis divitibus qualis adesse solet.
Errat si putat id voti prodesse gulosis;
  Nam quid lauta iuvat mensa, iacente fame?

96. *On the Death of Henry, Prince of Great Britain.*

Full-grown, his earliest mishaps left behind, desiring then new realms for his spirit, the British prince was seized by a common fever; hence like the flower which falls even as it begins to live, he died. Thus shall we die? Are we born to be mere playthings? Will the hope and fortunes of men fall in ruins so quickly?

97. *About Francis Drake.*[10]

By his name Drake was destined to inhabit the sea; for the British tongue calls a duck a drake.

98. *On the Death of James Huishe.*[11]

Alas you died when death was not ready for me, sweet Huishe, worthy as you weré of the years of Methuselah; you died of a disease which the deceit and greedy savagery of Synertius fostered; may God give much evil to that man; and with however many tears they weep for your death, with so many curses may they slay him in hateful wrath.

118. *On Nerva.*

Even poor and starving Nerva prays he'll have gout, usually a disease only of rich men. He is wrong if he thinks this prayer produces dainties. Indeed how does a laden table profit one while hunger lingers on?

[10] Epigram 94 also concerned Drake.

[11] James Huishe was admitted to Gray's Inn on February 4, 1595 (whence his acquaintance with Campion); the circumstances of his death, the identity of "Synertius," and other matters to which the poem alludes are unknown.

131. *Ad Chloen.*

Mortales tua forma quod misellos
Multos illaqueet, Chloe, superbis:
Hoc sed nomine carnifex triumphet.

143. *In Crispinum.*

Uxorem Crispinus habet; tamen indigus unam
    Vix alit, extremam sensit uterque famem.
Ipsam dives amat Florus; fremit ergo maritus,
    Quanquam rivali nunc opus esse videt.
Maechum saepe vocat, sed cum, qui sustinet, ipse
    Qua fruitur, victu, vestibus, aere domum,
Dispeream nisi sit vere Crispinus adulter:
    Sponsus, qui sponsi munia Florus obit.

151. *De horologio portabili.*

Temporis interpres, parvum congestus in orbem,
    Qui memores repetis nocte dieque sonos:
Ut semel instructus iucunde sex quater horas
    Mobilibus rotulis irrequietus agis,
Nec mecum quocunque feror comes ire gravaris,
    Annumerans vitae damna, levansque meae.

188. *De Regis reditu e Scotia.*

Nil Ptolomaeus agit, caelique volumina nescit,
    Nam nunc a gelido cardine (Phaebe) redis,
Et veris formosa rosis Aurora refulget:
    Hunc, precor, aeternum reddat Apollo diem.

131. *To Chloe.*

You plume yourself, Chloe, because your shape ensnares many wretched mortals: but a hangman may glory in this reputation.

143. *On Crispin.*[12]

Crispin has a wife; however, the poor man barely feeds her, and both are starving. A rich man Florus loves her; therefore her husband is raging although he sees that he needs a rival now. He often calls him an adulterer, but since he keeps the woman he himself enjoys in food, clothes, and pin money, may I die if Crispin is not really the adulterer: a husband for whom Florus takes on the duties of a husband.

151. *About the Portable Clock.*

Interpreter of time, packed into a small globe, who strike anew reminding sounds by night and day: as once wound you work happily, sleepless, with your little moving wheels for twenty-four hours, so you are not loath to be my companion wherever I go, keeping count of the lost parts of life, and easing the losses of mine.

188. *About the Return of the King from Scotland.*[13]

Ptolemy accomplished nothing and knows not the cycles of the sky, for now, Phoebus, you return from the icy pole and lovely Aurora sparkles with the roses of spring: may Apollo return this everlasting day, I pray.

[12] Compare *"Barnzy* stiffly vows" in the *Observations* (p. 305).
[13] This epigram celebrates the same event as *The Ayres That Were Sung and Played at Brougham Castle* in August of 1617, and is verbally quite similar to No. III, ll. 16–21 (see Doubtful Poems, p. 466).

189. *Ad ampliss. totius Angliae Cancellarium, Fr. Ba.*

Debet multa tibi veneranda (Bacone) poesis
   Illo de docto perlepidoque libro,
Qui manet inscriptus veterum sapientia; famae
   Et per cuncta tuae saecla manebit opus;
Multaque te celebrent quanquam tua scripta, fatebor
   Ingenue, hoc laute tu mihi, docte, sapis.

192. *Ad Ed. Mychelburnum.*

Nostrarum quoties prendit me nausea rerum,
   Accipio librum mox, Edoarde, tuum,
Suavem qui spirat plenus velut hortus odorem,
   Et verni radios aetheris intus habet.
Illo defessam recreo mentemque animumque,   5
   Ad ioca corridens deliciasque tuas;
Haud contemnendo vel seria tecta lepore,
   Cuncta argumentis splendidiora suis.
Haec quorsum premis? ut pereant quis talia condit?
   Edere si non vis omnibus, ede tibi.   10

189. *To the Most Noble Chancellor of All England, Francis Bacon.*[14]

Poetry owes you great reverence, Bacon, because of that learned and thoroughly charming book in which the wisdom of old is preserved; and this work will survive through all the ages of your fame; although many of your writings will glorify you, I say frankly, in this book it is *you*, learned sir, who seem to me splendidly wise.

192. *To Edward Mychelburne.*[15]

Whenever the nausea of our times grips me, I take your book forthwith, Edward, a book which breathes a sweet aroma like a garden in full bloom and holds within it the beams of a spring sky. With it I restore my wearied mind and spirit, laughing at your jokes and sallies; and the serious topics covered with no mean finesse are all the more splendid for their matter. To what end do you suppress these? Who creates such things to let them die? If you do not wish to publish for everyone, publish for yourself.

[14] Bacon's long-standing connection with Gray's Inn and his possible part in the entertainments for the Somerset wedding may account for Campion's acquaintance with him; this epigram compliments him on *De Sapientia Veterum* (1609), which draws scientific allegories out of several myths. Epigram 190 is also addressed to him.

[15] Edward Mychelburne (1565–1626) entered St. Mary's Hall, Oxford, in 1579 and later moved to Gloucester Hall (where Barnabe Barnes resided); though he took no degree because of his Roman Catholicism, he seems to have remained at Oxford the rest of his life. Campion was intimate both with him and his two brothers, Thomas and Laurence, and addressed a number of epigrams to them—e.g., 180, II, 77 and 121 to Edward; II, 69 to Thomas; and II, 34 to Laurence. According to Anthony à Wood, Edward was "the most noted Latin Poet of his time" (*Fasti Oxonienses*, under 1626), but published nothing save two prefatory poems to Peter Bales's *Art of Brachygraphy* (1597), exhibiting a reluctance to publish for which Charles Fitzgeffrey also scolded him, in *Affaniae* (see Campion's Epigram II, 70 and note). Bradner (*Musae Anglicanae*, p. 79) attributes the renewed interest in the epigram at Oxford in the 1580s to the work of the Mychelburne brothers.

211. *Ad Rusticum.*

Rustice, sta, paucis dum te moror, auribus adsis.
  Dic age, cuias es? Salsburiensis, ais?
Pembrochi viduam num tu Sidneida nosti?
  Non. Saltem natos, cum sit uterque potens?
A thalamis alter regis celeberrimus heros;   5
  Alter at in thalamis. Proh tenebrose, negas?
Inclitus ergo Senex Hertfordius an tibi notus?
  Tantumdem: coniux quid speciosa senis?
Non; non? anne tuum scis nomen? si id quoque nescis,
  Caetera condono hac conditione tibi.   10

222. *Ad Tho. Munsonium, equitem Auratum et Baronetum.*

Quicquid in adversis potuit constantia rebus,
  Munsoni, meritis accumulare tuis
Addidit, et merito victrix Dea, iamque sat ipse
  Fama et fortunis integer amplus eris.

211. *To a Peasant.*

Peasant, stop, listen while I delay you a few minutes. Tell
me, where are you from? Salisbury, you say? Don't you
know the Sidney woman, the widow of Pembroke?[16] No.
Surely the sons, since each is powerful? One is a very fa-
mous Gentleman of the King's Bedchamber;[17] but the
other in the bedchamber.[18] Ah, you dark fellow, do you
say no? But you do know the famous old man from Hert-
ford?[19] Just the same, what about the old boy's glorious
wife?[20] No. No? Do you know your own name? If you
don't, I pardon you for all the rest on this account.

222. *To Thomas Monson, Illustrious Knight and Baro-
net.*[21]

Whatever steadfastness in adversity could amass to your
credit, Monson, it added; the goddess of Justice was
rightly victorious, and now, spotless, you will be rewarded
by boundless fame and fortune.

16 Mary, Countess Dowager of Pembroke (1561–1621), sister of Sir Philip
Sidney, famous patroness of Daniel, Spenser, Thomas Watson, Abraham
Fraunce, and others, and mother of William Herbert, Earl of Pembroke
(1580–1630), and Philip Herbert, Earl of Montgomery (1584–1650), both
of whom danced in Campion's *Somerset Masque.* The Pembroke brothers
were the patrons of Shakespeare's first folio.

17 Montgomery, a Gentleman of the King's Bedchamber.

18 Pembroke, who married the Earl of Shrewsbury's daughter.

19 Edward Seymour (1539–1621), Lord Hertford.

20 Frances Howard, Hertford's third wife, whom he married in 1600
(Bullen); see *Umbra*, ll. 322 ff.

21 See headnote to *The Third and Fourth Booke of Ayres.*

EPIGRAMMATUM LIBER SECUNDUS

9. *In obitum Gual. Devoreux fratris clariss. Comitis Essexiae.*

Pilas volare qui iubebat impius
Forata primus igne ferra suscitans,
Ei manus cruenta, cor ferum fuit.
Fenestra quanta mobili hinc deae patet
Ferire possit ut malos, bonos simul.   5
Quid alta fortitudo mentis efferae,
Torive corporis valent? ruunt globi,
Praeitque caecitas, et atra nubila,
Sonique terror aethera; et solum quatit
Maligna fata; Devoreux, et unice,   10
Et alme frater incliti ducis, sacro
Tibi igne perdidere saucium caput.
Equo labansque funebri, heu, acerbum onus
Tuis, revectus arduum ad iugum redis.
Rotaque subgemente curribus iaces   15
Molesta pompa fratri, et omnibus bonis.
Peribit ergo Rhona, pulsa corruet
Fero canente classicum tuba sono,
Et ulta stabis inter umbra caelites.

SECOND BOOK OF EPIGRAMS

9. *On the Death of Walter Devereux, Brother of the Most Noble Earl of Essex.*[1]

Bloody hands and a savage heart had the wicked man who ordered the javelins to fly and was the first to take up firearms. Hence how great a window was opened for the fickle goddess [Fortune] to smite the bad and the good at once. What do the high courage of a spirited mind or strength of body avail? The balls rush in, and go ahead blindly, the black cloud, the holy terror of the noise; and evil fate shakes the ground; Devereux, you alone, dear brother of the illustrious leader, wounded by the cursed fire have lost your life. Borne on a funeral steed, a bitter burden to your kinsmen, you return carried to the steep ridge. You lie on the chariot with the wheels groaning beneath, in a procession grievous to your brother and to all good men. Therefore Rouen will perish and will sink down when the trumpet sings its blast with wild sound and you, a shade avenged, will take your place in heaven.

5

10

15

[1] Walter Devereux (b. 1569), the romantic younger brother of Robert Devereux, Earl of Essex, died on September 8, 1591, at the siege of Rouen conducted under his brother as part of the expedition to aid Henri IV against the Catholic League. A soldier in ambush killed him with a ball that entered his jaw and lodged in his head; there was a struggle over his body, which was eventually rescued by John Wotton and Sir Conyers Clifford, who had it embalmed and wrapped in lead so as to enter the gates of Rouen with the victorious army. Sir Robert Carey (see *Liber Primus*, 46), Barnabe Barnes, and, perhaps, Campion himself were also involved in this siege; Vivian maintains that the last three lines of this poem show it to have been written before the siege was lifted (Introduction, p. xxxii).

10. *Ad Melleam.*

O nimis semper mea vere amata
Mellea, o nostri pia cura cordis,
Quanta de te perpetuo subit mi
           Causa timoris!
Eminus quanquam iaculetur altus   5
Aureos in te radios Apollo,
Torqueor ne fictus amans in illis
           Forte lateret.
Et procul caelo pluvias cadentes
In sinus pulchros agitante vento,   10
Horreo, insanum placidus tonantem
           Ne vehat imber.
Somnians, et res vigilans ad omnes,
Excitor; noctuque pavens dieque;
Saepe si vestra potuit quis esse   15
           Quaero sub umbra.

11. *De obitu Phil. Sydnaei equitis aurati generosissimi.*

Matris pennigerum alites Amorum,
Quid suaves violas per et venustas
Nequicquam petitis rosas Philippum,
Dumis usque Philip, Philip, sonantes?
Confossum modo nam recepit Orcus,
Omnes dum superare bellicosa
Fama audet iuvenis; renunciate
Funestum Veneri exitum Philippi,
Vatem defleat ut suorum Amorum.

12. *In Melleam.*

Mellea mi si abeam promittit basia septem;
   Basia dat septem, nec minus inde moror:
Euge, licet vafras fugit haec fraus una puellas,
   Basia maiores ingerere usque moras.

10. *To Mellea.*

My Mellea, always too truly beloved, holy care of my heart, how great a reason for fear continually pervades me on your account! Although Apollo on high may cast his   5
golden rays on you from afar, I am tortured lest by chance a pretended lover lurks in them. And I shrink from the rains falling from heaven far off on the beautiful breasts,   10
driven by the wild wind, lest the peaceful rain bear the mad thunderer [Zeus]. Dreaming and waking, I am alert to every chance; trembling night and day, often I ask if   15
anyone could be beneath your shadow.

11. *On the Death of Philip Sidney, Most Noble and Illustrious Knight.*[2]

Birds of the mother of feathered Loves, why do you seek Philip in vain through the sweet violets and lovely roses, still calling Philip, Philip, in the thickets? For Orcus has just received him entombed while the warlike fame of the youth dares to surpass all; announce the sad death of Philip to Venus that she may weep for the poet of her Loves.

12. *On Mellea.*[3]

Mellea promises me seven kisses if I go away; she gives seven kisses and I don't linger any less for this: indeed obviously this one deceit escapes these crafty girls, that kisses make men stay still longer.

[2] For Campion's debts to Sidney, see headnote to songs appended to *Astrophel and Stella.* For the sparrows (ll. 1–4), see *Astrophel and Stella,* lxxxiii.

[3] a Latin version of "My love bound me with a kisse," *Canto tertio* of the songs appended to *Astrophel and Stella.*

18. *In Melleam.*

Anxia dum natura nimis tibi, Mellea, formam
  Finxit, fidem oblita est dare.

23. *Ad Lucium.*

Crassis invideo tenuis nimis ipse, videtur
  Satque mihi foelix qui sat obesus erit.
Nam vacat assidue mens illi, corpore gaudet,
  Et risu curas tristitiamque fugat.
Praecipuum venit haec etiam inter commoda, Luci,
  Quod moriens minimo saepe labore perit.

27. *De Catullo et Martiale.*

Cantabat Veneres meras Catullus;
Quasvis sed quasi silva Martialis
Miscet materias suis libellis,
Laudes, stigmata, gratulationes,
Contemptus, ioca, seria, ima, summa;
Multis magnus hic est, bene ille cultis.

40. *Ad nobiliss. virum Gul. Percium.*

Gulelme gente Perciorum ab inclita,
Senilis ecce proiicit nives hiems,
Tegitque summa montium cacumina;
Et aestuosus urget hinc Notus, gelu
Coactus inde Thracius, rapit diem   5

18. *On Mellea.*[4]

While solicitous nature has fashioned too much beauty for you, Mellea, she has forgotten to give loyalty.

23. *To Lucius.*

Too thin myself, I envy the fat man, he seems quite blessed to me who is fat enough. For his mind is always free, he rejoices in his body and dismisses cares and sorrow with a laugh. This is foremost among those blessings too, Lucius, the fact that dying he often goes with very little effort.

27. *About Catullus and Martial.*

Catullus used to sing only of loves; but Martial uses whatever topics he wishes in his little books, as many varieties as trees in the forest, praises, burning attacks, congratulations, contempt, jokes, serious topics, the depths, the heights; Martial is great for many men, Catullus for the very elegant.

40. *To the Most Noble Gentleman, William Percy.*[5]

William, of the illustrious line of Percys, see how the winter of old age piles up the snows and covers the highest peaks of the mountains; even the burning South Wind hurries away, the Thracian North Wind driven thence by   5

[4] See *The Fourth Booke of Ayres,* xvii, ll. 3–6.
[5] William Percy (1575–1648) had been an intimate friend of Barnabe Barnes since his college days at Gloucester Hall, Oxford (see l. 12); hence, probably, Campion's acquaintance with him. He was the author of the sonnet cycle *Coelia* (1594), which contains some friendly exchanges with Barnes, and of six manuscript plays for the children of St. Paul's: *The Cuck-queanes and cuckolds errants, The Faery Pastorall, Arabia Sitiens* (1601), *The Aphrodisial* (1602), *A Countrys Tragedy* (1602), and *Necromantes* (1602). Campion's poem is a free imitation of Horace *Odes* I. ix.

Palustris umbra, noxque nubibus madet.
Tibi perennis ergo splendeat focus,
Trucemque plectra pulsa mulceant Iovem.
Refusus intumescat Euhius sciphis,
Novumque ver amoenus inferat iocus,   10
Novas minister ingerat faces; ruit
Glocestriensium in te amica vis, simul
Furorem ut hauriant levem, facetiis
Simulque molle lusitent per otium.

53. *Ad Caspiam.*

Ne tu me crudelis ames, nec basia labris
    Imprime, nec collo brachia necte meo.
Supplex orabam satis haec, satis ipsa negabas;
    Quae nunc te patiar vix cupiente dari.
Eia age iam vici, nam tu si foemina vere es,
    Haec dabis invito terque quaterque mihi.

54. *Ad Amorem.*

Cogis ut insipidus sapiat, damnose Cupido,
    Mollis at insipidos qui sapuere facis.
Qui sapit ex damno misere sapit; o ego semper
    Desipuisse velim, sis modo mollis, Amor.

60. *In Lycium et Clytham.*

Somno compositam iacere Clytham
Advertens Lycius puer puellam,
Hanc furtim petit, et genas prehendens
Molli basiolum dedit labello.
Immotam ut videt, altera imprimebat   5
Sensim suavia, moxque duriora;
Istaec conticuit velut sepulta.
Subrisit puer, ultimumque tentat

the ice, the misty shade snatches away the day, and night drips from the clouds. Therefore may your hearth always glow for you and the notes of the lyre assuage the savage Jove. May the poured wine rise in the cups and the pleasant jest bring on a new spring, may your servant bring in new torches; the welcome vigor of Gloucester men flows upon you, and as soon as they drain this gentle inspiration, they keep bantering with witticisms through pleasant leisure.

10

53. *To Caspia.*[6]

Lest you love me, cruel as you are, do not press kisses on my lips nor twine your arms about my neck. As a suppliant, I begged for these things enough, you said no enough times; now I barely suffer them when you want to. Splendid! See, I have conquered! For if you are truly a woman, you will give these favors again and again when I don't want them.

54. *To Love.*[7]

You make foolish men wise, pernicious Cupid, but you gently make those who were wise foolish. He who is wise is wise because of his wretched loss; may I always be foolish, so you may be gentle, Love.

60. *On Lycius and Clytha.*[8]

The youth Lycius, noticing the maid Clytha lying stretched out asleep, stealthily approached her, and, taking her cheeks, placed a little kiss on her sweet little lips. As he saw her motionless, he gently planted a second round of sweet kisses, and soon more forceful ones; she was still as the tomb. The youth smirked and tested his

5

---

[6] a Latin version of *A Booke of Ayres,* Part I, xii.

[7] a Latin version of "Love whets the dullest wits," *Canto quarto* of the songs appended to *Astrophel and Stella.*

[8] See *A Booke of Ayres,* Part I, viii, and textual notes.

Solamen, nec adhuc movetur illa
Sed cunctos patitur dolos dolosa.   10
Quis tandem stupor hic? cui nec anser
Olim, par nec erat vigil Sibilla;
Nunc correpta eadem novo veterno,
Ad notos redit indies sopores.

61. *In eosdem.*

Assidue ridet Lycius Clytha ut sua dormit;
    Ridet et in somnis sed sua Clytha magis.

70. *Ad Carolum Fitz Geofridum.*

Carole, si quid habes longo quod tempore coctum
    Dulce fit, ut radiis fructus Apollineis,
Ede, nec egregios conatus desere, quales
    Nescibit vulgus, scit bona fama tamen.
Ecce virescentes tibi ramos porrigit ultro
    Laurus; et in Lauro est vivere suave decus.

utmost pleasure, and still she was not moved but treacher-
ously suffered all his treacheries. What trance was this, I   10
pray? she had neither goose[9] nor wakeful sybil; now this
same maid, overcome with a strange lethargy, returns every
day to her familiar slumbers.

61. *On the Same.*

Lycius smiles constantly as his Clytha slumbers; but his
Clytha smiles even more in her slumbers.

70. *To Charles Fitzgeffrey.*[10]

Charles, if you have something which finally becomes sweet
when ripened as fruit in the rays of the sun, publish it,[11]
and do not abandon these excellent attempts such as the
common mob will not know, but good reputation knows.
See how Laurel holds out her leafy boughs to you of her
own will; and it is pleasant to live in Laurel.

[9] The warning of a goose sacred to Juno saved the Roman Capitol in
the Gallic war; see Livy *Ab Urbe Condita* V. xlvii. 4.

[10] Charles Fitzgeffrey (1576–1637), an intimate friend of Campion, the
Mychelburnes, and other prominent Latin poets, was the author of the
English heroic poem *Sir Francis Drake, his Honorable Lifes Commendation
and his Tragical Deathes Lamentation* (1596) and of *Affaniae* (1601), a
collection of Latin epigrams in three books dedicated, respectively, to
Laurence, Edward, and Thomas Mychelburne. *Affaniae* contains several
epigrams addressed to Campion, as well as to William Percy, Daniel, and
Drayton.

[11] *"Ede"* is a play on words, and means both "publish" and "eat," the
latter meaning continued in the play on laurel as tree and reward for
poetic merit in ll. 5–6.

80. *In Barnum.*

Mortales decem tela inter Gallica caesos,
    Marte tuo perhibes; in numero vitium est:
Mortales nullos si dicere, Barne, volebas,
    Servasset numerum versus, itemque fidem.

85. *In Sannium.*

Quae ratio, aut quis te furor impulit, improbe Sanni,
    Foemineum ut sexum mente carere putes?
Cum mea diffusas foelix per pectus amantum
    Unica possideat Caspia centum animas?

88. *Ad Nashum.*

Commendo tibi, Nashe, Puritanum
Fordusum et Taciti canem Vitellum,
Teque oro tua per cruenta verba,
Perque vulnificos sales, tuosque
Natos non sine dentibus lepores   5

80. *On Barnes.*[12]

You vow that ten men were slain among the Gallic foe
when you played Mars; there is shame in this number:[13]
if you wished to say no men, Barnes, you would have kept
the meter of the verse and also the truth.

85. *On Sannius.*

What reason or what madness drove you, wicked Sannius,
to think that the female sex has no intellect? Why, my
Caspia alone has a hundred minds spread through the
heart of her lovers.

88. *To Nashe.*[14]

I commend to you, Nashe, the Puritan Fordusus and
Vitellus, the dog of Tacitus, and I beg you by your
bloody words, and by your wounding wit, and your humor
born not without teeth, and by that keen bolt of your   5

[12] another attack on the hapless Barnabe Barnes (see I, 17 and 143),
this time for boasting of his exploits in the Essex expedition to Normandy
in 1591 (see Epigram 9). Nashe enlarged the attack on Barnes's military
prowess in *Have with you to Saffron-Walden* (1596), and in the course
of the attack quoted the first line of this "universall applauded Latine Poem
of Master *Campions*" (*Works*, ed. McKerrow, III, 110). Compare the
epigram "All wonders *Barnzy* speakes" in the *Observations* (p. 308).

[13] The wordplay on *"numero"* as "number" and "verse" is explained in
l. 4: the first line needs the long syllable of *"nūllos"* instead of the short
"dĕcem."

[14] The improbable friendship between Campion and the harum-scarum
satirist Thomas Nashe may date from their residence at Cambridge, which
Nashe entered in 1582; Nashe wrote the preface to the surreptitious quarto
of *Astrophel and Stella* (1591) that contains Campion's first published work,
and praised Campion in *Have with you to Saffron-Walden* in 1596 (see
note to Epigram 80). The allusions in the poem are obscure; Bullen sug-
gests that the classical imitations of Harvey and others are meant. Line 2
perhaps alludes to the emperor Vitellius, a famous glutton whom Tacitus
compared to *"ignava animalia, quibus si cibum suggeras jacent torpentque,"*
cold-blooded animals who, if you keep them supplied with food, lie around
and grow torpid (*History* III. 36).

Istudque ingenii tui per acre
Fulmen insipidis et inficetis
Perinde ac tonitru Iovis timendum;
Per te denique candidam Pyrenen,
Parnassumque, Heliconaque, Hippocrinenque,   10
Et quicunque vacat locus camoenis,
Nunc oro, rogoque, improbos ut istos
Mactes continuis decem libellis;
Nam sunt putiduli atque inelegantes,
Mireque exagitant sacros poetas,   15
Publiumque tuum, et tuum Maronem,
Quos amas uti te decet, fovesque
Nec sines per ineptias perire.
Ergo si sapis, undique hos latrones
Incursabis et erues latentes;   20
Conceptoque semel furore nunquam
Desistes; at eos palam notatos
Saxis contuderit prophana turba.

93. *In Bretonem.*

Carmine defunctum, Breto, caute inducis Amorem;
    Nam numeris nunquam viveret ille tuis.

94. *Ad Ge. Chapmannum.*

Cottum perfidiae haud satis pudenter,
Chapmanne, insimulas, redarguisque
Neutiquam meminisse quod spospondit
Aequali, vel enim potentiori;
Quin eludere, si sit usus, ipsum   5
Audere intrepide suos parentes.
Responde mihi, vi'n fidem experiri?
I iam, ad coenam hodie vocato, vel cras,
Vel tu postridie, perendieve,
Si lubet, vel ad ultimas calendas;   10
Ni praesto fuerit, per et tabernas
Omnes undique quaeritans volarit,
Quas te nec meminisse iam nec unquam

genius to be feared by the unsavory and depraved even as
the thunder of Jove; in short by you white Pyrenees,
Parnassus, Helicon and Hippocrines and whatever place is
free of song, now I beg and I implore that you slaughter   10
these shameless men in ten books in succession; for they are
disgusting and distasteful and strangely criticize the sacred
poets, your Publius and your Maro,[15] whom you love as   15
you should, whom you cherish and preserve from death
through folly. Therefore, if you are wise, on all fronts you
will lay on these highwaymen in ambush and destroy them;   20
and with rage once aroused you will never stop, but you
will stone them to death, branded in public as an obscene
mob.

93. *On Breton.*[16]

You wisely introduced Love, killed by a song, Breton; for
never would he live by your meters.

94. *To George Chapman.*[17]

Chapman, not very honorably do you accuse Cottus of
bad faith and argue that he always forgets what he
promised an equal or even one more powerful; nay indeed,
that he himself dares fearlessly mock his parents if he has   5
occasion. Answer me, do you want his faith tested? Go
now, invite him to dinner today or tomorrow or next day
or the day after or the first of next month; if he is not on   10
hand, he may have flown through all the taverns, diligently
searching everywhere—through all the taverns which I
allow you to swear that you do not recall nor have ever

15 Ovid and Virgil.
16 This epigram mocks Nicholas Breton (ca. 1551–ca. 1623), the prolific
poet and pamphleteer; perhaps it alludes to *Brittons Bowre of Delights*
(1591).
17 George Chapman (ca. 1559–1634), the famous playwright and trans-
lator of Homer. There is no evidence of Campion's acquaintance with him;
but both later contributed to the festivities surrounding the Lady Elizabeth's
marriage in 1613. Three epigrams of the 1595 collection (one reprinted as
No. 36 of the present book, two not reprinted) likewise deal with Cottus
("Cook"?), whose eagerness for dining forms the basis of this ironic de-
fense.

Usurpasse oculis in hunc diem usque
Audacter mihi deierare fas sit: 15
Postremo nisi praeberit vocanti
Convivam memorem se, et impigellum,
Coenam coxeris hanc meo periclo.
Nullumne hoc specimen fidelitatis?

116. *Ad Cambricum.*

E multis aliquos si non despexit amantes,
    Si tua non fuerit rustica nata fremis?
Aut tam formosam tibi, Cambrice, non genuisses,
    Aut sineres nato munere posse frui.
Castae sint facies sua quas sinit esse pudicas,
    Pulchrior huic forma est quam decet esse probis.

117. *Ad Leam.*

Privato commune bonum, Lea, cum melius fit,
    Obscurum plane est foemina casta bonum.
Nam nulli nota, aut ad summum permanet uni,
    Omnibus atque aliis est quasi nulla foret;
Sin se divulget, mala fit. Quare illa bonarum
    Aut rerum minima est, aut, Lea, tota mala.

213. *In Pandarum.*

Scrotum tumescit Pandaro; tremat scortum.

225. *In Cambrum.*

Cum tibi vilescat doctus lepidusque Catullus,
    Non est ut sperem, Cambre, placere tibi.
Tu quoque cum Suffenorum suffragia quaeras,
    Non est ut speres, Cambre, placere mihi.

even glimpsed up to this very day: finally, if he does not 15
show you when you invite him that he is a mindful guest,
and not boring, you will have cooked this dinner at my
risk. Isn't this a token of sincerity?

116. *To Cambricus.*

Do you complain if your daughter has not spurned some of
her many lovers, if she has not been a simple country
girl? Either you should not have sired such a beauty,
Cambricus, or you should allow her to enjoy her natural
assets. Girls are chaste whose appearance allows them to
be modest, her figure is more beautiful than is proper for
honorable girls.[18]

117. *To Lea.*[19]

Since the common good is better than private good, Lea,
it is clear that a chaste woman is an obscure good. For if
she is known to none or remains faithful to one until the
end, it is to all others as if she did not exist; but if she
spreads her favors, she is bad. Therefore one of the good
women is either the least of possessions, or, Lea, she is all
bad.

213. *On Pandarus.*

Pandarus's jewels swell; his Jewel trembles.

225. *On Camber.*

Since the learned and witty Catullus is worthless to you, I
should not hope to please you, Camber. Also when you ask
for the votes of the Suffeni,[20] you should not hope to
please me, Camber.

[18] Compare *The Fourth Booke of Ayres,* xvii, l. 12.
[19] Compare *The Third Booke of Ayres,* vi.
[20] wealthy poetasters; see Catullus *Carmina* xxii.

227. *Ad Graios.*

Graii, sive magis iuvat vetustum
Nomen, Purpulii, decus Britannum,
Sic Astraea gregem beare vestrum,
Sic Pallas velit; ut favere nugis
Disiuncti socii velitis ipsi,
Tetrae si neque sint, nec infacetae,
Sed quales merito exhibere plausu
Vosmet, ludere cum lubet, soletis.

228. *Ad Librum.*

Verborum satis est; oneri sunt plura libello;
    Sermo vel urbanus multus obesse potest.
Partibus ex brevibus quae constat inepta figura est
    Si sit longa nimis; par modus esto pari.

227. *To the Grays.*[21]

Grays, or if your former name is more pleasant, men of Purpoole,[22] pride of Britain, thus Astraea blesses your flock, thus Pallas may wish; and, as scattered comrades yourselves, may you wish to approve these jests if they are neither offensive nor stupid but such as you yourselves usually put on with deserved applause, when you want to act.

228. *To the Book.*

Enough words; there are too many to burden this little book; indeed a long witty theme can be a hindrance. As everyone knows, a whole shape made of short pieces is awkward if it is too long; let the measure be equal to the measures.

[21] Campion was admitted to Gray's Inn on April 27, 1586, and apparently stayed there till 1595.

[22] The old name for Gray's Inn Lane was "Porte Pool," whence the characterization of the Inn as the "State of Purpoole" in the *Gesta Grayorum* of 1594.

EPIGRAMS FROM *POEMATA*, 1595

Ad Ed. Spencerum.

Sive canis silvas, Spencere, vel horrida belli
    Fulmina, dispeream ni te amem, et intime amem.

Ad Io. Davisium.

Quod nostros, Davisi, laudas recitasque libellos
    Vultu quo nemo candidiore solet,
Ad me mitte tuos; iam pridem postulo, res est
    In qua persolvi gratia vera potest.

Ad Io. Dolundum.

O qui sonora coelites altos cheli
Mulces et umbras incolas atrae Stygis,
Quam suave murmur! quale fluctu prominens
Lygia madentes rore dum siccat comas,
Quam suave murmur flaccidas aures ferit   5
Dum lenis oculos leviter invadit sopor!
Ut falce rosa dissecta purpureum caput

EPIGRAMS FROM *POEMATA*, 1595

To Edmund Spenser

Whether you sing of the forests or of the horrid bolts of war, Spenser, I swear I love you and love you dearly.

To John Davies[1]

Because you read and praise our books, Davies, with a franker expression than anyone else, send me yours; I asked long ago, this is an opportunity when a real favor can be repaid.

To John Dowland[2]

O you who soothe the dwellers high in heaven with your sounding lyre and those who inhabit the netherworld, how sweet your gentle murmur! On such a tide [of song] Lygia came forth drying her hair dripping with dew;[3] how sweetly your murmur falls on wearied ears while gently sleep softly steals over the eyes. As a rose clipped by the pruning shears droops its shining head, covering the

5

---

[1] Sir John Davies (1569–1626), whose *Orchestra* was probably written in 1594.

[2] John Dowland, the great musician, who set many of Campion's songs, and to whose *First Booke of Songs or Ayres* Campion contributed a prefatory poem in 1597 (see Occasional Poems, p. 195).

[3] Probably Ligea, one of the water nymphs; see Virgil *Georgics* IV. 336.

Dimittit, undique foliis spargens humum,
Labuntur, hei, sic debiles somno tori,
Terramque feriunt membra ponderibus suis.   10
Dolande, misero surripis mentem mihi,
Excorsque cordae pectus impulsae premunt.
Quis tibi deorum tam potenti numine
Digitos trementes dirigit? is inter deos
Magnos oportet principem obtineat locum.   15
Tu solus affers rebus antiquis fidem,
Nec miror Orpheus considens Rhodope super
Siquando rupes flexit et agrestes feras.
At, o beate, siste divinas manus,
Iam, iam, parumper siste divinas manus!   20
Liquescit anima, quam cave exugas mihi.

In se.

Olim fungus ego, silex verebar;
Ne non utibilis viro emineret
Penis, qui puero excitatus altum
Momentis caput extulit torosis.
Tum nec apposita manu fovere,   5
Nec sum tangere, nec repellere ausus,
Nimirum metuens adulta stirps haec
Ut posset pathico orbe comprehendi.
Vos iam intelligitis, viri et puellae,
Multo sed magis improbae puellae,   10
Quam stulte, illepideque rusticeque
Summae laetitiae meae dolebam.
Nec si grandior exiisset alnu
Idcirca fore mi magis verendam,
Aut plus penivorae arduam puellae.   15

ground all around with petals, alas, so the frail bodies
sink in sleep, and their limbs collapse on the ground of
their own weight. Dowland, you steal away my reason in   10
my misery, and the chords you strike overwhelm my foolish
heart. Which of the gods guides your trembling fingers
with his powerful spirit? He should hold first place among
the mighty gods. You alone bring truth to ancient history,   15
nor do I now find it marvelous that Orpheus sitting upon
Rhodope moved the rocks and beasts of the field.[4] But, O
blessed one, stay your divine hands, now, now for a mo-
ment, stay your divine hands! My spirit melts within me,   20
take care lest you exhaust me completely.

On Himself

Once I was a fool, an utter blockhead; I was afraid lest
the penis which lifted its head high with a twisting motion
when roused by the boy should not be of service to the
man. Then I did not dare to put my hand down to   5
fondle it nor to touch it or to push it away, fearing, of
course, that this sprout when full grown could not be
embraced by the lascivious orb. Now you all know, men
and maids, but far more do you know, you wicked girls,   10
how foolishly without grace or sophistication I suffered for
my supreme joy. If it had grown higher than an alder, I
would not have had to be any more afraid for my happi-
ness, nor would pleasure have been farther from the reach
of a penivorous girl.   15

[4] See *Ad Thamesin,* ll. 205-7.

DOUBTFUL POEMS

I have been very cautious in claiming for Campion any lyrics that he did not explicitly claim for himself in his publications. While attribution of unsigned poems is a difficult matter always, in the case of songs with music it reaches almost insurmountable difficulties. In the published songbooks, most lyrics are unsigned, and the reader has no way of knowing whether they are to be taken as the composer's own lyrics, or lyrics written for him by another, or common property. Furthermore, practices such as composing a new body and ending for the beginning of another's lyric, setting a lyric to new music and altering it slightly to fit, and merely taking a suggestion for one's own song from an old song were so widespread among both amateurs and professionals that what may seem a variant or first draft of a published lyric may well be merely someone else's "poetical descant" on it. The unsigned lyrics that may belong to Campion fall into three groups: *A Booke of Ayres,* Part II, *The Ayres That Were Sung and Played at Brougham Castle,* and a set of miscellaneous poems from manuscripts and other sources.

The attribution of *A Booke of Ayres,* Part II, to Campion is extremely doubtful. The statements of the printed book itself, for one thing, are inconclusive: Rosseter's claim that "the first ranke of songs are of his owne [Campion's] composition . . . to which I have added an equall number of mine owne" and the headnote labeling "the rest of the Songs contained in this Booke, made by Philip Rosseter," while they may indicate Rosseter's composition of the music alone, by no means suggest that it was Campion rather than someone else who wrote the words. The attribution of the second song to Campion in Davison's *Poetical Rhapsody* of 1602 was canceled in subsequent editions of 1608, 1611, and 1622, and replaced by "Anon." Furthermore, Ralph W. Berringer has shown, by a convincing analysis ("Thomas Campion's Share in *A Booke of Ayres,*" *PMLA,* LVIII [1943], 938–48), that the lyrics of Part II are stylistically quite unlike those of Part I: they lack the dramatic immediacy of Campion's genuine work, they are loose structurally, they contain little of the stanzaic variety and inventiveness typical of him, they are verbally and metrically very awkward, and they frequently fail to achieve metrical equivalence between strophes as his other songs do (for example, vii 5 and 13, xi 6 and 12, ix throughout).

Vivian assigns the words to George Mason and John Earsden's *Ayres That Were Sung and Played at Brougham Castle* in 1617 (published 1618) to Campion on several counts. First, there is his close connection with the Earl of Cumberland, who gave the entertainment (see headnote to *Two Bookes of Ayres* and Campion's epistle), and his household musician Mason. Then there is the close relation between Song III and *Epigrammatum Liber* I, 188, written for the same occasion, James I's return from Scotland into England; Vivian also finds the style typical of Campion, especially in Song VI. Finally, and most important, Vivian quotes (p. li) a letter from the Earl of Cumberland to his son Lord Clifford concerning the entertainment: "Sonn, I have till now expected your lettres according to your promis at your departure; so did George Minson [Mason] your directions touching the musick, whereupon he mought the better have writt to Dr. Campion. He is now gone to my Lord Presidents at York, and will be ready to do as he heares from you." This is pretty strong evidence, and on its basis *Grove's Dictionary of Music and Musicians* has accepted the attribution.

Of poems from manuscripts and printed books, I have confined myself largely to printing those claimed for Campion by Vivian (with the exception of two obvious errors: "Had those that dwell," which is a song from Jonson's *Masque of Beauty,* and "The hower of sleepy night," whose provenance and date he mistook), adding only five others on my own authority. The criteria for assigning manuscript songs to Campion are quite shaky. Attribution in the manuscripts is perhaps the surest, yet scribes assigned "Harke, al you ladies" (*A Booke of Ayres,* Part I, xix) to Sidney and "The man of life upright" (ibid., xviii) to Francis Bacon. Similarity of idea between a song and an established Campion song may indicate imitation as well as authenticity; and even quotation of some lines may afford no proof (for instance, Dowland took Sidney's line "O sweet woods the delight of solitarines" and made it the refrain of a new song). The frequent occurrence of a song amid other genuine Campion material may be a good criterion, but not all songbooks proceeded neatly composer by composer. Finally, there is the criterion of style, the pitfall of any editor; at its best, it leads to negative conclusions. For instance, Campion is seldom crabbed or awkward; his faults lie another way, toward the smoothly insipid. On grounds of style, therefore, one might summarily reject "My deerest mistrisse," "Could my poore heart," as well as *A Booke of Ayres,* Part II. I have indicated in the textual notes the evidence for acceptance or rejection of the doubtful poems from various sources. Of them, I propose that the following are genuine: "Of Neptunes Empyre," the three sonnets—"Thou shalt not love mee," "Thrice tosse," "Thou art not fayer"—from Harley MS. 6910, and "The peacefull westerne winde."

A BOOKE OF AYRES, PART II

I.

Sweete, come againe;
    Your happie sight, so much desir'd,
Since you from hence are now retir'd,
    I seeke in vaine.
Stil must I mourn   5
    And pine in longing paine,
Till you, my lives delight, againe
    Vouchsafe your wisht returne.

If true desire,
    Or faithfull vow of endles love,   10
Thy heart enflam'd may kindly move
    With equall fire;
O then my joies,
    So long destraught, shall rest,
Reposed soft in thy chast brest,   15
    Exempt from all annoies.

You had the power
    My wandring thoughts first to restraine,
You first did heare my love speake plaine,
    A child before: 20
Now it is growne
    Confirm'd, do you it keepe,
And let it safe in your bosome sleepe,
    There ever made your owne.

And till we meete,   25
    Teach absence inward art to find,
Both to disturbe and please the mind.
    Such thoughts are sweete,
And such remaine
    In hearts whose flames are true;   30
Then such will I retaine, till you
    To me returne againe.

II.[1]

And would you see my Mistris face?
    it is a flowrie garden place,
Where knots of beauties have such grace
    that all is worke[2] and nowhere space.

It is a sweete delicious morne,   5
    where day is breeding, never borne,
It is a Meadow yet unshorne,
    whome thousand flowers do adorne.

It is the heavens bright reflexe,
    weake eies to dazle and to vexe,   10
It is th' Idaea of her sexe,
    envie of whome doth world perplexe.

It is a face of death that smiles,
    pleasing, though it killes the whiles,
Where death and love in pretie wiles   15
    each other mutuallie beguiles.

It is faire beauties freshest youth,
    it is the fain'd Eliziums truth:
The spring that winter'd harts renu'th;
    and this is that my soule pursu'th.   20

III.

No grave for woe, yet earth my watrie teares devoures;
Sighes want ayre, and burnt desires kind pitties showres:
Stars hold their fatal course, my joies preventing:
The earth, the sea, the aire, the fire, the heav'ns
          vow my tormenting.

[1] Fellowes notes that a parody of this song occurs in *The Welsh Embassador* (ed. for the Malone Society by H. Littledale and W. W. Greg, Oxford, 1921), ll. 1396–1435. There is also a later 17th-century song beginning "Will you know my Mistress face/tis a garden full of roses" set by John Wilson (who reset several Campion texts), apparently derived from this song; it survives in Bodleian MS. Music b. 1 (fo. 19) and Edinburgh University Library Music MS. Dc. 1. 69 (fo. 67).

[2] ornament, like the "knots" or figured flower beds.

Yet still I live, and waste my wearie daies in grones,
And with wofull tunes adorne dispayring mones.
Night still prepares a more displeasing morrow;
My day is night, my life my death, and all but sence
                        of sorrow.

IV.

If I urge my kinde desires,
She unkind doth them reject;
Womens hearts are painted fires
To deceive them that affect.
I alone loves fires include,   5
Shee alone doth them delude.

Shee hath often vow'd her love,
But, alas, no fruit I finde.
That her fires are false I prove,
Yet in her no fault I finde: 10
I was thus unhappy borne,
And ordain'd to be her scorne.

Yet if humane care, or paine,
May the heav'nly order change,
She will hate her owne disdaine,   15
And repent she was so strange:
For a truer heart then I
Never liv'd, or lov'd to die.

V.

What harts content can he finde,
    What happy sleepes can his eies embrace,
That beares a guiltie minde?
    His tast sweet wines wil abhorre:
No musicks sounde can appease the thoughts   5
    That wicked deeds deplore.
The passion of a present feare
    Stil makes his restles motion there;
And all the day hee dreads the night,
    And all the night, as one agast, hee feares the morning light 10

But he that loves to be lov'd,
  And in his deedes doth adore heavens power,
And is with pitie mov'd;
  The night gives rest to his heart,
The cheerefull beames do awake his soule,   15
  Revived in everie part.
He lives a comfort to his friendes,
  And heaven to him such blessing sendes
That feare of hell cannot dismaie
  His stedfast hart that is enurd the truth still to obey   20

VI.

Let him that will be free and keep his hart from care,
  Retir'd alone, remaine where no discomforts are.
For when the eie doth view his griefe, or haplesse eare
            his sorrow heares,
  Th' impression still in him abides, and ever in one
           shape appeares.

Forget thy griefes betimes; long sorrow breedes long paine,   5
  For joie, farre fled from men, will not returne againe;
O happie is the soule which heaven ordained to live in
           endles peace:
  His life is a pleasing dreame, and everie houre his
           joyes encrease.

You heavie sprites, that love in sever'd shades to dwell,
  That nurse despaire, and dreame of unrelenting hell,   10
Come sing this happie song, and learne of me the Arte of
           true content,
  Loade not your guiltie soules with wrong, and heaven
           then will soone relent.

VII.

Reprove not love, though fondly thou hast lost
  Greater hopes by loving:
Love calms ambicious spirits, from their brests
  Danger oft removing:
Let lofty humors mount up on high,   5
  Down againe like to the wind,

While privat thoughts, vow'd to love,
   More peace and pleasure find.

Love and sweete beautie makes the stubborne milde,
   And the coward fearelesse,   10
The wretched misers care to bountie turnes,
   Cheering all thinges cheerelesse;
Love chaines the earth and heaven,
   Turnes the Spheares, guides the yeares in endles peace;
The flourie earth through his power   15
   Recceiv's her due encrease.

VIII.

And would you faine the reason know
   why my sad eies so often flow?
My heart ebs joy when they doe so,
   and loves the moone by whom they go.

And will you aske why pale I looke?   5
   tis not with poring on my booke:
My Mistris cheeke my bloud hath tooke,
   for her mine owne hath me forsooke.

Doe not demaund why I am mute:
   loves silence doth all speech confute.   10
They set the noat, then tune the Lute,
   harts frame their thoughts, then toongs their suit.

Doe not admire why I admire:
   my fever is no others fire;
Each severall heart hath his desire,   15
   els proofe is false, and truth a lier.

If why I love you should see cause:
   love should have forme like other lawes;
But fancie pleads not by the clawes,[3]
   tis as the sea, still vext with flawes.[4]   20

No fault upon my love espie,
   for you perceive not with my eie;
My pallate to your tast may lie,
   yet please it selfe deliciously.

---

[3] going point by point through each clause or proviso of a legal argument.
[4] sudden storms, with a pun on legal errors.

Then let my sufferance be mine owne: 25
  sufficeth it these reasons showne;
Reason and love are ever knowne
  to fight till both be overthrowne.

IX.

When Laura smiles her sight revives both night and day,
The earth and heaven viewes with delight her wanton play,
And her speech with ever-flowing musicke doth repaire
The cruell wounds of sorrow and untam'd despaire.

The sprites that remaine in fleeting aire 5
Affect for pastime to untwine her tressed haire,
And the birds thinke sweete Aurora, mornings Queene, doth shine
From her bright sphere, when Laura shewes her lookes devine.

Dianas eyes are not adorn'd with greater power
Then Lauras, when she lists awhile for sport to loure: 10
But when she her eyes encloseth, blindnes doth appeare
The chiefest grace of beautie, sweetlie seated there.

Love hath no fire but what he steales from her bright eyes,
Time hath no power but that which in her pleasure lyes:
For she with her devine beauties all the world subdues, 15
And fils with heav'nly spirits my humble muse.

X.

Long have mine eies gaz'd with delight,
Conveying hopes unto my soule;
In nothing happy, but in sight
Of her, that doth my sight controule:
But now mine eies must loose their light. 5

My object now must be the aire,
To write in water words of fire,
And teach sad thoughts how to despaire:
Desert must quarrell with desire.
All were appeas'd were she not faire. 10

For all my comfort, this I prove,
That Venus on the Sea was borne:
If Seas be calme, then doth she love,
If stormes arise, I am forlorne:
My doubtfull hopes like wind doe move.   15

XI.[5]

Though far from joy, my sorrowes are as far,
And I both betweene:
Not too low, nor yet too high
Above my reach, would I bee seene.
Happy is he that so is placed,   5
Not to be envi'd, nor to bee disdain'd or disgraced.

The higher trees, the more stormes they endure,
Shrubs be troden downe:
But the meane, the golden meane,
Doth onely all our fortunes crowne: 10
Like to a streame that sweetely slideth
Through the flourie banks, and still in the midst his
course guideth.

XII.

Shal I come, if I swim? wide are the waves, you see:
Shall I come, if I flie, my deere love, to thee?
Streames Venus will appease, Cupid gives me winges:
All the powers assist my desire
Save you alone, that set my wofull heart on fire.   5

You are faire; so was Hero that in Sestos dwelt;
She a priest, yet the heate of love truly felt.
A greater streame then this did her love devide,
But she was his guide with a light:
So through the streames Leander did enjoy her sight.   10

[5] Fellowes cites Horace *Odes* II. x as the source of this song; compare especially l. 7 with Horace's ll. 9-10:

saepius ventis agitatur ingens
pinus.

XIII.

Aye me, that love should natures workes accuse!
  Where cruell Laura still her beautie viewes,
River, or cloudie jet, or christall bright,
  Are all but servants of her selfe-delight.

Yet her deformed thoughts she cannot see,
  And thats the cause she is so sterne to mee.
Vertue and duetie can no favour gaine:
  O griefe, a death, to live and love in vaine!

XIV.

Shall then a traiterous kis or a smile
  All my delights unhappily beguile?
Shall the vow of fayned love receive so ritch regard,
  When true service dies neglected, and wants his due
        reward?

Deedes meritorious soone be forgot,   5
  But one offence no time can ever blot;
Every day it is renu'd, and every night it bleedes,
  And with bloudy streames of sorrow drownes all our
        better deedes.

Beautie is not by desert to be woon,
  Fortune hath all that is beneath the Sunne;   10
Fortune is the guide of love, and both of them be blind:
  All their waies are full of errors, which no true
        feete can find.

XV.

If I hope, I pine; if I feare, I faint and die;
  So betweene hope and feare I desp'rat lie,
Looking for joy to heaven, whence it should come:
  But hope is blinde, joy deafe, and I am dumbe.

Yet I speake and crie, but alas with words of wo;
    And joy conceives[6] not them that murmure so.
He that the eares of joy will ever pearse
    Must sing glad noates, or speake in happier verse.

XVI.

Unlesse there were consent twixt hell and heaven
That grace and wickednes should be combind,
I cannot make thee and thy beauties even;
Thy face is heaven, and torture in thy minde:
For more then worldly blisse is in thy eie,   5
And hellish torture in thy minde doth lie.

A thousand Cherubins flie in her lookes,
And hearts in legions melt upon their view:
But gorgeous covers wall up filthie bookes;
Be it sinne to saie, that so your eyes do you: 10
But sure your mind adheres not with your eies,
For what they promise, that your heart denies.

But O, least I religion should misuse,
Inspire me thou, that ought'st thy selfe to know,
Since skillesse readers reading do abuse,   15
What inward meaning outward sence doth show:
For by thy eies and heart, chose and contem'd,
I waver, whether saved or condemn'd.

XVII.

If she forsake me, I must die:
    Shall I tell her so?
Alas, then strait she will replie,
    No, no, no, no, no.
If I disclose my desp'rat state,   5
She will but make sport thereat,
    And more unrelenting grow.

[6] understands.

What heart can long such paines abide?
　　Fie uppon this love.
I would adventure farre and wide,　　　　　10
　　If it would remove.
But love will still my steppes pursue,
I cannot his wayes eschew:
　　Thus still helpeles hopes I prove.

I doe my love in lines commend,　　　　　15
　　But, alas, in vaine;
The costly gifts that I doe send
　　She returnes againe:
Thus still is my despaire procur'd,
And her malice more assur'd:　　　　　20
　　Then come, death, and end my paine.

XVIII.[7]

What is a day, what is a yeere
　　Of vaine delight and pleasure?
Like to a dreame it endlesse dies,
　　And from us like a vapour flies:
And this is all the fruit that we finde,　　　5
　　Which glorie in worldly treasure.

He that will hope for true delight
　　With vertue must be graced;
Sweet follie yeelds a bitter tast,
　　Which ever will appeare at last:　　　　10
But if we still in vertue delight,
　　Our soules are in heaven placed.

XIX.

Kinde in unkindnesse, when will you relent
And cease with faint love true love to torment?
Still entertain'd, excluded still I stand,
Her glove stil holde, but cannot touch the hand.

[7] This song bears an obvious resemblance to the popular "What if a day" ascribed to Campion; see p. 473 of this edition and notes thereto, and David Greer, " 'What if a day'—An Examination of the Words and Music," *Music and Letters,* XLIII (1962), 316–18.

In her faire hand my hopes and comforts rest: 5
O might my fortunes with that hand be blest,
No envious breaths then my deserts could shake,
For they are good whom such true love doth make.

O let not beautie so forget her birth
That it should fruitles home returne to earth: 10
Love is the fruite of beautie, then love one;
Not your sweete selfe, for such selfe love is none.

Love one that onely lives in loving you,
Whose wrong'd deserts would you with pity view:
This strange distast which your affections swaies   15
Would relish love, and you find better daies.

Thus till my happie sight your beautie viewes,
Whose sweet remembrance stil my hope renewes,
Let these poore lines sollicite love for mee,
And place my joyes where my desires would bee.   20

XX.

What thing is love but mourning?
    What desire, but a selfe-burning?
Till shee that hates doth love returne,
Thus will I mourne, thus will I sing,
    Come away, come away, my darling.   5

Beautie is but a blooming,
    Youth in his glorie entombing;
Time hath a wheel which none can stay:
Then come away, while thus I sing,
    Come away, come away, my darling.   10

Sommer in winter fadeth,
    Gloomie night heav'nly light shadeth,
Like to the morne are Venus flowers;
Such are her howers: then will I sing,
    Come away, come away, my darling.   15

XXI.

Whether men doe laugh or weepe,
Whether they doe wake or sleepe,
Whether they die yoong or olde,
Whether they feele heate or colde,
There is, underneath the sunne,　　　　5
Nothing in true earnest done.

All our pride is but a jest;
None are worst, and none are best;
Griefe, and joy, and hope, and feare
Play their Pageants every where:　　　　10
Vaine opinion all doth sway,
And the world is but a play.

Powers above in cloudes doe sit,
Mocking our poore apish wit
That so lamely, with such state,　　　　15
Their high glorie imitate:
No ill can be felt but paine,
And that happie men disdaine.

FINIS.

THE
AYRES
THAT WERE
SUNG AND PLAYED,

at *Brougham Castle* in *Westmerland*,

in the Kings Entertainment:

Given by the Right Honourable the EARLE of CUMBERLAND, and his Right Noble Sonne the LORD CLIFFORD.

COMPOSED
BY
Mr. GEORGE MASON, and
Mr. JOHN EARSDEN.

I.

A DIALOGUE SUNG THE FIRST NIGHT,

The King being at supper.

CANTUS. Tune thy chearefull voyce to mine,
    Musicke helpes digesting.

TENOR. Musicke is as good as wine,
    And as fit for feasting.

CANT. Melodie now is needfull here,   5
    It will helpe to mend our cheare.

BOTH.   Joyne then, one joy expressing.

CANT. Here is a guest for whose content
    All excesse were sparing.

TEN.   All to him present,   10
    Hourely new delights preparing.

CHORUS. Joy at thy board, health in thy dish,
    Mirth in thy cup, and in thy bed
    Soft sleepe and pleasing rest wee wish.

CANT. Earth and ayre and Sea consent   15
    In thy entertaining.

TEN.   All is old which they present,
    Yet all choice contayning.

CANT. Musick alone the soule can feast,
    It being new and well exprest;   20

BOTH.   Joyne then, sweet cords enchaining.[1]

CANT. Could we to our wisht ends aspire,
    Joy should crowne thy dishes.

TEN.   Proud is our desire,
    If thou dost accept our wishes.   25

CHORUS. Joy at thy board, health in thy dish,
    Mirth in thy cup, and in thy bed
    Soft sleepe and pleasing rest wee wish.

---

[1] with a pun on "cords": combine our voices into a chord, and tie our
voices together.

II.

Another Dialogue,

to be sung at the same time.

CANT. Now is the time, now is the hower
       When joy first blest this happy Bower:
TEN.   Here is a sight that sweetens every sower.
CANT.   So shines the Moon by night,
TEN.   So looks the Sun by day;   5
CANT.   Heavenly is his light,
TEN.   And never shal decay.

CHORUS. There is no voice enough can sing
         The praise of our great King.

CANT.   Fal, showers of sweet delight;   10
TEN.   Spring, flowers of plesant mirth;
CANT.   What heaven hath beams that shine more bright?
TEN.   Here heven is now, stars shine on earth.
CANT. In one all honor groweth,
TEN.   From one all comfort floweth: 15
BOTH. Dutie saith that to this one all it hath it oweth.

CHORUS. Let then that one of all be praised
         That hath our fortunes raised.

III.[2]

The Kings Good-night.

Welcome, welcome, King of guests
   With thy Princely traine,
With joyfull Triumphs and with Feasts
   Be welcom'd home againe.
     Frolicke mirth,   5
    The soule of earth,
   Shall watch for thy delight:

[2] Vivian compares "*De Regis reditu e Scotia,*" *Epigrammatum Liber* I, 188, a poem celebrating the same event, King James's return from his Scottish visit in 1617; the Latin poem contains the same conceit as ll. 16–21 as well as parallels to ll. 4 and 7.

Knees shall bend
From friend to friend
While full cups doe thee right: 10
And so, great King, good-night.

Welcome, welcome as the Sunne
When the night is past:
With us the day is now begunne,
May it for ever last.   15
Such a morne
Did nere adorne
The Roses of the East,
As the North
Hath now brought forth: 20
The Northerne morne is best.
And so, best King, good rest.

IV.[8]

Come follow me, my wandring mates,
Sonnes and daughters of the Fates:
Friends of night, that oft have done
Homage to the horned Moone,
Fairely march, and shun not light,   5
With such stars as these made bright;
Yet bend you low your curled tops,
Touch the hallowed earth, and then
Rise agen with anticke hops
Unus'd of men.   10
Here no danger is, nor feare,
For true Honour harbours here,
Whom Grace attends.[4]
Grace can make our foes our friends.

[8] apparently a night song addressed to the fairies (who are interestingly assimilated to trees in ll. 7-10).

[4] True honor resides wherever Grace (James) is.

V.

A Ballad.

Dido was the *Carthage* Queene
And lov'd the *Trojan* Knight,
That wandring many coasts had seene
And many a dreadfull fight:
As they on hunting road, a shower   5
Drave them, in a loving hower,
    Downe to a darksome cave:
Where *Aeneas* with his charmes
Lockt Queene *Dido* in his armes
    And had what hee could have.   10

Dido Hymens Rites forgot,
Her love was wing'd with haste:
Her honour shee considered not,
But in her breast him plac't.
And, when her love was new begunne,   15
Jove sent downe his winged Sonne
    To fright *Aeneas* sleepe;
Bad him by the breake of day
From Queene *Dido* steale away:
    Which made her waile and weepe.   20

Dido wept, but what of this?
The Gods would have it so:
Aeneas nothing did amisse,
For hee was forc't to goe.
Learne, Lordings, then, no faith to keepe   25
With your Loves, but let them weepe:
    'Tis folly to be true.
Let this Story serve your turne,
And let twenty *Didoes* burne
    So you get daily new.   30

VI.

The Dance.

CANT.   *Robin* is a lovely Lad,
         No Lasse a smother[5] ever had.

BASS.   *Tommy* hath a looke as bright
         As is the rosie morning light.

BASS.   *Tib* is darke and browne of hue,   5
         But, like her colour, firme and true.

TEN.   *Ginny* hath a lip to kisse
         Wherein a spring of Nectar is.

TEN.   *Simkin* well his mirth can place,
         And words to win a womans grace.   10

TEN.   *Sib* is all in all to me,
         There is no Queene of Love but she.

ALL.   Let us in a lovers round
         Circle all this hallowed ground.
         Softly, softly trip and goe: 15
         The light foot Fairies jet[6] it so.
              Forward, then,
              And backe againe;
              Here and there,
              And everywhere,   20
         Winding to and winding fro,
         Skipping hye and lowting[7] low.

CHORUS. And, like lovers hand in hand,
         March a round and make a stand.

[5] smoother.   [6] strut.   [7] bowing.

VII.

A Song.

The shadowes darkning our intents
   Must fade, and Truth now take her place,
   Who, in our right *Aegyptian* race,[8]
A chaine of Prophecies presents
   With which the starry Skye consents,   5
   And all the under-Elements.
Thou that art all divine, give eare,
   And grace our humble Songs
   That speak what to thy State belongs
Unmasked now and cleare;   10
   Which wee in severall straines divide,
   And heaven-borne Truth our Notes shall guide,
     One by one, while wee relate
     That which shall tye both Time and Fate.

VIII.[9]

CANT.   Truth, sprung from heaven, shall shine,
       With her beames divine,
       On all thy Land,
   And there for ever stedfast stand.

BASS.   Lovely peace,   5
       Spring of increase,
   Shall like a precious gemme
   Adorne thy Royall Diademe.

TEN.   Love, that bindes
       Loyall mindes,   10
   Shall make all hearts agree[10]
   To magnifie thy state and thee.

[8] Apparently the singers were dressed as Gypsies.

[9] This follows directly upon the previous unison sonnet, the singers now being in "severall straines" divided for the various prophecies promised in VII.

[10] a pun: consent, and come together (as in music, harmoniously).

TEN.   Honour, that proceeds
                Out of noble deeds,
            Shall waite on thee alone,   15
            And cast a sacred light about thy Throne.

BASS.   Long shall thy three Crownes remaine,
            Blessed in thy long-liv'd raigne.
            Thy age shall like fresh youth appeare,
            And perpetuall Roses beare.   20

TEN.   Many on earth thy dayes shall be,
            But endlesse thy posteritie,
            And matchlesse thy posteritie.

CHORUS. Truth, Peace, Love, Honour, and Long-life attend
            Thee, and all those that from thy loynes descend: 25
            With us the Angels in this *Chorus* meet:
            So humbly prostrate at thy sacred feet,
            Our nightly sports and prophesies wee end.

IX.

The Farewell Song.

O stay! sweet is the least delay,
    When parting forceth mourning:
O Joy! too soone thy flowers decay,
    From Rose to Bryer returning.
Bright beames that now shine here,   5
    When you are parted,
All will be dimme, all will be dumbe,
    And every breast sad hearted.

Yet more, for true love may presume,
    If it exceede not measure.   10
O griefe! that blest houres soone consume,
    But joylesse pass at leasure.
Since wee this light must lose,
    Our love expressing:
Farre may it shine, long may it live,   15
    To all a publique blessing.

X.

*The Lords Welcome, sung before the Kings
Good-night.*

Welcome is the word,
The best love can afford:
For what can better be?'
Welcome, Lords, the time drawes neare
When each one shall embrace his deare,   5
And view the face hee longs to see.
   Absence makes the houre more sweet
   When divided lovers meet.

Welcome once againe,
Though too much were in vaine: 10
Yet how can love exceed?
Princely Guests, wee wish there were
Joves Nectar and Ambrosia here,
That you might like immortals feed,
   Changing shapes like full-fed *Jove*   15
   In the sweet pursuit of love.

FINIS.

POEMS FROM VARIOUS SOURCES

I.

What if a day, or a month, or a yeare
Crown thy delights with a thousand sweet contentings?
Cannot a chance of a night or an howre
Crosse thy desires with as many sad tormentings?
  Fortune, honor, beauty, youth   5
  Are but blossoms dying;
  Wanton pleasure, doating love,
  Are but shadowes flying.
  All our joyes are but toyes,
  Idle thoughts deceiving;   10
  None have power of an howre
  In their lives bereaving.[1]

Earthes but a point to the world, and a man
Is but a point to the worlds compared centure:
Shall then a point of a point be so vaine   15
As to triumph in a seely[2] points adventure?
  All is hassard that we have,
  There is nothing biding;
  Dayes of pleasure are like streames
  Through faire meadowes gliding.   20
  Weale and woe, time doth goe,
  Time is never turning:
  Secret fates guide our states,
  Both in mirth and mourning.

[1] vanishing. [2] simple.

2.

A Hymne in praise of Neptune.

Of Neptunes Empyre let us sing,
At whose command the waves obay:
To whom the Rivers tribute pay,
  Downe the high mountaines sliding.
To whom the skaly Nation yeelds   5
Homage for the Cristall fields
          Wherein they dwell;
And every Sea-god paies a Jem,
Yeerely out of his watry Cell,
To decke great *Neptunes* Diadem.   10

The *Trytons* dauncing in a ring,
Before his Pallace gates, doo make
The water with their Ecchoes quake,
  Like the great Thunder sounding:
The Sea-Nymphes chaunt their Accents shrill,   15
And the *Syrens* taught to kill
          With their sweet voyce,
Make ev'ry ecchoing Rocke reply,
Unto their gentle murmuring noyse,
The prayse of *Neptunes* Empery.   20

Th. Campion.

*This Hymne was sung by Amphitryte, Thamesis, and
other Sea-Nimphes in Grayes-Inne Maske, at the
Court.* 1594.[3]

[3] It forms the introductory song to the masque; see *Gesta Grayorum*
(ed. for The Malone Society by W. W. Greg, Oxford, 1915), p. 58.

3.

Shadowes before the shining sunne do vanish,
The iron forcing Adamant doth resigne
His vertues where the Diamond doth shine;[4]
Pure holines doth all enchantment banish,
  And cullors of false Principallity   5
  Do fade in presence of true majesty.

Sheapheards sometymes in Lyons skins were cloathde,
But when the Royall Lyon did appeare,
What wonder though the sylly swaynes for feare
Theyr bravery and princely pale[5] have loathed?   10
  The Lyons skinn that graict our vanity
  Falls down in presence of your Majesty.

4.

Dolus[6]

Thou shalt not love mee, neither shall these eyes
Shine on my soule shrowded in deadly night.
Thou shalt not breath on me thy spiceryes
Nor rocke mee in the quavers[7] of delight.
Hould of thy hands, for I had rather dye   5
Then have my life by thy coye touch reprived.
Smile not on me, but frowne thou bitterly;
Slaye me out right: no lovers are long liv'de.
As for those lippes reserv'd so much in store,
Their rosy verdure shall not meete with myne.   10
Withhould thy proude embracements evermore,
I'le not be swadled in those arms of thyne.
  Now shew it if thou be a woman right:
  Embrace and kisse and love mee in despight.

finis Tho: Camp:

[4] These lines celebrate the mind-drawing "diamond" of Elizabeth's face over the magnetic rock of Proteus; see *Gesta Grayorum,* pp. 64–66.

[5] pall, cloak.

[6] *Dolus (Guile)* apparently refers to the speaker's cunning. Compare this sonnet and 6, "Thou are not fayer" following to *A Booke of Ayres,* Part I, xii, above.

[7] sixteenth notes in music; her breath is like music as well as spices.

5.

Thrice tosse those oaken ashes in the ayer,[8]
And thrice three tymes tye up this true-lovs Knott;
Thrice sitt you downe in this inchanted chaire
And murmure softe, *Shee will or shee will not.*
Goe burne those poysoned weeds in that blew fyre,   5
This *Cypres* gathered out a dead mans grave,
These *Scretchowles* fethers and the prickling bryer
That all thy Thornye cares an end may have.
Then come you *fairyes,* daunce with mee a round,
Daunce in a Circle, let my Love be Center.   10
Melodiously breath an inchanted sound,
Melt her hard harte, that some remorse may enter.
    In vayne are all the Charmes I can devise:
    She hath an arte to breake them with her eyes.

finis Idem.

6.

Beautie without Love deformitie

Thou art not fayer for all thy red and white,
For all those Rosye temperatures[9] in thee;
Thou art not sweet, though made of meere delight,
Nor fayer nor sweet unlesse thou pittie mee.
Thyne eyes are blacke and yet their glittering brightnes   5
Can night enlumine in her darkest den;
Thy hands are bloudy thoughts contriv'd of whitnes,
Both blacke and blooddy if they murder men.
Thy browe wheron my good happe doth depend
Fayerer then snow or lyllie in the springe,   10
Thy Tongue which saves at every sweete words end,
That hard as *Marble,* This a mortall sting.
    I will not soothe thy follyes: thou shalt prove
    That *Beautie* is no *Beautie* without Love.

finis Idem.

[8] Compare *The Third Booke of Ayres,* xviii, above.
[9] blendings.

7.

Do not, O do not prize thy beauty at too high a rate:
Love to be lov'd whilst thou art lovely, least thou love too
        late;
    Frownes print wrincles in thy browes,
    At which spightfull age doth smile,
    Women in their froward vowes   5
    Glorying to beguile.

Wert thou the onely worlds admired, thou canst love but one;
But many have before beene lov'd, thou art not lov'd alone:
    Couldst thou speake with heavenly grace,
    Sapho might with thee compare;   10
    Blush the Roses in thy face,
    Rozamond was as fair.

Pride is the canker that consumeth beautie in her prime,
They that delight in long debating feele the curse of time.
    All things with the time do change   15
    That will not the time obey;
    Some even to themselves seeme strange
    Thorowe their owne delay.

8.

    Some can flatter, some can faine;
    Simple trueth shall pleade for mee.
    Let not beautie trueth disdaine:
    Trueth is even as faire as shee.

    But, since Paires must equall prove,   5
    Let my strength her youth oppose:
    Love her beautie, faith her love;
    On ev'n terms so may we close.

    Corke or Leade in equall waight
    Both one just proportion yeeld;   10
    So may breadth be pays'd[10] with height,
    Steepest mount with plainest field.

[10] balanced.

Vertues have not all one kind,
Yet all vertues merits bee:
Divers vertues are combind,   15
Diff'ring so Deserts agree.

Let then love and beautie meete,
Making one divine concent,
Constant as the sounds, and sweete,
That enchant the firmament.   20

9.

My deerest mistrisse, let us live and love,[11]
And care not what old doting fools reprove.
Let us not feare their censures, nor esteeme
What they of us and of our loves shall deeme.
Old ages critticke and censorious brow
Cannot of youthful dalliance alow,
Nor ever could endure that we should tast
Of those delights which they themselves are past.

10.

Art thou that shee then whome noe fayrer is?
Art thou that shee desier soe strives to kisse?
    Say I am, how then?
Maids may not kisse
Such wanton humord men.   5

Art thou that shee the world commends for witt?
Art thou soe wise, and makst noe use of it?
    Say I am, how then?
My witt doth teach me shun
Such foolish foolish men.   10

[11] Compare "My sweetest Lesbia," *A Booke of Ayres*, Part I, i, above.

11.

As on a day Sabina fell asleepe,[12]
Into her bower by stealth then I did creepe:
And first spake softe, then loude unto my deare;
And still Sabina heard, but would not heare.

Then to my selfe more courage did I take.   5
When I preceiv'd shee did both winke and wake,
Then downe I lay'd mee by her on the ground,
And still awake, asleepe, Sabina found.

Then shew'd her sightes more strange to her then mee,
Yet still Sabina sawe, but would not see.   10
Now when as I had try'd all waies but one,
I lookt about, and found my selfe alone.

Then thought it best, the best waie for to wooe,
And still Sabina did, but would not doe:
Then did I touch each part from head to heele,   15
Yet still Sabina felt but would not feele.

Nowe from the doer whie should shee have hid it,
Yf it be true that twas Sabina did it?
But shee saies nay; I sweare and saie soe too:
Shee did both heare, and see, and feele, and doe.   20

12.

The peacefull westerne winde the wintrye stormes hath
              calmde,[13]
And nature hath in every kinde the vitall heate inflam'de;
The flowers so sweetlye breathe out of the earthlye bowers
That heaven, which seeth their pompe benethe, would faine
              be decte with flowers;
To grace the lyvely springe let all the shepheards singe,   5
Fa la la la.

[12] Compare *A Booke of Ayres,* Part I, viii, and *"In Lycium et Clytham,"*
Epigrammatum Liber II, 60, above.
[13] Compare *The Second Booke of Ayres,* xii, above.

See how the morninge smyles out of the easterne Cell,
And, softly stealinge forthe, beguiles them that in sleepe do
        dwell;
The frolicke birds do come from cliffs and Rocks unknowne
To see the treese and briers blow that late were   10
        overflowene:
All things do us invite to sing with sweete delite,
Fa la la la.

What Nature did destroye renewes, revives againe,
And now the wanton naked boye[14] doth in the woods
        remain:
Where he such Change doth Vewe in everye livinge thinge   15
As if the worlde were borne a newe to gratifie the springe.
To Cynthia then lett us recorde our musicke thus:
Fa la la la.

13.

Could my poore hart whole worlds of toungs employ,[15]
The greifes it ownes that number would out goe;
Its so enured to greife, s' estranged from joy,
That it knows not how it releife should know.
        Discurteous facts are cor'sives to true hearts,   5
        And those are pronest to dispayring smarts.

Noe caution, thought, nor alteration can
Assume affections place; change harder is
Fancied to be; use Lords it soe ore man
That it brooks worst what's strange as being amisse.   10
        And soe much witt should men in this age have
        As they should chuse what's good and what's not leave.

Those men are blest that can their freedom get
Whensoere they will, and free themselves from thrall;
That hope disdaines, on joy a rate doth set   15
Inferiour far to th' blisse that ease men call:
        A blest estate had better nere been knowne
        Then from the height thereof downe to be throwne.

14 Cupid.
15 Compare *The Third Booke of Ayres,* xxiv, above.

14.

Whether away my sweetest deerest?
Whether away will you depart?
Will you from mee that should bee neerest,
Will you from mee that have my hart?
No, no, no, no: bee with mee ever,
For on you my joyes do all relie;
Say then, o say, you'l leve mee never,
For if you forsake mee I must dye.

15.

Hide not, sweetest Love, a sight so pleasing
As those smalls[16] so light composed,
Those fair pillars your knees gently easing,
That tell wonders, being disclosed.
O show me yet a little more: 5
Here's the way, bar not the door.[17]

How like sister's twines[18] these knees are joined
To resist my bold approaching!
Why should beauty lurk like mines uncoined?
Love is right and no encroaching.   10
O show me yet a little more:
Here's the way, bar not the door.

16.

Verba volant; verum: quid enim velocius illis?
Arte (Balese) tua, nunc quoque penna volat.[19]
                                                            T.C.

---

[16] the round parts of pillars (Bullen).
[17] This is the refrain of *The Second Booke of Ayres,* xi.
[18] sewsters (or seamstress's) thread (Bullen).
[19] "Words fly; true: indeed, what can fly faster than they can? But now, by your art, Bales, the pen [wing—a pun] also flies." The poem alludes to Peter Bales's promise on the title page of *The Arte of Brachygraphie* (to which this poem is prefixed) that his method of shorthand will enable the reader "To write as fast as a man speaketh." The second line, with its pun on *penna,* alludes to the proverb *"Sine pennis volare haud facile est"* [Without wings it is difficult to fly].

17.

Tarry sweete love,
harke how the winds doe murmure at your Flyghte.
See how the trees in order growe,
the coole earth shodoinge belowe;
see the wanton streames how they playe by the banke
    side.
Then Stay in hope my lighte, my Joye, my life, my
    soule;
heere may you safe abide.

APPENDICES

SOURCES

A. MANUSCRIPTS

The British Museum, London

Additional MS. 10309. Margrett Bellasys' commonplace book, 17th century.

Additional MS. 10337. "Elizabeth Rogers hir virginall booke . . . 1656," including "Vocall lessons."

Additional MS. 11608. Songs, canons, dialogues, catches, and rounds, ca. 1646–1658.

Additional MS. 14934. *Rhapsodia* or miscellanies of Lewis Morris.

Additional MS. 15117. Songbook containing psalms and ayres, before 1630.

Additional MSS. 17786–17791. Part books, mostly instrumental fantasias, early 17th century.

Additional MS. 22603. Verse miscellany, 17th century.

Additional MS. 24665. "Giles Earle his booke," songbook ca. 1615–1626. Edited by Peter Warlock, London, 1932.

Additional MS. 27879. Bishop Percy's famous MS. Edited by John W. Hales and Frederick J. Furnivall as *Bishop Percy's Folio Manuscript,* 3 vols., London, 1867–1868.

Additional MS. 28253. Verse miscellany of the Caryll family, 16th and 17th centuries.

Additional MS. 29291. Songbook, 17th century.

Additional MS. 29386. Songbook, 18th century.

Additional MS. 29481. Songbook containing ayres and psalms, early 17th century.

Additional MS. 33933. Scottish metrical psalter, originally 1566, containing first lines and ayres (Tenor part) on additional leaves.

Additional MS. 34608. Commonplace book of John Stafford Smith,
    1785–1789.
Harley MS. 3991. Miscellany of poems and songs, 17th century.
Harley MS. 4064. Miscellany of verse and other writings.
Harley MS. 6910. Verse miscellany, late 16th century, dated 1596.
Harley MS. 6917. Verse miscellany, mid-17th century.
Egerton MS. 2013. Songbook, before 1644.
Egerton MS. 2230. Richard Glover's book, 1638.

The Bodleian Library, Oxford

MS. Don. c. 57. Songbook, before 1650. Described by John P. Cutts
    in *Music and Letters*, XXXIV (1953), 192–211.
MS. Music b. 1. Songs by John Wilson, ca. 1656. Described by Cutts
    in *Musica Disciplina*, X (1956), 142–209.

Christ Church College, Oxford

Christ Church MS. Mus. 87. Elizabeth Davenant's songbook, ca.
    1624. Described by Cutts in *Review of English Studies*, X
    (1959), 26–37.
Christ Church MS. 439. Songbook, probably before 1634.

The Fitzwilliam Museum, Cambridge

MS. 52 D. The John Bull MS., vocal and instrumental pieces, 17th
    century.

The Edinburgh University Library

MS. La. iii. 483. Scottish metrical psalter of 1566, containing Bass
    parts of songs at end; the counterpart of Additional MS. 33933
    and Dublin MS. F. 5. 13.
MS. La. iii. 490. John Squyer's music book, 1697–1701.
Music MS. Dc. 1. 69. Songbook, third quarter of the 17th century.
    Described by Cutts in *Musica Disciplina*, XIII (1959), 169–94.

The National Library of Scotland, Edinburgh

Advocates' MS. 5. 2. 14. Heber's MS., songbook, ca. 1630–1640.
Advocates' MS. 5. 2. 15. John Skene's tablature book, instrumental
    pieces, ca. 1615–1625. Partly transcribed by William Dauney in
    Ancient Scotish Melodies, Edinburgh, 1838.

Trinity College Library, Dublin

MS. F. 5. 13. Treble part only of part songs; the counterpart of
Additional MS. 33933 and MS. La. iii. 483.

The New York Public Library

Drexel MS. 4041. Earl Ferrer's MS. songbook, latter 17th century.
Drexel MS. 4175. "Songs Unto the Violl and Lute," ca. 1620. De-
scribed by Cutts in *Musica Disciplina,* XVI (1962), 73–92.
Drexel MS. 4257. John Gamble's music commonplace book, 1659.
Described by Vincent Duckles in *Journal of the American Musi-
cological Society,* I (1948), 23–40.

B. EARLY PRINTED EDITIONS

Thomas Campion. *Thomae Campiani Poemata. Ad Thamesin. Frag-
mentum Umbra. Liber Elegiarum. Liber Epigrammatum.* Lon-
don, 1595. Huntington copy.
————. *A Booke of Ayres. Set forth to be song to the Lute, Orpherian,
and Base Violl, by Philip Rosseter Lutenist.* London, 1601. Brit-
ish Museum copy.
————. *Observations in the Art of English Poesie.* London, 1602.
British Museum and Bodleian copies.
————. *The Discription of a Maske, Presented before the Kinges
Majestie at White-Hall, on Twelfth Night last, in honour of the
Lord Hayes.* London, 1607. British Museum, Bodleian, Folger,
Huntington, and Library of Congress copies.
————. *A Relation of the Late Royall Entertainment given By The
Right Honorable The Lord Knowles. . . . Whereunto is an-
nexed the Description, Speeches and Songs of the Lords Maske.*
London, 1613. British Museum, Bodleian, and Huntington cop-
ies.
————. *Two Bookes of Ayres. The First Contayning Divine and
Morall Songs: The Second, Light Conceits of Lovers.* London,
n.d. British Museum and Huntington copies.
————. *Songs of Mourning: Bewailing the untimely death of Prince
Henry. Worded by Tho. Campion. And set forth to bee sung
with one voyce to the Lute, or Violl: by John Coprario.* London,
1613. Bodleian and Huntington copies.
————. *The Description of a Maske: Presented in the Banqueting
roome at Whitehall, on Saint Stephens night last, At the
Mariage of the Right Honourable the Earle of Somerset.* Lon-
don, 1614. British Museum, Bodleian, and Huntington copies.

————. *The Third and Fourth Booke of Ayres.* London, n.d. British Museum and Huntington copies.

————. *A New Way of Making Fowre parts in Counter-point, by a most familiar, and infallible Rule. Secondly, a necessary discourse of Keyes, and their proper Closes. Thirdly, the allowed passages of all Concords perfect, or imperfect, are declared. Also by way of Preface, the nature of the Scale is expressed, with a briefe Method teaching to Sing.* London, n.d. British Museum copy.

————. *Tho. Campiani Epigrammatum Libri II. Umbra. Elegiarum liber unus.* London, 1619. British Museum copy.

Sir Philip Sidney. *Syr P. S. His Astrophel and Stella. Wherein the excellence of sweete Poesie is concluded. To the end of which are added, sundry other rare Sonnets of divers Noblemen and Gentlemen.* London, 1591.

John Dowland. *The First Booke of Songs or Ayres of foure partes with Tableture for the Lute.* London, 1597.

Robert Jones. *The Second Booke of Songs and Ayres, Set out to the Lute, the base Violl the playne way, or the Base by tableture after the leero fashion.* London, 1601.

Francis Davison. *A Poetical Rhapsody Containing, Diverse Sonnets, Odes, Elegies, Madrigalls, and other Poesies, both in Rime, and Measured Verse. Never yet published.* London, 1602.

John Dowland. *The Third and Last Booke of Songs or Aires, Newly composed to sing to the Lute, Orpharion, or viols.* London, 1603.

Francis Pilkington. *The First Booke of Songs or Ayres of 4. parts: with Tableture for the Lute or Orpherion, with the Violl de Gamba.* London, 1605.

Richard Alison. *An Howres Recreation in Musicke apt for Instrumentes and Voyces.* London, 1606.

Barnabe Barnes. *Foure Bookes of Offices: Enabling Privat persons for the speciall service of all good Princes and Policies.* London, 1606.

Robert Jones. *Ultimum Vale, with a triplicity of Musicke.* London, 1605.

————. *The First Set of Madrigals of 3. 4. 5. 6. 7. 8. Parts, for Viols and Voices, or for Voices alone; or as you please.* London, 1607.

————. *A Musicall Dreame. Or the Fourth Booke of Ayres.* London, 1609.

Alfonso Ferrabosco. *Ayres: By Alfonso Ferrabosco.* London, 1609.

William Corkine. *Ayres, To Sing and Play To The Lute And Basse Violl.* London, 1610.

Thomas Coryat. *Coryats Crudities. Hastily gobled up in five Moneths travells in France Savoy, Italy, Rhetia commonly called the Grisons country, Helvetia alias Switzerland, some parts of high Germany, and the Netherlands.* London, 1611.

William Corkine. *The Second Booke of Ayres, Some, to Sing and Play to the Base-Violl alone: Others, to be sung to the Lute and Base Violl.* London, 1612.

Thomas Ravenscroft. *A Briefe Discourse of the true (but neglected) use of Charact'ring the Degrees by their Perfection, Imperfection, and Diminution in Measurable Musicke, against the Common Practise and Custome of these Times.* London, 1614.

George Mason and John Earsden. *The Ayres That Were Sung and Played, at Brougham Castle in Westmerland in the Kings Entertainment: Given by the Right Honourable the Earle of Cumberland, and his Right Noble Sonne the Lord Clifford.* London, 1618.

Thomas Vautor. *The First Set: Beeing Songs of divers Ayres and Natures, of Five and Sixe parts: Apt for Vyols and Voyces.* London, 1619.

Select Musicall Ayres, And Dialogues, For one and two Voyces, to sing to the Theorbo, Lute, or Basse Violl. Composed by John Wilson, Charles Colman, Doctours of Musick. Henry Lawes, William Webb, Gentlemen. To which is added some few short Ayres or Songs for three Voyces, to an Instrument. London, 1652.

John Playford. *A Brief Introduction To the Skill of Musick. In two Books. The first contains the Grounds and Rules of Musick. The second, Instructions for the Viol, and also for the Treble-Violin. The Third Edition Enlarged. To which is added a Third Book entituled, The Art of Descant, or Composing Musick in Parts, By Dr. Tho. Campion. With Annotations thereon by Mr. Chr. Simpson.* London, 1660.

———. ———, *The Sixt Edition Corrected and Enlarged.* London, 1672.

———. *Select Ayres and Dialogues To Sing to the Theorbo-Lute or Basse-Viol. Composed by Mr. Henry Lawes, late Servant to His Majesty in His Publick and Private Musick: And other Exellent Masters. The Second Book.* London, 1669.

———. *The Musical Companion, In Two Books. The First Book containing Catches and Rounds for Three Voyces. The Second Book containing Dialogues, Glees, Ayres, and Songs for Two, Three, and Four Voyces.* London. 1673.

John Wilson. *Cheerfull Ayres or Ballads First composed for one single Voice and since set for three Voices.* London, 1660.

Thomas Davidson. *Cantus, Songs and Fancies. To Thre, Foure, or Five Partes, both apt for Voices and Viols. With a briefe Introduction of Musick, As is taught in the Musick-Schole of Aberdene.* Aberdeen, 1662.

C. MODERN EDITIONS

A. H. Bullen, ed. *The Works of Dr. Thomas Campion*. The Chiswick Press: privately printed, 1889.

————. *Thomas Campion, Songs and Masques, with Observations in the Art of English Poesy*. London and New York, 1903.

G. Gregory Smith, ed. *Elizabethan Critical Essays*. 2 vols. Oxford, 1904.

Percival Vivian, ed. *Campion's Works*. Oxford, 1909.

Edmund H. Fellowes, ed. *English Madrigal Verse, 1588–1632*. Oxford, 1920.

————. *Thomas Campian, Songs from Rosseter's Book of Airs*. 2 parts: The English School of Lutenist Song Writers, First Series, Nos. 4 and 13. London, 1922.

————. *Thomas Campian, First Book of Airs* and *Second Book of Airs*. The English School of Lutenist Song Writers, Second Series, Nos. 1 and 2. London, 1925.

————. *Thomas Campian, Third Booke of Ayres* and *Fourth Booke of Ayres*. The English School of Lutenist Song Writers, Second Series, Nos. 10 and 11. London, 1926.

NOTES

Songs Appended to Sidney's *Astrophel and Stella*

Canto Primo. See textual notes to the more authoritative version of this song in *A Booke of Ayres,* Part I, xix.

Canto tertio. Contained in Robert Jones's *Second Booke of Songs and Ayres,* 1601 (ii), La. iii. 490 (fo. 75), Adv. MS. 5. 2. 14 (fo. 4ᵛ), and La. iii. 483 (fo. 194), first line with Jones's ayre only. Variants: l. 3, "When I lost" (490); l. 4, "part away" (Jones, 490, 5. 2. 14); l. 5, "doth" (Jones, 5. 2. 14), "does" (490); l. 6, "kissing makes" (490). Both Jones and 5. 2. 14 add three further strophes, as follow:

> Yes she knowes it but too well,
> For I heard when Venus dove
> In her eare did softlie tell
> That kisses were the seales of love:
> O muse not then though it be so,
> Kisses make men loth to go.

> Wherefore did she thus inflame
> My desires, heat my bloud,
> Instantlie to quench the same
> And starve whom she had given food?
> I, I the common sence can show,
> Kisses make men loath to go.

> Had she bid me go at first
> It would nere have greeved my hart,
> Hope delaide had beene the worst;
> But ah, to kisse and then to part!
> How deepe it strucke, speake, Gods, you know
> Kisses make men loth to goe.

Canto quinto. Appears in Harl. MS. 6910 (fo. 156) with ll. 3–4 omitted.

A Booke of Ayres, Part I

II. First strophe appears without variation in both Add. MS. 24665 (fo. 26) and Ch. Ch. MS. 439 (fo. 6); and, reset by John Playford, in both *Select Ayres and Dialogues, The Second Book,* 1669 (p. 76) and *An Introduction to the Skill of Musick,* 6th. ed., 1672 (Part I, p. 67).

III. Occurs in Add. MS. 24665 (fo. 4–4ᵛ) with the following variants: l. 1, "those"; l. 13, "But if I"; l. 14, "I must give." The music has been rebarred, note values halved, and the third note in measure 17 changed from quaver to crotchet.

V. Appears in Add. MS. 34608 without variation.

VI. Appears in Davison's *Poetical Rhapsody,* 1602 (No. 154 in the ed. of Hyder E. Rollins, 2 vols., Cambridge, 1931) and Add. MS. 22603; the latter contains ll. 1–2, 5–6 only, and the former presents only two slight variants: l. 1, *"Corinna";* l. 11, "she doe."

VII. The first half of the second strophe reappears in *The Second Booke,* x. The attempts of Vivian and Fellowes to rearrange the strophe in order to remove the unrimed word "lips" (l. 10) seem unnecessary since the same word is repeated in the corresponding position in the second strophe (l. 22), thus creating a bonding rime *between* strophes (Campion does it again in xix). The other unrimed word, "changing" (l. 19), serves no such function; perhaps Bullen's emendation to "swerving" is correct, or perhaps a quantitative scansion is indicated by lack of rime (see further my article in *MLQ,* XXII [1961], 32–33).

XII. Appears in Thomas Vautor's *The First Set,* 1619 (xiii–xiv), *Select Musicall Ayres and Dialogues,* 1652 (Part I, p. 8), reset by N. Lanier, and the following MSS.: Harl. MS. 3991 (fo. 34); Bodleian MS. Don. c. 57 (fo. 40ᵛ), first strophe only; Drexel MS. 4041 (No. 4); Drexel MS. 4257 (fo. 80). Variants: l. 4, "unless you" (Don. c. 57); l. 5, "Nature affirmes & reason plaine doth prove" (Don. c. 57); "thy fancy" (Harl. MS., Drexel 4041); l. 6, "is not beautie" (Drexel 4257); l. 7, "nor seeke not to allure" (Vautor), "assure" (Harl. MS.); l. 8, "now divine" (Harl. MS); l. 9, "thy sighs" (Drexel 4257 and cancellation in 4041). There is also a version in sonnet form ascribed to Campion in Harl. MS. 6910 (fo. 155); see Doubtful Poems.

XIII. In the second strophe, ll. 18 and 19 were split in the original, but that arrangement produces an asymmetrical song and an unnecessary unrimed word, "raignes."

XIV. This song appears in Davison's *Poetical Rhapsody,* 1602 (No. 153 in Rollins' ed.) and Robert Jones's *Ultimum Vale,* 1605 (ix); both read "brest" in l. 11.

XVI. This song is listed as No. vii in the table of contents of Drexel MS. 4175, but is missing. It also appears slightly revised by Campion as "Beauty, since you so much desire" in *The Fourth Booke,* xxii.

XVII. Appears revised as "Your faire lookes urge my desire," *The Fourth Booke,* xxiii.

XVIII. This song reappears with some alterations in *The First Booke,* ii. It also appears in Alison's *An Howres Recreation in Musick,* 1606 (i and ii), Sloane MS. 4128 (fo. 14), Harl. MS. 4064, MS. 17 B. L. (fo. 2), Rawl. MS. Poet. 31, and Chetham MS. 8012 (p. 79); for a discussion of the text, see Catherine Ing, *Elizabethan Lyrics,* p. 156, n. 1. Variants as reported by Ing: l. 1, "upright of life" (Alison); l. 2, "life is free" (Harl. MS.); l. 6, "harmless joy" (Harl. MS.); l. 8, "Nor fortune" (MS. 17 B. L.), "sorrow" (Alison); l. 9, "tower" (Harl. MS.); ll. 13–16 omitted in Harl. MS.; l. 17, "But scorning all the chaunce" (Harl. MS.), "care" (Sloane MS. and MS. 17 B. L.); l. 19, "his heaven" (Alison); l. 22, "His life" (Sloane MS. and MS. 17 B. L.).

XIX. This song appeared first in the appendix to Sidney's *Astrophel and Stella,* 1591; it also occurs in two manuscript versions, in Add. MS. 28253 (fo. 5) without music as "A fantasye of Sir Phillipe Sydnys out of his Astrophel and Stella" and in Ch. Ch. MS. 439 (fo. 13ᵛ), strophes I and II only, with a new setting. Variants: l. 1, "Harke, harke all" (Ch. Ch. 439); l. 11, "Which shall pinch" (Ch. Ch. 439); l. 12, "faire hands and white armes" (Ch. Ch. 439—an attractive reading); l. 20, "No plaints nor grieves" (*Astrophel and Stella*); l. 24, "*Dianas* Dove" (*A and S*); l. 32, "they that have not yet fed" (*A and S*). In measure 12 of the music, an erroneous flat sign before the second note, *b,* has been removed.

Two Bookes of Ayres

The First Booke

II. See textual note to *A Booke of Ayres,* Part I, xviii.

V, l. 8. The original edition reads "All in darke, and foule within"; this may indicate a parallel between man and the dark world wherein he resides, but Vivian's emendation, followed here, fits the total context better.

VIII. In measure 7 of the music (Cantus part), *g* has been changed to *a*-flat in both the first and second notes.

IX, l. 3. The text underlying the Cantus part in the original reads "have ever trod"; the other three parts, and the text printed separately, all read "hath."

XIII, l. 23. Fellowes emends the original "humble" to "humbly."

XIV, l. 20. Vivian emends the original "And stone and by stone" to "And, stone by stone," as here.

The Second Booke

I. Appears in Adv. MS. 5. 2. 14 (fo. 7) without variants; the first line with air (treble and bass parts, respectively) appears in Add. MS. 33933 (fo. 83) and Edinburgh MS. La. iii. 483 (fo. 192).

II. In the music (Cantus part), the sixth note from the end has been changed from *d* to *c*, the fifth from the end from *c*-sharp to *b*.

V. Bullen emends l. 10 to "Her love thought to obtaine," a reading which ignores the antithesis between "love" and "grace." In l. 17, the original reads "prayes," probably a misprint caused by "praise" in the next line; Vivian emends to "prayers." Bullen emends l. 24 to "My words of zeale."

VI, l. 16. "Past recure" is Bullen's emendation of "most recure" in the original; "most secure" (firmly infixed), a more conservative emendation, would not fit the context as well.

IX. The first line and ayre appear in Add. MS. 33933 (fo. 82ᵛ) and MS. La. iii. 483 (fo. 187).

X. Lines 1–6 are reprinted from *A Booke of Ayres,* Part I, vii, ll. 12–17, without variation. In measure 10 of the music (Cantus part), the last note has been changed from *e*-flat to *d*.

XII. A reworking of this song into "poulter's measure" with totally different music appears in Add. MS. 15117 (fo. 10); see Doubtful Poems. In l. 6, the metrical text of the original reads "earthy," the words underlying the music, "earthly."

XIII. Appears without variation in Adv. MS. 5. 2. 14 (fo. 6).

XIV, l. 6. The printed text of the original reads "muse"; the text underlying the music reads "Muse."

XV. The first stanza alone, set by John Wilson, appears in Wilson's *Cheerfull Ayres or Ballads,* 1660 (pp. 134–35), Edinburgh Music MS. Dc. 1. 69 (fo. 42), and Bodleian MS. Mus. b. 1. Both MS. versions contain these two variants: l. 3, "That now I am of all"; l. 7, "loosing." See John P. Cutts, *Musica Disciplina,* XIII (1959), 183. In l. 24, "roving" is Vivian's emendation for "moving," erroneously repeated from l. 22 in the original.

XVI. This song appears in Robert Jones, *A Musicall Dreame,* 1609 (i); John Wilson, *Cheerfull Ayres or Ballads,* 1660 (pp. 40–41), reset by Wilson; Thomas Davidson, *Cantus, Songs and Fancies,* 1662 (No. 31); B. M. Egerton MS. 2230; Drexel MS. 4175 (No. xxv); Edinburgh Music MS. Dc. 1. 69 (fo. 59), first and third strophes only; Ch. Ch. MS. 439 (fo. 13ᵛ), first strophe only; Add. MS. 33933 (fo. 83) and La. iii. 483 (fo. 190), first line with treble and bass parts (respectively) only. Variants: l. 1, "Though your sadness" (439); l. 2, "I not complayne" (Jones, 4175); l. 6, "but a toy" (Jones, 4175); l. 8, "When your wisht sight I desire" (Jones, 4175); l. 12, "Thus a lover as you say" (Jones, 4175); l. 16, "Youle sweare" (Jones), "I have" (Dc. 1. 69); l. 17, "Whilst my rivall close doth stand" (Jones, 4175); l. 18, "I stand" (Dc. 1. 69); ll. 19–20 omitted in Dc. 1. 69, with ll. 26–27 substituted; l. 22, "Would a rivall" (Jones, 4175); l. 24, "Soe much the lesser" (4175); l. 26, "enjoy you every hower" (4175); l. 27, "Yet must I" (Jones, 4175, Dc. 1. 69). See Cutts in *Musica Disciplina,* XIII, 186. Vivian's emendation of "Some els" in the original to "Or els" makes the line say the opposite of what was intended. In the second measure of the music from the end (Cantus part), a dotted minim has been changed to a minim, and the bar lines reset to compensate for the change.

XVII, l. 3. The text printed separately from the music in the original reads "loves longing"; the text underlying the music in all parts reads "love and longing." Line 6 reads "pleasures" in the separate text, "pleasure" in the underlay.

XVIII. Appears in Add. MS. 24665 (fo. 3–3ᵛ); Add. MS. 10337 (fo. 48), first strophe only; and Ch. Ch. MS. Mus. 87 (fo. 1ᵛ), first strophe only. Variants: l. 3, "Thin'st thou to escape me thus" (24665); l. 4, "with flattring" (Mus. 87), "word" (10337); l. 5, "you lefte" (24665); l. 6, "When you were loose" (24665); l. 8, "from flyinge" (24665); l. 12, "hailes'" (24665); l. 14, "And th' fishe in th' sea devouring" (24665); l. 16, "your tyred lips" (24665); l. 20, "so fruitles" (24665); l. 21, "I would it were" (24665).

Songs of Mourning

1. In l. 5, the text underlying the music reads "Somewhile," the metrical text on the opposite page, "Sometime."

4. In the margin of the British Museum copy, a contemporary hand has corrected "love" in l. 6 to "fate"; Bullen and Vivian so

emend the line, but Fellowes lets "love" stand on the assumption that it refers to the god of Love. In the original, l. 12 reads "embarc't," which seems an obvious misprint for "embrac't."

6. In l. 2, the underlay of the music reads "insatiate," the metrical text "unsatiate." In l. 8, the underlay reads "Then now for ones fate," the metrical text "Thou now for ones fall."

The Third and Fourth Booke of Ayres

The Third Booke

II. Appears in Francis Pilkington's *First Booke of Songs or Ayres,* 1605 (viii), in Robert Jones's *Ultimum Vale,* 1605 (xvii), and in Add. MS. 29291 with Pilkington's setting. Variants: l. 2, "proves false" (Pilkington, 29291); l. 3, "so bewitched" (all three sources); l. 5, "new desires" (all sources); l. 6, "my deserts" (all sources); l. 9, "care did attend" (Pilkington, 29291), "heart did attend" (Jones); l. 11, "till the day of dying" (Pilkington, 29291), "to the day of dying" (Jones); l. 13, "Then false" (Pilkington, 29291), "Thou false" (Jones); l. 15, "that now so triumphs in thy love" (all sources); l. 17, "Were I as faire as divine *Adonis*" (Pilkington, 29291), "Were he as fayre as Adonis" (Jones); l. 18, "Love is not had" (Pilkington, 29291). These readings seem to come from an earlier draft.

III. First line with ayre in La. iii. 483 (fo. 187).

VI. Occurs in Adv. MS. 5. 2. 14 (fo. 11); La. iii. 483 (fo. 188), first line only with ayre; and John Playford's *A Briefe Introduction to the Skill of Musick,* 1660. Playford's text reads "nature or a curious eye can see" in l. 3.

VII. In the music, the Cantus line has been lowered a whole step in order to conform to the lute part.

X. First line with ayre in La. iii. 483 (fo. 191).

XI. Appears in Adv. MS. 5. 2. 14 (fo. 14); Add MS. 29386 (fo. 85); Drexel MS. 4257 (No. 10), with a new setting; La. iii. 483 (fo. 191), first line only with ayre; and both Playford's *Briefe Introduction,* 1660, and his *Musical Companion,* 1672. Drexel MS. 4257 alone contains variants: l. 2, "dissembling"; l. 3, "now kind of favour if they chance to prove"; l. 4, "a tempest straight their kindnes"; l. 5, "then like"; l. 6, "a storme"; l. 7, "women to deceave"; l. 8, "Or blame"; l. 9, "Both first"; l. 11, "in love may"; l. 12, "such by arte"; l. 16, "her divinest every parte to prove"; l. 17, "Yet this I wish what ever doth befall."

XIII. The repetition of the rime word "discourses" in ll. 3 and 5 seems erroneous, but the passage makes tolerable sense.

XIV. Appears in Adv. MS. 5. 2. 14 (fo. 10ᵛ) without variation, and in La. iii. 483 (fo. 193), first line with ayre only. The first line of the original, which I have emended from "What is it all that . . ." to "What is it that all . . . ," is subject to considerable variation, La. iii. 483 reading "What is all that men possesse, etc.," while the table of contents in the original reads "What is it that men possesse?" Fellowes suggests emending "conversing" in l. 1 to "dispersing" to avoid the repetition of the rime word in l. 3.

XVII. Appears in Add. MS. 29481 (fo. 20), first strophe only; Add. MS. 24665 (fos. 64–64ᵛ); and Cambridge, Fitzwilliam Museum MS. 52 D, two versions, fo. 97 as a piece for virginals with vocal part, fo. 105 first strophe only in a two-part setting. Variants: l. 2, "Nowe the evening beames" (24665), "be set" (52 D, both versions); l. 3, "refused be" (24665); l. 4, "wilt thou" (24665, 52 D, both versions); l. 5, "let not mee" (29481), "for pitty any more" (24665, 29481); l. 6, "thy dore" (all sources); l. 9, "for a pray" (24665); l. 10, "Or betray mee through despight" (24665; 52 D, first version, "with despight"); l. 11, "So alas may I dye" (52 D, first version), "Soe alas! shall I goe" (24665); l. 14, "disdain'd" (24665); l. 15, "in such a case" (24665, 52 D, first version); l. 16, "to expect" (24665); l. 17, "only doe not mocke" (24665); l. 18, "whil'st the cold" (24665), "least the cold night" (52 D, first version). 24665 interposes between the first and second strophes an additional strophe, as follows:

> When I first of love did thinke
> As a toy I it esteem'd,
> Never from it did I shrinke
> Cupids darts of lead I deem'd
> Now I find dispaire pursues the game,
> Night and day it doth inflame.

XVIII. First line only with ayre in La. iii. 483 (fo. 191); a version in sonnet form occurs in Harl. MS. 6910 (see Doubtful Poems).

XX. Appears in Playford's *Select Ayres and Dialogues, The Second Book,* 1669 (p. 56); Harl. MS. 6917 (fo. 163), text only; Drexel MS. 4257 (no. 83); Egerton MS. 2013 (fo. 49); Add. MS. 10337 (fos. 47–47ᵛ); and Bodleian MS. Don. c. 57 (no. 47, fo. 60), first strophe only; in all the sources with music, it appears reset by Nicholas Lanier. Variants: l. 1, "fire" repeated only once (all five MS. sources); l. 2, "Loe howe I burne" (2013, Don. c. 57), "Oh how I burne in hott desire" (6917); l. 3, "For all the teares" (6917); l. 4, "From an empty love-sick brain" (6917, 4257), "From my empty love-sicke braine" (2013, 10337), "From my troubled lovesick braine" (Don. c.

57); l. 5, "your scorching paine" (Don. c. 57); l. 6, "Humber Trent and silver Thames" (all sources); l. 7, "Great Ocean" (6917), "ocean com" (4257); l. 8, "if they" (4257), "my fires" (Don. c. 57); l. 9, "Then drown" (6917); l. 10, "fire" not repeated (2013); l. 11, "no helpe for" (6917), "no helpe to" (4257); l. 12, "see how the Rivers" (2013), "back retire" (4257); l. 13, "The Oceans do their ayde denye" (6917), "the Ocean doth his ayde" (2013, 4257); l. 14, "Least my heat" (6917), "my hearte" (4257); l. 15, "Come heavenly powers" (2013), "come pouring down" (6917); l. 16, "yee that once" (6917); ll. 17–18 repeated from ll. 8–9 in 6917; l. 18, "that else might burne" (10337, 2013), "and like me fall" (2013). See John P. Cutts, *Music and Letters,* XXXIV (1953), 201. In measure 25 of the music (Cantus part), a rest which would add an extra beat has been removed.

XXI. Appears in Egerton MS. 2013 (fo. 9ᵛ) with the following variants: l. 3, "are soe well plac't"; l. 7, "Golden Age"; l. 12, "Which till eyes ache, let you fond men envye."

XXIV. Appears in Add. MS. 10309 (fo. 85) with the following variants: l. 4, "can aske"; ll. 7–10 and 13–16 switched; l. 7, "Happy men"; l. 9, "hope or joy"; l. 11 "should demeane man soe"; l. 12, "As she should all thinges foreknow"; l. 13, "But no thought nor"; l. 14, "Grow on affections easie"; l. 16, "That it." There is also on fo. 94 of the same MS. source a very similar song which may be a draft of this one; see Doubtful Poems.

XXV. First line only with ayre in La. iii. 483 (fo. 193).

XXVI. Appears in Add. MS. 24665 (fos. 53–53ᵛ) with the following slight variants: l. 7, "heaven which"; l. 8, "But nor"; l. 14, "not like to the summers frost"; l. 15, "untill her day of dying." The first line only with ayre also appears in La. iii. 483 (fo. 193).

XXVII. First line with ayre in La. iii. 483 (fo. 190).

XXIX. First line only with ayre in La. iii. 483 (fo. 193).

The Fourth Booke

II. First line only, with ayre, in La. iii. 483 (fo. 192).

III. First line with ayre in La. iii. 483 (fo. 188).

VII. Appears in Richard Alison, *An Howres Recreation in Musicke,* 1606 (xix–xxi), and Robert Jones, *Ultimum Vale,* 1605 (x); there is also a five-part instrumental piece entitled "There is a garden" in Add. MSS. 17786, 17787, 17788, 17789, and 17791 (no. 20, fo. 11 in each). Variants: l. 4, "Wherein these" (Jones); l. 5, "that none" (Alison); l. 11, "no Peere" (Jones), "may buy" (Alison and Jones); l. 15, "piercing shaftes" (Jones); l. 16, "that approch" (Alison), "that presume" (Jones); l. 17, "These" (Alison).

IX. Appears in Alfonso Ferrabosco's *Ayres,* 1609 (viii); *Select Musicall Ayres and Dialogues,* 1652 (Part II, pp. 22–23), reset by Nicholas Lanier; Playford's *The Musical Companion,* 1673 (pp. 204–205); Ch. Ch. MS. 439 (fo. 43ᵛ); Harl. MS. 6917 (fos. 113–114); Add. MS. 14934 (fo. 192), with the second strophe lacking; Add. MS. 24665 (fos. 56–56ᵛ), first strophe only; Add. MS. 11608 (fo. 58), first strophe only, with Lanier's setting; Adv. MS. 5. 2. 14 (fo. 8ᵛ); La. iii. 483 (fo. 194), first line only, with ayre. Variants: l. 8, "or to dispaire" (Ferrabosco, 439); l. 15, "did bide" (439); l. 21, "'tis" (Ferrabosco, 439, 6917). Adv. MS. 5. 2. 14 adds a sixth strophe, as follows:

> Maried wyves may take or leave,
> When they list refuse receave
> We poor maydes may not doe soe,
> We must answere ay with noe.
> We must seame strang coy and curst.
> Yet do we would faine if we durst.

The second strophe of the original edition is corrupt, repeating ll. 3–6 for ll. 9–12; the missing lines have been supplied from Ferrabosco.

XI. Line 11 in the original repeats l. 7, an obvious error which I have not, however, been able to correct.

XVII. Appears in John Dowland's *The Third and Last Booke of Songs or Aires,* 1603 (xvii); Add. MS. 15117 (fo. 19); and Ch. Ch. MS. 439, two versions (fos. 31ᵛ–32 and 34ᵛ–35). Variants: l. 1, "she doth enjoye my love" (439, both versions); l. 2, "beauties parts" (Dowland, 15117), "bewtius parte" (439 at 34ᵛ), "bewtius partes" 439 at 31ᵛ); l. 3, "Hence" (15117); l. 4, "arte" (439 at 34ᵛ); l. 5, "To frame her" (15117); l. 7, "Should I have grieved and wisht" (15117); l. 9, "new suters" (Dowland); l. 10, "This kindles" (15117). The sources differ greatly in strophic arrangements. Dowland has the two-strophe version of Campion's original; 15117 prints it too, but adds a third strophe:

> Thus my complaynts from her Untruthe aryse,
> accusinge her and nature boathe in one
> for Beautie stainde is but a false disguise,
> a comon wonder which is quicklye gone,
> A false faire face cannot with all her feature,
> without a trew hart make a trew faire creature.

The version on fos. 34ᵛ–35 of Ch. Ch. 439 contains the first strophe of the original and the third strophe (given in 15117) only, while the three-strophe version on fos. 31ᵛ–32 contains the first, third, and a new one:

> whatt need't thou playne, iff thou be still rejectted
> the fayrest creature sumtime may proove strange
> continuall playntes will make the still rejeckted
> if that her wanton mind be given to range
> and nothing bettere fitts a mans true partes
> than with dissdayne t' encounter ther false hartes.

John P. Cutts prints the three-strophe version of Ch. Ch. MS. 439 in *Seventeenth Century Songs and Lyrics* (Columbia, Missouri, 1959), p. 178.

XVIII. Appears in a quite different three-strophe version in William Corkine's *Ayres*, 1610 (xi), as follows:

> Thinke you to seduce me so with words that have no meaning?
> Parets can learne so to speake, our voice by peeces gleaning:
> Nurses teach their Children so about the time of weaning.

> Learne to speake first, then to woe: to woeing much pertaineth:
> He that hath not Art to hide soon falters when he faineth,
> And as one that wants his wits he smiles when he complaineth.

> If with wit we be deceived, our fals may be excused:
> Seeming good with flatterie grac't is but of few refused,
> But of all accurst are they that are by fooles abused.

XX. First line only, with ayre, in La. iii. 483 (fo. 192).

XXII. First line only, with ayre, in La. iii. 483 (fo. 192).

XXIV. Appears in Thomas Davidson's *Cantus, Songs and Fancies*, 1662 (No. 58) and Edinburgh University Library MS. La. iii. 490 (fos. 80–81) with a few lines turned in order to form a male parody of Campion's song (whose music is used). Variations: l. 1, "a fair young maid"; l. 4, "I heard them say"; l. 7, "But this foolish mind of mine straight looks the thing resolved" (quite a telling parody). There is also an arrangement for virginals by Richard Farnaby in *The Fitzwilliam Virginal Book*, cxcvii.

Occasional Poems

"To. Campiani Epigramma de instituto Authoris." Vivian emends "sibi" in l. 2 to "tibi," perhaps taking "Dolandi" for the vocative.

"In Peragrantissimi . . ." This poem reappears, without variation, in the pirated edition of the prefatory matter of *Coryats Crudities* entitled *The Odcombian Banquet* (1611). Whether "undigenas" in l. 5 is a misprint for "indigenas" ("native") or meant as a pun ("wave-native"), I cannot tell.

The Lord Hay's Masque

P. 208, l. 12, "Ducere, et unam" printed incorrectly as "ducer, et uname" in the Bodleian, Folger, and Huntington copies of this masque; corrected in that of the Library of Congress, which also corrects a few smaller errors.

P. 215, "Now hath *Flora.*" The version of this song printed at the end of the masque with its music compresses "bowers" and "flowers" in ll. 1 and 2 to monosyllables: "bowres," "flowres."

P. 217, l. 27. "Hear" is "here" in the original.

P. 220, l. 11. "Can musicke then joye?" is obviously a corrupt line, both lacking two syllables and fostering obscurity. Perhaps it should read, "Can musicke? then can joye!"—implying that the power of joy is as great as that exhibited by music.

P. 221, "Move now with measured sound." The version with music at the end has "groves" for "grove" in l. 2.

P. 226, "Of all the starres." I follow Vivian's corrected lineation of this song.

P. 227, l. 18. "In elves" is Bullen's emendation of the original's "id elves."

The Caversham Entertainment

P. 239, l. 30. "Begin" is "begins" in the original.

P. 239, l. 37. "Lower Garden" in the Huntington copy, "Bower Garden" in the British Museum and Bodleian.

P. 242, l. 8. "Our thoughts" is "your thoughts" in the original.

P. 243, l. 8. "Irrationals" in British Museum and Bodleian copies, correcting "Orrationals" in the Huntington copy.

P. 244, l. 8. *"A la mode . . ."* is Bullen's emendation of *"A la more . . ."* in the original.

The Lords' Masque

P. 250, l. 26. *"Joves* will then" is Bullen's emendation of *"Joves* willing then" in the original.

P. 254, l. 18. Perhaps "adoring" should read "adorning."

P. 257. The version of "Wooe her and win her" with music appended to *The Somerset Masque* reads "venter" for "venture" in l. 16.

P. 257, l. 20. The stage direction *"While this Song is sung . . ."* is misplaced in the original, after the full song "Supported now" on p. 256.

P. 260, l. 26. "Monumentum" is Bullen's correction of "momumentum" in the original.

The Somerset Masque

There were apparently two impressions of this masque, an early one represented by the Bodleian copy and a corrected one represented by the British Museum and Huntington copies. In the former, the lines following Campion's name on the title page are as follows: "Whereunto is annexed divers choyse *Ayres* that / may be sung with a single voyce to the / Lute or Base-Viall." The early copy contains a few errors, most of them negligible; in the first and third songs with music at the end the Basso part is placed above the Cantus instead of below it, and is upside down (sigs. C2 and C4).

P. 268, l. 16. *"Inchauntments"* corrected for "Inchauntmens" in all copies.

P. 270, l. 16. All copies read "lighning" for "lightning."

P. 272. In the version of "Bring away" printed at the end with its music, l. 6 reads "her blest hand."

P. 272, l. 33. "Destinies" in British Museum and Huntington copies, "destanies" in Bodleian.

P. 273. The version of "Goe, happy man" at the end reads "thy raised Bow" in l. 6. In the transcription of the music, the fourth note from the end in the top line of the Bass has been changed from *b*-flat to *c*.

P. 274. The version of "While dancing rests" at the end, which omits the echo effect for solo singing, reads "Spring" in l. 9.

Observations in the Art of English Poesie

There are four copies of this work extant, one in the British Museum, one in St. John's College, Oxford, one in the Bodleian Library; and one formerly belonging to the Royal College of Physicians, now owned by H. B. Martin. The Bodleian copy lacks pp. 7–8 and 21–22, in the original pagination.

P. 293, l. 25. "Or *Rithmus* and *Metrum*": in the original, "of *Rithmus* and *Metrum*."

P. 300, l. 15. "Fourth verse": erroneously "fift verse" in the original.

A New Way of Making Fowre Parts in Counter-point

The sole copy of the original edition is contained in the British Museum. I have made no attempt to collate it with the editions issued after Campion's death by Playford in 1660 and after.

P. 334, second example. Campion's black notes (to distinguish his second from his first way) have been retained in the transcription.

P. 336, first example. First note in Meane changed from semibrief to minim; third and fourth from crochets to minims; and third note in Tenor from crotchet to minim.

P. 339, example. As in on p. 334, the black notes have been retained.

LATIN POEMS

Ad Thamesin

From the *Poemata* of 1595; this was not reprinted with the other Latin poems in 1619. Vivian records a correction of "imbrifer" in l. 198 to "imbricus" in the Bodleian copy.

Umbra

Lines 1–230 of this poem appeared as *Fragmentum Umbrae* in the *Poemata* of 1595 with the following variants: l. 1, "O dea foemineos nigro quae"; l. 6, "Abreptos"; l. 79, "Nec saturat spectando sitim, tangendo, fruendo"; l. 114, "Tristis, ut expleret miseros plangendo dolores"; l. 154, "Accurit." The fragment ended thus (replacing ll. 229 ff.):

> Dum loca percurrit, Veneres et mutua libans
> Oscula, prospexit recubantem forte Melampum,
> Et quid ait, . . .

The fragment was preceded by the following prose argument:

ARGUMENTUM

Iole Berecynthiae filia magicis carminibus sopita ab Apolline vitiatur, et ex eo gravida fit, puerumque nigrum parit nomine Melampum. Hunc, postquam adoleverat, Morpheus amare coepit, dormientemque variis imaginibus cum diu frustra tentasset, Proserpinam adit, cuius sub ditione formosarum omnium manes habentur. Ibi Troianas, Graecas, Romanas, aliarumque gentium formas cum satis spectasset, tandem ad Britannicarum exemplum figuram sibi longe pulcherrimam effingit eaque indutus Melampum denuo aggreditur, qui falsa pulchritudinis specie deceptus in miserrimum amorem dilabitur, siquidem patris interuentu mox expergefactus umbrae ipsius quam per somnium viderat desiderio tabescit, et in umbram mutatus est.

Elegiarum Liber

Elegeia I (1595). The first elegy of the 1595 collection; not re-printed in 1619. "Depinxit" in l. 21 is Vivian's correction of "depixit" in the original.

Elegia I (1619). The first elegy of the 1619 set, replacing that of 1595. "Fetas" in l. 11 is Vivian's correction of "faetas" in the original, as is "coepit" for the original's "cepit" in l. 19.

Epigrammatum Liber Primus

These epigrams all first appeared in 1619.

143. *In Crispinum.* In l. 1, "unam" is Vivian's emendation of "unum" in the original.

Epigrammatum Liber Secundus

Most of these epigrams are revisions of poems that appeared in the *Poemata* of 1595.

9. *In obitum Gual. Devoreux.* Appeared in 1595 as *In obitum fratris claris. comitis Essexii;* variants: l. 1, "quisque iussit impius"; l. 18, "Canentque Nemesin fero tubae sono."

10. *Ad Melleam.* Appeared in 1595 with l. 7 reading "ne doctus amans in illis."

11. *De obitu Phil. Sydnaei.* Appeared in 1595 as *De interitu Philippi Sydnei* with the following variants: l. 1, "Passeres Cypriae alites petulci"; l. 2, "per et niventes"; l. 3, "Et rubras petitis"; l. 4, "Usquequaque Philip, Philip"; and the following in ll. 5 to the end of the poem:

> Mars illum insidiis modo interemit
> Rivalem metuens, renunciate
> Flebiles Veneri exitus Philippi,
> Victus involvit caput tenebris.

12. *In Melleam.* Appeared in 1595 without variation.

18. *In Melleam.* Appeared in 1595 without variation.

40. *Ad nobiliss. virum Gul. Percium.* Appeared as *Ad. Gu. Percium* in 1595 with "locus" instead of "iocus" in l. 10.

53. *Ad Caspiam.* Appeared in 1595 with "Invito dabis haec" in l. 6.

60. *In Lycium et Clytham*. An extensive revision of *De Thermanio et Glaia* in 1595:

> Somno compositam iacere vidit
> Glaiam Thermanius puer puellam,
> Diducit tacita manu solutas
> Vestes, illa silet, femur prehendit,
> Suaviumque levi dedit labello,
> Illa conticuit velut sepulta:
> Subrisit puer, ultimumque tentat
> Gaudium nec adhuc movetur illa,
> Sed lubens patitur dolos dolosa.
> Quis novus stupor? ante Glaya molli
> Ansere, aut vigilans magis Sybilla,
> Lethargo quasi iam gravi laborans
> Noctes atque dies trahis sopores.

80. *In Barnum*. Appeared in 1595 with the following last line: "Servassent versus et numerum atque fidem."

85. *In Sannium*. Appeared in 1595 as *In Calvum* with the following variants: l. 1, "improbe Calve"; l. 2, "Ut dubites animam foemina an ullam habeat?"; l. 3, "Cum mea conclusas foelici pectore amantum."

88. *Ad Nashum*. This is the text of 1595, which is more personal in tone than its revision *Ad Nassum* in 1619; variants in the revised text of 1619: l. 1, "Nasse, paedagogum"; l. 2, "Sextillum . . . canem Potitum"; l. 4, "Et per"; l. 7, "Fulmen, ridiculis"; l. 8, "Irati ut tonitru"; l. 9, "denique Pierum serenum"; l. 16, "Nasonemque tuum"; l. 17, "Quos ut te decet aestimas, tegisque"; l. 18, "Nec possint per"; l. 19, "Quare si sapis."

93. *In Bretonem*. Appeared in 1595 with "Nempe tuis nunquam viveret in numeris" in l. 2.

94. *Ad Ge. Chapmannum*. As with No. 88, the text of 1595 has been used; revised in 1619 as *Ad Corvinum* with the following variants: l. 1, "Sextum perfidiae"; l. 2, "Corvine, insimulas"; l. 3, "Nequaquam"; l. 7, "Laesam dic age vi'n"; l. 8, "Hunc ad coenam"; l. 10, "Sin mavis vel"; l. 16, "nisi praebeat."

116. *Ad Cambricum*. Appeared in 1595 without variation.

Epigrams from *Poemata* of 1595

These are among the 41 epigrams of the 1595 collection not reprinted in 1619.

DOUBTFUL POEMS

A Booke of Ayres, Part II

I. The first strophe of this song occurs in Ch. Ch. MS. 439 (fo. 5ᵛ), without variation.

II. Appears in Add. MS. 34608, Harl. MS. 4286 (fo. 56), Add. MS. 24665 (listed in the table of contents as on fo. 27, but missing from the MS. itself), and Davison's *Poetical Rhapsody* (no. 152 in Rollins' edition). Variants: l. 3, "knots of beauty" (Davison); l. 10, "Which" (Davison); l. 18, "It is fayned" (4286); l. 19, "A face which winter'd" (4286); l. 20, "And this is it" (4286).

IX. Fellowes suggests "The wanton spirits" to supply the missing pair of syllables in l. 5.

X. Appears in Drexel MS. 4257 (No. 118), with the following variants: l. 3, "happy in nothing"; l. 5, "That now"; l. 6, "Their object"; l. 7, "And write"; l. 8, "Teaching"; l. 10, "All were content"; l. 12, "on the seas"; l. 14, "If stormes do rise"; l. 15, "My fortunes as the wind doth move." This MS. further adds fourth and fifth strophes, as follows:

> My fortunes which have robb'd myne eies
> And drawne her picture in my hearte
> With sighing makes me soe to rise
> That still it seemes to breake in parte
> Hold hearte or else thy picture dies.

> Then Mistris myne take this farewell
> A bleeding hearte a blubberd eie
> Disquiett thoughts which still rebell
> A broken hearte that can not dye
> If ever man were crost—'tis I.

XIII. "Her selfe-delight" is Vivian's punctuation of "her selfe delight" in the original, l. 4. "O griefe, a death," l. 8, emendation of "A greife, O death" in the original.

XVIII. Add. MS. 24665 (fos. 25–25ᵛ) contains this song with the following slight variants: l. 11, "if in vertue wee still delight"; l. 12, "in heaven shalbe placed."

XX. A better copy of this song is contained in Add. MS. 24665 (fos. 65–65ᵛ); from it I have adopted the following readings: l. 1 (and table of contents), "What thing" for "What then" in the original; l. 8, "Time hath a wheele" for "Time hath a while" in the original. Other variants from this source: l. 11, "Sumer and winter fadeth"; l. 12, "heavens light"; l. 13, "morne or venus flower."

XXI. The first strophe appears without variation in Edinburgh University Library MS. La. iii. 490 (fo. 77).

The Ayres That Were Sung and Played at Brougham Castle

V. Appears in Add. MS. 27879 (fo. 220) with the following variants: l. 1, "a Carthage queen"; l. 8, "Whereas"; l. 10, "would have"; l. 15, "their loves were"; l. 18, "Who bade"; l. 28, "And let."

VIII. Fellowes considers the repeated word "posteritie" in ll. 22 and 23 a misprint, and suggests emending l. 22 to "prosperity."

Lyrics from Various Sources

1, "What if a day." Though Bullen, Vivian, Fellowes, and others assert that this song was attributed to Campion by Richard Alison in *An Howres Recreation in Musicke,* 1606 (xvii–xviii), David Greer (see article cited below) is unable to locate this attribution in any of the extant copies; the present editor confesses the same inability. However, Alexander Gil does refer to it as *illo perbello cantico Tho. Campiani* in *Logonomia Anglica,* 1619 (p. 140), so that the possibility of its being Campion's is still open. The version of Alison is printed here; for variants and other versions of three, five, seven, and even ten strophes, the reader is referred to two articles: A. E. H. Swaen, "The Authorship of 'What if a Day' and Its Various Versions," *Modern Philology,* IV (1907), 397–422, and David Greer, " 'What if a day'—An Examination of the Words and Music," *Music and Letters,* XLIII (1962), 304–19. Swaen believes that Campion reset an old text (perhaps tidying it up in the process) and hence became credited as its author, while Greer admits the possibility of his being composer of both words and music. To their lists of versions, one might add only Edinburgh MS. La. iii. 490 (fos. 18–21), five strophes.

2, "Of Neptunes Empyre." This song formed part of the Masque of Proteus and the Adamantine Rock included in the festivities of *Gesta Grayorum* at Shrovetide, 1594. It was attributed to Campion by Francis Davison in *A Poetical Rhapsody* in 1602, and, since there is positive evidence that Campion took part in the festivities, the attribution seems reasonable. The version printed here is Davison's (No. 151 in Rollins' edition); the *Gesta Grayorum* was printed much later, in 1688, with the following variants for this song: l. 3, "To whom Rivers"; l. 6, "for their Chrystall Fields"; l. 8, "And every Sea-God praise again"; l. 13, "The Waiters with their Trumpets quake"; l. 18, "every echoing Voice"; l. 20, "In praise."

3, "Shadowes before the shining sunne." This is the other song from the Masque of Proteus; Davison did not reprint it, but E. K. Chambers has suggested that Campion wrote it as well as the other

(*The Elizabethan Stage,* III, 240). The version printed here is from Harl. MS. 541 (fo. 145); in the printed version of *Gesta Grayorum* of 1688, the following variants occur: l. 4, "Inchantments blemish"; l. 5, "And Councellors of false Principality"; l. 8, "Lyon doth"; l. 9, "What wonder if"; l. 12, "of Her Majesty."

4, 5, 6, "Thou shalt not love mee," "Thrice tosse," "Thou art not fayer." All three sonnets appear, attributed to Campion by the scribe, in Harl. MS. 6910 (fos. 150–151ᵛ), written apparently in the late 1590s (a date of 1596 in the same hand appears on fo. 74ᵛ). The early date and attribution make the hypothesis that these sonnets are early drafts of *A Booke of Ayres,* Part I, xii and *Third Booke of Ayres,* xviii seem probable.

7, "Do not prize thy beauty." Appears in Robert Jones's *Ultimum Vale,* 1605 (i), unascribed; Vivian (p. liv) assigns it to Campion on grounds of style alone; to this might be added the resemblance of its second strophe to both *The Second Booke,* vii and *The Third Booke,* vi. It also appears in Edinburgh MS. La. iii. 490 (fo. 31), Adv. MS. 5. 2. 14 (fo. 5), and La. iii. 483 (fo. 190), first line only with ayre; in the second and third of these it occurs in Campion groups—after "Never love unlesse you can" in Adv. MS. 5. 2. 14, and between "My love bound me" and "Come away" in La. iii. 483. The version printed is from Jones; variants from the other sources: l. 3, "prints" (490); l. 7, "Thou can love" (5. 2. 14); l. 8, "And many" (both 490 and 5. 2. 14); l. 9, "Could thou" (5. 2. 14); l. 14, "the course of time" (490); l. 15, "with time" (490), "doth change" (5. 2. 14); l. 17, "seemes strang" (5. 2. 14); l. 18, "in rough [and rue?] their owne delay" (490).

8, "Some can flatter." From William Corkine's first book of *Ayres* 1610 (ii); Vivian attributes it to Campion because of its similarity to *The Fourth Booke,* xii, especially in its fourth line.

9, "My deerest mistrisse." From William Corkine's *The Second Booke of Ayres,* 1612 (xi); Vivian attributes it to Campion because of its obvious resemblance to "My sweetest Lesbia," but it seems rather to be a clumsy imitation.

10, "Art thou that shee." The first strophe alone appears in a Campion set including "Silly boy" and "Young and simple though I am" in "Giles Earle his booke, 1615" (Add. MS. 24665, fos. 55–55ᵛ). The version printed here is the two-strophe one contained in Ch. Ch. MS. 439 (fo. 18ᵛ); 24665 reads "none fairer" for "noe fayrer" in l. 1. This song was printed by Cutts, *Seventeenth Century Songs and Lyrics,* p. 18.

11, "As on a day Sabina fell asleepe." Comes after "Come you pretty false-ey'd wanton" and "I care not for these Ladies" in Add. MS. 24665 (fos. 5–5ᵛ); Vivian (p. 356) attributes it to Campion on grounds of its resemblance to *A Booke of Ayres,* Part I, viii and to one of the Latin epigrams (see footnote).

12, "The peacefull westerne winde." A very close reworking, in "poulter's measure," of *The Second Booke,* xii, from Add. MS. 15117 (fo. 10). Vivian attributes it to Campion, but the fact that its setting is totally unlike his printed one suggests that it may just as well be someone else's alteration of his text to fit another tune.

13, "Could my poore hart." Either a first draft or a close imitation of *The Third Booke,* xxiv; it occurs on fo. 94 of Add. MS. 10309, which also contains the text as printed in Campion's original edition on fo. 85.

14, "Whether away." Occurs directly after "Come you pretty false-ey'd wanton" in Ch. Ch. MS. Mus. 87, ca. 1624 (on fo. 1ᵛ); the similarity of both text and music to the preceding song makes it likely that this is intended as a sequel to it. Cutts prints it in *Seventeenth Century Songs and Lyrics,* p. 413.

15, "Hide not, sweetest Love." Printed by Bullen from an un-specified mid-17th-century MS. commonplace book owned by the Duke of Buccleugh; Vivian attributes it to Campion because it uses the refrain of *The Second Booke,* xi, but it could just as easily be a parody of that song. Bullen records original MS. readings of "smales" for "smalls" (l. 2), "blood" for "bold" (l. 8), and "like mine eyes" for "like mines" (l. 9).

16, "Verba volant." Prefixed to Peter Bales' *The Arte of Brachy-graphie* (1597). The identification of "T. C." as Campion rests on the style of the Latin and the fact that Campion's friend Edward Mychel-bourne (see *Epigrammatum Liber* I, 192, above), along with Thomas Newton and Thomas Lodge, also contributed prefatory verse to Bales' book.

17, "Tarry sweete love." From Ch. Ch. MS. 439 (fo. 3). Claimed for Campion by Mary Joiner in "Another Campion Song?" *Music and Letters,* XLVIII (1967), 138-9, mainly because its second line is nearly identical with the line illustration "Th' English Iambick licentiate" in his *Observations* (p. 298, l. 10, above).

BIBLIOGRAPHY

The reader may wish to consult the following secondary studies:

Ralph W. Berringer. "Thomas Campion's Share in *A Booke of Ayres.*" *Publications of the Modern Language Association of America*, LVIII (1943), 938–48.

Leicester Bradner. *Musae Anglicanae: A History of Anglo-Latin Poetry, 1500–1925.* New York: The Modern Language Association of America, General Series X, 1940.

Giovanni Coperario. *Rules how to Compose.* Facsimile edition with an introduction by Manfred F. Bukofzer. Los Angeles, 1952.

Walter R. Davis. "A Note on Accent and Quantity in *A Booke of Ayres.*" *Modern Language Quarterly*, XXII (1961), 32–36.

———. "Melodic and Poetic Structure: The Examples of Campion and Dowland." *Criticism*, IV (1962), 89–107.

Vincent Duckles. "The Gamble Manuscript as a Source of *Continuo* Song in England." *Journal of the American Musicological Society*, Vol. I, No. 2 (Summer 1948), 23–40.

John Hollander. *The Untuning of the Sky: Ideas of Music in English Poetry, 1500–1700.* Princeton, 1961.

Catherine M. Ing. *Elizabethan Lyrics: A Study in the Development of English Metres and Their Relation to Poetic Effect.* London, 1951.

Miles M. Kastendieck. *England's Musical Poet, Thomas Campion.* New York, 1938; reprinted 1963.

Thomas MacDonagh. *Thomas Campion and the Art of English Poetry.* Dublin, 1913.

Wilfrid Mellers. "Words and Music in Elizabethan England." In *The Age of Shakespeare,* edited by Boris Ford. Harmondsworth: Pelican Guides to English Literature, 2, 1955.

Allardyce Nicoll. *Stuart Masques and the Renaissance Stage.* New York, 1938.

Bruce Pattison. *Music and Poetry of the English Renaissance.* London, 1948.

Catherine W. Peltz. "Thomas Campion, An Elizabethan Neo-Classicist." *Modern Language Quarterly,* XI (1950), 3–6.

Paul Reyher. *Les Masques anglais: Étude sur les ballets et la vie de cour en angleterre (1512–1640).* Paris, 1909.

Andrew J. Sabol. *Songs and Dances for the Stuart Masque.* Providence, 1959.

R. W. Short. "The Metrical Theory and Practice of Thomas Campion." *Publications of the Modern Language Association of America,* LIX (1944), 1003–18.

Hallett D. Smith. *Elizabethan Poetry: A Study in Conventions, Meaning, and Expression.* Cambridge, Massachusetts, 1952.

Frederick W. Sternfeld. "A Song from Campion's *Lord's Masque.*" *Journal of the Warburg and Courtauld Institutes,* XX (1957), 373–75.

John E. Stevens. *Music & Poetry in the Early Tudor Court.* London, 1961.

John Thompson. *The Founding of English Metre.* New York, 1961.

Enid Welsford. *The Court Masque: A Study in the Relationship between Poetry & the Revels.* Cambridge, 1927; reprinted 1962.

G. D. Willcock. "Passing Pitefull Hexameters: A study of Quantity and Accent in English Renaissance Verse." *Modern Language Review,* XXIX (1934), 1–19.

INDEX OF FIRST LINES

In the Norton Library

LITERATURE